CONFIRMATION

Presbyterian Practices in Ecumenical Perspective

Richard Robert Osmer

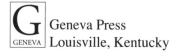

Geneva Press
Louisville, Kentucky

Scripture quotations from the New Revised Standard Version of the Bible are copyright © 1989 by the Division of Christian Education of the National Council of the Churches of Christ in the U.S.A. and are used by permission.

Book design by Jennifer K. Cox
Cover design by Kim Wohlenhaus
First edition

Published by Geneva Press
Louisville, Kentucky

This book is printed on acid-free paper that meets the American National Standards Institute Z39.48 standard. ♾

PRINTED IN THE UNITED STATES OF AMERICA

97 98 99 00 01 02 03 04 05 — 10 9 8 7 6 5 4 3 2

Library of Congress Cataloging-in-Publication Data
Osmer, Richard Robert, 1950–
    Confirmation : Presbyterian practices in ecumenical perspective /
Richard Robert Osmer. — 1st ed.
       p.   cm.
    Includes bibliographical references.
    ISBN 0-664-50000-5 (alk. paper)
    1. Confirmation—Presbyterian Church.   2. Confirmation—Comparative
studies.   3. Presbyterian Church (U.S.A.)—Membership.   4. Presbyterian
Church—United States—Membership.   I. Title.
BX9189.C7075   1996
264'.0508—dc20   95-46244

With love, to my parents, Richard and Bernice Osmer,
my first and most important teachers

Contents

Acknowledgments

The end of this book leaves me with many thanks to render. Thomas Long and Daniel Migliore, my colleagues at Princeton Theological Seminary, have read portions of this book and their comments proved to be invaluable. Likewise, conversations with Richard Fenn, Elsie McKee, George Hunsinger, and Bruce McCormack about various topics, also proved to be a valuable source of insight. My teaching and conversations with Janet Weathers, growing out of our doctoral seminar, "History and Method in Practical Theology," have been enormously stimulating. Kenda Creasy Dean, Director of the Princeton Institute for Youth Ministry, read chapter 3 and has served as a wonderful conversation partner on the place of youth in our society today, as have Emily Anderson and Amy Vaughn. Increasingly, I have come to believe that conversation and writing go hand in hand. William Harris, Librarian for Archives and Special Collections, Luce Library at Princeton Theological Seminary, has been extraordinarily helpful in locating primary source material and has been genuinely interested in this project. Special thanks goes to Timothy Staveteig, my editor at Geneva Press. His patient guidance and depth of scholarly knowledge made him the ideal editor for this project.

As I wrote this book, my children, Richard and Sarah, entered adolescence and began to make their way through this special stage of the life cycle. The joys and trials we have shared as they negotiated this part of their lives has taught me more than I can possibly put into words. The combination of communal nurture and personal initiative that I have attempted to combine in my understanding of confirmation is undoubtedly a result of the insights I have gained from our relationship. Richard read Part 1 of the book during his senior year of high school and served as an important reality check on the perspective I was trying to develop. My wife Sally, a minister and social activist in her own right, has been the source of countless insights and was particularly helpful in the editing of chapter 7. To my family goes my heartfelt thanks.

This book is dedicated to my parents. As a longtime superintendent of the Sunday school and active churchman, my father served as the model for the calling I have chosen as a minister, Christian educator, and practical theologian. My mother's encouragement and support throughout my years in school instilled in me many of the values I hold dearest and taught me the importance and power of education.

Introduction
Troubling Questions

What could be more endearing? A group of young people in their early teens, well-scrubbed and nicely dressed, standing before the congregation. This is their moment, the day of their confirmation. Excitement and earnestness are found on their faces. Friends and family sit near the front of the sanctuary. The eyes of the entire congregation watch as the minister moves through the confirmation liturgy, especially at those moments when they are asked to affirm their faith and to receive the blessing of the church as the minister lays hands on each one. The service is upbeat. Many of the confirmands will celebrate the step they have taken at a special meal with their family and friends, where they will be given gifts and memorabilia.

In thousands of churches across the United States, scenarios similar to this one get played out each spring. There are many positive things that can be said about the approach to confirmation it represents. Long before the young people gather in the sanctuary to be confirmed, they enter an educational process with their peers. Whether the confirmation class lasts six weeks or two years, it represents an honest effort by the congregation to give its young people a chance to understand the faith into which most of them were baptized as infants. The minister frequently is more involved in the teaching of confirmation than any other educational program the congregation offers. Most parents want their children to participate in the confirmation program, even if their family is only marginally related to the church. They often lend more support to this program than the youth group or Sunday school, believing that this may be the last chance the church will have to influence their child before the experimentation and rebellion of adolescence hit full force.

What, indeed, could be more endearing . . . and more important? Surely, confirmation remains one of the bright spots in the somewhat dark horizon of contemporary mainline Protestantism. Reality, unfortunately, tells us a different story. Recent research has made it all-too-clear that the long-term effect of confirmation is limited. The commitments made and the promises offered seem as lasting as the spring flowers adorning the altar during the confirmation service. It is with the present practice of confirmation that we begin our practical theological reflection. Here the problems guiding the historical investigation of the second part of this book and the constructive work undertaken in the third part begin to take shape. The questions before mainline Protestantism about the nature and purpose of confirmation are troubling indeed. They arise from the seeming failure of this practice to have any long-term impact on its members.

Recent Research on Confirmation

As early as the 1960s, the Episcopal Church began to raise questions about confirmation on the basis of pastoral concerns. Baptisms and confirmations were decreasing. It was widely recognized that many baptized and confirmed young people were beginning to leave the church during their teenage years. In response to this sense of looming crisis, and to research already undertaken by the Church of England, the Episcopal Church undertook a relatively modest survey of twelve parishes across the country.[1] The findings and reflections were published in *Confirmation Crisis*.[2] As reported in this study, the leaders of the church found their pastoral concern well justified. More than 50 percent of the people who had been confirmed in the parishes surveyed were found to be inactive.[3] The breakdown by parish is striking. Only three parishes reported more active than inactive confirmed members.

Not surprisingly, this same finding is borne out thirty years later. The most substantial, recent research on the long-term impact of confirmation is found in *Vanishing Boundaries* by Dean Hoge, Benton Johnson, and Donald Luidens.[4] These three sociologists identified 500 people born between 1947 and 1956 who were confirmed in the Presbyterian Church. When the research was done in 1989, this group was between the ages of thirty-three and forty-two. Only 29 percent of those who were confirmed as Presbyterians remained in the Presbyterian Church.[5] Ten percent participated in other mainline churches, 6 percent had joined fundamentalist congregations, and 7 percent had joined other Christian groups. Fully 48 percent of the confirmands were at that time classified as unchurched.

The criteria used to include persons in the churched category are minimal.[6] They must be a member of a church body and have attended worship at least six times in the previous year. In other words, to be classified as among the churched, a person need attend church only once every two months. If this were to be increased to once a month, the number of those classified as churched would decline from 52 to 49 percent.[7] If two or three times a month were the criterion, this would decline further still to 43 percent. The findings based on this somewhat stricter means of classification are shocking.

Of those confirmed in the Presbyterian Church who have now reached their early thirties and forties, 57 percent no longer can be found among the churched. This study raises serious questions about the long-term effect of confirmation. The study does not focus on young adults who are still in flux, sorting out various life choices. It examines those who are well on their way to mid-life and have established a relatively stable life structure.[8] Among more than half of this group, the promises made and the commitments entered into during confirmation seem long forgotten.

Research of this size and sophistication on the long-term impact of confirmation in other mainline denominations is not available. There are indirect indications that a similar process is at work in other denominations, however. In the Search Institute's recent study of six major American Protestant denominations, it found perplexing data about the Evangelical Lutheran Church in America.[9] In comparison to the other mainline denominations, the Evangelical Lutheran Church had a much higher rate of participation in its Christian education program by youth grades seven through nine: the Lutheran Church showed 70 percent; the Southern Baptist Convention, 52 percent; the United Methodist Church, 45 percent; and the Presbyterian Church, 48 percent. When the rate of participation of the Lutheran Church's youth in grades ten through twelve was examined, however, it was the *lowest* of any of the denominations, declining to 32 percent.

When asked to interpret this precipitous decline, many Lutheran pastors and Christian educators noted that confirmation in Lutheran congregations often is offered between the seventh and ninth grades. As soon as the confirmands finish this program, their participation in the church begins to decline. As one pastor put it: "Once they've finished confirmation, they act like they've graduated from the Sunday school." Although this interpretation is speculative, it adds to the questions raised by the findings of *Vanishing Boundaries*. If confirmation does not even influence the church participation of youth who have just been involved in the program, what kind of long-term impact can we expect it to have when they become adults?

In order to better understand this research on confirmation from the perspective of confirmands themselves, I have conducted a number of informal interviews of people confirmed during the period examined by Hoge and his colleagues.[10] Half were interviews of those who no longer participate in the church. I received many answers such as the following from persons currently among the unchurched in response to the question, Why did you get confirmed?

"I didn't want to let my family down. I knew my parents really wanted me to get confirmed, so I went ahead and did it to please them. Remember, I was only eleven years old at the time."

"My minister encouraged me to go ahead and do it. He knew that I had a lot of questions about Christianity but assured me it was OK to join the church, even though I wasn't sure I believed it all. I really liked him, so I went ahead and got confirmed."

"All my friends were joining the church, so I guess I kind of went along. We all knew that it would be a special day. We'd get new clothes and presents from our relatives. Some of my friends were even going to have special parties like their Jewish friends have when they have their bar mitzvah."

"Actually, it was a special time for me. I took it really seriously and got a lot out of it. Once I went to college, though, I began to question everything. Confirmation was more a part of my childhood faith than what I came to believe as an adult."

Many who remained involved in the church offered similar comments. When asked to indicate confirmation's importance to their present faith, less than half of the churched group identified a strong positive relationship. The following comment is typical of those who did:

"It was important for me. Many of my friends were already starting to drop out of church. My parents used confirmation as a time to explain to me why the church was so important to them. My pastor made it clear right from the beginning that he wasn't going to put any pressure on us to join the church. It was our decision. I think I made the best commitment that a ninth-grader can make. This doesn't mean that I stopped asking questions. A lot of that took place later. Even then, however, I think I knew deep down inside that I believed because of the influence of my church and my parents. Confirmation kind of pulled it all together for me."

This kind of positive comment, however, was offset by an equal number of negative ones offered by persons who are actively involved in the church today. The following are representative:

"My confirmation doesn't really have anything to do with what I believe now. Frankly, I don't remember anything we learned. The pastor didn't know how to teach at all. It was boring, and I only went because my parents made me."

"It was pretty quick, only four or five weeks if I remember right. We had confirmation classes right before Easter and got confirmed on Palm Sunday. I don't think I really understood what I was supposed to believe."

"Confirmation wasn't the place that I made a commitment to Christ. That came much later when I was involved in a Christian organization at college. Frankly, my church didn't do a very good job of evangelism, especially of its own members. It still doesn't."

No doubt many pastors and Christian educators have heard similar comments. They give expression to widespread ambivalence about the role of confirmation in mainline Protestantism today. Research by Hoge and his colleagues and the Search Institute only serves to deepen this ambivalence. Without question, confirmation is an important educational practice in many congregations. It receives family support, elicits pastoral leadership, and gets young people involved, many of whom would otherwise have little participation in the church. This is offset by the failure of confirmation to have a long-term impact on its participants. Pastors and educators have wondered if this were the case for some time. They now have hard evidence to back up their intuitions. What are we to make of the current state of confirmation? Is it possible to give more definite shape to the ambivalence felt by many church leaders?

Bringing Our Questions into Focus

Two basic questions lie beneath the contemporary church's uncertainty over confirmation: What is the purpose of the practice of confirmation? What form should this practice take in the modern context? These questions cannot be totally separated, but they can be distinguished for purposes of examination. They lie at the heart of the twofold task of practical theology: (1) a critical and constructive account of some aspect of the Christian life as it is lived both inside and outside the church; and (2) a description of this life in relation to relevant contextual factors: social, psychological, environmental, and so forth. The history of practical theology will be described briefly in the epilogue, as will be the practical theological method informing this book throughout.

In response to the first question raised above, the first task of practical theology is to articulate a normative understanding of some aspect of the Christian life through a critical and constructive assessment of contemporary practice and a fresh encounter with the sources of theology. This task is theological through and through. It will become apparent as our story unfolds that confusion about the role of confirmation in the contemporary church stems from long-standing uncertainty about the meaning of this practice in the theology of the church. From the outset, the church has been unclear about the status of confirmation. Is it a Sacrament? What is its relationship to Baptism and the Lord's Supper? Does it represent an individual's personal profession of faith, a matter of "owning" the vows made on his or her behalf at Baptism? Does it represent a deeper understanding of and assent to the basic teachings of the church, teachings that lay a foundation for the mature pursuit of Christian vocation in the world and participation in congregational life? Or does it represent a rite of passage, a transition out of childhood faith into adolescent faith?

These questions can only be answered theologically. Until the church is clear about its theological understanding of confirmation, uncertainty and ambivalence will surround this practice. The first question, however, cannot be answered independently of the second one raised above: What form should confirmation take in the modern context? The church's witness to the gospel is always concrete. It takes form in a particular time and place. Although dependent on what God did "then and there" in Jesus Christ, the church seeks to communicate and live out the significance of this work to humans who are situated in concrete social and historical contexts. The forms the church devises to carry out its ministry of witness are not unchanging. Practices as basic as preaching and the administration of Baptism have changed across the centuries.

This is especially true with regard to confirmation. Understanding the story of its gradual emergence out of the practice of adult Baptism during the fourth and fifth centuries, through the various trajectories emerging out of the Reformation, makes the contextual nature of confirmation apparent. This contextuality is not something to be feared, as if one form of confirmation created at a certain point in history is the only one appropriate to Christianity. In every age, the church must discern the appropriate form its witness should take in relation to the context in which it is situated. It must ask the first, normative question posed by practical theology anew within the particular circumstances of the second, contextual question.

This means that the second task of practical theology is equally important. In its most comprehensive sense today this involves placing Christianity in the context of the changing function of religion in modernity. This is an exceedingly complex task and involves the examination of economic, cultural, and psychosocial factors as they impinge on the role of religion in contemporary life. Within the space of this book, it is not possible to take up every aspect of this task; only those aspects of modernization will be examined that are directly relevant to our consideration of confirmation. It will become apparent, however, that it is not possible to answer the question of the purpose of confirmation today without locating it in relation to the recent social and historical context.

Modernization has placed enormous pressure on mainline Protestant churches over the last two hundred years. One of the great ironies of the story we will tell is how the church's attempt to make the traditional, catechetical approach to confirmation more up-to-date gradually weakened its ability to offer the children and youth of the church a compelling witness to the gospel. Becoming educationally "modern" rendered it relatively feeble in responding to the challenges of modernization. The task before the church is not to turn back the clock and attempt to repristinize older practices of catechesis and confirmation. Rather, it is to ask anew the question of the theological meaning of confirmation in relation to the emerging context of late modernity or what some would prefer to call "postmodernity."

Questions about the purpose and form of confirmation inform all that follows. The fact that the second is taken up first does not indicate the order of importance. Telling the story of confirmation's emergence as a practice and the theological meaning ascribed to it will take longer and, therefore, is given more space. The constructive proposal made in the final part of this book, however, can only be made by answering both questions. Everything that needs to be said in this regard cannot be offered at once. We begin, therefore, with where we are, reflecting on the vicissitudes of adolescence in the modern context.

Part 1

Confirmation as a Current Challenge

1

Adolescence: The Emergence of a New Stage in the Life Cycle

That so many people confirmed in the Presbyterian Church are no longer actively involved in Presbyterian congregations should not be surprising. Nor should the fact that young people appear to greatly reduce their participation in the Lutheran Church immediately after confirmation. These are matters of common knowledge among church leaders and parents. The struggle to keep young people involved in the church is a hard one. Even when involvement is relatively great during high school years, it often drops dramatically during college.

Contextualizing the Problem

One study after another has revealed a pattern of "decline and departure" among mainline Protestant youth. This body of research also has discovered an increase in denominational switching among Protestants in general. It is important to view the research on confirmation examined in the Introduction in relation to these broader trends. This helps us see that the challenge before the church with regard to confirmation is not merely one of improving its teaching methods, timing, or format. Powerful social forces outside the church pose a major challenge to the plausibility of Christianity in the modern world. Many of these begin to have a dramatic impact on individuals during adolescence. As Erik Erikson points out, the link between adolescence and social history is particularly close: "Adolescence, thus, is a stage in which the individual is much closer to the historical day than he is at earlier stages of childhood development. While the infantile antecedents of identity are more unconscious and change very slowly, if at all, the identity problem itself changes with the historical period: this, in fact, is its job."[1]

Erikson provides us with two important clues here. First, he points us to the reality of the identity problem. Adolescence as a unique stage in the life cycle is a relatively new social phenomenon. It is during this period that young people struggle with the identity crisis. The gap between confirming one's faith during early adolescence and participating in the church as an adult is filled precisely with the psychological work of this stage. It may well be that the inherited practices of confirmation do not adequately take this work into account.

Erikson's comment also provides us with a second clue. Adolescence, he notes, is a time when persons are especially close to the historical period in which they live. As surely as toddlers need the mirroring of parents, adolescents need the mirroring of the surrounding culture. They are struggling to construct a coherent

3

sense of self that not only knits together the unique events of their own lives but also projects possible futures in the adult social world.

These insights invite us to place the practice of confirmation in a much broader social and historical context. Practices that were adequate for Calvin's Geneva or Coe's New York may not be adequate to the task before the church at the end of the twentieth century. What major changes have taken place over the course of this century and how do they impact adolescent faith?

Declining Population

In the study of confirmands examined in the Introduction, only 29 percent of those confirmed in the Presbyterian Church continued to be a part of the Presbyterian Church by the time they reached their early thirties and forties. Only an additional 10 percent were involved in mainline Protestantism. Forty-eight percent could at that time be classified as unchurched.[2] What is going on here? Two trends identified by recent sociological research help us put these statistics in broader perspective: the declining participation of youth in mainline Protestantism and the widespread pattern of denominational switching.

The first of these refers to the pattern of declining church participation characterizing childhood, adolescence, and young adulthood. An overwhelming number of parents in the United States want their children to receive some form of religious education. According to research of the Gallup organization, as many as 82 percent of all adults in the American population receive some sort of religious instruction as children.[3] Even parents who do not belong to a religious organization express a strong desire to have their children exposed to religious teaching. In one recent study of unchurched adults, 96 percent reported wanting their children to receive a religious education, even though they personally had no desire to be involved in religion.[4] Many pointed out that the church is one of the few places left in American society that offers moral education. The importance of the church in teaching children a basic moral code seems to be appreciated by churched and unchurched alike.[5]

By the time they reach early adolescence, however, a notable decline in participation begins to be apparent.[6] Fifty-six percent of all those between the ages of thirteen and fifteen attend church. This drops 10 percent among sixteen- and seventeen-year-olds. This same pattern of diminished participation during adolescence also is evident in their involvement in the educational programs of the church. In the five denominations studied by the Search Institute, approximately 60 percent of the children in grades K–6 were actively involved in the educational program of the church; 52 percent in grades 7–9; and 35 percent in grades 10–12.[7] This pattern of declining participation during adolescence is even found among those adults who currently are active in the church. Sixty percent report that they dropped out of the church for at least two years during this period.[8] Another 20 percent report a period of diminished involvement. In short, a staggering 80 percent of the adult members of the church under age forty experienced a period of departure from the church.

A pattern of high participation during childhood, diminished involvement during adolescence, and departure during late adolescence and young adulthood is widely established in mainline Protestantism, even among those who eventually return to the church. It is a pattern that first began to emerge in the 1960s.[9] The fact that so many people confirmed during early adolescence later appear among the unchurched is no accident. It reflects a much broader social trend. There are powerful forces shaping adolescent faith that are located far beyond the reach of the confirmation program or the church as a whole.

A second trend also helps us understand the gap between confirmation and adult faith in relation to broader social forces: the increased reality of "switching." This term characterizes a widespread phenomenon in contemporary American religion: the movement of members of one denomination or religious group to another.[10] Denominational ties no longer hold the same kind of power they once did in American history. When a family moves from one location to another, it no longer automatically affiliates with a congregation in the same denomination as the one it just left. This is equally true of adolescents. When they leave home, they may or may not affiliate with a congregation in the same denomination as the one in which they were raised.

A particularly important dimension of this phenomenon with regard to adolescents is their movement to the unaffiliated sector of the population. Adolescents are far more likely to leave the church altogether than they are to join another religious group. This belies the argument that mainline Protestantism is losing its members to more conservative religious groups. As Roof and McKinney aptly put it: "The challenge to liberal Protestantism comes not so much from the conservative faiths as from the growing secular drift of many of their not-so-highly-committed members."[11] This observation was upheld in the research on Presbyterian confirmands. Only 6 percent of those confirmands affiliated with fundamentalist churches as adults, whereas a staggering 48 percent could be placed in the unchurched category.[12]

The reasons behind this increase in religious and denominational switching are complex.[13] For our purposes, it is enough to point out that congregations and denominations find themselves in a very different situation today than the one that existed as recently as the middle of this century. Increasingly, they are in a "market" situation in which they must compete for members. Individuals and families enter this market with a desire to find those organizations that meet their needs most adequately. Childhood denominational affiliation no longer weighs as heavily as other factors that emerge during adulthood: the arrival of children, spouse's religious orientation, personal crises, the search for a deeper grasp of spiritual matters, and the hunger for a stronger sense of community.[14]

Taken together, the trends of declining church participation during adolescence and denominational switching help us see that the relative lack of influence of confirmation on adult church membership is more complex than it might appear on the surface. External factors related to the broader social context have made the older pattern of Baptism-confirmation-adult membership less and less of a seamless whole. Adolescence has become a period of time in which many young people no longer actively participate in the church, even if they continue to hold to a minimal set of Christian beliefs. What is going on during this period? Does the current theology and practice of confirmation represent an adequate response to this phenomenon?

Emergence of Adolescence as a Distinct Stage in the Life Cycle

The emergence of adolescence as a distinct stage in the life cycle is a relatively recent phenomenon. In large measure, it has taken place during the twentieth century and is the by-product of social changes related to advanced industrialization. Two factors in particular can be seen as contributing to its emergence: industrial mechanization and prolonged education.

Industrial mechanization refers to the shift from manual labor to machines. Prior to industrialization, young people entered the work force at a relatively early age. Children raised on farms were expected to work as soon as they were able, and the tasks they were asked to carry out grew progressively more difficult as they grew older. Throughout their teens and early twenties, young boys remained in a state of semidependence on their parents, continuing to farm their parents' land and owning no property of their own.[15] The same situation held for young men working in the family business. As long as their parents were actively involved in the business, they remained dependent on them, even if they had married and started their own families.

The major alternative pattern was that of apprenticeship. It involved leaving home in order to learn a trade under the tutelage of a skilled practitioner. This was the most common pattern in semiskilled trades such as iron casting, tailoring, and blacksmithing. By the time they reached their early teens, many young people lived far from home with relative strangers. They were expected to work hard to compensate their employers for teaching them a trade and providing them with room and board.

The first stages of industrialization, which took place in the United States immediately after the Civil War, changed both of these patterns. Mechanization of farm equipment and the assembly line made it possible to carry out tasks with machines that were once performed solely by human labor. Tailors were not needed, for example, when clothing could be mass produced. During the early phases of industrialization, young people were still employed in factories to tend simple machines.[16] In some factories as much as 45 percent of the work force was between sixteen and twenty years of age.[17] As industrial equipment became more automated and efficient, this type of labor was unnecessary. The result was the gradual removal of young people from the work force. Where did they go? Many of them moved into educational institutions.

Initially, allowing children to attend high school was a luxury that only the middle class and wealthy could afford. Even though the public school movement had been successful in establishing elementary public education during the nineteenth century, its reforms had not yet been as successful with high school edu-

cation. As recently as 1900, only 6.4 percent of the American population graduated from high school.[18] By 1940, however, over 50 percent of the population
graduated from high school, and by 1956, over 60 percent. The emergence of the
high school as a major educational institution for young people during the first
half of this century was one of the most important institutional factors allowing
adolescence as we think of it today to come into existence. By prolonging education and freeing young people from major economic responsibilities, it created a
new social space and set of psychological tasks for the youth.

The gradual increase of the importance of the high school during the first half
of the twentieth century was actually preceded by an upsurge of involvement in
college and professional education during the last quarter of the nineteenth century. In 1850, there were 38 undergraduates for every 100,000 persons; in 1900,
123. Between 1890 and 1894, undergraduate enrollment increased almost 40 percent.[19] Increased enrollment in professional education was even more dramatic.
Between 1878 and 1899, the proportionate increase in dentistry was 988 percent,
medicine 142 percent, law 249 percent, and theology 87 percent. During that
decade and the next, public teaching as a profession grew 400 percent.[20]

During the latter part of the nineteenth and first part of the twentieth century,
a professional class began to emerge. Those aspiring to be professionals needed
both high school and college education. Even those who could not become doc-
tors and lawyers realized that advancement in the business world increasingly depended on attending college. As industrialization spawned large corporate bureaucracies, a wide range of managerial positions came into being. "Getting an
education" and "getting ahead" became synonymous. It was this ideology, first
spawned by the newly emerging professional middle class, that gave impetus to
the expansion of the high school.

Two major trends thus contributed to the emergence of adolescence as a new
stage in the life cycle: industrial mechanization and prolonged education. The former displaced young people from the work force. The latter provided an institutional context in which they were given a new social role and set of psychological tasks.

It is no accident that explicit social definition of adolescence took place among
psychologists in close conjunction with educators. Stanley Hall's two-volume
work *Adolescence* was enormously influential in this regard.[21] Written in 1904, it
was widely used by educators, guidance counselors, and others closely associated
with high schools and colleges. Hall's book was the most popular and influential
of many written on adolescence. The amount of writing done on this topic during
the first decades of this century was enormous, ranging from research on adolescent conversion to manuals for guidance counselors.

Although we take adolescence for granted today, it is important to realize how
new this stage of the life cycle is historically. From Calvin's Geneva and Luther's
Wittenberg through much of the nineteenth century, most young people were already making a contribution to the economic well-being of their families by the
time they entered the pastor's catechetical class in preparation for first communion. Some would be leaving home soon and entering apprenticeships. Others

would be assuming more adult responsibilities on the farm or in the family business. Many would be married and begin families within a few years. Only a relative few could afford the luxury of prolonged education. Adolescence as a socially established stage in the life cycle simply did not exist.

The challenge this poses to inherited practices of confirmation is not always recognized. Adolescence not only emerged during the modern period but it also mediates the freedoms and burdens of this period in a special way. It is during this stage that both the problems and the possibilities of modernity are first experienced by individuals in a self-conscious way. Forming and sustaining religious identity among adolescents has become increasingly difficult, as the trends of declining participation during adolescence and religious switching well attest. In order to better understand the challenge this represents to inherited practices of confirmation, we must take a closer look at the shape of adolescence today.

2

Confirmation in Modern Context: Individualization and Identity Formation

Adolescence as a social category has evolved over the course of this century. If the early psychologists and educators viewed it as a time of idealism and moral introspection, contemporary interpreters are just as likely to view it as a time of age-appropriate narcissism and moral relativism. In part, these shifting definitions reflect the different institutional contexts giving shape to adolescence over the course of this century. Although the high school continues to be an important context, church-related youth movements and organizations such as Christian Endeavor, the YMCA and YWCA, and Boy Scouts and Girl Scouts have declined in importance, replaced by institutions like the broadcast media and an identifiable (and marketable) youth culture. The very definition of adolescence has shifted as the social contexts giving it shape and form have changed. As we approach the end of the twentieth century, what is the shape of this stage in the life cycle? I believe that it can be captured in terms of two basic concepts: individualization and identity formation. The former describes adolescence sociologically, and the latter, psychologically.

Individualization describes the ways modern society gives more freedom to and places more burden on the individual. The shift to an advanced industrial economy characterized by large-scale corporate and governmental bureaucracies has greatly diminished the power of older forms of community found in small towns and rural life. Relatively stable communities with a high degree of face-to-face interaction no longer are the primary mediators of economic, civic, and moral values in contemporary society. As these forms of community have lessened in importance, more burden has been placed on individuals to organize the various aspects of their lives.

Much of this is encountered first during adolescence. Indeed, adolescence can be viewed as a special social role in which the individualizing effects of modernity are mediated to people. Adolescents face three important tasks: (1) They must ready themselves to leave home, establishing some measure of economic and psychological independence from their families of origin; (2) they must learn how to make their way through the maze of relatively autonomous institutions and roles characterizing modern society; and (3) they must construct a personal system of moral meaning. Each of these tasks is indicative of the way modern societies are asking individuals to carry more of the burden of their lives' meaning and purpose, while providing them with less support.

At the same time, adolescence is more than a social role. It also is a psychological process, what we are calling here *identity formation,* following Erik Erikson. Too often, sociologists operate with an "over-socialized" view of the self, reducing its complexity and relative autonomy "upward" to broad social processes and forces.[1] Individuals do not move through institutional contexts and social roles in the same way. These things are mediated, in part, through the self, which negotiates these contexts and roles. Two adolescents may go to the same church, attend the same high school, and even come out of the same family but make markedly different life choices. At their best, psychological processes give an account of the self, which interacts with, but is not reducible to, broader social processes.

Understood psychologically, adolescence is a period during which young people struggle to construct a coherent sense of identity. This involves a process of looking backward and piecing together the various identifications formed during earlier stages of life. It also involves the task of projecting possible futures. Much of the inner work of this period involves adolescents' exploration of what and whom they might become, from jobs or careers they might enter, to persons they might marry, to places they might live, to lifestyles they might pursue. Past and future must cohere in a meaningful sense of self in the present. This sense of self must be confirmed socially. Significant others and realistic life chances must confirm adolescents' budding sense of self. Otherwise, it will be extremely difficult to bring the hard work of identity formation to fruition.

Adolescence, then, must be investigated from two perspectives: as a social role mediating the individualizing trends of modernity and as a psychological process in which personal identity is constructed. As we examine each of these in turn, it will begin to become apparent why it is no longer possible to assume a large measure of continuity between childhood and adulthood. Although Luther and Calvin could assume that the children in their catechetical classes would soon step into adult-like roles as apprentices and contributors to the farm or household, this is no longer the case today. A whole new stage in the life cycle has appeared in modern society, raising questions about the inherited practice of confirmation.

Individualization and the Social Role
of Adolescence

Adolescence represents a special kind of social role in contemporary society. Although given shape in specific contexts—for example, the youth group, the high school and university, the mall, and the rock concert—this role stretches beyond any of these contexts and embraces young people in their totality. Whether walking down the street listening to a Walkman or negotiating use of the car with their parents, adolescents are viewed as "youth," "teenagers," "young people," or any number of labels identifying them as occupants of a specific stage in the life cycle. They carry this role with them from context to context, something that is relatively unique in terms of the way social roles ordinarily function.

In virtually every social setting, human behavior is influenced by the roles that are appropriate to that setting.[2] Such roles represent a repertoire of general expectations about how one is to behave and communicate with others who also are participating in that setting. Take a college classroom, for example. Imagine the roles of professor and students respectively. In a large, lecture-oriented class, professors are generally expected to offer a comprehensible lecture at an assigned time and place, ask and answer student questions, and handle administrative matters related to course papers, exams, and assigned reading. Students, in contrast, are expected to arrive before the professor begins, to take notes, and to ask questions by raising their hand and waiting for the professor to call on them. These expectations become apparent when they are violated: by a student who constantly arrives late or one who stands up in the middle of the lecture and offers a lengthy diatribe against the professor's position.

Human interaction in virtually every domain is governed by social roles, from schools to families to businesses to sports. Much of the time, roles are confined to specific domains. Persons usually do not relate to their children when playing a parenting role, for example, in the same way they prosecute a case when practicing law. Some roles, however, are not confined to a specific domain but spill over into many other areas. This is particularly true of roles that have a symbolic function in representing the social order as a whole. Monarchs and presidents, for example, play this kind of special role.[3] In modern society, adolescence has come to occupy this kind of general social role, representing a special time of transition from childhood to adulthood. It is during adolescence that young people are expected to gain the knowledge and skills necessary to function in a highly differentiated, loosely bounded society.

The transition from childhood to adulthood is acknowledged in virtually every society. In many tribal societies, for example, special rites of passage exist to initiate pubescent girls and boys into adult society. Typically, the initiates are set apart for a period of time, entering what the anthropologist Victor Turner calls a liminal state.[4] There they must prove themselves as ready to make the transition to adulthood and receive the knowledge and skills necessary to carry out adult tasks. This kind of clear-cut transition from childhood to adulthood begins to disappear in traditional societies and is absent altogether in modern societies. In place of rites of passage, we see the emergence of special milestones, marking the shift from one social status to another.

Getting one's automobile license, registering to vote, matriculating at college, or losing one's virginity might qualify as modern equivalents, but none of them are invested with the same public quality as archaic rites of passage. This is because the transition from childhood to adulthood is spread out over many years. A single moment cannot be held up and ritualized as *the* defining transitional moment. Instead of a specific rite of passage, adolescence as a transitional social role has come into being in modern society. Entry into and exit from this role are not clearly demarcated. Over the course of many years, young people must carry out three tasks that will allow them to function as adults in a highly differentiated, loosely bounded society:

1. renegotiating their relationship with their family of origin, moving from a position of economic and psychological dependence to a relationship of relative independence;
2. acquiring the repertoire of knowledge and skills necessary to participate in the wide range of institutional contexts characterizing modernity; and
3. constructing a personal system of moral meaning in response to the challenges posed by cultural pluralism, generational discontinuity, and instrumental reason.

Each of these tasks relates to the way a modern society individualizes its members' relationship to its major institutions and roles. If premodern societies were characterized by relatively static social roles determined by family of origin, class, and gender, then modern societies afford people a high degree of freedom in the roles they choose. Peter Berger refers to this as the movement from "fate to choice."[5]

Rules and roles that would have been taken for granted in the past, must be constructed and negotiated by individuals. Although this affords them a large measure of freedom, it also incurs a cost: the loss of supportive communities, the fragmentation of experience, the erosion of lasting moral commitments, and the anxiety of making major life decisions. It is largely the social function of adolescence to teach people how to handle both the burdens and freedoms involved in individualization. This will become evident as we examine each of the three tasks outlined above.

Renegotiating Relationship with Family of Origin

Modern societies expect children to grow up and leave home. It is an expectation their children share. I recently asked a group of forty high school seniors how many of them would still be living at home by the time they reached twenty-three. Not a single person raised a hand. While economic pressures have led more and more adolescents to live at home in recent years, the expectation is widespread in our culture that young people will achieve some measure of economic and psychological independence from their families of origin by the time they enter young adulthood. This social expectation is driven by several broad social forces.

The most important of these is the individualization of a person's relationship to the economy, emerging during the early phases of industrialization in the last half of the nineteenth century. The industrialization of the economy brought about a major shift from an agricultural and local economy to one that was corporate and national.[6] Between 1860 and 1900, investments in manufacturing plants rose from $1 to $12 billion and the annual value of manufacturing products jumped from $1.9 to $11 billion. The number of workers employed in U.S. factories increased almost fivefold. During this same period, agriculture declined from 50 percent of the total national wealth to 20 percent.

The shift to a national economy based on modern business planning and technological innovation individualized people's relationship to the economy. The primary economic unit no longer was the family but the individual. As farming and family owned businesses became a much smaller proportion of the economy, chances for upward mobility began to be found elsewhere. The extended family declined in importance, and geographical mobility became more prevalent. Persons had to leave their home town in order to find work. If they were involved in a managerial position, this often became the first of many moves, as corporate transfers became an accepted practice.

The result of these trends was the establishment of a new social expectation: Children are expected to grow up and leave home. They must be ready to support themselves economically and psychologically by the time they reach young adulthood. Even as the U.S. economy has shifted in recent years from a manufacturing base to an information and service orientation, this fundamental expectation has not changed. Most young people feel they are odd if they are still living at home by the time they reach their mid-twenties.

The social expectation of leaving home holds true for women today every bit as much as for men. As more women have entered the work force, the expectation that they too will become economically independent when they enter young adulthood has become prevalent. This has been supported ideologically by the modern women's movement, which has argued successfully that women should not be confined to the domestic sphere if they want to pursue careers and jobs outside the home. Moreover, marriage is taking place later in life and no longer represents the point of departure from the home for an increasing percentage of women. The high incidence of divorce and the recognition that two incomes are needed to sustain a middle-class lifestyle, also have contributed to the social expectation that women should be able to support themselves economically.

The result of these broad trends on the shape of adolescence has been enormous. We recall that adolescence first emerged as a distinct stage in the life cycle precisely when large-scale industrialization began to take place. Mechanization of factory jobs and farm labor and increased emphasis on high school education removed adolescents from the work force. This created the single most important paradox defining adolescence. Adolescence is viewed as a time of life in which young people ready themselves to leave home and achieve some measure of economic and psychological independence. This is accomplished, however, by lengthening the period of time they depend on their parents. Learning independence while prolonging dependence creates many of the difficulties characteristic of this period.

Economic support through college means that many parents will continue to spend enormous portions of their income supporting their adolescent offspring through their early twenties. However, their adolescents have long since stopped looking to them as their primary source of guidance. They are oriented toward their peers, boyfriends and girlfriends, college professors, and other trusted adult mentors. They begin to mature sexually during their early teens and frequently become sexually active before leaving home. They achieve the ability to engage in abstract reasoning and can reflect critically on their parents, projecting ideal alternatives.[7] Often they make life choices that stand in tension with the values of their parents.

In short, adolescents achieve milestone after milestone of social and intellectual maturity while remaining economically dependent on their parents. They are involved in an extensive and ongoing renegotiation of their relationship with their family of origin. The stresses and strains inherent in this task are defining features of adolescence in modern societies.

Acquiring Knowledge and Skills for Participation in Modern Society

This task grows out of the highly differentiated nature of modern societies. Differentiation means the relatively autonomous nature of modern institutions. Modernization is characterized by the gradual separation of political, economic, educational, familial, religious, and other life spheres into relatively autonomous subsystems that play different roles in society as a whole.[8] Each sphere pursues its own functional purpose and, accordingly, develops its distinctive language, practices, and norms. So much of everyday life is governed by structural differentiation that it is easy to overlook the ways it shapes experience in the modern world.

Imagine a woman who lives outside a major metropolitan area. She drops off her youngest child at a neighborhood day-care center on her way to work each day, while her husband, who drives to work, makes sure their oldest child gets on the school bus safely. The woman takes a train into the city, where she then catches a bus to the large insurance company where she works. The company is one of the largest in the world and has its corporate headquarters in another part of the country. This woman is part of the regional marketing team for the local office. She rarely socializes with her co-workers who live in different parts of the city. Her friends come from other sources: her church, the neighborhood swimming/tennis club, and the persons she has gotten to know through her oldest child's activities. Once a week a woman comes to clean her house. She communicates with this woman by writing notes, because she has to leave for work so early. She and her husband take turns shopping in a large supermarket on weekends. Even though they have been shopping in the same store for more than five years, they know none of the employees. They go there because it is located nearby and allows them to shop quickly and at competitive prices. In the little leisure time she has available during the week, this woman collapses in front of the TV late at night. On weekends, she and her husband play tennis and do things with their children, including taking them to church.

It is not difficult to see the reality of differentiation in this brief vignette. The clear demarcation of different life spheres is apparent. Work, religion, family, recreation, and shopping are all carried out in contexts that are relatively independent of one another in daily life. Different roles and norms are adopted in each sphere. At work, this woman plays the role of the corporate planner, devising marketing strategies that will maximize the profits of her company. At church, she is more passive, rarely volunteering to provide leadership, and primarily seeking help in raising her children to be morally responsible persons. At home and with friends, she is more expressive, showing what she refers to as her "real self." She is openly affectionate with her family and fun-loving with her friends.

The differentiation of modern societies has an individualizing effect on its members. As the German sociologist Niklas Luhmann points out, this affords individuals a high degree of freedom.[9] No one life sphere dictates to the individual the way life should be lived. Choice is maximized. This woman is free to shop where she likes, join the volunteer organizations she pleases, and look for employment in a new company if it seems more lucrative or convenient.

Along with this expanded range of choice, however, there are real losses. These stem from the absence of any meaningful community in this woman's life and the fragmentation of her experience. There is no community to which she feels deep affectional ties outside her family. Even the church is given only a carefully measured modicum of loyalty. She simply is too busy. Likewise, this woman's experience is fragmented. As she moves from one life sphere to another, no one knows her "wholeself." Her life feels chopped up into bits and pieces as she plays one role after another.

How and when do the members of modern societies learn to make their way through this maze of institutions? Largely, this is something they learn as they pass through adolescence. It is during this period that they begin to take part in a wider range of institutional contexts with a larger degree of personal freedom. Adolescents have been going to schools, malls, movies, and churches since they were children. Once they reach their teens, however, they can enter these settings without their parents, either being dropped off or, better yet, driving themselves. Parental expectations begin to change. It is now appropriate for teens to stay out later, to date, to drive themselves to school, and to spend their allowance as they please. Their personal freedom will increase dramatically when they leave home to attend college or when they get their first apartment and job.

One of the most important expectations attached to the social role of adolescence is that persons will be able to make their way through various institutional contexts with increasing autonomy as they grow older. This involves a two-step process. First, adolescents must learn the appropriate rules and roles governing a particular context. Behavior appropriate at school and in the movie theater are not the same. Adolescents must expand their repertoire of knowledge and skill of different life spheres in order to enter into them successfully. Second, they must learn to distance themselves from the roles they adopt in each sphere.

Role distancing is one of the most powerful individualizing forces in modern society. As adolescents learn how to recognize the boundaries separating one life sphere from another and to modulate their personalities accordingly, they gradually acquire the ability to distance themselves from the various roles they play. They can engage in what Irving Goffman calls "impression management," presenting thoughts and feelings appropriate to a role yet one step removed from the self.[10] They "play" the roles of athlete, student, child, friend, and church member, but identify themselves fully with none of them. The individual is given an increased measure of freedom in the "social space" created by differentiation. He or she also is given the task of constructing a self that can negotiate these various domains.

Constructing a System of Moral Meaning

The final aspect of individualization that we will examine focuses on the freedom and burden placed on individuals in the construction of moral meaning. The concept of moral meaning is used here in a broad, Durkheimian sense, referring to those interpretive categories by which persons construct an understanding of the ultimate context of their existence and determine how they ought to live in relation to this ultimate context.[11] Until the advent of modernity, religious traditions provided the interpretive categories by which persons constructed an understanding of life's meaning and purpose. Typically, these categories played an integrative function in society, binding groups together with a shared vision of the sacred foundations of the community and legitimating or criticizing the moral norms of everyday life.

Religion no longer plays this integrative function in modern society. No overall system of moral meaning can bind together every sphere of life in a highly differentiated society. This has resulted in three trends: cultural pluralism, generational discontinuity, and the extension of instrumental reason. Each of these has the effect of individualizing the construction of moral meaning and is closely associated with the social role of adolescence.

It is almost impossible to escape the reality of cultural pluralism in contemporary American society. Whether this takes place directly through a multicultural education curriculum in the school or informally through the media and contact with others, individuals learn that there are other persons and groups that view the world very differently than they do. The taken-for-granted quality of their family's, church's, or class's perspective is challenged as it becomes one among many possible ways of being in the world.

The overall effect of this pluralism is to relativize the values and beliefs of the groups that carry out individuals' primary socialization. These values and beliefs are placed alongside those of other groups. Whether persons respond to the awareness of pluralism defensively, stereotyping all positions that are different from their own, or embrace it, refusing to make evaluative judgments altogether, more of a burden is placed on individuals in the construction of moral meaning. Values and beliefs that could have been taken for granted in a relatively homogeneous, integrated society now must be self-consciously chosen in the face of cultural pluralism.

Adolescence is the stage of life when this first takes place for most persons in our society. Cognitively, many young people are now capable of constructing the perspective of other groups.[12] Simultaneously, they are placed in contexts such as the high school, youth culture, and the media exposing them to a multiplicity of perspectives. Recent research has revealed that the relativizing effects of this kind of pluralism have begun to set in by the time young people graduate from high school.[13] Adolescents already are asking questions such as these: "Surely, you don't still believe that Christians are the only people who are saved?" "Why shouldn't a couple divorce if there is no love in their marriage? Just because your church won't remarry divorced people, that doesn't make it the only way to do things." "Are you trying to tell me that it's wrong to practice birth control? That's your parents talking, not you." "I personally wouldn't get an abortion, but I can see why some of my friends might. Why shouldn't they have the chance to do what's best for them?"

College intensifies the experience of cultural pluralism, frequently making it a guiding curricular principle. Students are systematically and intentionally exposed to a wide range of intellectual perspectives and learn how to "locate" themselves in terms of class, ethnicity, and sexual orientation. As numerous psychological studies of college students have found, the overall effect is to encourage students to go through a period of ethical relativism.[14] This often proves to be temporary. Nonetheless, it remains an important step in the individualization of moral meaning. As students relativize the perspectives of all moral positions, they must accept the burden of constructing their own system of moral meaning. Most colleges offer very little to help them construct a moral framework beyond this relativism, lacking both the curricular coherence and the social will to educate their students toward a shared moral vision and set of virtues.

The experience of pluralism in college has a decidedly negative impact on religious commitment. Study after study since the 1950s has found that higher education and increased secularization go hand in hand.[15] It seems that the one perspective not receiving a fair hearing in the academy is a religious perspective. The relativizing effects of an intellectual encounter with pluralism are coupled with a negative evaluation of religion. The result is the portrayal of religion as a residual of childhood and the diminishment of its potential as a resource for the individual in the construction of moral meaning. All too often, this leaves college graduates with little more than a form of ethical egoism or utilitarianism to guide their lives. While such a framework has a certain plausibility in the face of pluralism, it has little to offer in framing issues of the common good that transcend the special interests of either individuals or groups.

A second factor contributing to the individualization of moral meaning is generational discontinuity.[16] This is the diminished role of trusted adult figures as moral exemplars for the generation following them. This is due in large measure to the rapid pace of social change and technological innovation in contemporary society. Knowledge and skills that were useful for one generation seem to be outdated by the time the next one comes along. Parents who are computer illiterates suddenly are faced with children and youth who are adept at using computers and have grown up playing video games. Attitudes that seemed to work well with one generation of women suddenly appear unattractive to their daughters. The strong company loyalty of one generation appears naive and unrealistic to another, faced with managerial downsizing and the export of manufacturing jobs. The search for sexual freedom in one generation seems like little more than a gateway to AIDS in another.

The result is generational discontinuity. The role of parents, teachers, ministers, and other adult authorities who traditionally have served as moral exemplars is diminished. The social context shifts so rapidly that the problems faced by one generation are not those of the next. Again we see more of a burden placed on the individual. Traditionally, young people have been able to look to their elders as repositories of the community's wisdom. They have received from them trusted moral guidance and a broader historical perspective on the problems facing them in the present. Generational discontinuity makes it more difficult for this type of exchange to take place.

Indeed, we often see a kind of role reversal in modern societies: older generations look to adolescents for the cutting edge of fashion, music, and language. Adolescents, moreover, repeatedly have shown themselves to be one of the most important sources of social change (for example, the antiwar movement of the sixties and the evangelical movement of the eighties). This kind of role reversal comes at a high cost. Cut off from the sources of historic memory, the younger generation is more easily manipulated by the media, youth culture, and charismatic leaders. Individuals, moreover, are faced with the task of constructing moral meaning "from scratch," unable to link the traditional repositories of wisdom to the emerging problems they face.

A third factor leading to the individualization of moral meaning is an expansion of the influence of instrumental reason from the realms of science and technology to other spheres of life. Modernity is closely related to the advent of scientific reason and its critical, empirical spirit. Industrialization is largely the result of the application of scientific reason to the means of production. Over the course of the past two centuries, most spheres of life have been "rationalized," in Max Weber's sense.[17] The law, government, economy, school, and home are all subject to rational procedures and organization. The dominant form of reason in these spheres is instrumental, strategic, problem-solving reasoning. Ends are rationally derived and the most efficient means to achieve these ends are calculated.

It is primarily during adolescence that people in our society learn how to engage in problem-solving reasoning.[18] While the rationalization of life has been a part of their everyday experience since childhood, they are capable of the cognitive procedures involved in problem-solving reasoning only after entering the Piagetian stage of formal operations during early adolescence. This has a tremendous influence on adolescents' construction of moral meaning.

If they have been raised in a religious community, the "mythic" dimensions of their religion seem unreal in comparison to the findings of science. The Bible may describe Jesus as carrying out healing miracles, for example, but modern science makes it clear to the adolescent that sound medicine is more likely to bring about healing than laying on of hands. Likewise, the Christian community may teach believers to pray, but modern reason tells them they are more likely to get what they desire by reflecting on the most efficient ways of pursuing their goals, that is, approaching them instrumentally. Many adolescents begin to find it difficult to relate religious categories and ethical guidelines to spheres of life that are primarily governed by instrumental reason. When this source of moral meaning becomes problematic, where else can the young person turn to receive help? There are two important sources: the peer group and the school.

Although public education has backed away from the explicit teaching of morality, it often teaches a style of moral reasoning indirectly based on the paradigm of instrumental reasoning. This is what is frequently called utilitarian individualism.[19] In its popular forms, this style of moral reasoning grants individuals the power to determine those goals that they deem worthy. How should they decide? By calculating the costs and benefits to the individual. Think of how sex education is taught in most public schools. Along with basic physiological information, young people are encouraged to decide their own values and to rationally calculate the dangers of sexual activity (for example, disease or pregnancy) in relation to the gains.

The other major source of guidance for adolescents is the peer group. This can encourage a wide range of moral perspectives, depending on the values of the group with which a young person identifies. Since the 1960s, however, youth culture consistently has communicated a style of moral reasoning sometimes called expressive individualism.[20] Here too the primary locus of meaning is the individual. Rather than engaging in rational calculation, individuals are encouraged to turn to their inner feelings, intuitions, and desires in making everyday decisions.

On the surface, this style of moral reasoning seems to stand in opposition to a utilitarian approach. The valuing of spontaneity and expressivity in rock music, for example, frequently is portrayed as standing over against the cool, rational calculation of the adult world. It is a theme that gets replayed endlessly on the videos of MTV and teen-oriented movies. The contrast is more apparent than real, however. Expressive individualism, like youth culture in general, fits quite nicely with the consumptive patterns of advanced capitalism.[21] "Spontaneous" desires and needs are shaped by the media and peer fashion to fuel an endless round of purchases that are supposed to give self-expression in dress, music, and experience. Like utilitarianism, it reflects the shape of modern institutions and their individualization of moral meaning.

Thus far, we have examined adolescence from the perspective of society. We now turn and consider it from the perspective of the self. Although everything that has been explored to this point is assumed in what follows, it does not determine the psychology of adolescence in a direct manner. This is because the self cannot be reduced "upward" to broader social processes and trends. It has its own integrity and relative autonomy. Adolescence as a social role confronts the self with a set of socially established expectations. These expectations form only part of the agenda facing adolescents. Equally important are tasks related to physiological and psychological maturation. It is the coordination of inner and outer realities that characterizes the psychological work of the self during this period.

Identity Formation

The psychological work of the self during adolescence can be described in terms of the concept, *identity formation*. This concept is taken from the theory of Erik Erikson.[22] According to Erikson, identity formation is the construction "of a sense of sameness, a unity of personality now felt by the individual and recognized by others as having consistency in time."[23] Adolescence is that stage in the life cycle during which young people construct, for the first time, a sense of self that binds together their past, present, and future into a coherent whole. Simply put, they must answer three fundamental questions: Who am I? Where have I come from? and Where am I going?

Why do these questions come to the fore during adolescence? Erikson's answer is twofold. On the one hand, physiological and psychological maturation not only make it possible to ask these identity questions but motivates the adolescents' search for their answer. Cognitive advances, for example, allow them to construct a perspective on themselves that simply was not possible during childhood. They now can construct complex temporal sequences and a richer understanding of their own subjectivity to form a sense of themselves as having continuity through time. Bodily maturation also motivates the search for identity. It stimulates young people to make sense out of the adultlike appearances they are beginning to acquire and the capacity for sexual intimacy they now possess.

On the other hand, identity also involves the social confirmation of these changes in the self. It is forged out of the negotiation of self-definition and social definition. In the previous section, we examined some of the most important expectations attached to adolescence as a social role. As young people mature physically and intellectually, society expects them to take up the tasks of readying themselves to leave home, to learn how to make their way with greater independence through various institutions, and to construct a personal system of moral meaning. It is significant to recognize the importance that culture plays in the mediation of these social expectations. Different cultural groups communicate them in markedly different ways.

Asian Americans and African Americans, for example, communicate somewhat different expectations to their youth than do the white, middle class.[24] Asian Americans, for example, often maintain a more traditional, hierarchical pattern of kinship obligations between generations. This can create a strain between the role expectations of adolescence communicated through the media, the schools, their peers, and those of the Asian-American church and home.[25] Adolescents may chafe against the deference toward authority expected at home and yearn for the greater freedom their peers seem to have. The self not only must negotiate the expectations of dominant social institutions but also those of its own cultural group. This complicates the psychological work of adolescence.

Culturally based gender differences also influence the psychology of adolescence. Sex role stereotypes influence sexual identity very early in life. Research has shown repeatedly that infants and children of different genders are treated differently. They are dressed differently, provided different toys, and encouraged to develop along different lines. Some of the most important research in this regard has emerged out of the investigation of women's development.[26] As will become clear below, this research helps us see why identity formation presents a special set of problems for adolescent girls. If the dominant set of expectations surrounding the role of adolescence focuses on individualization, these expectations can be experienced as doubly difficult and threatening to adolescent girls whose selves are relational. Being a relational self in an individualizing world is analogous to being an ethnic minority with cultural patterns at variance with the dominant society.

It is important, then, to take the psychosocial nature of identity formation quite seriously. Identity is the negotiation of self-definition and social definition. Society provides a ready-made stock of cultural "scripts" shaping adolescents' understanding of their past, present and future life course. Unless emerging definitions of the self are in some way confirmed by the social scripts provided by the surrounding world, it will be difficult for the adolescent's search for identity to be sustained.[27]

Although Erikson's account of identity formation is crucial to the understanding of adolescence adopted here, two critiques of his position must be taken into account: those found in the structural developmental tradition and recent research on women's development. On the surface, these critiques appear to move in diametrically opposed directions. Both have something to offer our understanding of the psychological work of the self during adolescence.

The Structural Developmental Critique

The structural developmental tradition—growing out of the work of Jean Piaget and developed in the thinking of Robert Selman, Lawrence Kohlberg, Robert Kegan, James Fowler, Sharon Parks, Thomas Lickona, and the early work of Carol Gilligan—points out that identity formation as described by Erikson does not necessarily include the psychological processes involved in *individuation* (not to be confused with individualization focusing on the social effects of modernization described in the previous section).[28] Individuation, the members of this tradition argue, involves the psychological work of disembedding the self from the various roles, relationships, and symbolic meanings that compose an adolescent's world in order to construct a self that is brought to and expressed through these roles, relationships, and symbolic meanings. This is something that is only achieved during late adolescence, if it takes place at all.[29]

Observers of adolescence frequently have noted the highly conformist nature of this stage of life. Whether young people are clean-cut scholar athletes or wear long hair and grungy clothes, they often are merely conforming to the norms of the peer group with which they identify. It is possible for young people to answer the questions of identity formation solely on the basis of these social reference groups with which they identify. Research based on Erikson's work, moreover, has revealed that many adolescents do not achieve fully individuated identities.[30] Identity foreclosure may take place in which young people enter into adultlike commitments and relationships without really choosing them for themselves. Or they may construct a diffuse identity in which they are unable to make long-lasting adult commitments on the basis of an internal sense of who they are and what they value.[31] They drift aimlessly from one relationship and job to another.

The structural developmental tradition helps us gain a better understanding of the kinds of psychological processes involved in constructing an individuated identity. Drawing on the capacities for abstract reasoning and systemic perspective taking that emerges during middle adolescence, the self engages in the work of differentiating itself more fully from the roles and relationships in which it participates. It is not that these things cease to be important during this process. Rather, they are engaged in a qualitatively new way. To borrow Robert Kegan's language, persons move from an identity in which "I am my relationships" to one in which "I have my relationships."[32] The self is disembedded from the roles and relationships by which identity is formed, constructing a clearer sense of its boundaries, needs, and values.

Why is this kind of individuation an important part of identity formation? In large part, it is important because of the possibilities and problems confronting the self in modernity. We have just examined the individualizing effects of modern society. In its relation to the economy, to differentiated institutions, and to moral meaning, the self is confronted with much more freedom than in traditional and archaic societies. Modernity creates the *social space* in which psychological individuation can take place on a wide scale for the first time. The much tighter fit of social roles and moral meanings characterizing traditional societies has disappeared.

Not only is the development of an individuated identity possible on a wider scale in modern societies, but it is desirable in this context as well. Individuation allows persons to make their way through the wide range of differentiated institutions in which they participate on the basis of a coherent and self-conscious understanding of themselves. Moreover, it helps them achieve a voice and moral perspective that can be brought to the pluralistic conversation of contemporary life. It also enables them to reflect critically on sources of cultural value and meaning, making them more adept at resisting the manipulation of the media, charismatic leaders, and political propaganda.

Individuation is particularly important with regard to the construction of moral meaning. Several decades ago, Gilligan and Kohlberg described adolescents as growing up in a "postconventional" world.[33] It is not necessary to adopt the neo-Kantian moral framework in which their argument was originally made in order to agree with their point: Modern societies confront individuals with the task of constructing critically examined, self-chosen moral perspectives. A variety of postconventional moralities are available for this purpose. Gilligan herself has broken with Kolhberg's "rights" approach in recent years and developed a care morality representing a different, postconventional moral framework, for example. The relativizing effects of cultural pluralism and the critical rationality of modern science create conditions in which it is increasingly difficult to accept moral perspectives on the basis of authority or convention alone. One of the psychological tasks of the modern self is to individuate in a postconventional moral and religious world.

In many ways, mainline Protestantism already recognizes this fact. It attempts to support the development of the kind of religious identity that offers a real alternative to religious fundamentalism. Fundamentalism often seems to encourage a pattern of identity foreclosure among its adolescents. This is based on the encouragement of precocious conversions during early adolescence, protection of adolescents from perspectives different from those of the religious group, and reinforcement of conformity to the values and beliefs of adult leaders.[34] At every point, mainline Protestantism stands at the opposite end of the spectrum from this pattern. It encourages many of the things that promote individuation: exposure to pluralism, use of critical thinking, and a refusal to force group conformity. As the departure of so many mainline youth makes clear, however, these things in and of themselves are not enough. Something more is needed if mainline Protestantism is to support the development of a postconventional religious identity and not merely to represent one more pathway to conventional, secular relativism.

The Critique from Research on Women's Development: The Relational Self

Erikson's portrayal of identity formation also has been criticized from the perspective of theorists carrying out research on women's development: Carol Gilligan, Blythe McVicker Clinchy, Jean Baker Miller, Judith Jordan, Ruthellen Josselson, Janet Surrey, Lyn Mikel Brown, Mary Belenky, and others.[35] Taken together, the emerging theoretical perspective they represent serves as an alternative to certain aspects of Erikson's model.

Erikson's description of adolescence is viewed as reflecting a male bias. It identifies maturation with greater levels of autonomy and independence. His description of identity formation implies that persons must first disconnect from relationships during adolescence in order to reconnect during young adulthood when they are capable of achieving intimacy. It is not just Erikson's description of adolescence that is problematic here. The problem is the model of the self and its development that he assumes. As Jean Baker Miller puts it: "In Erikson's scheme, for example, after the first stage, in which the aim is the development of basic trust, the aim of every other stage, until young adulthood, is some form of increased separation or self-development."[36]

In contrast, research on girls and women has discovered the ongoing importance of relationality at every point in their development. New psychological models have begun to emerge in which the self is seen as inherently relational (self-in-relationship) and development as a matter of complexifying and deepening responsive engagement with others.[37] Particularly suggestive in this regard is the role afforded empathy in development.[38] First nurtured in the mother-daughter relationship, this is portrayed as involving both cognitive and affective processes and as a key trajectory in the growth of the self. As empathetic communication becomes more complex and nuanced, greater sensitivity to differentness and sameness with others is achieved, contributing to a more differentiated self.

Changes like these in the core concepts used to portray the development of the self have both grown out of and contributed to new understandings of the problems faced by adolescent girls. Research indicates that many girls during early adolescence begin to experience a paradox that colors this entire period: In order to sustain relationships, they must diminish their relational orientation.[39] It is not that relationships stop being the primary context in which they struggle with identity issues. Rather, the contexts in which they find themselves do not support the relational orientation that they prefer, forcing their natural styles of interacting, learning, and knowing to go underground. From school settings that reward competition and objectifying forms of knowledge rather than cooperative learning and connected teaching to relationships based on sexual objectification rather than empathetic sharing, adolescent girls do not find their relational selves socially confirmed.

This social disconfirmation can make the process of identity formation excruciatingly difficult. Many girls experience a kind of psychic split during adolescence.[40] They may excel in the classroom but not feel that it reflects the way they really construct knowledge. High achievement does not engender high self-esteem. They may strive to make themselves sexually attractive to boys but dislike being treated as sexual objects and being forced to compete with their female peers. They may feel angry at themselves when they give in to others to avoid conflict but feel guilty when they assert themselves. Identity splits begin to appear, making it hard to achieve a coherent sense of self.

In short, identity formation can be especially difficult for adolescent girls in a world that does not provide social confirmation of their patterns of development. It is not hard to see why the individualizing expectations attached to the social role of adolescence could be particularly disconfirming of a relational self: so much emphasis is placed on standing apart from others to achieve greater autonomy. Is this necessarily the case? Do the individualizing social tendencies of modern life necessarily lead to psychological individuation understood along the patterns of male development? It may well be that patterns of development supporting growth in relationship may be better suited to the possibilities and problems of modern life.

Home-leaving does not necessarily mean separating altogether from your parents. It can mean gaining the capacity for more adult-to-adult relationships. This is precisely what many college-age women strive to achieve.[41] Learning to distance yourself from roles as you make your way through a highly differentiated society does not necessarily lead to self-fragmentation. It can mean becoming critical about the roles you choose to play and reconstructing them when they are experienced as oppressive.[42] The breakdown of systems of moral meaning providing large-scale social integration need not lead to moral individualism and relativism. It can create the conditions for a critically chosen, postconventional ethical position in which clearer lines between society, religion, and the self are maintained.

The social processes of individualization thus may serve as the conditions for new patterns of adolescent development that are more consistent with the relational needs of women and men alike. As mainline Protestantism struggles to discern the emerging patterns of adolescent development that it will support, one of the most perplexing questions before it is the role of psychological individuation. Here, theories of women's development seem to move in a direction diametrically opposed to that of the structural developmental tradition.[43] Rather than accentuating individuation, as the structural developmentalists seek to do, it redefines the tasks of adolescence by conceptualizing the self as inherently relational and development as the elaboration and complexification of this relationality.

The issues involved in a comparison of these two positions are complex and cannot be fully treated here. I believe it is important to retain the structural developmentalists' focus on individuation, while acknowledging that this can take place along different lines. Indeed, we would do well to reconceptualize individuation as a process of self-differentiation or differentiation in relationship rather than as a matter of increased autonomy and separation.[44] Although much of the research on women's development seems ambivalent about how to describe this process, it is clear that many of the theoretical perspectives emerging from this research point to some kind of process of self-differentiation as an important part of the development of adolescent girls.

Gilligan's research on moral reasoning, for example, describes the shift from a style of moral caring in which the needs of the self are subordinated to the needs of others to a moral style in which self and others are interdependent.[45] Similarly, research has found college women struggling to integrate separateness and conflict into their primary relationships.[46] Likewise, many women college students have been found to be involved in shifting from a cognitive style that is highly subjective to one that draws on the shared procedures of communities.[47] In each case, a new form of self-differentiation is taking place, albeit one that continues to be located squarely within the context of significant relationships.

Jacobs and Salzman adamantly affirm the importance of this self-differentiation in adolescent girls' development.[48] Jacobs argues that "idealization of the nurturing female has come to replace the image of the dependent woman" and that "it is essential that we develop models of female autonomy along with the relational perspective."[49] Her research has uncovered adolescent girls who are over-identified with others and are worn out by meeting their needs. These girls desire to be left alone and are willing to risk isolation and loneliness in order to construct a clearer sense of their self-boundaries and commitments.[50]

This kind of self-differentiation is an important part of the psychological work of adolescence. While it may take place along different lines in women and men, it cannot be omitted from an account of identity formation in the present context. It may well be that further research on this process in adolescent girls will reveal developmental patterns that are better able to hold together the social tasks of individualization with the psychological work of self-differentiation. If this is the case, then mainline Protestantism has a stake in supporting these kinds of patterns in its various ministries with adolescents.

At present, it appears that individuation means leaving the church. Adolescents seem to feel that they must separate from this context in order to grow. The promise of research on adolescent girls is the uncovering of patterns of development in which self-differentiation involves deepening and complexifying relationships, not separating from them. Mainline Protestantism has a stake in learning how this takes place and forming practices that confirm this sort of growth in relationship, not inadvertently encouraging an image of development based exclusively on a male model and encouraging the departure of its adolescents.

Facing the Realities of Adolescence

There are several important conclusions that we can draw from our discussion to this point. These conclusions, in turn, give rise to certain questions. First, the emergence of adolescence as a new stage in the life cycle should give the church pause to reflect on the nature and purpose of confirmation. Until the twentieth century, this practice could assume a social context in which children moved fairly quickly from childhood to adult roles and responsibilities. This is no longer the case. Between the intellectual growth and personal commitments of late childhood and those of young adulthood, a new stage of development now exists. Is it still appropriate to locate confirmation prior to this stage?

Second, the nature of adolescence in the modern context makes this question particularly pressing. Socially and psychologically, individuals must bear the burdens of constructing a coherent sense of life's meaning and purpose as never before. The highly differentiated, pluralistic character of modern society has an individualizing effect on its members. This creates social conditions in which constructing a personal identity becomes a widespread psychological task of the self for the first time in history. Can the church afford to ignore this social reality? The exodus of adolescents from the church during this stage of life seems to indicate that it cannot. What sort of implications does this have for the practice of confirmation?

Third, religion can be seen as responding to modernity in a variety of ways. It can respond defensively, attempting to shelter its members from modernity's individualizing effects and foreclosing the struggle to achieve personal identity. Religion can accommodate to modernity, furthering its individualization of moral meaning by maximizing elements of diversity and choice in its programs. Or it can seek a transformational role in relation to modernity, providing a communal context in which persons are given support in achieving a postconventional religious identity. If it chooses the latter, it may well be that the church can learn much about how to nurture this sort of identity from patterns of development being uncovered in research on girls and women. Here, development is not viewed as separation from relationships and primary communities but as deepening and complexifying persons' primary connections. Do individuals really have to leave the church in order to form a more differentiated self? If not, what sort of educational contexts allow them to grow in relationship rather than separating themselves from their primary relationships?

In short, our discussion to this point has issued in questions, not action-prescribing conclusions. This is because analysis of the social context alone cannot tell the church what it should do and be. How the church should shape the practice of confirmation in response to modernity must be discerned on theological grounds. The nature and purpose of confirmation is derived from theological reflection on the nature and purpose of the church. Only after engaging the story of confirmation from a theological perspective will we be able to decide how and if we should reconstruct confirmation in response to the social and psychological conditions that have been described.

Part 2

Confirmation in Historical Perspective

Introduction to Part 2

3. Antecedents and Origins of Confirmation

Before Confirmation: Antecedents in the New Testament?
"Confirmation" in the Context of Adult Initiation
The Emergence of Confirmation as a Sacrament

4. Changes in Confirmation and Catechetical Instruction in the Reformation

Catechetical Instruction during the Middle Ages
The Influence of Renaissance Humanism
The Influence of Erasmus
Martin Luther and the Emergence of Catechetical Instruction
Consensus: The Importance of Catechetical Instruction
Ulrich Zwingli and Baptism, Catechetical Instruction, and Covenant
    Theology
Martin Bucer and the Emergence of an Evangelical Confirmation
John Calvin and Crystallizing the Pattern of Reformation Catechesis

5. Lutheran, Anglican-Episcopal, and United Methodist Confirmation Practices

The Lutheran Tradition
The Anglican-Episcopal Tradition
The United Methodist Traditon

6. American Presbyterian Confirmation Practices

Early Reformed Liturgical Traditions
Antecedents of the American Tradition: The Westminster Assembly
The American Appropriation of the Westminster Heritage: Two
    Models of the Christian Life in the Early Tradition
Admission to the Lord's Supper: The Two Models in Practice
The Break-up of the Reformation Paradigm
From the Civil War to the 1930s
From the 1940s to the Present

Introduction to Part 2

The second part of this book tells the story of confirmation. By adopting a narrative-historical approach, it strives to employ a method that is appropriate to the nature of confirmation as a practice. It is important to pause at the beginning of this section and reflect briefly on why this sort of historical investigation is an integral part of the work of practical theology.[1]

Over the past decade a rich discussion has taken place about the nature of social practices.[2] As used here, "practices" are socially shared activities of such richness and depth that they shape the character of their participants and engender goods that are ends in themselves and not means to other ends.[3] Practices are special forms of social interaction. They have sufficient richness and depth to shape the dispositions and actions of those who participate in them. Worship, for example, is a practice, whereas the coffee hour following it is not.

Worship, then, is undertaken to glorify and enjoy God, not to provide a psychic "lift" for the coming week. Alasdair MacIntyre makes a similar point when he argues that practices generate "internal goods."[4] By this, he means that the beneficial effects of a practice cannot be gained in any other way than by participation in that practice. Certain knowledge and skills can only be acquired from the inside. Furthermore, only those who have acquired these things are competent to pass judgment on when a practice is performed well. It is the depth and power of practices to generate internal goods that makes their role unique in communities.

An important part of the recent discussion of practices has centered on the ways they are narrative-dependent. They are portrayed thus in two ways. First, narratives provide the cognitive framework in terms of which the goods engendered by practices are interpreted to and internalized by their participants. Second, practices have histories. To understand the goods they generate over time, it is necessary to construct a narrative by which their history is displayed. A few words about each of these will clarify why a historical-narrative approach is employed in the second part of this book and its importance to practical theology.

Like the concept "practice," narrative also has generated a rich discussion in recent years.[5] The center of this discussion is the unique role narrative plays in the construction of temporal meaning. Narratives have the capacity to knit together the interaction of persons and events as they unfold through time. They do so through "emplotment": the placement of particular occasions in a larger temporal framework.[6] Narratives serve as the larger gestalt in which the parts (events and people) are located. In the passion narrative, for example, Judas's kissing Jesus is one event in a larger pattern that sets forth the meaning of the cross. It is part of a story line that accentuates the singularity of Jesus' work, especially the way he was betrayed and abandoned by even his closest followers.

Typically, practices provide their participants with narrative scripts by which they can understand the meaning of the actions in which they are participating.[7] Sometimes these stories are implicit. At other times they are explicitly rehearsed. The meaning of worship is not articulated clearly every Sunday, for example. It is assumed and enacted in the dramatic sequence of events that unfold during the service of worship. On occasion, however, the assumed story is expressed directly and the meaning of the various parts of the service placed in a larger whole. Narratives thus play a key role in interpreting and generating the internal goods of practices.

This brings us to the second reason it is important to tell the story of confirmation. The meaning of confirmation has shifted over the course of time, reflecting a change in the goods prized by this practice. In order to understand and evaluate the remnants of these goods as they continue to inform the present, to retrieve past goods that have been lost, and to make a constructive proposal about which ones should be fostered today, it is necessary to tell the story of this practice as a whole.

Another way of making this point is to say that practices have histories.[8] They do not make up their meanings on the spot. The goods they generate are part of a much longer and broader complex of meanings that are inherited from the past and socially shared in the present. Only when the story of a practice is displayed can the goods that have been a part of this history become apparent. Such a narrative telling is itself a constructive act, an argument for a particular way of "reading" a practice with implications for its present form. This is especially important with regard to confirmation, which continues to have a wide range of meanings ascribed to it on the basis of its convoluted history.

In the following chapters, we will tell the unfolding story of the practice of confirmation. To provide an overview of the story line that will be set forth, a brief description of the primary purpose of confirmation at different points in history can be described briefly. As this purpose has shifted, so have the primary goods fostered by confirmation and the narrative by which these goods were framed.

During the first centuries of the church's life, confirmation was part of a much broader *catechumenal* process. Firmly embedded in the practice of adult initiation, its primary purpose was to shape the habits of thought, action, and feeling of those who were joining the church. During this period, confirmation was not a separate rite or even a clearly distinguishable moment in all baptismal rites. In those places that did include an anointing, consignation, and some similar act by the bishop it was an integral part of the baptismal service, symbolizing the initiate's reception of the Holy Spirit. The story told by the whole process of initiation placed emphasis on the importance of new Christians breaking away from the surrounding world and entering a community oriented toward the heavenly city of God. Catechumens were to demonstrate moral and spiritual readiness before they were qualified to enter this community.

As the adult catechumenate disintegrated and the practice of infant Baptism became more prevalent, confirmation was separated from Baptism and became a freestanding rite. Over many years, increased importance gradually was attached to this rite, and it came to serve a *sacramental* purpose. Primary emphasis was placed on God's action communicated through the church's sacramental action. It was not until the Middle Ages, however, that Thomas Aquinas gave explicit theological definition to confirmation along these lines. Aquinas described it as a Sacrament that communicates the fullness of the Holy Spirit, strengthening confirmands and allowing them to take up the tasks of the Christian life with greater maturity. The story told by the practice of confirmation at this point centered on God's confirming action in and through the church's sacraments and the special grace individuals receive when confirmed, allowing them to grow in sanctification and grace.

The Reformers ascribed a *catechetical* purpose to confirmation. They rejected the sacramental system of the medieval church, leading them to reject a sacramental definition of confirmation. The earliest generations of Reformers were ambivalent about retaining the concept of confirmation at all. Whether they called it confirmation or not, however, all of the Reformers advocated a special educational practice that handed on the basic doctrinal teachings of the church to every baptized member. This typically preceded First Communion and often was accompanied by a solemn ceremony marking admission to the Lord's Supper. The primary purpose of this practice was catechetical: instruction providing every baptized Christian with the theological knowledge necessary to make an intelligent confession of the church's faith. It also was viewed as enabling responsible participation in the life of the congregation and preparing persons to pursue their vocations in the world. The story told by the practice during this period focused on the uniqueness of God's saving action in Christ, available to individuals through faith, and the calling of all Christians to serve God in every sphere of their worldly existence.

The Reformation also saw the emergence of a *professional* understanding of confirmation. By "professional," we are not referring to a person who participates in one of the professions such as medicine or law. Drawing on language that begins to appear in various baptismal and confirmation services, we are pointing to the act by which an individual ratifies the covenant into which that person was baptized as an infant. This is viewed as a deeply personal act, a matter of the heart as well as the mind. Typically, it is portrayed as involving a declaration of trust and belief in the God revealed in Jesus Christ and a pledge of loyalty and obedience to that God. Among the first generation of Reformers, Martin Bucer was virtually alone in making this the primary good of confirmation, although it played a secondary role in Luther's and Calvin's thought as well. Although Bucer was a strong advocate of catechetical instruction, he came to believe that confirmation should be separated from this instruction and focus on a heartfelt profession of faith and pledge of obedience. This understanding came to the fore in the work of Richard Baxter among the English Puritans and later was emphasized in certain parts of American Presbyterianism. The primary goods attached to confirmation understood in this way centered around the individual's personal response to God's claim upon her or his life. The story told by the practice when this purpose was dominant was governed by covenantal themes. The confirmand was located in God's covenants with humanity, Israel, and the church and was invited to take up the vows of the covenant of grace made explicit in Jesus Christ.

During the last half of the twentieth century, a *developmental* understanding of confirmation has emerged. Based on the insights of developmental psychology, modern education, and liberal theology, this understanding of confirmation can be found in various confirmation curriculums and liturgical texts since the 1930s. The primary goods of confirmation understood along these lines focus on helping confirmands engage in a significant act of faith exploration and discovery on an unfolding journey of faith. Participatory, experiential pedagogies are advocated, over against the internalization approaches of earlier forms of confirmation. The story told by a developmental understanding of confirmation draws heavily on the journey motif. The Christian life is portrayed as an ongoing journey in which openness and risk are as important as certainty and commitment. Confirmation is an important step, but it is only one step on an ongoing journey of faith.

It will become apparent in the following chapters that each of these purposes is partially present at every point in the unfolding story of confirmation. The catechumenate of the early church, for example, had catechetical, sacramental, and confessional dimensions. Likewise, the Reformers sought to shape the habits of thought and action of those they instructed and to allow them to understand and confess personally the catechism they were learning. Typically, however, one purpose was primary at each point in history and governed the goods generated by confirmation at that time.

Understanding the story of confirmation brings before us the range of possible purposes this practice might play today. No doubt something can be learned from each part of this story. The construction of the narrative that follows thus has a deeply practical purpose. It is to guide the contemporary church in its attempt to discern how the present chapter of this practice should be written. This is the constructive task of practical theology, and it will be taken up in Part 3 of this book.

3

Antecedents and Origins of Confirmation

Where does the story of confirmation begin? Some scholars locate the first chapter of the story in the New Testament period, whereas others place it much later.[1] Oscar Cullmann, for example, argues that we can discern in the book of Acts two distinct liturgical components of Baptism that correspond to its two central meanings: water-washing, associated with the forgiveness of sins, and laying on of hands, associated with the reception of the Holy Spirit. From the very beginning, he says, Baptism ran "the danger of falling apart into two different sacraments."[2] Along different lines, Dom Gregory Dix claims that confirmation was fully present during the apostolic period and "originated as the Christian equivalent of the circumcision imposed on proselytes to Judaism."[3]

Before Confirmation: Antecedents in the New Testament?

What are the antecedents of confirmation? Can they be found in the New Testament period? In order to answer these questions, we must examine key biblical texts that seem to indicate the existence of a separate rite in the apostolic church that transmitted the Holy Spirit to new members. The most important of these are found in Acts 8 and 19.[4] A second group of passages focus on Jesus' baptism by John. Some scholars have argued that the descent of the Holy Spirit is a second act that follows Jesus' immersion, the founding analogy of confirmation's relationship to Baptism.

Proto-Confirmation in Acts?

The biblical passages providing the strongest evidence for those who argue that a kind of proto-confirmation can be found during the apostolic period are Acts 8 and 19. In both chapters, the laying on of hands by official representatives of the church is closely identified with the bestowal of the Holy Spirit. In both cases, moreover, it is clear that this bestowal follows Baptism. In Acts 8, Philip travels to Samaria after the stoning of Stephen. There he preaches the gospel and performs miracles. Those who respond in faith are baptized. Later, the apostles in Jerusalem hear what has taken place and send Peter and John so that the new disciples might receive the Holy Spirit. The text explicitly points out that the Spirit had not yet come upon any of them and goes on to say: "Then Peter and John laid their hands on them, and they received the Holy Spirit" (8:17).

We find a similar, if more complex, pattern in Acts 19:1–7. Traveling through

Ephesus, a center of John the Baptist's disciples, Paul comes upon some followers of Jesus. He asks them if they received the Holy Spirit when they became believers? They respond that they have never heard of the Holy Spirit. Paul asks, "Into what then were you baptized?" (v.3). They respond that they have only received John's baptism. Paul then baptizes them in the name of the Lord Jesus. This is followed by a crucial verse: "When Paul had laid his hands on them, the Holy Spirit came upon them, and they spoke in tongues and prophesied" (v.7).

It is not difficult to see why these two accounts have fueled speculation about the existence of confirmation in the early church. The Holy Spirit does not seem to be bestowed by baptism alone but through the laying on of hands by the apostles. Does this represent a kind of proto-confirmation or even confirmation itself? As early as Tertullian, teachers and theologians of the church began to attach great importance to the imposition of hands after Baptism on the basis of Acts 8 and 19.[5] What are we to make of this claim?

The first thing we must do is complicate matters. When the entirety of Acts is taken into account, it becomes clear that Acts 8 and 19 do not set forth a standard pattern in which the Holy Spirit is bestowed after Baptism through the laying on of hands. At least four patterns at variance with these passages also can be discerned in Acts.[6]

1. *The Spirit operates independently of Baptism, often in close association with the preaching of the gospel.* This pattern describes in part what occurs on Pentecost as portrayed in Acts 2. There is an outpouring of the Holy Spirit on the disciples, leading them to speak the languages of many nations. No mention is made of their subsequent baptism, presumably because they already are followers of Jesus. A similar pattern is found in Acts 10 where the Spirit directs Peter to go to the house of a Roman centurion, Cornelius, following a vision in which he is told that all that God has made is clean. Cornelius is a "God-fearer," a term used to describe persons who were loosely associated with the synagogue. As Peter preaches to the Gentiles who have gathered at Cornelius's house, the Holy Spirit comes upon them, and they begin to speak in tongues and extol God. Only then are they baptized. A version of this pattern also is present in Acts 9:10–19. Ananias is directed by the Holy Spirit to visit Paul not long after he has been blinded on the road to Damascus. Ananias tells Paul that he must lay his hands on him so that he may regain his sight and "be filled with the Holy Spirit" (9:17). Only after this happens is Paul baptized.

2. *The Spirit is given through Baptism in the name of Jesus.* This is the pattern found in the second half of the Pentecost account. When a crowd gathers after the Spirit's initial outpouring on the disciples, Peter begins to preach to them. He culminates his sermon by telling them: "Repent, and be baptized every one of you in the name of Jesus Christ so that your sins may be forgiven; and you will receive the gift of the Holy Spirit" (Acts 2:38). About 3,000 people are baptized.

3. *Baptism takes place following proclamation of the gospel with no mention of the Holy Spirit.* This pattern is found in a number of places. In Acts

8:26–40, Philip comes upon an Ethiopian eunuch reading Isaiah 53. Then, "starting with this scripture, he proclaimed to him the good news about Jesus" (Acts 8:35). Philip baptizes the eunuch and is snatched away by the Holy Spirit. No mention is made of the Spirit's descent on the eunuch. Similarly, in response to Paul's preaching, Lydia and her household are baptized, but no mention is made of their reception of the Holy Spirit (Acts 16:14–15). In the same chapter, the Philippian jailer and his household also are baptized with no mention of the Spirit (16:33–34). The same pattern is found when Crispus and his household are baptized (18:8). In all of these passages, persons respond to the preaching of the gospel and are baptized with no explicit mention made of their reception of the Spirit.

4. *An unusual case: A teacher of the church who seemingly has the Spirit is not baptized.* This pattern is found in Acts 18:24–28, and it is full of difficulties. The passage refers to Apollos who "knew only the baptism of John" (v. 25). Yet the way he is described squares with Acts' account of a person who is filled with the Spirit: He speaks with "burning enthusiasm"; he is "bold" before the synagogue and is able to refute their leaders' arguments; he is of great assistance to those who are already believers, helping them understand scripture. At no point, however, does the text explicitly say that Apollos has received either the Spirit or Christian Baptism.

Taken together, these passages make it clear that there was no single pattern in the early church governing the relationship between the bestowal of the Holy Spirit, Baptism, and the laying on of hands. The Spirit is given before, during, and after Baptism. What is important is the close relationship between proclamation, faith, Baptism, and the reception of the gift of the Spirit. Each of the elements is an important part of a person's incorporation into Christ and the new community that he has brought into being.

What then are we to make of Acts 8 and 19? The answer resides in the theology of the Holy Spirit that informs the composition of the book as a whole. The author of Acts generally is considered by New Testament scholars to be the author of the Gospel of Luke. In both books, the Holy Spirit plays a special role. In Luke, for example, the Spirit plays a much broader role in the events surrounding Jesus' birth than in Mark and Matthew and Luke even goes so far as to describe John the Baptist as "filled with the Holy Spirit" (1:15). Following Jesus' baptism by John and the beginning of his public ministry, the Spirit is confined to Jesus alone. It is bestowed on the church only after his ascension (24:49). The contrast between the disciples before and after the bestowal of the Spirit tells us a great deal about the special role Luke sees the Spirit as playing in the church.[7] Prior to Pentecost, the disciples lack understanding and do little teaching and healing. After the outpouring of the Spirit, they are full of "power" and manifest signs of the Spirit's work: boldness before the authorities, healing, prophesying, speaking in tongues, and so forth. The Spirit who had empowered Jesus' ministry now empowers theirs.

An important part of Luke's depiction of the Spirit's activity in the church is the way it directs the church's mission to the Gentiles. This mission is given special emphasis by Luke even in his depiction of the ministry of Jesus. Jesus' baptism, for example, is followed by a genealogy tracing his lineage back to David and then on back to Adam, reminding his readers of Jesus' fundamental kinship with humanity, not just with Israel.[8] In Acts, the Holy Spirit is portrayed as directing each significant step in the fulfillment of the church's universal mission. It is here that we find the key to the meaning of the laying on of hands in Peter's and John's visit to the Samaritans in Acts 8.

This episode is part of a series of steps by which the church is portrayed as fulfilling its commission to proclaim "repentance and forgiveness of sins in his name to all nations" (Luke 24:47).[9] The first step takes place on the Day of Pentecost itself. Not only is the Holy Spirit poured out on the disciples, but they begin to speak in other languages (Acts 2:4, 6). The gift of the Spirit is symbolically related to the church's fulfillment of its universal mission. The second step takes place in the mission to the Samaritans, of which Peter's and John's laying on of hands are a part. We will turn to this shortly. The third step is Peter's baptism of the Gentile Cornelius and those gathered in his household. Here the church's worldwide mission reaches fruition for the first time.

The events leading up to Peter's baptism of Cornelius are portrayed as involving the special intervention of God at every step of the way. An angel tells Cornelius to seek Peter out. Peter falls into a trance in which it is revealed that all things created by God are clean. When Peter later travels to Cornelius's household and begins to preach, the Holy Spirit falls on the Gentiles who have gathered to hear him, leading them to speak in tongues and extol God. Only then is Peter willing to baptize Gentiles for the first time, in spite of his own surprise and that of the circumcised believers who accompanied him. What we have here is a kind of second Pentecost, effecting a crucial turning point in the mission to the Gentiles. Peter makes this connection himself: "The Holy Spirit fell upon them just as it had upon us at the beginning" (11:15).

Peter's and John's trip to the Samaritans is situated between Pentecost and this "second Pentecost" involving the Gentiles. This is no accident, for the Samaritans were located religiously between the Jews and the Gentiles. Moreover, long-standing animosity existed between the Jews and Samaritans, as evidenced in the story of the Samaritan woman at the well and the parable of the good Samaritan. Philip travels to Samaria after Stephen is stoned to death and successfully converts and baptizes a number of people. This represents a significant step beyond Judaism in the fulfillment of the universal mission of the church. The Jerusalem church sends Peter and John to see what has taken place, just as it would later send Barnabas to Antioch to examine what has taken place there after the conversion of a number of Hellenists. The apostles lay hands upon these new Christians, and they receive the Holy Spirit.

What is the significance of this symbolic action? It is important to remember that the laying on of hands is used for a number of purposes in both the Old and New Testaments: blessing, transfer of power, and commissioning.[10] What is its purpose here? The answer resides in the important step being taken in including the Samaritans into the Christian community. The church is moving beyond the Jewish community and is on its way to the inclusion of the Gentiles. G. W. Lampe points out the significance of this for our interpretation of the laying on of hands: "An unprecedented situation demanded quite exceptional methods."[11] Something more than Baptism is necessary to demonstrate to the Samaritans that they really are members of the church. The laying on of hands represents their incorporation into the church, the bestowal of the Holy Spirit, and their commission to carry out the ministry of the gospel. A new nucleus of the missionary church has been established, and Luke makes it clear that the gospel, henceforth, will emanate outward from this center.[12]

Something similar seems to be happening when Barnabas lays his hands on Paul. Healing is involved, to be sure. But Luke also portrays Paul as receiving the missionary spirit, for immediately after receiving the Spirit the apostle is described as beginning to preach the gospel and as becoming "increasingly more powerful" (9:20, 22). Here, as in the laying on of hands on the Samaritans, a significant turning point is taking place. Paul, the apostle to the Gentiles, is empowered to carry out his mission. At every such turning point, Luke portrays the Holy Spirit as involved in a special way.

Is this what is happening in Acts 19 where Paul lays hands on the twelve disciples? It is quite possible. Ephesus was a center of Gentile missionary activity, and Luke may have wanted to make it clear that the Spirit is at work in establishing the outpost as well. A somewhat different explanation, however, is perhaps even more plausible. The primary focus of this story seems to be on the contrast between John's baptism of repentance and Jesus' baptism of the Holy Spirit. The twelve who are baptized and have hands laid on them had only received John's baptism of repentance. Ephesus was known to be a center of John's former disciples, and it is fitting that Luke would use Paul's trip there as an occasion to make it clear that John's baptism has been surpassed by that of the church "in the name of the Lord Jesus" (19:5). Luke even seems to recall language used by the Baptist in his witness to Jesus prior to his baptism.

By viewing Acts 8 and 19 in light of Luke's theology of the Spirit, we can draw several conclusions about their relationship to confirmation. First, it is easy to see why the church later would associate the laying on of hands with the bestowal of the Spirit, especially when practiced by the bishops of the church. It also is easy to see why the church would look to these passages to justify the emergence of confirmation as a distinct rite. Acts 8 and 19 lend themselves to this sort of interpretation, especially when taken out of the context of Luke's theology of the Spirit and the universal mission of the church.

Second, when these passages are placed in Luke's theological framework, however, they do not point to a kind of proto-confirmation. If anything, they represent exceptional practices marking significant steps in the church's mission to the Gentiles. Third, when the entire range of baptismal practices found in Acts is taken into account, no single pattern emerges. The Holy Spirit is found before, during, and after Baptism. In Acts, God is not portrayed as binding the Spirit mechanically to any particular rite.[13] Reception of the Holy Spirit is a part of the entire process of incorporation into Christ and the new community that he has brought into being.

In short, Acts 8 and 19 cannot be used to justify the existence of confirmation during the New Testament period. Although the laying on of hands was practiced for a number of different purposes in the early church, there is no evidence that it represented a widespread, normative practice by which the Holy Spirit was communicated to believers following Baptism. This does not exhaust our investigation, however. Appeal also has been made to the descent of the Spirit on Jesus as indicating the separation of Baptism and the bestowal of the Spirit. This is an equally important area to examine, for the relation of Baptism and the Holy Spirit became deeply problematic when confirmation was given sacramental status and viewed as "completing" or "perfecting" the work first begun in Baptism.

Jesus' Baptism by John the Baptist
and the Descent of the Spirit: The Origins of Confirmation
in the Synoptic Tradition?

Cyril Pocknee's comment is representative of those modern scholars who would look to the narrative of John's baptism of Jesus to find the origin of confirmation: "A careful reading of the Gospel narratives shows that the act of water-baptism and the descent of the Spirit are two different things, however closely linked. . . . It is not surprising that Christian Initiation has been influenced by these accounts of Christ's baptism and that we should expect that in liturgical practice the gift of the Holy Spirit would follow on and not immediately coincide with the act of water-baptism."[14] Pocknee reflects a line of thinking that appeared as early as the patristic period: Baptism is associated with the forgiveness of sins and the postbaptismal anointing, consignation, or laying on of hands with the bestowal of the Holy Spirit. Does this distinction stand up to scriptural evidence? The synoptic tradition alone portrays John as baptizing Jesus, and our focus thus will be on it.

The synoptic tradition describes John as the forerunner of Jesus (Matt. 11:10; Mark 1:2). He is "Elijah," who was portrayed as returning at the dawning of the end time (Matt. 11:14; cf. Mal. 4:5–6).[15] His message and his baptism represented a call for Israel to repent in preparation for the coming Messiah. As Mark puts it, he offered a "baptism of repentance for the forgiveness of sins" (1:4, cf. Matt. 3:6b). This posed something of a problem for the early church. Why would Jesus submit to a baptism involving repentance for sin? The synoptics answer this question in two ways: (1) They differentiate between the forerunner and the Messiah, and (2) they describe the theological significance of Jesus' baptism as representative of his ministry as a whole; that is, in submitting to John's baptism, something of great significance is being said about the kind of Messiah Jesus would be.

To begin with the first of these, all three of the synoptics portray John the Baptist as giving direct witness to the difference between his ministry and that of Jesus. He baptizes only with water, but the Messiah will baptize with the Holy Spirit (Matt. 3:11; Mark 1:8; Luke 3:16). Baptism is used metaphorically here, referring to the general outpouring of the Holy Spirit that would accompany the Messiah's coming. The Spirit had been quenched since the demise of Old

Testament prophecy, and this return would be a sign that the new age had dawned.[16] John himself thus is portrayed as subordinating his ministry to that of Jesus. It is one of preparation; Jesus' is one of fulfillment. John's baptism is of water; Jesus' of the Spirit. The descent of the Spirit onto Jesus during his baptism by John marked a transition point from preparation to fulfillment. It cannot be separated from what is going on in the baptismal account as a whole.

This becomes even clearer when we turn to the second issue noted above, the theological interpretation of the Baptism offered by the synoptics. This comes to expression in God's declaration about Jesus, accompanying the descent of the Spirit: "This is my Son, the Beloved, with whom I am well pleased" (Matt. 3:17). This statement is a conflation of two passages from the Old Testament.[17] "This is my Son, the Beloved" comes from Psalm 2:7. This is a royal psalm, describing the adoption of the king of Israel by Yahweh at the monarch's enthronement and his endowment with special gifts to rule God's chosen people.[18] The kings of Israel received a special anointing with oil during their enthronement, endowing them with the Spirit and allowing them to carry out their work with wisdom and justice.[19] The second half of this conflation, "With whom I am well pleased," comes from Isaiah 42:1. This is one of several passages describing the Servant of the Lord, culminating in the suffering servant passage of Isaiah 53. The servant is closely identified with the Spirit in 42:1, immediately following the passage used in Matthew: "I have put my Spirit upon him."

The theological meaning of this conflation is unmistakable. The One who is God's royal Son is the One who will play the role of the suffering servant. He is endowed by the Spirit to carry out this ministry. It is here that we find a clear answer to the question: Why did Jesus submit himself to John's baptism, a baptism of repentance for the forgiveness of sin? It is an act of identification with a lost and suffering Israel and, by implication, a lost and suffering humanity. It anticipates the ministry of suffering and death that lies before Jesus. Cullmann captures this nicely: "Thus the Baptism of Jesus points forward to the end, to the climax of his life, the Cross, in which alone all Baptism will find its fulfillment. There Jesus will achieve a general Baptism. In his own Baptism in Jordan he received commission to do this."[20]

Without the declaration attending the descent of the Spirit, this meaning is unclear. With it, it is crystal clear. Baptism and the reception of the Spirit are integral parts of a theological whole. The One who is the long-awaited royal Messiah, empowered by the Spirit of God, is the One who will endure the suffering and humiliation of the cross.

This interpretation makes it very difficult to view the descent of the Spirit on Jesus as indicative of a separate rite of confirmation lying behind the baptismal accounts. It is only much later, when Baptism develops into a complex of differentiated rites, that we find the beginnings of the separation of water-washing and the bestowal of the Spirit. This can only be read back into the New Testament community if the literary and theological unity of the baptismal account is denied. To do so, I believe, is to forfeit the clear meaning of scripture. We are left with a question: If confirmation cannot be found in the New Testament, where did it come from? To answer this question, we move beyond the New Testament period and examine developments taking place in the practice of Christian initiation.

"Confirmation" in the Context of Adult Initiation

The first five centuries of the church's life saw the emergence of one of the most dramatic and powerful practices in its entire history: the adult catechumenate. The catechumenate emerged out of the teaching and formation offered new converts in the early church. Its purpose was *catechumenal:* a process of formation designed to shape the habits of thought, action, and feeling of persons seeking membership in the church.

It is not difficult to see why this purpose was so important during this period. Throughout the first part of the church's life, it was a minority in relation to the surrounding culture. At times it experienced extreme forms of persecution. Even when it was not directly under duress, it represented an alternative to the dominant ideas and values of the Roman Empire. The practice of initiation was designed to prepare prospective members for participation in a community that was embattled. It was a lengthy and demanding process. Ironically, this demanding process of initiation was offered precisely as the church was growing in leaps and bounds.[21] This practice has much to teach the contemporary church about the importance of holding together catechetical instruction, spiritual direction, and liturgical formation. Its potential contribution goes beyond its historical role in the emergence of confirmation as an independent rite.

Over a period of several centuries, the preparation leading up to Baptism gradually became more formalized and elaborate. Baptism began as a straightforward washing with water, signifying the forgiveness of sins offered in Christ and the reception of the Holy Spirit. As the catechumenate became more complex, this central rite was supplemented with other rites. The baptismal service itself became more complex. It is in this context that we find the origin of confirmation.

Throughout this period, confirmation was not a separate rite. It was an integral part of the baptismal service. Various ritual acts began to accompany the water-washing, including anointing with oil, consignation, and the laying on of hands. It was out of these supplementary rites that confirmation slowly evolved. Ambrose, near the end of the third century, was the first to use the term "confirmation" to refer to this part of the baptismal ceremony, and it is clear that he used the term to refer to the "completing" of Baptism.[22] It was not until the ninth century that it became a technical term referring to an independent rite.

It is for this reason that we have put the term confirmation in quotations in the heading of this section. Confirmation as an independent rite did not exist during this period. Indeed, it is inaccurate to argue, as some contemporary liturgical theologians do, that three clearly differentiated moments in the practice of initiation existed throughout the church during this period: Baptism, confirmation, and First Communion. Empirically, this simply is not accurate. Wide variety existed throughout the church with regard to the ritual actions accompanying the water-washing.[23] At least two distinct patterns, for example, are evident in the earliest available evidence.[24] The Western pattern involved two separate anointings: one before the water-washing and a second immediately after. The Syrian pattern only had one anointing, immediately before the water-washing. Even much later, when postbaptismal anointings began to appear in the East, wide variety continued to be present in the church. Theodore, bishop of Mopsuestia, tells us that candidates had a cross made on their foreheads, describing them as "sealed with the oil of baptism."[25] John Chrysostom, in contrast, only mentions a prebaptismal anointing and says that the Holy Spirit is conferred by the bishop at the baptismal font. In some churches, the bishop laid hands on the ones who were being baptized and made the sign of the cross above or on their heads.[26] In other churches, this signing was performed with oil. In still others, a combination of these rituals was administered.

The theological interpretation of these gestures also reveals great variety. In some instances, they were identified with the bestowal of the Holy Spirit. Ambrose associated them with the bestowal of the sevenfold gifts of the Spirit, for example, recalling Isaiah 11:2–3. In other cases, these postbaptismal acts were interpreted as signifying the reception of the candidates into the church and their blessing by the bishop. In still other instances, consignation was interpreted as marking persons with the sign of Christ, signifying to Satan that they no longer belonged to him and identifying the members of the church as belonging to Christ when he returns.

In short, we should not fall into the trap of idealizing the practice of initiation during this period or assume more uniformity was present than actually existed. What we find during this period is proto-confirmation, a range of ritual actions following the water-washing that later developed into the rite of confirmation as the power of the Roman church was consolidated and began to regularize the liturgical practices of the church. During this period, these liturgical actions were an integral part of Baptism, not an independent rite or even a clearly distinguishable moment.

This variety should be kept in mind as we move to two accounts of adult initiation during this period, those found in Hippolytus's *Apostolic Tradition* and the writings of Cyril of Jerusalem, supplemented with the diary of Egeria, a pilgrim to Jerusalem. The former is our earliest account of the emerging adult catechumenate. The latter describes the catechumenate in full bloom, near the end of the fourth century. Both give clear indication of the ritual actions that eventually will evolve into confirmation as a separate rite. At this point, however, they do not represent a uniform practice existing throughout the Eastern and Western churches.

Hippolytus's Apostolic Tradition: *Developments in the Practice of Initiation*

One of the oldest accounts of Christian initiation during this period is found in Hippolytus's *Apostolic Tradition*.[27] Many scholars have come to associate this work with the church of Rome, for certain features of its baptismal rite are analogous to the practice of the Roman church in later centuries.[28] The church order is of great antiquity and provides insight into church practice at an early point in history. It would be too much, however, to appeal to it as an authoritative piece of tradition that can warrant contemporary practice. The authorship and church home of the work cannot be established with any certainty. No ancient text survives except in the context of other manuscripts in Coptic, Arabic, Ethiopic, and Latin. The church orders of these documents do not completely correspond with one another. It is well-known that such orders were often gathered into collections from the fourth century onward and at times were rewritten in the process.

What we have today then is a scholarly reconstruction on the basis of manuscripts far removed from the original source in time and space. Accordingly, the *Apostolic Tradition* cannot be appealed to uncritically as a definitive example of influential (probably Roman) church practice. We simply do not know with certainty when or where it was written, who its author was, and what kind of role it actually played in church life. A more appropriate use of this church order (we will be following the reconstructed text of Geoffrey Cuming) is to use it to catch a glimpse of developments beginning to take place in the practice of initiation during the first centuries of the church's life. The simple water-washing of the early church was being supplemented with other liturgical and instructional activities, creating a rich and powerful practice by which new members were incorporated into the church.

The church order of Hippolytus identifies two classes of people in the preparatory phase of confirmation: hearers of the word and baptismal candidates. The former (also known as catechumens) are persons just learning about the Christian faith. The latter are persons who have been in this preparatory phase for at least three years and desire to become full members of the church by being baptized. Each of the phases of initiation begins with an examination of the candidate. Hippolytus describes how this takes place for hearers of the word. They are to "be questioned about their reason for coming to the faith."[29] Sponsors who know the candidates must come forward and testify to their sincerity. Special attention is paid to their "state of life."[30] By this, the text means their moral conduct, including their sexual practices and marital relations. Inquiry also is made into how the person makes a living. Whole classes of occupations are deemed incompatible with Christianity and prospective members are told they must leave them if they wish to join the church. From the outset, persons desiring to join the church were faced with a choice. What is more important: their worldly occupation or their allegiance to Christ? This emphasis on concrete moral and behavioral changes continued throughout the first phase of the catechumenate. During this period they received special teaching and participated in special liturgical practices.[31]

After an extended period of formation, persons could become baptismal candidates. Once again, they were examined. At a later point, this would be known as the scrutiny and would include exorcism, as well as examination. At this point, it involves only the latter. Sponsors were required to testify on each candidate's behalf. As Hippolytus puts it: "And when those who are to receive baptism are chosen, let their life be examined: have they lived good lives when they were catechumens? Have they honored the widows? Have they visited the sick? Have they done every kind of good work?"[32]

This marked the final stage of their preparation for full initiation into the church and took place in the weeks immediately preceding Easter or Pentecost when Baptism was normally offered. This final phase involved intensive, prebaptismal teaching and participation in special liturgical rites. It was taken extremely seriously. Even after entering this phase, persons could be set aside by the bishop if their conduct was deemed not worthy.

Hippolytus does not provide insight into the kind of teaching that was offered during this period, only that it took place.[33] He does provide, however, insight into the liturgical formation taking place during this phase. From the time baptismal candidates entered this phase, they were exorcized daily. Hippolytus does not describe what this involves, but the *Gelasian Sacramentary* of the fourth century describes three scrutinies or special Lenten services that focused on the exorcism of catechumens.[34] In these services, prayers of intercession were offered that focused on events of deliverance in biblical history. Prayer was made for a similar deliverance of the candidates who were moving toward Baptism. In Augustine's day, exorcism involved a contemptuous hissing at baptismal candidates, blowing all evil out of their lives.[35] As this took place, the candidates stood without shoes on a rough rag or animal skin, symbolizing the vices on which they must learn to tread and the first clothing worn by Adam and Eve after their expulsion from the garden.

All that Hippolytus tells us is that exorcism involved the laying on of hands. He does reveal, however, that it was an intimate part of the candidates' final preparation for Baptism. On the Thursday immediately prior to Baptism, persons were to bathe for the first time since becoming baptismal candidates. They were to fast the following day and assemble at a place designated by the bishop. The bishop then administered a final exorcism that concluded with his breathing on the faces of the candidates and making the sign of the cross on their foreheads, ears, and noses. This ritual was later known as the Effeta and symbolized the opening of the candidates' faculties to the sacraments. The candidates then spent the night before Easter in vigil, having the Bible read to them and receiving final instruction.

With the break of dawn, the candidates proceeded to the baptistery. The water to be used in the baptismal service was blessed. The candidates then removed all their clothing. The bishop blessed two vessels of oil that were used in the service: the oil of thanksgiving and the oil of exorcism. A priest then took each of the candidates and asked if he or she renounced Satan, to which the response was: "I renounce you, Satan, and all your service and all your works." The candidates then were anointed with the oil of exorcism. In Tertullian's description of the renunciation of Satan, he uses the phrase "*pompa diaboli,*" the procession of the devil. A *pompa* was a festive procession marking a special occasion such as a military victory or an anniversary.[36] In Baptism, Christians were dropping out of the devil's procession and following Christ alone.

Following this renunciation and anointing with oil, Hippolytus tells us that candidates were handed over to the bishop, who descended with them, one by one, into the water. There they were asked three questions in which they affirmed their faith in the Father, Son, and Holy Spirit. After each question, candidates responded "I believe," and the bishop would immerse them in the water. On coming out of the water, they were anointed a second time with oil, this time with the oil of thanksgiving. They put on their clothes and entered the main sanctuary of the church. The bishop would then engage in three acts. He would begin by laying his hands on their heads, one at a time, praying that just as God had made them worthy of receiving the forgiveness of sins in the baptismal water, God also might make them worthy of receiving the Holy Spirit. He then would anoint them with oil and "seal" them on the forehead. This was followed by the kiss of peace. At this point, the newly baptized Christians would join the rest of the congregation, where they prayed with them and exchanged the kiss of peace for the first time. They then received First Communion and were given a special drink of milk and honey.

Hippolytus's description of the conclusion of the baptismal service is important, for he presents it not so much as an ending but as a beginning of ongoing growth in the Christian life: "When these things have been done, each one shall hasten to do good works and to please God and to conduct himself rightly, being zealous for the Church, doing what he has learnt and advancing in piety."[37] This is followed by a somewhat cryptic reference to further instruction in the meaning of Baptism by the bishop. This is to be done in private, he says, for non-Christians are not capable of understanding its meaning.

It is not difficult to enter imaginatively into the practice of initiation as described in the reconstructed church order of Hippolytus. Not only does it include moral, spiritual, and doctrinal teaching, but it also involves liturgical formation at every point. The culminating event of Baptism must have been especially powerful. We sense the depth and power of this practice and can only wonder if there is anything comparable in the mainline Protestant church today.

The Blossoming of the Adult Catechumenate

The acceptance of Christianity by the Roman Emperor Constantine marked an important turning point for Christianity at many levels. No longer an embattled minority, the church was now viewed by the emperor as the glue holding a declining empire together. This shift in the church's relationship to the powers that be had a marked impact on the church. The most obvious change was the influx of new converts that followed the emperor's acceptance of Christianity. Suddenly, belonging to the church was no longer a liability in a person's advancement in the empire's bureaucracy, but a positive gain. Not only did more people begin to seek affiliation with the church, but they did so for less worthy reasons.

This had an impact on the adult catechumenate. One effect was a shortening of the process. The three-year period in which persons were hearers of the word was largely abandoned.[38] Persons were admitted immediately into the final phases of the catechumenate for an eight-week intensive period of instruction and formation leading up to their baptism. Moreover, a large number of people began to become *clinici:* persons taking part in the catechumenate but refraining from Baptism until they were near death. This was done on the belief that the Sacrament would wipe out all sins committed to that point in a person's life at the moment of its administration. Constantine himself was a *clinici,* and Augustine constantly railed against this group of people, portraying them as "halfway" Christians. Another effect of the influx of new members on the practice of initiation was greater formality and regimentation. Teaching, by necessity, became more formal as it was offered to larger groups. The various phases of the catechumenate became more clearly demarcated.

The adult catechumenate can be described as reaching full bloom during this period. Persons such as Augustine and Ambrose, with extensive education prior to their conversions, began to reflect on this practice. Building on the developments of the previous centuries, they clarified and elaborated the theological meaning of its various parts. It is during this period that many of the theologians of the church began to identify the bestowal of the Holy Spirit with the ritual actions taking place after the water-washing. As we have seen, signs of this trend were evident as early as Hippolytus. Our examination of the practical side of initiation during this period will focus primarily on the Jerusalem church in the middle of the fourth century. We are fortunate to have an extensive series of catechetical sermons preached by Cyril, the bishop of Jerusalem during this period.[39] We also have the diary of a woman pilgrim, Egeria, who visited this city in the 380s, providing us with a firsthand account of the catechumenate and baptismal rite.[40] It is important to keep in mind the variety that continued to exist throughout the church, however. The blossoming of the adult catechumenate did not lead to uniformity. Significant regional differences continued, even in the baptismal liturgy.[41]

Cyril became bishop of Jerusalem around the year 350. Neither Cyril nor Egeria mention a lengthy waiting period prior to entry into the final phase of the catechumenate, beginning their accounts with the enrollment of persons for prebaptismal instruction and formation.[42] Those so enrolled were a special class of people in the church. In the East, they were called *photizomenoi* and in the West, *competentes.* Entry into this class continued to involve examination of the character of candidates and the testimony of neighbors or friends who knew them well. This took place on the first Monday of Lent.

In the Jerusalem church, Lent began eight weeks before Easter. By the fourth century, it had become a time of repentance and examination for the entire church. All baptized members were encouraged to participate vicariously in the intense preparation of the catechumens as a way of renewing their own commitment to the faith. They were free to attend the catechetical lectures and to witness the various liturgical events that accompanied this process. The first catechetical lecture, the Procatechesis, took place in the presence of the entire congregation, reminding every member of the seriousness of this step.

The catechumens then began a daily routine that was followed throughout Lent. They would come to the church before daybreak each morning, where they were exorcized. This remained one of the most personal elements of the catechumenate. The office of exorcist was of a lower clerical rank, making it possible for a large number to be available to administer this rite to individuals and small groups.[43] The candidates then gathered in the Martyry, where the bishop, seated upon his throne and surrounded by presbyters and priests, offered catechetical instruction for three hours. While this seems an intolerably long time to us today, Egeria reports that these lectures included periods of discussion and that the audience greeted the teaching with loud exclamations.[44]

Of the eighteen lectures delivered by Cyril during this period, the first five deal with general matters. The remaining thirteen focus on the articles of the Jerusalem Creed. Egeria describes these lectures as focusing on the key events of the Bible and a detailed explanation of the Creed.[45] This focus upon the creed is indicative of one of the important new elements in the catechumenate that appeared during this period: the "Handing over of the Creed."[46]

Prior to the fourth century, Baptism included only one moment of creedal affirmation by the catechumens, when they gave assent to the Trinitarian questions asked during their baptism. By Cyril's day, a second moment of affirmation had appeared: the "Handing over of the Creed" (mentioned above). During the final stages of instruction, the bishop would share the creed with the candidates, and they were expected to memorize it. Many of the teachings and practices of Christianity were kept secret from outsiders during this period, a practice later described by scholars as the Disciplina Arcani. As Ambrose put it, "The creed should not be written down. You have to be able to repeat it, but no one must write it down."[47]

Egeria reports that in the Jerusalem church the handing over of the creed took place at the beginning of the sixth week of Lent. Henceforth, the bishop's instruction of the catechumens focused on explaining the creed's meaning. In many places, catechumens took part in a ceremony called the "Giving back of the Creed," in which they repeated it from memory and offered it as a personal confession of the church's faith. Egeria reports that in the Jerusalem church this took place on Palm Sunday. Each candidate would come before the bishop, accompanied by a sponsor, and repeat the creed to him.[48] Augustine describes this as taking place on a raised platform in front of the entire church.[49] He also describes a similar process of "handing over" the Lord's Prayer to the catechumens on the same day they "give back" the creed to the bishop. They were to repeat this prayer a week later.

In many ways, the "giving back" of the creed and Lord's Prayer represented the culminating moment of catechetical instruction. The candidates now gave public testimony to their personal assent to the basic doctrines of the faith as summarized in the creed. In "handing back" the Lord's Prayer, they gave public testimony to their acceptance of a life of prayer and the other disciplines of the Christian community learned during their period of instruction.

It is uncertain whether the postbaptismal sermons that have come down to us were given by Cyril or by his successor as bishop, John. They were designed to explain the meaning of the sacraments and provide us with an excellent description of the baptismal service as practiced in the Jerusalem church. The candidates gathered in the outer hall of the baptistery, a special building next to the central sanctuary. They began by renouncing Satan. Facing west, toward the darkness of the night, they stretched out their hands and rejected Satan and all his works, pomp, and service. They then turned toward the east, facing the rising sun, and affirmed their faith by saying: "I believe in the Father, and in the Son, and in the Holy Ghost, and in one Baptism of repentance."

Entering into the baptismal chamber, they disrobed and were anointed with the oil of exorcism. They were led one by one into the baptismal pool, where they confessed the Trinitarian faith in response to questions asked by the bishop. Coming out of the water, they received an anointing. Following this anointing, the newly baptized Christians would put on white garments and proceed to the Martyry carrying torches. There they would participate in the Lord's Supper for the first time. During the week following Easter, the *neophytes* (those who were newly baptized) received further instruction called the Mystagogy. This teaching provided detailed theological interpretation of the various parts of the sacraments in which they had just participated.

Of special importance for our purposes is the mystogogical sermon in which Cyril (or his successor) explains the meaning of the anointing taking place immediately after the water-washing. It is portrayed in a manner that is similar to the Effeta received prior to Baptism in the *Apostolic Tradition*. In the Jerusalem church, the candidates were anointed on their foreheads, then their ears, nostrils, and breasts. The major analogy Cyril uses to explain the meaning of this act is based on the baptism of Jesus by John. "Christ bathed in the river Jordon, and having invested the waters with the divine presence of his body, he emerged from them, and the Holy Spirit visited him in substantial form, like coming to rest on like. In the same way, when you emerged from the pool of sacred waters you were anointed in a manner corresponding with Christ's anointing. That anointing is the Holy Spirit . . ."[50] The sacramental overtones of Cyril's interpretation in his mystagogical sermon are unmistakable. He implores his hearers not to regard the oil with which they were anointed as mere oil, but like the Eucharist as transformed: " . . . so the holy charism after the invocation is no longer ordinary ointment but Christ's grace . . ."[51] Likewise, the anointing of various parts of the body is connected with special gifts conferred by the Spirit: the ability to understand the sacraments, to resist the devil, and to identify with Christ. The anointing is viewed typologically as prefigured in anointings of the kings and priests of Israel and as established definitively in the Spirit's descent on Jesus. Christians can now be called "anointed ones" by virtue of their reception of this sign of the Spirit.

There are broad similarities of Cyril's description of Christian initiation to that of Hippolytus. Both provide insight into a powerful practice combining moral, spiritual, and doctrinal instruction with a process of liturgical formation. Of special importance for our purposes is the way both relate the anointing following the water-washing to the bestowal of the Holy Spirit. They reflect both the liturgical complexification of Baptism accompanying the development of the practice of initiation and the theological interpretation of scripture used to explain its various parts. Both refer to Jesus' baptism to differentiate the role played by the water-washing and the episcopal actions of anointing that follow. Elsewhere, Cyril appeals to Acts 8 and 19 to warrant the claim that Christ gave the apostles the power to bestow the Holy Spirit through the laying on of hands.[52] The scriptural practice of laying on of hands is now being fused with the episcopal practice of consignation with oil, indicating the way biblical interpretation is being shaped by liturgical developments.

It is important to emphasize that confirmation, as an independent rite, does not exist during this period. What we do see are the conditions that at a later point will lead to its development: the liturgical elaboration of Baptism and a process of theological interpretation and scriptural justification of these liturgical developments. What had been a straightforward washing with water in the early church was increasingly surrounded by a wide range of supplementary liturgical acts. Moreover, as the catechumenal process of membership began to stretch over a longer period of time, new liturgical developments began to accompany the doctrinal and moral instruction offered prospective members: exorcism, enrollment, and the rendering of the Creed, to name but a few. No doubt these added to the drama of initiation and contributed much to its ability to shape the habits of thought, action, and feeling of its participants. There was a downside to these developments, however.

Nathan Mitchell aptly compares the liturgical elaboration taking place during this period to the kind of growth found in a tropical rain forest.[53] In such a forest, the accumulated vegetation can become so thick and variegated that any semblance of order is hard to find. As the various parts of the practice of initiation became more elaborate and differentiated, so too the theological meaning of this practice and the inner coherence of its various parts were harder to find. If Baptism had served as the theological core of the early practice of initiation, this was increasingly less apparent as liturgical and theological permutations began to abound.

The liturgical actions that followed the water-washing are an important case in point. Development of a range of episcopal actions at this point in the service—from anointing to consignation to laying on of hands—created the conditions for certain theological confusions. Scripture was misinterpreted to justify later liturgical developments. Postbaptismal actions were, in some instances, portrayed as completing or perfecting the water-washing.[54] Most important of all, the bestowal of the Holy Spirit began to be closely associated with a specific point in the service administered exclusively by a particular rank of church official, the bishop. Where the book of Acts had portrayed the Spirit as working in freedom before, during, and after Baptism, it now was in danger of being domesticated. Such is the ambiguity of the liturgical and theological developments represented by the practice of initiation. While a dramatic practice serving a powerful need in the early centuries of the church's life, it was the seed bed of theological confusion that would plague confirmation throughout its history. Throughout the period of the adult catechumenate, the postbaptismal actions from which confirmation would emerge are neither uniform nor freestanding. Certain developments would soon take place, leading to the emergence of confirmation as a separate rite in the church, one that eventually would be ascribed sacramental status.

The Emergence of Confirmation as a Sacrament

It was only gradually, over the course of many centuries, that confirmation was differentiated from the practice of initiation to become an independent rite. The story begins with the dissolution of the adult catechumenate. Like a ship breaking up on the rocks surrounding an island, the practice of initiation disintegrated as the church moved into the Middle Ages. The various parts of the original ship were put to new use. What had been the mast was the frame of a bamboo hut. The wine barrel was used to store fruit. Cooking knives were used to hunt game. So too various parts of the practice of initiation began to appear in new contexts and serve new purposes. Catechetical instruction dissipated in many parts of the church. Where it did appear, it often came after Baptism and was closely related to the practice of confession. Exorcisms and scrutinies that had been an integral part of the lengthy process of preparation of catechumens for Baptism were tacked on to a baptismal service administered to infants. So too the postbaptismal actions that evolved into the Sacrament of confirmation were granted new significance as they were separated from the baptismal service and took on a life of their own.

Tracing the story of the separation and development of confirmation will not be easy. It was only gradually, over the course of many centuries, that this part of the baptismal service developed into a separate rite and was officially recognized by the Western church as a sacrament. These developments do not follow a single, unfolding trajectory.[55] The Eastern church, for example, never separated Baptism and confirmation and hold them together in a single, unified, ritual occasion to the present. In the West, the theology and practice of confirmation developed in fits and starts. In some regions, certain practices would emerge that largely were absent in other parts of the church. Theological interpretations of confirmation would be offered in some periods, only to be rejected in others. As late as the high Middle Ages, when confirmation was given explicit theological definition as a sacrament, there was much debate over what it represented.

The unevenness of the history of confirmation in the Middle Ages is an important part of the story we are telling. It is inaccurate to portray the process by which this rite attained sacramental status as the gradual unfolding of a universally established, early tradition. What we see is a complex, historical process, unfolding along different lines in various parts of the church. Five trends can be pointed to that contributed to the emergence of confirmation as a separate rite. These should not be viewed as clear-cut chronological steps, but as interpenetrating trends that together eventuated in the gradual differentiation of confirmation from the practice of initiation and its theological definition as a sacrament of the church.

1. Separating confirmation from Baptism and the ascendancy of the Roman rite of initiation
2. Shortening the period of time between birth and Baptism

3. Lengthening the period of time between Baptism and confirmation
4. Debate over the significance of confirmation in scholastic theology
5. Official declaration of confirmation as a sacrament of the church by various church councils

Separation of "Confirmation" from Baptism
and the Ascendancy of the Roman Rite
of Initiation

Like a nineteenth-century English novel, each step we follow in the story of confirmation's definition as a sacrament contains subplots within the larger movement of the story. Two such subplots are particularly important in the early stages of this story: the gradual separation of confirmation from Baptism and the ascendancy of the Roman rite of initiation throughout the Western church. Neither leads to the definition of confirmation as a sacrament. Indeed, ascendancy of the Roman rite of initiation in the Western church had a conservative impact on the theology of confirmation. This rite maintained a great deal of continuity with the older baptismal rite that had been used in the adult catechumenate. Even when infants were being addressed, rubrics originally designed for adults were retained. Especially important for our purposes is the way it encouraged maintenance of the bishop's role in the postbaptismal acts of confirmation, even in circumstances that made this difficult.

Probably the most important reason that Baptism and confirmation were separated was strictly a practical one: the expansion of Christianity, especially to the countryside. Early Christianity was largely an urban phenomenon.[56] Most of its congregations were situated in major metropolitan areas. This made it possible for bishops to participate in all parts of the practice of initiation, from catechetical instruction to the baptismal service. The expansion of Christianity made this more difficult in metropolitan areas and virtually impossible in rural areas. The legitimation of Christianity by Constantine and the influx of new members this precipitated already had put pressure on the church along these lines. The collapse of the Roman Empire made episcopal participation in all parts of initiation an impossibility. It resulted in the decline of city life and made transportation more difficult and risky. Travel to metropolitan areas where bishops could preside over Baptisms became harder, and it was equally difficult for bishops to travel around the countryside.

The church responded to this situation in several ways. One of the most important patterns was that of the church of Rome. Local priests were given the right to baptize adult converts and infants but not to "confirm" them. This liturgical act was referred to in a variety of ways—as a completing, perfecting, and sealing—and was reserved for the bishop alone. For the first time, a gap appeared between Baptism and the postbaptismal acts carried out by the bishop. Persons were baptized at one point and had to wait until some point in the future for the completion of their baptism by the bishop.

This was not the only way the church responded to the difficulties posed by expansion to rural areas. Throughout northern Italy, Gaul, and Germany there were extended periods of time in which the baptismal rite, including the postbaptismal anointing, could be administered entirely by a local priest when it was not possible for a bishop to be present.[57] It was not until the twelfth century that the Roman practice became universal throughout the West. The difficulties inherent in the Roman pattern are obvious. Either those who have just been baptized or the one doing the confirming must travel. As we shall see, Baptism was increasingly administered to infants, making travel doubly difficult. Why then did the Roman practice prevail? Why did the church not allow local priests to baptize *and* confirm new members? There are several reasons.

The postbaptismal anointing and laying on of hands had been closely associated with the episcopacy throughout the patristic period, lending the weight of tradition to its preservation. As early as A.D. 305, the Council of Elvira instructed priests who had baptized persons living far from a church (or who were deathly ill) to bring them to a bishop "that the catechumen may profit through the laying on of hands."[58] Jerome, likewise, states that this prerogative is reserved for the bishop. This tradition was repeated in a number of church councils and was portrayed as the accepted practice of the bishop of Rome. The *Apostolic Constitutions* of 370 and the first and second councils of Carthage codified this tradition and made it a matter of church law. Pope Innocent I, in 416, and Pope Gelasius I, around 492, set forth an identical policy. Episcopal confirmation thus had the weight of tradition and church law behind it from a very early period.

Just as important, however, was the increasingly important role bishops began to play in the church and broader culture during this period. Although the last Roman emperor was not deposed until 476, the empire had long been in decline. Throughout the latter part of the empire's existence, its various governmental institutions had become less effective and had contracted in scope. This created a power vacuum of major proportions, and the church began to fill this void. It was the one major institution of transregional proportions with administrative offices and procedures in place. It also was one of the few institutions staffed with well-educated leaders, as classical education began to decline.[59]

With the decline and fall of the empire, bishops increasingly were called on to provide leadership for broad sectors of life. They were symbols of church unity and political stability in a time of uncertainty. It is not difficult to see why this would add to the weight of tradition, lending credence to retaining an important element of episcopal participation in Christian initiation. Bishops were effective symbols of the church universal and represented the role of the church around the world.

As we have noted, however, the Roman baptismal rite and its designation of confirmation as the exclusive prerogative of the bishop was not immediately accepted in all parts of the church. This did not take place throughout the West until the twelfth century.[60] The story of how this finally occurred is indicative of the convoluted process by which confirmation was finally established as an independent rite with sacramental status. A key step in this direction took place during the reign of Charlemagne.

Charles the Great, commonly known as Charlemagne, inherited a kingdom that was first established by Clovis in the last part of the fifth century. Unlike other Germanic leaders, Clovis converted to Catholicism, not Arianism, creating a long-lasting alliance between his dynasty and the church. When Charlemagne came to power in 768, his military strength was such that the pope was able to renounce his nominal allegiance to the emperor of the eastern Byzantine empire and give it exclusively to the ruler of the Carolingian empire. Charlemagne, in turn, allowed himself to be crowned by the pope. Thus the Holy Roman Empire was born.

Charlemagne nearly doubled the size of his kingdom through military conquest and ushered in an era of political and economic stability. Following the fall of Rome, Europe had lacked a centralizing governmental agency that could offset the growth of feudalism, a political system vesting local nobles with a tremendous amount of power and keeping a large percentage of the population in serfdom. Charlemagne sought to offset the power of local, feudal lords by consolidating the political and religious unity of his kingdom. Working closely with the church, he sponsored a series of reforms. The most important of these were promulgated in *Admonitio Generalis,* issued in 789.[61] Three years before this document was issued, Pope Hadrian had sent Charlemagne a copy of the Roman sacramentary. *Admonitio Generalis* had the effect of making the Roman pattern of Baptism standard throughout his kingdom. Baptism, now, was only allowed at Easter and Pentecost. The final portion of the service, the "confirmation," could be administered solely by a bishop, the long-standing Roman practice.

The effect of this policy was the creation of a gap between Baptism and confirmation throughout most of the Holy Roman Empire. Much of the kingdom was rural, and there were relatively few bishops. The way this pattern was actually put into effect reveals an attempt to accommodate it to local custom. We noted above that Gaul and Germany had allowed priests to administer the entire baptismal service, including the postbaptismal anointing.[62] Even after Charlemagne's reforms were put into effect, the older pattern was retained and episcopal laying on of hands merely added a week later.[63]

We can summarize the first trend. The expansion of Christianity, especially to rural areas, made it increasingly difficult for bishops to preside over all Baptisms. In response, priests in many parts of the church were gradually allowed to carry out the entire baptismal service. In those areas that used the Roman pattern of initiation, however, the postbaptismal anointing or consignation still was the prerogative of the bishop alone. This reflected ancient tradition and the symbolic and political importance of the bishop during the early Middle Ages. The practical effect of this policy was the gradual separation of "confirmation" from Baptism in many parts of the church. Priests baptized, and bishops conducted periodic tours to "complete" these Baptisms. It was not until the twelfth century that this pattern became universal in the Western church. An important step had been taken, however. What originally had been united in a single baptismal service, in many parts of the church was separated by a period of time. A second important step was the increased prevalence of infant Baptism.

Shortening of the Period of Time
between Birth and Baptism

The debate over the existence of infant Baptism in the early church has been long and inconclusive.[64] While there are no clear references in the New Testament to infant Baptism *per se,* there are references to household baptisms in Acts, Paul's Letters, and the pastoral letters.[65] It is quite possible that there were children in these households who were baptized. The term "house" (*oikos*) had a technical meaning in Judaism during this period, indicating that children were especially in mind.[66] The practice of baptizing an entire household reflects the importance placed on corporate identity in ancient Israel and in Judaism during the New Testament period.[67]

While it is possible that infant Baptism was practiced during the New Testament period, it is clear that adult Baptism represented the norm. This is to be expected in light of the minority status and missionary orientation of the church at this point. Emphasis was placed on helping adults make the transition from their pagan lives to a new life in Christ. The entire catechumenate, culminating in Baptism, was organized around this task. As early as Hippolytus, however, we find incontrovertible evidence that children were participating in Baptism on a regular basis. Along with instructions about the baptism of adults, *The Apostolic Tradition* also tells church leaders: "They shall baptize the little children first. And if they can answer for themselves, let them answer. But if they cannot, let their parents answer or someone from their family."[68]

Although adult Baptism was the norm, infant Baptism already was beginning to gain ground. With the legitimation of Christianity, this trend was accelerated. The general population was Christianized, and the presentation of children and infants for baptism by their Christian parents became much more common.

It is important to remember that Baptism was only administered at Easter and Pentecost in those places under the influence of the church of Rome. Even when infant baptism became more dominant, the Roman pattern was prescribed by canon law until the thirteenth century, with a few notable exceptions such as the British Isles.[69] Emergency Baptisms by priests, parents, and midwives could be performed at any time, if the baby's life was in danger. By the thirteenth century, however, the practice of allowing Baptism at any time of the year became widespread throughout many parts of the church, as evidenced in the councils of Cognac (1259) and Bourges (1255). By the fourteenth century, various councils positively mandated parents to bring their infants for Baptism as quickly as possible. The *Constitutions of Padua* (1339), for example, required Baptism within eight days of birth, and the Synod of Avignon (1337), within twenty-four hours of birth.[70]

There were several reasons for the trend toward shortening the period between birth and Baptism. The most obvious is the high incidence of infant mortality.

When conjoined with Augustine's theology of original sin and his view of Baptism as having salvific power, it created a kind of "logic" in which early Baptism made sense: All persons are born in sin and stand under God's judgment; Baptism saves them from this judgment by removing the curse of original sin and applying the medicine of immortality to those who are washed with its laver of regeneration. This "logic" echoed throughout the theology and practice of the Western church and was still highly influential on theologians and councils of the twelfth and thirteenth centuries.[71] Robert Pulleyn, for example, wrote that gehenna hung over unbaptized infants; Hugh of St. Victor argued that Baptism was indispensable for the salvation of infants.[72]

The practical effect of shortening the interval between birth and Baptism was the removal of bishops from the process of Baptism. Most Baptisms were now performed by a local priest soon after a child was born in the parish. Confirmation thus not only was separated from Baptism in time, but it also was differentiated from Baptism in terms of the authorized officiant.

Lengthening the Period of Time between Baptism and Confirmation

A third trend was the movement of First Communion and confirmation to a later age, generally referred to as the "age of discretion." This age was not clearly defined but generally referred to a child's ability to discern right from wrong. Again, the trend toward increasing the interval between Baptism and confirmation was not something that happened in a straightforward, chronological fashion. As late as the twelfth and thirteenth centuries, infants were still being confirmed and served First Communion in conjunction with their baptism, under the influence of Roman practice harking back to the adult catechumenate. During this period, however, a number of councils began to recommend a much later date for confirmation. The Council of Cologne in 1280 declared that anyone under the age of seven was too young to be confirmed. Other councils placed the age of confirmation as late as fourteen.

This trend gradually was accepted throughout the Western church. It reflects the extent to which confirmation was viewed as a freestanding rite with its own liturgical power and theological meaning. Indeed, as scholastic theology struggled to define the meaning of confirmation during this period, it gave support to the later date for confirmation. The theological meaning given confirmation did not really fit with infancy, whereas it did with the age of discretion.

Debate over the Significance of Confirmation in Scholastic Theology

The theological meaning of confirmation did not emerge overnight. By and large, it developed in tandem with the emergence of confirmation as a differentiated liturgical rite. Theological reflection on the meaning of confirmation, however, began while the adult catechumenate was still intact. As we have seen, theologians began to set forth the meaning of the various parts of the baptismal service in their mystagogical teaching. Building on the insights of the church fathers, two lines of thinking about confirmation began to emerge during the early medieval period.[73] In one, confirmation was described as necessary to become fully Christian, adding things not present in Baptism. In the other, it was portrayed as bestowing a further installment of a gift already bequeathed in Baptism. Although these two positions overlapped, they led to important distinctions in medieval theology.

The first finds its antecedents in a highly influential Pentecost sermon given by Bishop Faustus of Rietz. In this sermon, he describes the Holy Spirit as giving all that is necessary for innocence in Baptism but as bestowing the strength necessary to battle against sin in adulthood in confirmation. He poses a hypothetical question about confirmation: "What good can it do to me, after the mystery of baptism, to have the ministration of one to confirm me? So far as I can see, we have not obtained everything from the font, if after the font we still need the addition of something new."[74] In his answer to this question, he uses a military analogy that was destined to become famous.[75] Baptism represents the enlistment of a soldier in the kingdom of Christ, and confirmation indicates reception of the arms to wage the battle against evil and sin.

Faustus's theological understanding had an enormous impact on the later Middle Ages by its incorporation into the *False Decretals*. This was a collection of letters and decrees by popes and early councils that was supposedly put together by Isidore of Seville, an influential Spanish bishop of the early 600s. In reality, it was a combination of authentic and forged documents put together by a group of church leaders in order to consolidate the church's power in the Holy Roman Empire. Whereas Charlemagne had worked closely with the bishops to unify his kingdom, his death was followed by a power struggle between local nobles, the emperor, and the bishops. In order to strengthen their position, a group of church leaders decided to "discover" the *Decretals*. Parts of Faustus's sermon, including the quotation given above, were included in this document. It was attributed to Isidore himself. Other statements about the theological significance of confirmation set forth a similar meaning. One, for example, allegedly written by Urban I, reads as follows: "For all the faithful must after baptism receive the Holy Spirit through the laying on of the hand of the bishops, so that they may become fully Christians."[76]

Throughout the Middle Ages, the *False Decretals* was thought to be genuine and had an important impact on one way of thinking about confirmation. Baptism was viewed as incomplete: everything is *not* given at the font. Confirmation is necessary to seal or perfect the Christian life, strengthening persons to take up the struggle against sin and evil and characterizing maturity in faith. A second line of thinking was found in Rabanus Maurus, who was a disciple of Alcuin, Charlemagne's most influential adviser. Maurus described Baptism as bestowing the Holy Spirit and confirmation as a further donation of this gift.[77] As he puts it:

> The Holy Spirit, the Paraclete is bestowed immediately on the baptized by the bishop through the imposition of the hand, that they may be strengthened

through the Holy Spirit for preaching to others the same gift which he bestowed in baptism, given by the grace of eternal life. For the baptized are signed with charism by the priest on the top of the head, but by the bishop on the forehead, so that in the first anointing the descent of the Holy Spirit upon them is signified, to consecrate the dwelling for God, and that in the second anointing, the sevenfold grace of the same Holy Spirit is declared to come upon people with all fullness of sanctity and knowledge and power.[78]

Two things are important here. First, the Holy Spirit is received in *both* the first unction immediately after Baptism and in the bishop's "confirmation" of Baptism. The latter is a further installment of something already received. Second, confirmation is described as enabling persons to preach the gospel to others, a gift that they themselves received in Baptism.

The difference between these two lines of thinking may not seem great to us, but in the detailed distinctions created by scholastic theology they were developed into different positions.[79] Recall the practical situation before the medieval theologians: Baptism was administered as close to birth as possible and confirmation much later, when the age of discretion was reached. What was the status of this rite? In Lombard's *Sentences* and other theological works, it already was being portrayed as a Sacrament. But what was the purpose of this Sacrament? Just how necessary was it? The medieval theologians knew full well that many people who were baptized as infants were not confirmed before they died. Were they not saved? Just how necessary for salvation was confirmation? If it was necessary, what was the purpose of Baptism?

Building on the lines of thinking described above, two positions appeared.[80] Some theologians described confirmation as "conditionally necessary," as adding spiritual strength necessary to combat sin as an adult. Salvation from the curse of original sin and the Holy Spirit, however, had already been bestowed in Baptism. This was the position of Peter Lombard, William of Auxerre, and Bruno of Segni.[81] Other theologians portrayed confirmation's necessity in stronger terms. It was "mortally necessary," for Christians were obligated to equip themselves for the struggle against sin.[82] Hugh of St. Victor, for example, argued that there was justifiable concern for persons who, though baptized, did not avail themselves of the grace conferred in confirmation. Similarly, Peter of Poitiers divided the sacraments into two classes: those necessary for salvation and those not. Baptism and confirmation were placed in the former, with marriage and ordination in the latter. Although not denying that baptized infants who died before being confirmed were saved, they argued that Christians who live to adulthood and are not confirmed did not possess the sanctifying grace necessary to fulfill their calling as Christians. They were not equipped to ward off the temptations facing them as Christian adults.

In typical fashion, Thomas Aquinas brilliantly synthesizes both lines of thinking and represents the definitive statement of the meaning of confirmation by scholastic theology. He draws on the *False Decretals* at points to cite various authorities, but his theological reasoning is not sullied by the dubious status of this document. Aquinas begins his discussion of confirmation in the *Summa Theolog-*

ica by providing justification for its sacramental status.[83] Unlike some of his contemporaries, he believed that all of the sacraments had to be directly instituted by Christ and could not merely develop out of the tradition of the church. Christ, he argues, instituted this sacrament, not by bestowing it, but by promising it, for the fullness of the Holy Spirit could only be poured out after his resurrection and ascension.[84]

He then tackled the problematic question of confirmation's relation to Baptism, mediating the two positions described above. Confirmation is necessary for salvation but only in that it brings to perfection what is already conferred in Baptism. If death intervenes before confirmation takes place, Baptism is sufficient for salvation.[85] He describes their relation succinctly: ". . . just as Baptism is a spiritual regeneration unto Christian life, so also is Confirmation a certain spiritual growth bringing man to perfect spiritual life."[86] Similarly, he writes: "Confirmation is to Baptism as growth to birth."[87] Baptism is the Sacrament that breaks the curse of sin and regenerates persons to new life. Confirmation is the sacrament of growth. After persons have reached the age of discretion, they are ready to receive the "fullness of the Holy Ghost," enabling them to live a sanctified life.[88]

Aquinas echoes traditions examined above: ". . . in this sacrament the Holy Ghost is given for strength in the spiritual combat."[89] Similarly, he writes: "Though he who is baptized is made a member of the Church, nevertheless he is not yet enrolled as a Christian soldier."[90] He also describes confirmation as conferring the ability to make a public confession of faith, even in the face of adversity.[91] In confirmation, then, baptized Christians are given the grace necessary to fight against the sin and evil that will assail them throughout their adult lives. Its purpose is different than that of Baptism and equally important in its own right.

Official Declaration of Confirmation as a Sacrament of the Church by Various Church Councils

The work of scholastic theologians on confirmation stood in a reciprocal relation to its practice. It both reflected and influenced this practice. Theological distinctions, such as those made by Aquinas, had the effect of reinforcing the trend toward increasing the interval between Baptism and confirmation. Even in the thirteenth century, infants could still be confirmed. As confirmation was viewed as a "sacrament of growth," conferring the grace necessary for spiritual combat and perfection, it was clear that infant confirmation did not make theological sense, and practice was altered accordingly.

The theology and practice of confirmation as a sacrament culminated in its canonization by the Council of Florence in 1439. This document was written for Armenian Christians who wanted to join the Roman Catholic Church, and it set forth basic doctrines and practices. Confirmation is described as one of the church's seven sacraments. Its purpose is explained as follows: "The effect of the sacrament is that in it the Holy Spirit is given for strength, as it was given to the apostles on the day of Pentecost, and namely that a Christian may boldly confess the name of Christ."[92] Drawing on Acts 8, the decree states that ordinarily the bishop alone can administer this sacrament, just as the apostles alone had communicated the Holy Spirit through the imposition of hands.[93] Along with Baptism and ordination, it is described as conferring an "indelible character on the soul" and thus is not repeatable.[94]

Following the Reformation, this position was repeated in the anathemas attached to various doctrinal statements of the Roman Catholic Church. They portrayed confirmation as communicating the Holy Spirit through the ritual action of the bishop and as imprinting an imperishable character on the soul, making it not repeatable. These statements responded to the new understanding of confirmation the Reformers were beginning to champion: "If people say that confirmation of the baptized is an idle ceremony and not rather a true and proper sacrament, or that once it was nothing other than a kind of catechesis by which those close to adolescence explained the reasoning of their faith before the assembly, let them be accursed."[95]

The contrast here between confirmation as a sacrament and confirmation as a form of catechesis is clearly drawn. The five trends noted above lead to the former, not the latter. The theology and practice of the medieval church portray confirmation as a sacrament conferring a "strengthening" grace through the power of the Holy Spirit. As a sacrament, it was viewed as communicating the Holy Spirit objectively. It did not depend on the worthiness of the officiant or the worthiness of the recipient.

As a practice, confirmation had become severely truncated, reduced to a single ritual occasion unaccompanied by teaching, spiritual guidance, or other measures of formation. Aquinas mentions teaching in relation to this sacrament only once, in his justification of a place for sponsors who stand with the confirmand.[96] What happened to catechetical instruction during the period we have just been describing? It was an integral part of the practice of initiation in the adult catechumenate, just as confirmation had been. Did it disappear altogether during the Middle Ages, only to reappear during the Reformation? Did the Reformers define confirmation so exclusively in catechetical terms that their practice was condemned by the Roman Catholic Church? If so, what was at stake in the move? These questions lead to the next part of our story, dealing with the Reformers' critique of the medieval developments we have just been describing.

4

Changes in Confirmation and Catechetical Instruction in the Reformation

Confirmation, as many branches of contemporary Protestantism have come to think of it, emerged out of the broader reforms of the Reformation. The Reformers looked askance at the medieval rite of confirmation. Its sacramental definition, its close association with the privileges of the episcopacy, and its diminishment of Baptism were all offensive to them. This led some of the leaders of the reform movement to cast aspersions on confirmation. John Calvin, for example, referred to the inherited rite of confirmation as a "misborn wraith."[1] Others such as Philip Melanchthon and Martin Bucer were more sympathetic, advocating an evangelical rite of confirmation that was part of a broader practice. Martin Luther was ambivalent about confirmation, referring to the medieval, sacramental form of this rite as "mumbo jumbo" and "monkey business," but lending his support to others in the reform movement attempting to reconstruct its meaning.[2]

No single understanding of confirmation thus emerged out of the Reformation period. Indeed, the alteration of confirmation was *not* a primary concern of the Reformers, even among those who advocated reclaiming this rite in Reformed congregations. Far more emphasis was placed on the establishment of the practice of catechetical instruction. On this point, all of the Reformers agreed: Establishment of a form of teaching allowing every baptized member of the church to understand and confess the faith of the church and equipping them to take up their Christian vocations in the world was crucial to the success of the reform movement. Catechetical instruction, not confirmation, was the key focus of the Reformers' work. To the extent that confirmation was retained, or a new rite put in its place, it was defined within the parameters of the goods generated by the practice of catechetical instruction.

The primary purpose of confirmation during this period thus is best described as *catechetical*. It represented the liturgical culmination of a practice focusing on the study of the catechism. This instruction was viewed as entailed by Baptism and was held in such high esteem that it was carried out by many different people and institutions. It was seen as a prerequisite for admission to the Lord's Supper. While emphasis was placed on fostering real understanding in those being instructed and on their personal ratification of the baptismal covenant, the primary good fostered by this practice was preparation of individuals to make an intelligent confession of the church's faith. Bucer alone drew a clear distinction between the learning taking place in catechetical instruction and the personal profession or pledge associated with ratification of the baptismal covenant in confirmation. His influence on the Lutheran Church (by way of Melanchthon) and the Church of England (by way of Cranmer) helped spark the emergence of several distinct understandings of confirmation among Protestant churches.

Accordingly, much of our attention in this chapter will focus on the establishment of catechetical instruction among churches involved in reform and only secondarily on the new understandings of confirmation emerging alongside this practice. Martin Luther clearly was the creative force behind the emergence of catechetical instruction in the reform movement, and we will turn to his pioneering work in this area first. Not only did he bring a new literary genre into being—the catechism—but he also was responsible for many of the educational innovations associated with its use in the home, school, and church. Calvin and Zwingli built on Luther's work, shaping it to fit their somewhat different theological convictions. Their work will be examined as well. We will begin, however, by placing the Reformers' innovations in a larger historical context. It is just as easy to idealize the innovations taking place during the Reformation as it is for contemporary liturgical scholars to idealize the liturgical practices of the adult catechumenate. History teaches us that efforts at repristinization are doomed to failure. Catechetical instruction did not begin with the Reformation nor did it end when the catechism stopped being widely used. Our task is to locate the Reformers' innovations in relation to prior developments in the Middle Ages, tracing catechetical instruction to the present.

Catechetical Instruction during the Middle Ages

Recall the image of the shipwreck, offered in the previous chapter. There the practice of initiation was portrayed as breaking apart with the collapse of the Roman Empire and its various pieces put to different uses as they were placed in new ecclesial contexts. One important piece of the catechumenate that survived in a highly diminished form was catechetical instruction. With the fall of the Roman Empire, most of the institutional support for education disappeared. As Pierre Riché has put it, one by one the lights of classical education went out around the Mediterranean.[3] Although monasteries and bishops' schools kept the rudiments of reading and writing alive, support for the full range of the classical curriculum was rare. Education in these contexts was tailored to the rudiments necessary to chant the psalter, read the Bible, and carry out general pastoral responsibilities.

The long-term effect of this decline in general education was to undermine the regular offering of catechetical instruction. The church could no longer depend on a steady supply of literate clergy, much less clergy who were the beneficiaries of a well-rounded liberal arts education. Clergy and bishops frequently were not well-grounded in the basic doctrines of the church, making it difficult for them to teach the rudiments of theology to adult converts or those baptized as infants. Catechetical instruction fell on hard times. It did not disappear altogether, however. The memory of the older teaching was kept alive by several serious attempts to reestablish catechetical instruction initiated at various points in the Middle Ages.

The earliest attempt took place during the reign of Charlemagne. In the previous chapter, we saw how Charlemagne sponsored a series of church reforms in

Admonitio Generalis designed to strengthen the unity of his kingdom. These reforms placed great emphasis on the renewal of catechetical instruction in the church. For the first time since the demise of the adult catechumenate, an organized effort was made to teach the laity the rudiments of the Christian faith on a regular basis. This effort was directed in two directions simultaneously: (1) toward the Germanic tribes conquered by Charlemagne, who had converted to Christianity en masse after their defeat; and (2) toward the ordinary members of the church, most of whom had been baptized as infants and subsequently received little general education or catechetical instruction.

One of the most important innovations, championed by Alcuin, Charlemagne's most influential adviser, was to teach both groups in the vernacular.[4] Collections of basic instructional material in the native language of different regions began to appear. Translations of the "Weissenberg Catechism," for example, were written in various dialects. This document included the Gospel of Matthew, the Lord's Prayer, the Apostles' Creed, the Athanasian Creed, and selected psalms.[5] Similarly, the reform councils of Theims and Tours encouraged the teaching of the Apostles' Creed and the Lord's Prayer in the vernacular. Teaching of the Athanasian Creed also was common.[6] The traditional catechetical material—the Lord's Prayer, Apostles' Creed, and Ten Commandments—began to appear in psalters and was recited in worship. Bishops' capitularies urged priests to teach them on a regular basis.[7]

Going hand in hand with these reforms was greater emphasis on the education of clergy. More schools for basic education were established. Bishops developed working libraries for their priests and began to publish handbooks designed to help them carry out their pastoral duties, especially their teaching responsibilities.[8] Catechetical homilaries began to appear: collections of sermons, written in Latin, that could be translated by the priest into the language of the people and used to instruct them.[9] Rabanus Maurus, one of Alcuin's disciples, compiled a homilary of seventy sermons aimed primarily at rural populations.[10]

The reforms of the Carolingian period were the high point of catechetical instruction during the early Middle Ages. The decline of the Holy Roman Empire following Charlemagne's death was swift. As feudalism gained ground once again, education declined and catechetical instruction declined along with it. It was not until the rise of cathedral schools in the eleventh and twelfth centuries and the medieval university in the thirteenth that general education received enough institutional support to influence catechetical instruction.

In the cathedral schools, famous scholars such as Abelard, John of Salisbury, and Hugh of St. Victor offered lectures to students from all over Europe. These "schools" were not organized around an integrated curriculum supported by a number of teachers and courses but were governed by the interests of the teacher.[11] The rise of the medieval university in the thirteenth century marked the beginning of a better organized course of study. More than one professor would lecture on a subject, and they would engage one another in public disputation. Albert, Aquinas, Bonaventura, and the other great theologians of this period were all located in a university setting.

The rise of the university took place precisely at a time when the reconquest of Spain gave scholars access to manuscripts from Greece and Rome that had been preserved by Muslims. Of particular importance in this regard was the recovery of the full range of works written by Aristotle. For the first time since the early years of the church, Christian scholars had access to Aristotle's logic and, somewhat later, to his natural and metaphysical works. The impetus this gave to scholarship can hardly be underestimated. Not only were scholars fascinated with the task of retrieving and translating these classical texts but they began to draw on Aristotle's understanding of science and logic to frame their approach to theology and philosophy. It was not enough merely to cite the authorities of the past, important as they continued to be. These authorities now were to be approached dialectically and their truth arranged in a logical system.[12] A new genre of theology emerged in conjunction with this dialectical method, the summa, of which Aquinas's *Summa Theologica* is the greatest example. This recovery of Aristotle gradually came to exert an enormous influence on medieval education. Dialectic stood at the apex of the curriculum, while rhetoric, the telos of classical education, was crowded between grammar offered to boys and logic to young adults.[13]

The revival of scholarship and general education during this period had an important impact on catechetical instruction at several levels. Not only was increased emphasis placed on the education of clergy, but also, theological reflection on the duties of the priest as preacher, confessor, and teacher began to take place. As the role of theologian-teacher received greater respect in the cathedral schools and universities, so too did the teaching role of the bishop and priest.

One of the most important results of this renewed emphasis on teaching was the association of catechetical instruction and the practice of confession. Priests were encouraged to use a young person's first confession as a time to assess religious knowledge and to prescribe remedial instruction, if needed. How could persons be held accountable for their beliefs or actions if they did not even have a rudimentary understanding of the doctrines and moral tenets of the church? The association of catechetical instruction and confession is an important development because it sets the stage, in part, for the catechetical reforms that Luther engendered. It is worth pausing to better understand what was at stake in this development.

The practice of confession and penitence had long been a part of the Christian tradition. As early as the New Testament, the practice of excommunicating and reinstating sinners existed. This developed extensively as the church gained more power under the Roman empire, and the practice of public penance was increasingly regularized by canon law. During the early part of the Middle Ages, however, public penance was gradually replaced with a new form of penance originating in Ireland. This focused on private confession to a priest, followed by assignment of penance. By the eighth century, various bishops and councils began to make confession of serious sins mandatory before communion. This became the norm for the entire Western church in the Fourth Lateran Council in 1215. By the high Middle Ages, an elaborate system of confession and penance was in place.

The Council of Lambeth in 1281 reveals the kind of links that were beginning to be made between confession and catechetical instruction. Convened under the auspices of the influential Archbishop of Canterbury John Pecham, the Council issued an elaborate code that dealt with a number of topics of practical importance to parish priests: the administration of the sacraments, the hearing of confession, and so forth. It made a direct link between the offering of catechetical instruction and confession. One section, *De informatione simplicium,* outlined a program of instruction that priests were to expound to the people in the vernacular at least four times a year: the fourteen articles of faith (the Apostles' Creed), the Ten Commandments and the Two Commandments of the Gospels, the seven works of mercy, the seven virtues, the seven vices, and the seven sacraments. The Council of Lambeth brought into being a series of pastoral helps designed to assist priests in assessing penance and carrying out this program of instruction. Archbishop Thoresby, for example, wrote his *Instructions,* commonly known as the "Lay Folks' Catechism," in 1357.[14] It covered all the basic teachings mentioned by the Council that were to be expounded in English by parish priests.

Catechetical instruction then was not altogether absent from the Western church during the Middle Ages. In many ways, its fate paralleled that of general education. With the collapse of the Roman Empire, both general education and the adult catechumenate declined, making it difficult for the church to find priests with enough education to teach the laity on a regular basis. The reforms of the Carolingian period and the high Middle Ages kept the memory of catechetical instruction alive.

On the eve of the Reformation, developments irradiating from scholastic theology and the medieval university had an important influence on the shape of this instruction. It was closely associated with the practice of confession. Even though confirmation had received official definition by the church and been treated extensively in scholastic theology, it was not the focal point of catechesis. Rather, emphasis was placed on topics with a close relationship to confession: the Ten Commandments and the vices and virtues. Luther's first catechetical sermons stood in this tradition, and an important part of his reform of this practice was to shift its focus theologically, ordering it in a way that gave clear witness to the doctrine of justification.

Equally important were the reforms of general education supported by the leaders of the Reformation. These were put forward by the leading representatives of Renaissance humanism, and they exerted more influence on the Reformers' vision of catechetical instruction than is commonly recognized. Before turning to Luther's innovations in this area, we will examine briefly the humanistic critique of scholastic education, noting the important ways it influenced the Reformers' understanding of the role of teaching in the church.

The Influence of Renaissance Humanism

The Reformers' new vision of catechetical instruction was the result of their reforms in two closely related areas: Baptism and education. Reform in these areas did not take place simultaneously. The Reformers did not really turn their attention to Baptism until the Anabaptists began to challenge the legitimacy of infant Baptism.[15] Once this took place, catechetical instruction became an important part of the Reformers' defense of infant Baptism. It allowed them to maintain infant Baptism, while simultaneously affirming the importance of a personal confession of faith.

Long before this line of argument began to emerge, however, the Reformers were calling for the establishment of catechetical instruction in reform congregations. Indeed, Luther began to initiate a new approach to catechetical instruction in his preaching even before he provoked an open conflict with the church hierarchy by posting his Ninety-five Theses. His reforms in this area were only intensified by his break with Rome. Zwingli followed suit shortly in Zurich. Why was catechetical instruction viewed as so important to the reform movement from the very beginning? The primary answer to this question is theological, and it grew out of the Reformers' new vision of the church, the laity, and Christian liberty. But an important, secondary answer is found in their positive attitude toward the educational reforms being championed by the renaissance humanists.[16]

Virtually all of the Reformers studied under prominent humanists and made their own contribution to humanist studies. During the early phases of the Reformation, humanists and Reformers made common cause in their opposition to medieval scholasticism. It was no accident that the first people giving public support to Luther after he posted his Ninety-five Theses were German humanists. They viewed his call for religious reform as having much in common with their own goals.[17] Conversely, the Reformers were sympathetic to many aspects of the humanists' program, especially in the area of education.

One of the first areas of reform in which Luther was successful, for example, was the curriculum of the University of Wittenberg. By 1520, he and Philip Melanchthon had gotten the older scholastic curriculum thrown out and a new one instituted along the lines of humanistic higher education. This was a harbinger of things to come. As the Reformation advanced, one town after another placed a humanistic program of studies in their schools. John Sturm's amalgamation of humanistic education and reform theology in the Gymnasium of Strassburg served as a model for Calvin's Academy in Geneva and, by way of the Academy, mediated humanism to the new schools being set up throughout Europe under the auspices of the reform movement.[18]

Renaissance humanism was a complex movement, and scholars increasingly have become aware of the diversity of forms it took. In virtually all of its forms, however, humanism placed great emphasis on education. Two central tenets of its educational program exerted influence on the Reformers' understanding of catechetical instruction and education in general: (1) its retrieval of classical models of education, and (2) its belief in the power of education, as an agency of the community, to shape the basic dispositions of its students.

The recovery of classical models of education was only one facet of the humanists' broader interest in recovering classical culture. They were deeply suspicious of the "near" traditions of the Middle Ages and attempted to reach behind them to those of antique culture. A recovery of ancient Greek and Roman texts and classical modes of writing and expression lay at the heart of their program. Likewise, their educational proposals were modeled on classical education.[19] They placed rhetoric once again at the apex of the curriculum, making the capacity to speak and write in an eloquent and morally informed fashion the crowning achievement of education. This stood in sharp contrast to medieval education's emphasis on logic and dialectic.

How did one learn to speak and write eloquently? This was accomplished through an application of the principle of "authoritative usage," a principle the humanists also took over from classical education.[20] It focused on the importance of imitating authoritative texts that embody good speech and writing. A canon of classics had stood at the heart of antique education, and the humanists began to construct their own canon, placing the authors whom they were busy recovering and translating at the heart of their curriculums: Cicero, Virgil, Horace, Sallust, and many others.

Just as important as the models the renaissance humanists took over from classical education was their adoption of the accompanying belief in the community's power, through education, to shape the fundamental dispositions of its members. At its best, classical culture had articulated a broadly based humanism in which humanity was viewed as capable of developing in a wide variety of directions both for better and for worse.[21] This humanistic vision was revived during the Renaissance, reflecting a confidence in human possibilities long missing from the West. It was given apt expression in Erasmus's famous dictum: "Humans are fashioned, not born." Humans were seen as incomplete at birth and as capable of being shaped in many different directions. The accent here was not on the nurture of individual creativity, a theme that would emerge much later in Rousseau. It was on the *community's* capacity to form humans in ways that allow them to develop their humanity to the fullest and to contribute to the public realm. Individual creativity and artistry only emerge on the basis of a prior internalization of the highest expressions of the community's culture.

The Reformers did not share the humanists' confidence in human nature. What they did share was their general critique of scholasticism, especially scholastic education. This influenced their vision of catechetical instruction in several ways. First, like the humanists, the Reformers rejected scholastic education's concentration on logic and dialectic. In their view, this had led to the degeneration of theology into frivolous and highly technical discussions. Theology, they believed, should be practical, not speculative. It should edify the church. There was no clearer expression of this than in the writing of catechisms. There the basic theological beliefs of the church were offered in a manner accessible to ordinary Christians.

Second, like the humanists, the Reformers saw themselves as reaching behind the "near" tradition to recover ancient sources that had been lost under the influence of scholasticism. With regard to catechetical instruction, they sought to revive the early catechumenate's attention to the Apostles' Creed, the sacraments, and the other basic teachings of the church. Although their knowledge of the history of the catechumenate was faulty, they were correct in discerning its emphasis on teaching the basic elements of the faith in conjunction with Baptism.[22]

Third, the Reformers shared the humanists' confidence in the power of the community to form persons through education, as well as their understanding of how this is best done: through imitation and internalization of acknowledged communal authorities. To be more specific, their willingness to make an authoritative text—the catechism—such an important part of catechetical instruction reflects their acceptance of the humanistic pedagogical principle of authoritative usage. Although the traditional catechetical pieces had long been used in the church, the Reformers were the first to gather them into a catechism and organize them in a manner reflecting the way of salvation. Like a classic in the general curriculum, the catechism was to serve as an authoritative teaching and learning model, assisting the individual in internalizing the church's common faith.

The Influence of Erasmus

Desiderius Erasmus played an important role in mediating the insights of humanistic education to the Reformers. Luther, Zwingli, Bucer, and Calvin were all familiar with Erasmus's works and knew well his proposals on catechetical instruction.[23] His humanistic scholarly orientation toward this practice, his recognition that it was closely linked to Baptism in the ancient church, and his concrete suggestions about when and how it should take place left their mark on the Reformers' thinking.

Erasmus, of course, came to be critical of the reform movement, and the Reformers came to be critical of him. In his theological writings, he argued for a voluntarist form of mysticism that seemed to the Reformers to border on pelagianism.[24] This is particularly evident in his sacramental theology, which placed great emphasis on the individual's subjective (especially moral) appropriation of grace. In large measure, the role of catechetical instruction in relation to all of the sacraments was to allow this kind of self-conscious, subjective appropriation to occur. It was primarily Erasmus's understanding of how this should take place in relation to Baptism that sparked the Reformers' thinking.[25]

As a humanistic scholar, Erasmus was committed to a historical approach. His research on the patristic period made him aware that a catechumenate had preceded the baptism of adults during this period. In his own proposals, he saw himself as harking back to this earlier practice. He also was aware of criticisms of confirmation offered by Wycliffe and Hus during the fourteenth and fifteenth centuries. Their ideas had influenced the Bohemian Brethren, who placed great emphasis on postbaptismal instruction and used a special rite to admit to the adult community young persons who had been baptized as children. Erasmus had firsthand knowledge of the Bohemian rite, and he included many of its elements in his own service of baptismal renewal: a summary of prior, doctrinal instruction, examination of the candidates, personal profession, and laying on of hands.[26]

The key theological basis of Erasmus's understanding of the relationship between Baptism, catechetical instruction, and the rite of baptismal renewal was his distinction between the external sign of a sacrament and the grace it signifies.[27] As he put it with regard to Baptism: "The body is moistened with water, but the mind is anointed with invisible grace."[28] Grace is not given *by* the water, but *with* it.[29] Catechetical instruction, he argued, should be offered all Christians so they can appropriate the grace into which they were baptized as infants. Following Tertullian, he noted that this kind of self-conscious appropriation was implicit in the Latin term *sacramentum,* which originally referred to a military oath of allegiance. In Baptism, an oath or agreement is made with God; catechetical instruction allows persons to understand and keep this oath.

In his *Paraphrase on St. Matthew's Gospel,* Erasmus provided a description of what catechetical instruction should involve.[30] Recalling ancient practice, he recommended offering a series of catechetical sermons during Lent that are designed for youth who have reached the age of discretion. These sermons should help young people understand what was at stake in their baptism in two ways: (1) by offering instruction in the basic tenets of the faith based on the Apostles' Creed and certain biblical material; and (2) by helping them recognize their moral weakness and their need for God's mercy. Erasmus advocated an examination of each young person who had received this instruction to make sure each understood and remembered what he or she had been taught and to see if each personally accepted the oath of loyalty made on his or her behalf by sponsors at Baptism. If the response was affirmative, each was to participate in a rite of baptismal renewal. Erasmus does not provide many details of this rite, but he does describe it as an occasion in which young people were to reaffirm their baptismal profession in public "with solemn ceremonies, fitting, pure, serious, and magnificent."[31]

Although the Reformers did not follow Erasmus in his sacramental theology, they did take up his call for catechetical instruction. He pointed them to an important need in the church and reminded them that catechesis had been closely associated with Baptism during the patristic period. He also raised the question of the kind of rite that should be associated with this instruction. Should it serve as a renewal of the vows made on the catechumen's behalf at Baptism or some other purpose? In their answer to this question, the Reformers did not fully agree.

Martin Luther and the Emergence of Catechetical Instruction

Of all the Reformers, Martin Luther was most responsible for fashioning the new practice of catechetical instruction. Not only did he originate a new genre — the catechism — but provided a theological vision in which catechetical instruction was portrayed as playing a key role in the successful reform of the church. Luther's work in this area represents a brilliant synthesis of theory and practice. So successful were his reforms that they were universally adopted in the reform movement and, eventually, even by the Roman Catholic Church. Whereas Luther had little to say about confirmation, he had a great deal to say about the importance of catechetical instruction. The educational dimension of his thinking ultimately gave rise to a new way of thinking about confirmation, one in which the *catechetical* goods of this practice were dominant.

Even before his decisive break with Rome, Luther already had laid the groundwork for the establishment of a new practice of catechetical instruction. He began this work in a series of catechetical sermons preached to congregations in the vicinity of Wittenberg.[32] His earliest catechetical sermons followed traditional medieval lines, linking catechesis and confession. They dealt with the Ten Commandments and the Lord's Prayer. During this same period (1517–19), he also wrote brief expositions of these topics for the laity, designed to help them prepare for confession. The brief tract, *A Short Explanation of the Ten Commandments,* for example, was designed to assist Christians in preparing for confession. Even this tract, however, reveals Luther's innovative energies at work. It pointed out the superfluous nature of the traditional catalogs of vices and virtues that had been central to the catechesis attached to penance, and it argued that the Ten Commandments provide Christians with all they need to know to examine their lives in preparation for confession. We see here a trend that would characterize many aspects of the reform movement: the desire to sweep away accumulated human traditions that obscure the central meaning of a rite or practice.

Luther's first major reform of catechetical instruction took place in 1520. He brought together his earlier writings on the Ten Commandments and the Lord's Prayer and added a third part dealing with the Creed. Together, they were published as *A Brief Explanation of the Ten Commandments, the Creed, and the Lord's Prayer*.[33] This rightly has been called the first evangelical catechism.[34] For the first time, the traditional catechetical pieces were brought together in a single book and arranged on the basis of a self-conscious theological principle. We see here the beginnings of a new genre: the catechism. In the preface, Luther described the theological rationale governing the way he ordered the material: "Three things a man needs to know in order to be saved. First, he must know what he ought to do and what he ought not to do. Second, when he finds that by his own strength he can neither do the things he ought, nor leave undone the things he ought not to do, he must know where to seek and find and get the strength he needs. Third, he must know how to seek and find and get this strength."[35]

The catechism thus mirrored Luther's understanding of the order of salvation. The law, represented by the Ten Commandments, serves as a mirror that shows humanity its sin. Lists of transgressions derived from each commandment were placed in the appendix for self-examination in preparation for confession.[36] An awareness of their sinfulness drives persons to the saving work of the triune God, represented by the Creed. This is placed second in the catechism. Luther underscores the Trinitarian character of the Creed by dividing it into three parts instead of the traditional twelve. It is offered to teach us how to "put my trust in Him, surrender myself to Him and make bold to deal with Him. . . ."[37] Help in learning how to live, on the basis of trust in God's parental care, then is offered in Luther's exposition of each petition of the Lord's Prayer, the final piece contained in the catechism. The three traditional catechetical pieces thus were ordered on the basis of Luther's theology.

Throughout the next decade, catechetical instruction remained an important priority for Luther, and he continued to make innovations in this practice. He preached catechetical sermons on a regular basis, many of which were published as catechetical tracts. One such tract was *Five Questions Concerning the Lord's Supper.* The material in this piece was used to examine those seeking to take communion for the first time. Gradually, teaching on the sacraments became a standard part of Luther's catechetical instruction.

During this same period, Luther encouraged yet another innovation: the hiring of a catechist for young people. He had Agricola called to this position in Wittenberg and encouraged the establishment of schools both in that city and the surrounding villages to make sure that Christian and general education would take place.[38] In 1525, he commissioned Agricola and Justus Jonas to prepare a catechism, using this term for the first time to refer to a book and not to oral instruction.[39] In the *German Mass,* published the following year, he continued this call, placing great emphasis in the preface on the need for "an easily understood, plain, simple catechism."[40] He also gave instructions on how it might be used to teach children and youth. Once more, Luther showed his creative genius, advocating for the first time the use of a question and answer format in catechetical instruction. He argued that it would promote understanding: "They should not merely learn to say the words by heart, as heretofore, but with each part they should be asked questions and give answer, what each part means and how they understand it."[41]

Luther was not yet finished with his innovations in this area. Immediately after the publication of the *German Mass,* he threw himself into the task of composing his own catechism, for it had become clear that Agricola and Jonas would not be successful in this venture. He encouraged others to do the same. Between 1522 and 1530, around thirty such catechisms were written by members of the reform movement.[42] It is likely that Luther began working on the material that came to comprise the *Large Catechism* during this period.[43] He came to realize that it would be too long and difficult for the ordinary Christian, leading him to write a much shorter and simpler catechism that could be published on placards. This material, later, was published in book form as the *Small Catechism,* generally acknowledged as a classic of the catechetical genre.[44]

In both these catechisms, Luther continued to use the theological rationale first found in the *Brief Explanation.* Questions and answers on the Ten Commandments were placed immediately before those on the Creed, mirroring the manner in which the law prepares the way for the gospel. The third section, on the Lord's Prayer, was portrayed as teaching the central features of the Christian life. Significant new material extending beyond the traditional catechetical trilogy also appeared. A section on Baptism and the Lord's Supper was included, recalling Luther's earlier teachings on the sacraments. This was followed by a section providing prayers for individuals and table graces for families. A final section provided a table of duties describing the Christian responsibilities of pastors, magistrates, parents, children, and widows as they live out their vocations in the world.

Not only did Luther institute a variety of innovative catechetical practices, but he also provided a theological rationale for the importance of catechetical instruction. He linked this practice with admission to the Lord's Supper in a manner that was to become paradigmatic for the reform movement as a whole, instructing pastors not to allow children or adults to partake of this Sacrament until they had learned the catechism.[45] He wanted to make sure that the members of reform congregations had thrown off the vestiges of Roman Catholic sacramental theology and could receive in faith the word of grace to which the Lord's Supper gives witness. The Lord's Supper is not a magical rite, he argued. It is a visible expression of the gospel and must be received in faith. Although faith is a gift of God, it is the responsibility of the church to provide its baptized members with the "minimum of knowledge" they need to understand what is at stake when they participate in the Lord's Supper.[46] This was one of the most important tasks of catechetical instruction, in Luther's view, and the reason he repeatedly emphasized the importance of helping persons go beyond memorization of the catechism to achieve genuine understanding of its meaning.[47]

In Luther's theological reflection on catechetical instruction, it is clear that more was at stake in this practice than preparing Christians to participate in the Lord's Supper;[48] Luther's entire view of the Christian life hangs in the balance. Christians, he believed, are not merely passive participants in a sacramental system controlled by the church hierarchy. They are recipients of the gospel, freeing them to take up their ministries in the congregation and in the world. Catechetical instruction was an attempt to enable the laity to fulfill their calling as the priesthood of all believers, providing them with the knowledge to understand the gospel and to live lives of joyful obedience. It also was a key means of equipping them to carry out their vocations in the world.

In comparison to his work in the area of catechetical instruction, Luther wrote relatively little in the area of confirmation.[49] Indeed, his desire to place Baptism once more at the heart of the Christian life led Luther to reject the medieval, sacramental understanding of confirmation. The Roman Catholic doctrine of confirmation, he argued, has no foundation in scripture and mocks "God in saying that it is a sacrament of God, when it is a merely human invention."[50] What particularly rankled Luther about the medieval doctrine of confirmation was the way it diminished the importance of Baptism: "You hear: the water, that is the bath: you hear: to be born again, that is the regeneration and the renewal, and Spirit, whom here St. Paul interprets as the Holy Spirit. And here it is to be noticed that the apostle knows nothing of the sacrament of confirmation. For he teaches that the Holy Spirit is given in baptism, as Christ also teaches, indeed, in baptism we are reborn by the Holy Spirit."[51]

As Luther rightly discerned, the medieval understanding of confirmation implied that the Holy Spirit is not given fully in Baptism and had to be supplemented with the grace bestowed in confirmation. Luther vehemently rejected this theological perspective. Baptism is not merely the first step in the Christian life that gives way to other sacramental helps. It is *the* sacramental sign under which all the Christian life is lived. He drives home this point repeatedly in the *Babylonian Captivity:* ". . . the sacrament of baptism, even in respect to its sign, is not the matter of a moment, but continues for all time. Although its administration is soon over, yet the thing it signifies continues until we die, nay, until we rise at the last day. For as long as we live we are continually doing that which our baptism signifies—we die and rise again."[52]

Baptism represents the basic pattern of the Christian life: dying of the old self and rising to new life in Christ. Christians never really progress beyond Baptism. In that the medieval theology and practice of confirmation detracted from the centrality of Baptism, Luther rejected it outright.

This did not mean, however, that he rejected any role for confirmation at all. As he puts it at one point: "Confirmation should not be observed as the bishops desire it. Nevertheless we do not find fault if every pastor examines the faith of the children to see whether it is good and sincere, lays hands on them, and confirms them."[53] Although Luther did not write a liturgy of confirmation himself, he gave his approval to several liturgies for a new evangelical rite of confirmation written by others. One such liturgy was the *Brandenburg Church Order* of 1540, written by Johannes Bugenhagen. The preface of this service describes its purpose as follows:

> It is our will that confirmation be retained in accordance with the old practice, namely, that when those who have been baptized come to an age when they know what they should believe and how to pray, and also know how they should lead a Christian life and behave honestly, as it is set out in the catechism, they are to be summoned before the bishop at his visitation and examined, and if it is found that they have a good understanding of the faith and Christian life, the bishop shall, as we said above, lay his hands upon them and pray to almighty God that they may remain constant in the faith and may be preserved and strengthened yet more in the same, and then confirm them.[54]

Luther also supported the confirmation service found in the *Wittenberg Church Order,* written by Melanchthon in 1545.[55] In the rationale accompanying this order, the church is told to offer catechetical instruction throughout childhood to all who have been baptized. When such persons reach the "age of discretion," they are to make a public profession of their faith and to promise that they will remain loyal to the doctrine and practice of the church. Following this confession, hands are to be laid on the confirmand and a prayer offered.

Luther's support for these attempts to reform confirmation was passive. His own energies clearly were directed toward the reform of the sacraments and the establishment of catechetical instruction. He remained ambiguous about the possibilities of an evangelical rite of confirmation. This led to a wide range of attitudes toward confirmation in the Lutheran tradition. Repp identifies as many as six different trajectories of confirmation in Lutheranism after the Reformation period. It was catechetical instruction, not confirmation, that lay at the heart of Luther's reforming efforts in this area.

Consensus: The Importance of Catechetical Instruction

Whereas Luther was the creative force behind the making of catechetical instruction such an important part of the reform movement, many other Reformers played important roles in shaping the form this practice took: Zwingli in Zurich; Zell, Capito, and Bucer in Strassburg; and Calvin in Geneva. These are but a few of the theologians and pastors who made a contribution to this practice. The 1520s represented a period of experimentation in which a wide variety of catechisms were written and different avenues of catechetical instruction attempted. By the 1530s, the general shape of catechetical practice had begun to appear. Its key elements can be identified.

First, virtually all of the churches interested in reform had adopted the catechetical genre as formulated by Luther. Theologians might argue with Luther about the arrangement and theological meaning of the traditional catechetical pieces, but they did not differ with him over the effectiveness of placing these pieces together in a single book and presenting them in a question and answer format. The catechism was acknowledged as an indispensable tool in promoting theological literacy and Christian unity. It provided Christians with a basic doctrinal framework, enabling them to reflect theologically on their work in the church and ordinary life. The church did not seek to control every aspect of a person's life; only to provide a sure foundation on the basis of which liberty and conscience could be exercised. At the same time, the catechism was seen as a promoting unity among Christians. Confession based on such instruction was of the church's one, true faith, not the individual's particular, idiosyncratic beliefs. The catechism thus was viewed as promoting both individual freedom and church unity.

Second, there was consensus about the location of this practice. It was seen as making its primary contribution after Baptism and before First Communion, although persons continued to be instructed after they had been admitted to Communion through catechetical sermons and special teaching on the larger catechisms. As we have seen, infant Baptism was widely defended by the early Reformers against the Anabaptists. Catechetical instruction was viewed as entailed by this Sacrament, affording baptized Christians the opportunity to understand and accept the obligations of the covenant into which they were initiated already. Participation in the Lord's Supper was not allowed until a person had demonstrated an adequate mastery of the catechism through an examination by the minister and elders.

Third, consensus emerged about the contribution of three institutions in catechetical instruction: the home, the school, and the congregation. The home was viewed as playing a critical role in catechetical instruction. Luther's practice of publishing wall and door tables of key catechetical verses was widely imitated, and catechisms were frequently owned and used by individual families. Parents were expected to teach those in their charge and were held accountable if they did not.[56] Schools also were centers of catechetical instruction. In both Latin and vernacular schools, memorization and explanation of the catechism was a standard part of the curriculum. Bucer called for the establishment of schools so young people might "learn the writings and catechism of our faith," and it is no accident that he refers to the questioner in his catechism as the *Lehrer* or *Meister,* common designations for the schoolmaster or teacher.[57]

Likewise, congregations were important centers of catechetical instruction. Although practices varied somewhat from one congregation to another, virtually all of them offered special catechetical services and classes, typically on Sunday afternoon or evening. In these services, the traditional catechetical pieces were the focus of preaching. Collections of these sermons designed especially for children began to circulate.[58] Catechetical classes were occasions not only for examining the progress of young persons in memorizing the catechism but also for establishing a living dialogue between the teacher and learner. As all the Reformers repeatedly emphasized, *understanding* was their goal, not rote memorization. Along with this preaching, young people also were examined on their mastery of the catechism. In addition to these special services, many congregations included a reading from the catechism as a regular part of their Sunday evening worship. Moreover, ministers and elders were expected to make catechetical examination and instruction a regular part of their home visitation.

In Zurich, Wittenberg, Strassburg, and other centers of the reform movement during the 1520s and 1530s, a common pattern began to emerge around the practice of catechetical instruction. Catechisms were written to serve as a pedagogical tool for instruction offered to children who had been baptized as infants but could not yet participate in the Lord's Supper. This instruction was offered by families, schools, and congregations. On one key point, however, a consensus did not emerge about this practice. Should catechetical instruction culminate in a special worship service in which youth were given an opportunity to make a confession of faith before the entire congregation? Three different trajectories can be identified.

In the first, catechetical instruction culminated in a private examination of the young person, followed by First Communion.[59] Typically, this took place during Lent and was conducted in the minister's home. It often was preceded by a special course of instruction for the youth by the minister, to supplement what they had learned in the home, school, and congregation. There was no thought of an additional rite following this examination.

In a second trajectory, young persons participated in a special service of admission to the Lord's Supper, following their adequate mastery of the catechism and examination by the pastor and elders.[60] This was the position of Calvin and Zwingli. In Geneva, this service involved the recitation by the candidates of a brief "catechism" of questions and answers summarizing the essential doctrinal tenets of the longer catechism they had studied throughout childhood. It served as a demonstration of the candidates' understanding and acceptance of the church's faith as set forth in the catechism. Reflecting his critique of medieval theology and practice, Calvin studiously avoided the term "confirmation" for this service, preferring others such as "the admission." At certain points in his writings there are hints of a more positive attitude toward an "ancient" practice of confirmation, however, closely related to instruction in the faith.

Bucer, Melanchthon, and others represented a third trajectory. They argued for the establishment of a full-scale evangelical rite of confirmation that assumed the acquisition of basic doctrinal knowledge through catechetical instruction. In some cases, this stood in the same position as Calvin's service of admission: at the culmination of catechetical instruction. In his later writings, however, Bucer began to draw a sharper line between catechetical instruction and confirmation. The knowledge provided by the former was not enough, he argued. To be confirmed, persons must make a "heartfelt" profession of faith and show signs of the Spirit's work in their lives. Confirmation thus represented the individual's personal ratification of the baptismal covenant and the church's acknowledgment that the Spirit truly was at work in his or her life, bringing the promises of Baptism to fruition.

In the remainder of this chapter, we will examine three theologians who portrayed catechetical instruction and confirmation along somewhat different lines: Zwingli, Calvin, and Bucer. They provide insight into the theological variety existing within the reform movement, as well as a vantage point on developments that were to take place in the centuries that followed.

Ulrich Zwingli and Baptism, Catechetical Instruction, and Covenant Theology

Along with Luther, Ulrich Zwingli was one of the earliest advocates of catechetical instruction in the reform movement. The leader of the Reformation in the Swiss city of Zurich, he placed catechetical instruction in the context of covenant theology. His successor in Zurich, Henrich Bullinger, developed this theology more fully and it became an important theological trajectory in the Reformed tradition. In many ways, it came to represent an alternative to the "high Calvinism" of Reformed orthodoxy, which placed such emphasis on the doctrine of double predestination that it seemed to imply a kind of determinism in matters of salvation. In contrast, covenant theology portrayed God's electing grace as establishing the human capacity for a free response. This perspective was to play an important role in English Puritanism and, through this movement, American Presbyterianism. Zwingli's early attempt to place catechetical instruction in the context of covenant theology thus is of importance in the unfolding story being narrated in this book. Covenant themes, moreover, will appear in my own constructive proposal, although placed in the context of a different theological framework.

Born in a village in the proximity of Zurich, Zwingli left his home to study in Vienna and Basel. At Basel, he first encountered humanism, an intellectual current that was to grow even stronger when he became the priest of the rural parish of Glarus. While in Glarus he became acquainted with the writings of Erasmus and had the opportunity to meet him in 1515. The two men began a correspondence that lasted until the late 1520s, when they parted over the course of church reform. During his early years in Zurich, where he began serving as the people's priest in 1518, Zwingli was deeply immersed in the humanistic critique of scholasticism and was especially sympathetic to Erasmus's formulation of this critique. He had ample exposure to Erasmus's interest in the ancient catechumenate and his proposals on catechetical instruction. It is no accident that he announced a program of catechetical instruction in Zurich the year after Erasmus published his *Paraphrase on St. Matthew's Gospel* in 1522.[61]

Zwingli began to develop his covenant theology in response to the Anabaptists. This group rejected infant Baptism, arguing that Baptism is properly reserved for those who have undergone a conversion experience and can make a personal confession of faith. Baptism is a sign of faith that is present already and represents a public declaration of this faith. When the Anabaptists cast this in covenant terms, they portrayed it as a contract between two consenting parties, that is, between the individual and God.[62]

Zwingli wrote several treatises refuting this position and defending infant Baptism. The most important of these were *Of Baptism* (1525), to which he appended a new baptismal rite, *On Baptism, Rebaptism and Infant Baptism* (1525), and *Refutation of the Tricks of the Catabaptists* (1527).[63] Also important for our purposes was his treatise, *Of the Education of Youth* (1523).[64] During this same period, he placed his thoughts on these topics in what has been called the "earliest truly comprehensive treatise of Protestant theology": *Commentary on True and False Religion* (1525).[65]

Zwingli's conflict with the Anabaptists was not an academic matter. Influential representatives of this position were beginning to influence the members of reform congregations. In order to diminish their influence, he took part in several public disputations with the prominent Anabaptists, in which he collaborated with his young colleague, Henrich Bullinger.[66] It was in this context that he first began to use covenant theology to conceptualize the relationship between Baptism and catechetical instruction.

Even as he attempted to refute the Anabaptists' position, he acknowledged the kernel of truth it contained. There is an important role in the Christian life for the rendering of a personal confession of faith. It should not be placed, however, on an equal footing with the true source of salvation: God's covenanting activity in Jesus Christ. Consequently, Zwingli develops the covenant theme in a way that retains the sovereignty of God in the covenant relationship without eradicating a corresponding subordinate role for the human covenant partner. First, the covenant is portrayed as a divine promise of grace initiated and fulfilled by God. Even faith must be seen as the product of God's electing, predestining, and calling work.[67] God's covenanting activity, however, enables individuals to render a free response.

It is not difficult to see why this theme would be such a powerful way of defending infant Baptism and conceptualizing the relationship between Baptism and catechetical instruction. Zwingli's early treatise, *Refutation of the Tricks of the Catabaptists,* represents the theological argument he develops.[68] He begins by arguing that there is only one eternal covenant of grace running throughout the Old and New Testaments. As he puts it: "Therefore the same covenant which he entered into with Israel he has in these latter days entered into with us, that we may be one people with them, one church, and may have also one covenant."[69] On the basis of the essential unity of the covenant throughout biblical history, he then argues for parallels between the signs that God has instituted to represent this covenant. In the Old Testament, God instituted circumcision as a sign of the covenant made with Abraham and his posterity.[70] With the coming of Christ, this sign was replaced by Baptism, providing a clearer witness to the washing away of sins and the renewal of life that Christ brings. While the external form of the sign has changed, its inner meaning has remained the same: the one covenant of grace. Both circumcision and Baptism are properly administered to infants born to members of the covenant community.

As Zwingli developed a clearer statement of his theology of the sacraments, he began to make a sharp distinction between the sacramental "sign" and the reality to which this sign points. As signs of God's covenanting activity, Baptism and the Lord's Supper have both commemorative and promissory dimensions. As a memorial, they recall God's prior saving work by which the covenant is established. As a promise, they point forward to the inward appropriation of this covenant by the individual through the power of the Holy Spirit. The outward washing of the individual in Baptism thus looks forward to the inward washing of the Spirit that will lead the person to a self-conscious confession of faith and a life of obedience. The one covenant of grace pointed to in Baptism must be taken up and ratified by the individual through the power of the Spirit.

It is within this framework that Zwingli located the role of catechetical instruction. In *Of the Education of Youth,* for example, he points out that "faith comes by hearing" and that it is the responsibility of the church to teach children and youth about Christ, confident that God can use this teaching to create faith. Likewise, in his discussion of Matthew 28:19–20 in *Of Baptism* he argues that the Greek text makes it clear that Jesus is telling his followers they are to make disciples by baptizing and teaching.[71] Contrary to Anabaptist interpretations of this passage, they are not told to make disciples first and then baptize them; they are to make disciples through baptizing *and* teaching. This is consistent, he notes, with the clear admonition to Christian parents in Ephesians 6:4, where they are told to bring their children up in the *paideia* of the Lord, a classical Greek term rich with educational connotations.

This relationship between Baptism and catechetical instruction in the context of a covenant is found in the baptismal liturgies Zwingli developed. In *The Order of the Christian Churches of Zurich,* probably written in 1526, he placed Baptism in a covenantal framework, referring to it as a "sign of the covenant." In the prayer of invocation, he makes it clear that baptism with water points backward to God's saving action in Christ and forward to the work of the Holy Spirit by which inner baptism is accomplished. As the liturgy puts it: "Therefore, let us pray God that this child receive faith and that the outward baptism be, through the work of the Holy Spirit, inwardly accomplished with the rich water of grace."[72] He abandons the medieval practice of having parents or godparents make the baptismal vows and recite the Creed on the child's behalf.[73] No vows are made on behalf of the one being baptized; rather, the entire congregation is invited to pray the Lord's Prayer and recite the Apostles' Creed as an expression of the covenant into which the infant is being baptized. Godparents are admonished to "bring up this child to the glory of God."[74] This involves a significant role for catechetical instruction: ". . . those who have been baptized before the age of discretion should when they reach that age of understanding make an affirmation themselves of a faith which they have come to understand. That is, they should first do this after they have been instructed in the matter of salvation."[75]

The heart of this instruction will be the Creed and Prayer offered by the congregation, along with teaching on the Ten Commandments and the Sacraments.[76]

In his theology and practice, Zwingli thus offered a covenant framework in which he knit together Baptism and catechetical instruction. Baptism, he believed, entails catechetical instruction. In Baptism, persons are marked with the sign of the one, eternal covenant of grace. Their external washing looks forward to the inner washing by the Holy Spirit that allows them to take up and self-consciously claim the vows of the covenant. Although the Spirit uses all the ordinary means of the church to bring about this confession, catechetical instruction plays a special role, providing children and youth with an understanding of the essential elements of the faith.

Zwingli's development of the beginnings of a covenant framework in which Baptism and catechetical instruction were held together is his major contribution to our story. He has almost nothing to offer on the topic of confirmation. Like Luther, this simply was not a matter of pressing concern for him, whereas reform of Baptism and establishment of catechetical instruction was. For creative work in this area, we must turn to Martin Bucer.

Martin Bucer and the Emergence of an Evangelical Confirmation

As a young Dominican monk, Martin Bucer had the opportunity to hear Martin Luther defend himself publicly at Heidelberg, and then to dine with him the next day. Bucer quickly became an advocate of Luther's reforms, which led eventually to Bucer's excommunication and exile. Shortly after his exile, Bucer began to correspond with Ulrich Zwingli and to read his writings. Almost from the beginning of his work in the reform movement, Bucer played a mediating role between Luther and Zwingli. He is best known for his efforts to overcome their bitter conflicts over the meaning of the Lord's Supper. Although unsuccessful in this endeavor, he was able to chart large areas of consensus about the essentials of church reform. At the same time, Bucer made his own creative contribution. His emphasis on the role of the Holy Spirit in the Christian life, his advocacy of church discipline as a mark of the true church, and his understanding of the sacraments were areas in which he left his distinctive stamp on the Reformation.

Nowhere is this combination of consensus building and personal creativity more apparent than in Bucer's work on catechetical instruction and confirmation. On the one hand, he reflects the common pattern of catechetical instruction that was beginning to emerge in the reform movement during the 1530s. On the other hand, his establishment of an "evangelical" rite of confirmation was based on theological themes that were uniquely his own among the early Reformers.[77] Although Bucer shared the central theological tenets of the reform movement, interpreters of his thought have long drawn attention to the special emphasis he placed on the work of the Holy Spirit in his theology.[78] This influenced his understanding of justification and sanctification. The former is described as involving both imputed and imparted righteousness.[79] God does not merely declare the elect righteous but, through the power of the Holy Spirit, actually makes them righteous. The regenerate show signs of the inner working of the Spirit, just as a good tree bears good fruit.

Bucer's emphasis on the Holy Spirit also played an important role in his doctrine of the church. In his early work, under the influence of Zwingli, he made a sharp distinction between the inner work of the Spirit and the external signs of the church, especially in his discussion of the sacraments. Many who participate in the church, hearing the external word and partaking of the sacraments, are not among the elect. Only the inner work of the Spirit makes the gospel a reality in persons' lives. During the thirties, as the controversy with the Anabaptists became heated, Bucer placed his emphasis elsewhere. Although maintaining the distinction between the external sign and the inner reality, he now emphasized God's institution of the church as the ordinary instrument through which the Spirit works. As he puts it in his *Shorter Catechism,* written in 1537: "The Holy Spirit makes those who believe in Christ our Lord unite and hold to one another as members of one body. It is by using word, sacraments, and discipline in the church that the Spirit builds up Christians in faith."[80]

The term "discipline" here is telling. Bucer alone among the early reformers made this a mark of the true church, along with Word and sacrament. What Bucer meant by discipline went beyond the connotations of punishment or correction typically associated with this concept today. In some ways it is closer to what we might call formation, pointing to the ways the church supports the sanctity of its members through the ordering of its internal life. Just as we might refer to a team as well-disciplined, referring to the willingness of its members to follow a common strategy and to use their individual gifts within the goals of the team, Bucer thought of church discipline as a mark of a congregation's ordering of its life according to the larger purposes dictated by Christ. The Holy Spirit uses the relationships and practices of the community to shape its members' habits of thought, feeling, and action. Here, as in the areas of preaching and the sacraments, Bucer differentiates the external sign and the inner reality. Church discipline alone cannot make a person a Christian; only the Holy Spirit can do this. But the Spirit uses church discipline the same as preaching and the sacraments to do the work.

It is this larger theological framework that informs Bucer's understanding of the relationship between catechetical instruction and confirmation. Of all the Reformers, Bucer alone developed his understanding of catechetical instruction in relation to confirmation. Zwingli and Calvin believed that Baptism entails catechetical instruction, and Bucer argued that catechetical instruction entails confirmation. By this he meant a heartfelt profession of faith and pledge of obedience in which the essential tenets of the faith are not merely grasped intellectually but are appropriated personally. This alone is a sign that the Spirit is at work in a person's life, leading to ratification of the baptismal covenant.

Bucer developed this distinction between catechetical instruction and confirmation only gradually over the course of many years.[81] During the early part of his work in Strassburg, he focused most of his attention on the reform of Baptism and the establishment of catechetical instruction. In one of his early writings, *Grund und Ersach,* he described their relationship in Zwinglian terms, distinguishing the external sign of baptism and the inner baptism of the Spirit.[82] Catechetical instruction is portrayed as an ecclesial practice used by God to effect this inner baptism. In his later writings, the accent has shifted considerably. In *De Regno Christi* and the *Censura,* both written near the end of Bucer's life when he was living in England, the important contrast is between catechetical instruction and confirmation.[83] Persons should only be confirmed when there are clear signs that the Spirit is at work in their life, and there is no guarantee that this is the case just because they can recite the catechism correctly. As Bucer puts it: "A confession of faith should be required of such a kind as might be judged not to originate in the mouth and not be merely a preparation of human teaching: it should be accompanied by signs in the conduct and manner of life of the candidate which the churches might accept as proceeding from a heart which truly believes the gospel and from the teaching of the Holy Spirit."[84]

Accordingly, confirmation should not represent the automatic culmination of catechetical instruction. To administer it to everyone who memorizes the catechism is to "mock" both God and the church, introducing into congregations leaven that could spoil the whole lump.[85] For this reason, "children who show in their life and conduct no signs yet or only modest signs of the faith" should be "left among the catechumens" and their education continued.[86] To do otherwise would violate God's freedom to call those whom God wills and would undercut the disciplinary function of the church in encouraging faith, not merely external conformity to religious convention. Bucer thus draws a clear line between catechetical instruction and confirmation, which should represent a personal response of ratification of the baptismal covenant reflected in a heartfelt confession of faith and pledge of obedience.

This is not to say that Bucer opposes confirmation and catechetical instruction. Indeed, an important part of the individual's act in the service is confession of the church's faith. This confession is entailed by Baptism and builds on catechetical instruction. In both of his confirmation services, the close links between confession of the church's faith and study of the catechism are evident.[87] In both, the minister is told to examine all confirmands the week before the service to make sure they understand the catechism. Moreover, a "minicatechism" of questions and answers is used in the service to represent the individual's understanding and acceptance of the essential tenets of the faith that have been studied in the catechism. Although only one child must answer these questions before the entire congregation, all confirmands must know them by heart and be willing to affirm: "I believe and confess the same and yield up myself to Christ and his congregation trusting in the grace and help of our Lord and Saviour, Jesus Christ."[88]

The combination of catechetical questions and questions eliciting a personal response by the candidates is striking. The first question is addressed directly to the candidates: "Dost thou profess thyself to be a Christian?" to which the confirmands are to reply, "I profess." The questions then move to traditional material, including recitation of the Apostles' Creed and specific inquiries about its meaning. This is followed by more personal concerns in which the confirmands ask God to confirm the faith just confessed in their lives, and a prayer by the minister also requesting that God do so. The questions then shift to a personal act of commitment in which the confirmands renounce Satan and his works and pledge their loyalty to Christ. This renunciation and profession goes all the way back to the early church.

This part of the service is followed by a prayer in which the minister asks God to confirm the work begun in Baptism, increasing in the confirmands' lives the gift of the Holy Spirit that they might grow in their knowledge and obedience of the gospel.[89] The minister then lays hands on the confirmands one by one, praying once more for God to "confirm this thy servant with thy Holy Spirit, that he may continue in the obedience of thy gospel, and strongly resist the devil and his own weakness."[90] The order explicitly excludes the use of chrism because it was thought to breed superstition. The biblical practice of laying on of hands is deemed sufficient to represent God's blessing of the confirmands.

This became the first evangelical service of confirmation. It combines the Reformers' interest in allowing every baptized Christian to confess the faith of the church on the basis of their study of the catechism with more personal elements of profession and pledging. Bucer's understanding of confirmation exerted much influence on the Lutheran and Anglican traditions. Why did Calvin, who followed Bucer in so many areas, not accept this service of confirmation? Is it simply a matter of being fearful of any remnant of the old Catholic order or is something more at stake theologically?

John Calvin and Crystallizing the Pattern
of Reformation Catechesis

John Calvin represents the second generation of church reformers. By the time of his conversion, the reforms of Martin Luther, Ulrich Zwingli, and Martin Bucer were already under way. Calvin could assume the theological and practical groundwork these men had laid in the area of catechetical instruction. His contribution was one of crystallization, pulling together facets of practice and theological argumentation that were already in existence to form a unique and striking example of reformation catechesis. Geneva came to serve as a model for catechetical instruction throughout Europe and, much later, the new world.

Calvin became involved in catechetical instruction not long after his conversion. Forced to flee from Paris because of his allegiance to the reform movement, he traveled to Basel where he began work on the *Institutes of the Christian Religion.* It is noteworthy that he originally described this as a "simple and . . . elementary form of teaching," terms virtually identical to his later descriptions of the catechism.[91] When William Farel successfully drafted Calvin to assist him in the reform of Geneva, the two presented the governing council of the city with a set of articles outlining the most essential reforms that needed to take place.[92] Among these reforms was the establishment of catechetical instruction. Even at this early point, Calvin justified the need for this practice by linking it to Baptism, arguing that it would enable young people to "testify their faith to the Church, to which they were unable at their Baptism to render witness."[93] He also called for a "brief and simple summary of the Christian faith" that could be taught to all the children, and he set out to fill this need by writing the first of two catechisms. Titled *Instruction in Faith,* this catechism provided a short, popular exposition of doctrinal material covered in the *Institutes* of 1536.[94]

Calvin's quick exit from Geneva turned out to be a blessing in disguise. Largely through Bucer's persistent efforts, he ended up in Strassburg, where he became the pastor of a congregation composed of refugees from France, as well as a regular lecturer of exegesis in the college established by John Sturm. He followed Bucer and the other Strassburg ministers in making catechetical instruction obligatory for every child in his congregation, establishing special catechetical services. His work on a new catechism during this period, later known as the *Genevan Catechism,* reveals the influence of Bucer's catechism of 1534.[95]

By the time Calvin and Farel were asked to return to Geneva, Calvin had extensive pastoral experience in the practice of catechetical instruction. He outlined his program of reform in the *Ecclesiastical Ordinances,* once more making catechetical instruction a top priority. The pattern he advocated in this document, and eventually established in Geneva, reflected the consensus that was beginning to emerge throughout the reform movement during the 1530s. Children were to receive instruction in the catechism from their parents, the congregation, and the school. This culminated in special catechetical classes offered by the minister and a service in which those who had mastered the catechism made a public confession of the church's faith before the congregation and were admitted to the Lord's Supper. To support this practice, Calvin completed work in 1541 on his second catechism, *The Catechism of the Church of Geneva,* adopting a question and answer format and arranging the material in a way that reflected the development of his own theological position. Faith was presented prior to consideration of the law, and the law's third use (its positive role in sanctification) was emphasized.

In his theological reflection on the importance of catechetical instruction, Calvin also gives indications of the influence of Luther, Zwingli, and Bucer. He takes elements of their positions and forges them into comprehensive explanation of the importance of catechetical instruction. Following the lead of the other Reformers, he locates his discussion of catechetical instruction in the context of the sacraments, especially Baptism. He appropriates Zwingli's description of the sacraments as signs of the covenant, though modifying Zwingli's position along the lines of Bucer's thought. The sacraments are not "mere" signs; they are "means of grace." When Calvin refers to the sacraments as means of grace, he has three things in mind: (1) the sacraments are established by God; (2) they are visible forms of the Word, serving as signs of the covenant of grace; and (3) they are used by the Holy Spirit to effect union with Christ, arousing, nourishing, and confirming faith.[96] They are more than a memorial or a promise of God's activity. They "cause and communicate" that which they signify. As means of grace, they are established by Christ as special instruments by which the Word is communicated to the elect through the power of the Spirit.

But what of the baptism of infants? They do not yet have the capacity to understand what is being set before them in Baptism. Does Baptism generate faith, as Luther thought in the latter part of his life?[97] Calvin's thinking on this point goes through several stages.[98] In his mature thought, he denies that this is the case. Infants "are baptized into future repentance and faith, and, even though these have not yet been formed in them, the seed of both lies hidden within them by the secret working of the Spirit."[99] Calvin could make this statement only on the basis of his doctrine of election. Salvation, he argues, does not depend on Baptism, catechetical instruction, or any of the earthly means of grace. It depends on God's free and sovereign election of some to salvation and others to damnation before the foundation of the world. The means of grace are instruments God has established to effect this salvation among the elect through the power of the Holy Spirit. The church can baptize the children of believers, confident that the Spirit will bring their baptism to fruition if they truly are among the elect.

This did not mean, however, that the church could shirk its earthly responsibilities in communicating the benefits of God's grace, sitting idly on its hands and waiting for the Holy Spirit to do its work. Calvin exhibited an activistic streak throughout his life, and it is reflected in his doctrine of the church. The church must do everything it can to place itself at God's disposal, attempting to serve as a faithful witness to the gospel. The use to which this witness is put rests in God's hands.

It is this broader theological framework that determines Calvin's understanding of the relationship between Baptism and catechetical instruction. As did the other Reformers, the latter is viewed as entailed by the former. Infant Baptism serves as a powerful witness to the fact that it is God alone who effects salvation. Catechetical instruction affords those who have received this Baptism the opportunity to understand and personally appropriate its meaning at a later point in life. This will take place, however, only if they are among the elect. In the passage quoted above, Calvin thus could argue that infants are baptized into future faith and repentance and, simultaneously, claim that the seed of faith and repentance has been planted in them by the Holy Spirit. The Holy Spirit uses Baptism to engraft those who are among the elect to Christ, setting in motion a lifetime of exposure to the gospel through the nurture of parents, church members, and the ministries of the church. These function as the ordinary means of grace by which the seed that has been planted is brought to fruition in a confession of the church's faith.

Calvin shapes his baptismal liturgy along the lines of his theological convictions.[100] He eliminated from his baptismal service any notion that the minister, parents, or sponsors were confessing the faith on the infant's behalf. In the Order for Baptism in the *Genevan Psalter* of 1542, the parents make four vows. None of them has anything to do with a confession of faith for their child.[101] Rather, parents affirm their own faith in the gospel and promise to raise their children in a manner that will allow their offspring to confess this faith themselves when they are capable of doing so.

This is pointed to in the very first question parents are asked: "Because this is a matter of receiving this child into the company of the Christian Church, do you promise that when he comes to the age of discretion that he will be instructed in the teaching which is received by the people of God as it is summarized in the confession of faith, which we all hold?"[102] This question is followed by the recitation of the Apostles' Creed. For the present, only the parents can affirm their faith in the teaching represented by the Creed. At a future point, the infant being baptized will be given the chance to affirm this faith for himself or herself. Indeed, there is a kind of parallelism between the affirmations the parents are asked to make and the catechetical instruction that later will be offered the child. Just as parents are asked to affirm their belief in the Creed, the authority of Scripture, the law, and a life of self-denial, so too the infant being baptized will receive at a future time instruction in the importance of these elements of the Christian life.

When we move forward in time and look at the service that Calvin developed to admit persons to the Lord's Supper, the close relationship between catechetical instruction, Baptism, and First Communion is evident.[103] This service followed catechetical instruction and assumed an examination of those being admitted. Through their study of the catechism, they have been given the opportunity to learn the meaning of the Creed, the Ten Commandments, the Lord's Prayer, the sacraments, and Christian vocation. They have been examined to make sure that they understand what these mean and that they believe them. The service of admission represents the opportunity to make a public declaration of their acceptance of the articles of faith they have studied and to take up the covenant promises and responsibilities into which they were baptized as infants. As Hughes Old points out, the service constitutes a profession of the candidates' baptismal faith.[104] No vows were made on their behalf during Baptism; those who were baptized long ago now make these vows themselves.

It is likely that this service took place in the context of a regularly scheduled catechetical service on the Sunday before Easter, Pentecost, Christmas, or the first Sunday in October when Communion was regularly offered. At the heart of this service was a kind of minicatechism of questions and answers representing a summary of the essential elements of the faith that the young person had learned through his or her instruction in the catechism.[105] The personal nature of this "catechism" is apparent in the first question: "In whom do you believe and in whom do you put your complete trust?"[106] Likewise, the service ends on a personal note:

Minister: Is it necessary for us, therefore, to have true faith before we are able to rightly participate in this sacrament?

Child: Yes.

Minister: And how can we have this faith?

Child: We have it through the Holy Spirit, who dwells in our hearts and who makes sure to us the promise of God, which we have in the gospel.

Minister: Go then in peace, and may the good God increase more and more his graces in you, and to us all his children.

Child: So be it, through our Lord Jesus Christ. Amen.[107]

The remainder of the questions and answers are based on the traditional catechetical trilogy. Following an initial question, the young person recites the Apostles' Creed, accompanied by questions about its meaning. This is followed by recitation of the Ten Commandments and then the Lord's Prayer, each of which also are accompanied by questions about their significance. This is followed by questions on the sacraments. The way they are arranged here reflects the order in which Calvin had put them from the time he began writing the *Genevan Catechism* in Strassburg. The Ten Commandments come after the Creed, just as the law follows the gospel. The Lord's Prayer flows into a discussion of the sacraments.

There are many parallels between this service and that formulated by Bucer. Why did Calvin refuse to follow Bucer's lead and refer to it as an evangelical service of confirmation? We gain important clues in his extended discussion of confirmation in the *Institutes*.[108] There he argues in two directions simultaneously. He is sharply critical of the current theology and practice of confirmation in the Roman Catholic Church. But he also describes the practice of confirmation as found in the early church, and he uses this to frame his own proposal.

Building on Erasmus's misleading historical portrait of ancient confirmation, Calvin describes a practice in which children and adolescents, having been instructed in the faith, were examined by the bishop "according to the form of the catechism."[109] This examination concluded, he believed, with the laying on of hands. Calvin adds: "I warmly approve such laying on of hands, which is simply done as a form of blessing, and wish that it were today restored to pure use."[110] Although Calvin is drawing on faulty historical scholarship at this point, what is important is the openness he shows to the practice of "true" confirmation. He draws on it directly to paint his own picture of what this practice might look like if restored in the contemporary church. As he puts it:

> How I wish that we might have kept the custom which, as I have said, existed among the ancient Christians before this misborn wraith of a sacrament came to birth! Not that it would be a confirmation such as they fancy, which cannot be named without doing injustice to baptism; but a catechizing, in which children or those near adolescence would give an account of their faith before the church. . . . A child of ten would present himself to the church to declare his confession of faith, would be examined in each article, and answer to each; if he were ignorant of anything or insufficiently understood it, he would be taught. Thus, while the church looks on as a witness, he would profess the one true and sincere faith, in which the believing folk with one mind worship the one God.[111]

There are several things of importance in this passage and the larger discussion of which it is a part.[112] First, Calvin provides us with a clear statement as to why he did not use the term "confirmation" to refer to the practice he is advocating, even though he believes it to be the restoration of "true" confirmation as practiced in the early church. In the above passage, he says that confirmation "cannot be named without doing injustice to baptism." The thrust of his whole argument in this section is a rejection of confirmation because of the damage it does to Baptism. Not only does it represent bad theology, but bad practice. It was a striking example, he believed, of the substitution of human tradition for the simple and straightforward teaching of the gospel. Whereas his friend and colleague Martin Bucer was quite willing to reform this practice and hold on to the rubric "confirmation," Calvin was not.

Second, this passage reveals Calvin's openness to the practice of confirmation in its "original," ancient form. It is this practice that he is seeking to restore. Moreover, he offers a special service marking the culmination of catechetical instruction, confession of the church's faith, and admission to the Lord's Supper. Contemporary scholars such as J.D.C. Fisher, who argue that Calvin "provided no ceremony for children when they were examined in the faith," clearly are wrong.[113] It is one thing for an Anglican like Fisher, with an axe to grind, to make this charge; it is quite another for members of the Reformed tradition to ignore Calvin's positive comments about confirmation and his actual practice in a service of admission.

Third, this passage reveals Calvin's understanding of the primary goods the practice engenders: access to the essential tenets of scripture summarized in doctrinal form in the church's catechisms and public confession of the church's faith. It allows those baptized as infants to understand and confess the "one true and sincere faith," as he puts it in the concluding sentence. If this practice were followed in the present church, he argues, "it would certainly arouse some slothful parents, who carelessly neglect the instruction of their children."[114] Fourth, the passage reveals the fact that Calvin gives sanction to a concluding rite in conjunction with the candidates' public confession. Elsewhere, he writes that such a rite gives this confession greater "reverence and dignity."[115] As in the ancient church, the minister is to place his hands on each young person, representing a "solemn blessing."[116]

Calvin and Bucer clearly share much in common. Although the latter attempted to establish an evangelical service of confirmation and the former did not, both emphasized the importance of catechetical instruction, the individual's confession of the church's faith, and the church's blessing of this public affirmation of faith. The really significant difference between the two men is the relative independence of confirmation from catechetical instruction that Bucer came to advocate. The brief concluding service advocated by Calvin is the culmination of catechetical instruction. For him it was the end point of a practice that primarily was *catechetical,* marking the individual's confession of the church's faith. Although it clearly includes personal elements, the accent falls on the individual's internalization of the beliefs of the church. The comparable service of confirmation developed by Bucer came to represent something more. It serves a *professional* purpose. Although it includes confession of the church's faith on the basis of study of the catechism, it places its primary emphasis on the individual's personal act of profession and pledging. The service is no longer the natural outgrowth of a catechetical program. It marks the individual's heartfelt acceptance of the faith, reflected experientially in signs of the Spirit's work in her or his life and by acts of renunciation and profession in the confirmation service.

Whereas Calvin's caution about the use of the rubric "confirmation" was to exert a lasting influence on the Presbyterian Church, Bucer's attention to the personal elements of profession and pledging also were given equal attention in early Presbyterianism. Perhaps it is only today, in the face of the emergence of adolescence as a new stage in the life cycle and the individualizing features of modern life, that the Reformed tradition can appreciate the cogency of Bucer's argument.

5

Lutheran, Anglican-Episcopal, and United Methodist Confirmation Practices

Following the Reformation, a broad consensus about the importance of catechetical instruction was present in the various churches emerging out of the reform movement. This instruction was located between Baptism and First Communion and represented the church's attempt to allow persons baptized as infants to understand the basic tenets of the Christian faith in preparation for responsible participation in the Lord's Supper and, more generally, in the life of the church. In virtually all Protestant traditions, the practice of catechetical instruction was viewed as the middle term in a comprehensive paradigm: infant Baptism, catechetical instruction, and admission to the Lord's Supper. No such consensus existed, however, about the role of the rite of confirmation in this catechetical practice. A wide range of perspectives were present in Protestantism. In some cases, confirmation was viewed as merely summing up goods generated by this practice, affording individuals the opportunity to make a public confession of the church's faith. In other cases, it stood in a more indirect relationship to this practice and even began to redefine it. In still other instances, it was seen as having no role at all.

Our task in this chapter is to provide an overview of the history of three Protestant traditions: the Lutheran, Anglican-Episcopal, and United Methodist. This will afford us a perspective on their similarities and differences and underscore the importance of the recent steps taken by each of these traditions toward a convergence of liturgical practice. This also will allow us to place the story of American Presbyterianism told in the following chapter in an ecumenical context. Recent liturgical developments in that tradition are an outgrowth of contemporary scholarship and dialogue between various branches of Protestantism. The constructive proposal offered in the third part of this book is an attempt to enter this dialogue from the perspective of the Reformed tradition.

The Lutheran Tradition

It is no accident that diversity has characterized the Lutheran tradition's understanding of the rite of confirmation from the beginning. Luther, we recall, placed his primary emphasis on the practice of catechetical instruction, not confirmation, lending his support rather passively to the attempts of others to establish a rite of confirmation consistent with Reformation theological principles. It was Martin Bucer's creative work in this area that was to be the driving force of reform, influencing the Lutheran tradition through the writings of Melanchthon. Melanchthon's *Wittenberg Church Order* of 1545 offered a confirmation service at the end of catechetical instruction, which included a confession of the church's faith on the basis of the catechism, a personal profession of loyalty to Christ and the church, prayer on the confirmand's behalf, and the laying on of hands.[1] Martin Chemnitz constructed a confirmation rite that included remembrance of Baptism, personal confession, questions based on the catechism, admonition to remain faithful to the baptismal covenant, and the laying on of hands.[2]

Diversity in the Post-Reformation Era

Melanchthon's and Chemnitz's understandings of confirmation represented only two of several that emerged in the Lutheran tradition during the post-Reformation period. Arthur Repp has identified four different perspectives on the rite of confirmation appearing at this time and others emerging at later points.[3] It is not possible, consequently, to point to a single understanding of confirmation in the Lutheran tradition. Rather, we must point to a range of liturgical practices and theological understandings that have coexisted and comingled at different points in Lutheran history.

Immediately after the Reformation, four different understandings of confirmation first appeared: the instructional, hierarchical, sacramental, and traditional.[4] The *instructional* approach to confirmation did not use the term "confirmation." Building on catechetical instruction in the home, congregation, and school, it emphasized the special instruction offered by the pastor, which reviewed and "confirmed" that which had taken place already. This concluded with an examination by the pastor and admission of the young person to the Lord's Supper. Sometimes admission was signified by a special rite but often not. The *sacramental* understanding of confirmation stood at the opposite end of the spectrum, going back to Luther's and Bucer's distinction between "sacramental ceremonies" and sacraments proper.[5] The *Cassel Church Order,* penned by Bucer and Melanchthon, referred to three sacramental ceremonies, including "Confirmation and the Laying on of Hands." While they were clear that the laying on of hands did not involve a sacramental bestowal of the Spirit completing Baptism, others interpreted their service in this manner. Andreas Hyperius, for example, described the *Hessian Church Order* as distinguishing between forgiveness of sins, granted in Baptism, and bestowal of the Holy Spirit, in confirmation.[6]

The *hierarchical* type of confirmation drew on Bucer's understanding of church discipline. Vows were included in the confirmation service in which confirmands promised loyalty and obedience to God and the church.[7] In the Waldeck confirmation service of 1556, for example, both these elements were prominent.[8] The *traditional* type of confirmation separated confirmation from First Communion and made administration of confirmation by a bishop normative. The best example of this approach is the *Brandenburg Church Order* of 1540 in which the bishop is instructed to lay hands on confirmands, pray over them, and "confirm" them.[9] This liturgy was used in Sweden during the latter part of the sixteenth century, leading to a sharp reaction against it in which confirmation was rejected altogether.[10]

It is important to point out that in spite of these differences, Lutherans were of one mind in their affirmation of the importance of the practice of catechetical instruction. Over time, Luther's *Small Catechism* came to hold pride of place in this instruction. Many commentaries building on his work were written. In Germany alone, around 300 catechisms were produced before 1600.[11] The catechism was *the* center of the church's educational ministry, not merely one element in a broader program. The various forms of confirmation described above all stood in a subordinate relationship to this practice. Even the *sacramental* and *traditional* approaches to confirmation were not seen as communicating goods as important as those gained by studying the catechism over a long period of time.

Lutheran Orthodoxy and Pietism

The most significant, early changes of catechetical instruction and confirmation in the Lutheran tradition took place under the influence of *orthodoxy* and *pietism*. Both movements began to ascribe goods to confirmation that were not originally present in their classical Reformation formulations. Orthodoxy's excesses begat those of pietism, and pietism was to have an important influence on early American Lutheranism.

Regardless of its good intentions, orthodoxy's zeal for the purity of doctrine and conservation of the past gave rise to theological authoritarianism and interchurch polemics.[12] It brought about real changes in the practice of catechetical instruction and led to many of the excesses that later gave it such a bad name. These were an outgrowth of its preoccupation with the rational ordering of doctrine, resulting in an expansion of the amount of doctrinal material included in catechisms and the use of increasingly technical language. Catechetical sermons began to resemble university lectures.[13] A change in the spirit of catechizing also began to take place. Catechisms were viewed less as resources enabling a living dialogue between teacher and student than as a set of doctrinal standards to be memorized. Conrad Dietrich's *Institutiones catecheticae* (1613) is illustrative of these trends. It attempted to introduce children to an entire dogmatic system and considered any resistance on their part to be the work of Satan. It portrayed itself as defending the pure doctrine of Luther from the corruption of other Christian traditions, transforming "children into fully armed soldiers against any danger which might threaten the Lutheran Church."[14] This defensive spirit led to changes in confirmation as well. Questions about the differences between the Lutheran Church and other churches were placed in the confirmation service for the first time. Some church orders went so far as to elicit a solemn vow from confirmands that they would remain loyal to the Lutheran Church as long as they lived.[15]

This kind of catechetical instruction was never universal in Lutheranism, even when orthodoxy was dominant. Where it was present, however, the effect was negative. Attendance at catechetical services began to decline. A practice that initially had been seen as equipping the laity for ministry and breaking the tyranny of the church hierarchy was now used as a tool of ecclesiastical partisanship and control. It is not surprising that critical responses to orthodoxy began to emerge. This took place on two levels. Educators began to criticize the parrot-like quality of learning in catechetical instruction. Students might be able to repeat the catechism, educators argued, but they did not understand it, much less believe it. It is during this period that Comenius created his model Christian schools, which were to have such an important impact on the English Puritans.[16] Even more important was the response of Lutheran pietism. It fostered changes in the relationship of catechetical instruction and confirmation that were to have a major impact on the Lutheran tradition.

Philip Jacob Spener is generally considered the father of Lutheran pietism. A Lutheran pastor, Spener was deeply concerned with the formalism and over-intellectualization of Lutheran orthodoxy. In his own words, he sought to bring "the head into the heart," placing emphasis on the subjective dimension of the faith.[17] He argued that adolescence represented the most important period for catechetical instruction, because it is the time "when the human heart, like a field, should be well plowed and sown before it is overgrown with the thorns of worldliness."[18] Reacting to the changes in this instruction made by orthodoxy, he argued that its primary purpose was not the handing on of the basic tenets of the faith but the creation of an "impulse" that would lead young persons to freely take up a pious life.[19] This was precisely how Spener defined confirmation. It was portrayed as the "renewal of the baptismal covenant" by the individual's heartfelt acceptance of the faith and promise to lead a Christian life. Confirmation as such was viewed as the "fulfillment" and "completion" of Baptism.

An extremely important shift was beginning to take place. Instead of confirmation being viewed as the culmination of catechetical instruction, it was portrayed as the defining purpose of this instruction. A *professional* understanding of confirmation, focusing on the individual's personal ratification of the covenant through an act of profession, was replacing a *catechetical* understanding, focusing on the individual's confession of the church's faith. This is evident in the new catechetical material and methods that Spener began to use. His teaching still took its bearings from Luther's *Small Catechism* but placed less emphasis on memorization and the catechism's question and answer format. Even more important, Spener instructed his classes in a manner that placed great emphasis on the personal experience of the students. His goal was to repeat in their religious experience the order of salvation found in the catechism.

Pietists coming after Spener placed great emphasis on this subjective element of baptismal renewal in confirmation. Christoff Pfaff, for example, encouraged catechists to bring students to "holy tears" as part of the recapitulation of the order of salvation in their experience.[20] August Hermann Francke believed that the use of an official confession in the confirmation service was too formal, and he encouraged confirmands to express their faith in their own words.[21] The spread of pietism led to the spread of confirmation and a renewal of interest in catechetical instruction. An important change had taken place, however. Confirmation was no longer defined in terms of the practice of catechetical instruction; it was now the defining purpose of this instruction. It was this pietistic understanding of confirmation that was dominant among the first Lutherans coming to America.

The Enlightenment, Rationalism, and Cultural Protestantism

Throughout the seventeenth century, a new critical spirit began to emerge in intellectual circles. Responding to the awful results of the Thirty Years' War and advances in the natural sciences, it attempted to free intellectual inquiry from dogmatic constraints. René Descartes epitomizes this new critical approach.[22] All things are to be doubted, he argued. Nothing is to be accepted on the basis of tradition or authority alone. The result was a series of cultural and political enlightenments, taking place at somewhat different times and along different lines in various regions.[23]

Broadly speaking, these enlightenments influenced catechetical instruction and confirmation in three ways. First, they resulted in a defensive reaction on the part of Lutheran orthodoxy and pietism. In the face of the modern, critical spirit, there was an attempt to intensify efforts to inculcate the one true faith (orthodoxy) or to elicit a personal profession (pietism). Second, the new critical spirit began to influence the way catechetical instruction and confirmation were viewed by liberal theologians. They were seen as an opportunity for young people to reflect critically on the meaning of the Christian faith and to decide if it was something they accepted. This was the approach advocated by the father of modern theology, Friedrich Schleiermacher.[24] Third, a new critique of catechetical instruction and confirmation began to be made. They were viewed as a particularly pernicious form of indoctrination: A religious authority, the catechism, which children cannot really understand but only memorize, is used to inculcate a dogmatic point of view without any real reflection on its validity. Calls were made for the replacement of Luther's catechisms as the focus of catechetical instruction.[25] Teaching approaches consistent with modern educational theory were advocated.

The impact of these trends was not the immediate elimination of catechetical instruction and confirmation but the subtle diminution of their importance. What had been widely accepted as a practice essential to the reform movement was seen as needing the "correction" of modern pedagogy and theology. An important source of theological education for the laity was slowly transformed into a kind of family festival. Widely established by the spread of pietism, but uncertain of its role in the modern church, confirmation and catechetical instruction continued to be practiced in the eighteenth and nineteenth centuries through the momentum of cultural forces rather than a clear theological understanding of their purpose. As schooling became compulsory, confirmation became closely associated with the completion of education and even with the bestowal of civic and economic privileges.[26] It sank so low in some places that young women's social debuts influenced the time that it was offered.[27] Various attempts at reform during this period were unsuccessful. Repp points out why reform was so widely resisted: "Confirmation had become so deeply rooted in the social life of the people that no major modification was possible. As long as confirmation was enforced by law and had so many extraneous privileges associated with it, it seemed next to impossible to correct what had become a serious situation with the Lutheran Church."[28]

Lutheranism in America

Lutheran immigrants coming to America brought with them the pattern of catechetical instruction and confirmation they had experienced in Europe. Accordingly, each type of confirmation emerging out of the Reformation is found in American Lutheranism. Among the earliest Lutherans immigrating to this country, the pietistic understanding of confirmation was strongest. Under the influence of Heinrich Melchior Muhlenberg, colonial Lutheranism viewed confirmation as the renewal of the baptismal covenant. Muhlenberg went so far as to say that the "unction" of Baptism is lost quite early in life through sin, leading to the breaking of the baptismal covenant.[29] Catechetical instruction, he argued, should focus on helping young people "renew their broken baptismal covenant."[30]

Frontier conditions added to the plausibility of this perspective. New families were constantly arriving and departing on the frontier. The practice of having all persons enter catechism class when they reached a set age was difficult to follow. Typically, a broad spectrum of ages were involved in these classes in frontier congregations.[31] The result was less emphasis on providing all young people of a certain age with instruction in the tenets of the faith than on helping them make a personal commitment to God, regardless of their age. The catechisms used by Muhlenberg and his followers were based on the "order of salvation" approach developed in German Lutheran pietism, particularly in the form developed by Ziegenhagen.[32] This is reflected in the first official statement on confirmation by American Lutheranism, formulated by the Pennsylvania Ministerium in 1786. Pastors were charged with making sure that their teaching offered more than head knowledge and that "the hearts of the children were improved."[33]

This understanding of confirmation proved to be vulnerable to the two great awakenings and revivalism sweeping across America during the latter part of the eighteenth and nineteenth centuries. Why should confirmation be maintained as the means of awakening the heart when the methods of revivalism were proving to be even more effective? In many parts of Lutheranism during this period, confirmation declined in importance or was dropped altogether.[34] It took a new wave of Lutheran immigrants during the 1830s to breath fresh life into this practice. Influenced by the more catechetical approach still operative in certain parts of Europe, many of these immigrants brought with them an emphasis on the teaching of Luther's *Small Catechism*. Still other immigrants from Sweden maintained Swedish Lutheranism's long-standing antipathy toward a confirmation ceremony.

In short, American Lutheranism reflected the wide diversity of understandings and practices characterizing Lutheranism in Europe. No single pattern emerged. One final aspect of the American experience must be mentioned before turning to the contemporary Lutheran discussion of confirmation: the rise of the Sunday school movement. Originating in England through the work of Robert Raikes in the latter part of the eighteenth century, this movement spread like wildfire in American Protestantism.[35] Lay-led and evangelically oriented, it viewed its mission as the spread of Christianity across the American frontier. So successful was it in the pursuit of this goal that it became the dominant pattern of Protestant Christian education. During the nineteenth century, the Sunday school movement made its way into all of the major Protestant denominations, including the Lutheran Church.

When the Sunday School Union began to produce its own literature, reflecting its nonconfessional, individualistic, evangelical theology, the denominations rightly sensed a threat to their ability to hand on the core tenets of their heritage. The initial response was to encourage pastors to renew their efforts to maintain a strong program of catechetical instruction and confirmation in their congregations. When it became apparent that the pattern of Sunday school education was going to triumph, the denominations attempted to co-opt this movement, producing their own denominational literature that could be used on Sunday morning.[36] Even catechetical instruction was adapted to this format, with questions and answers of Luther's catechisms added to Sunday school lessons.

For the most part, however, Lutheran congregations resisted a total reduction of catechetical instruction to the Sunday school. Special classes focusing on the catechism or comparable doctrinal material were still taught by the pastor. These classes culminated in a rite of confirmation. In some parts of Lutheranism, this service was understood along pietistic lines and served a *professional* purpose: the individual's heartfelt profession of faith. In other parts, it was viewed as having a *catechetical* purpose: allowing the individual to confess the faith of the church. These two purposes often were conjoined, with personal profession seen as a subordinate dimension of confession. Although a relatively common practice of catechetical instruction followed by confirmation was widely established in American Lutheranism, the goods this practice was seen as serving varied widely.

The Contemporary Lutheran Discussion

Over the past four decades American Lutheranism has undertaken a serious examination of the theology and practice of confirmation. In large measure, this was sparked by the unification of several branches of Lutheranism to form the Evangelical Lutheran Church in America (ELCA). In both the initial, exploratory stages of this unification and after its completion, these denominations examined their doctrinal and liturgical heritage in conjunction with the creation of a worship book for the new denomination. This process was informed by the wealth of new liturgical scholarship emerging during this period and various attempts at liturgical reform taking place in different denominations.[37] During this period, an attempt has been made to lead the church into a new and clearer understanding of what is meant by confirmation. The diversity present in Lutheranism from the beginning has continued to be a part of the American Lutheran experience. Empirical studies carried out as recently as the 1970s found a wide range of confirmation practices and understandings in the Lutheran Church.[38] In a sense, the unification served as an occasion for the ELCA to reflect on its internal diversity and clarify exactly what is at stake in confirmation. The long-term effect this will have on congregational life remains to be seen.

The first and most important step in this process was taken in *The Report of the Joint Commission on the Theology and Practice of Confirmation* written in 1970.[39] Responding to an invitation of the Lutheran Church in America, the American Lutheran Church and The Lutheran Church–Missouri Synod formed a study commission on the theology and practice of confirmation in 1964. The study was part of a broader series of efforts to explore the possible unification of various Lutheran denominations and to recommend "a uniform practice suitable in North America at the present time."[40] One of the members of the commission was Arthur Repp, whose book on confirmation appeared the year the commission began its work.[41] Repp's prior work on the history of Lutheran confirmation, in which he characterizes Bucer's perspective as "hierarchical" and portrays pietistic and sacramental understandings of confirmation in a negative light, was incorporated into the committee's report and, by and large, has been accepted uncritically in much of the subsequent discussion.[42]

The commission offered the following definition of confirmation: "Confirmation ministry is a pastoral and educational ministry of the church which helps the baptized child through Word and Sacrament to identify more deeply with the Christian community and participate more fully in its mission."[43]

One of the most important aspects of the commission's work was its attempt to set this definition in a solid Lutheran theological framework.[44] It does so admirably, pointing to the centrality of justification by grace in the Lutheran tradition and the church's status as a means of grace through which the gospel is proclaimed. In the context of this discussion, it makes several important points:

1. Confirmation is *not* a sacrament. Only Baptism and Communion are. Confirmation belongs to the well-being of the church and not its essence. It can be changed as need arises.
2. Confirmation is *not* a renewal of the baptismal covenant along the lines of pietism. It should not focus on the individual's religious experience but on God's "confirming" action through the church and the individual's response.
3. While sharing identical gospel content, Baptism and Communion are different. "The former is the initiating sacrament; the latter, the sustaining."[45] Baptism grants "sonship"; Communion maintains and strengthens it.
4. Confirmation is grounded primarily in Baptism. It does not complete or complement Baptism in any way, for Baptism grants all the benefits and privileges of membership in the body of Christ.
5. Confirmation should be separated from First Communion.

This final point marks a break with the inherited Reformation paradigm of infant Baptism, catechetical instruction, and admission to the Lord's Supper. As described in the explanatory material by Frank Klos that accompanied the commission's report, the call to separate admission and confirmation was seen as part of an integrated series of changes.[46] Confirmation was to be offered later (tenth grade is recommended) and admission to the Lord's Table, earlier (fifth grade is recommended). Moreover, the nature of confirmation education was to be altered, being broadened considerably beyond catechetical instruction. As the definition cited above puts it, the goal of confirmation is "identification" with the Christian community. Study of the catechism is one objective among several. Each confirmand is still "to know and confess as his own the Christian faith" based on "the central teachings of the church as expressed in Luther's *Small Catechism.*"[47] But the confirmand also is "to learn his role as a child and servant of God," as well as "what it means to continue to grow in the life of the Christian community and its mission."[48] Liturgically, the commission called for a rite of admission to the Lord's Supper along with a rite for confirmation. In its discussion of the latter, it stressed repeatedly the importance of strengthening the link between Baptism and confirmation.

Although the Commission's report marked the end of the older Reformation paradigm, it maintained strong continuity with it in many ways. A rite of confirmation, not admission to the Lord's Supper, was to mark the end of a special confirmation program designed to deepen the many things young people have learned through the nurture and care of the church. Included in this program were certain catechetical elements, but these were balanced by a desire to help confirmands gain a sense of their vocation in the world and to identify more fully with the mission of the church. We can accurately call this understanding of confirmation *catechetical* only in the broadest of senses. It retains a strong educational focus and even includes the longtime emphasis on study of Luther's catechism. But this program is opened out to the broader processes of formation by which youth have learned the Christian life since they were baptized.

This understanding of confirmation has exerted enormous influence on contemporary mainline Lutheranism. It was adopted by the Lutheran Church in America in 1970 and 1971. Subsequently, the Inter-Lutheran Commission on Worship's subcommittee on Confirmation and First Communion drew on the basic understandings of the report as it began to formulate liturgical rubrics for the new denomination (ELCA).[49] The work of this subcommittee provided the foundation for the rubrics on confirmation incorporated into the *Lutheran Book of Worship* (*LBW*), published in 1990.[50] This book of worship is deeply informed by contemporary liturgical developments and scholarship, particularly in the area of the rite of initiation. Although it maintains continuity with the Lutheran tradition, it also reaches behind the Reformation to the patristic period, bringing together elements of initiation that had long been separated in the Western church: renunciation and profession, water-washing, laying on of hands, prayer for the Holy Spirit, consignation, and Eucharist.

The baptismal service of the *LBW* continues the Lutheran tradition's strong emphasis on God's action through this rite, describing it as granting forgiveness of sin and liberation from sin's power by joining the one baptized to the death and resurrection of Jesus Christ. Everything of importance takes place here. This

service also maintains the Lutheran tradition's close linkage of Baptism and catechetical instruction, especially with regard to infant Baptism. Parents and sponsors promise to teach the one being baptized the traditional catechetical trilogy
and to live out the baptismal covenant so the infant will come to know what it
means. The close linkage with instruction also is maintained in the profession of
the Apostles' Creed, which follows the renunciation and precedes the water-
washing. This represents a summary of the history of God's mighty acts in which
the one who is being baptized is now being placed, a history also rehearsed in the
prayer of thanksgiving. The final portion of the service is significant because it includes the elements of laying on of hands and consignation. These, of course, are
the very things that broke off from Baptism during the early Middle Ages, leading to the development of confirmation as an independent rite. By including them
here, the *LBW* makes it clear that the bestowal and the sealing of the Spirit take
place in Baptism. Nothing remains to be added at a later point.

Accordingly, the confirmation service is portrayed as closely related to Baptism. It is located under the general heading, "Affirmation of Baptism," along with
services for the reception of new members and those who wish to renew their
faith. One rite is used for all three occasions. This rite also can be used by the
members of the entire congregation to reaffirm their baptismal covenant. Moreover, the close relation of confirmation and Baptism is made clear throughout the
entire service. The opening explanation of the rite reads: "Those who have completed this program were made members of the Church in Baptism. Confirmation
includes a public profession of the faith into which the candidates were baptized,
thus underscoring God's action in their Baptism."[51] Likewise, the bestowal of full
membership in Baptism is emphasized in the ministerial address to the candidates.
Confirmation does not add to Baptism; it represents a deeper affirmation of that
which has already been given. The invitation, renunciation, and profession of faith
are the same as those used in the baptismal service. Especially significant is the
language used in conjunction with the minister's laying on of hands. The rubric
asks God to "stir up" the gift of the Spirit and "confirm" his or her faith. The assumption is that the Spirit has already been bestowed in Baptism, where the prayer
reads "pour your Holy Spirit."

What, then, does confirmation represent? It seems to involve several things. As
the passage cited above from the *LBW* puts it, "public profession" is involved.
This seems to include a personal dimension but not in the pietistic sense. The accent is on the individual's acceptance of a reality in which he or she already participates by virtue of Baptism. It also involves a confessional element, indicated
by use of the Apostles' Creed in interrogatory form. The individual has studied
the catechism and now can join the entire company of Christians in confessing the
one faith of the church. Finally, it represents an acknowledgment of God's past
and present actions that have brought the young person to this place. God has
worked through the nurture and care of the church to strengthen and confirm the
work begun in Baptism. By pointing to God's work in the confirmand's life, the
service expresses confidence that this will continue to take place in the future.

Each of these dimensions of confirmation is grounded in its relation to Baptism.

This is consistent with Lutheran tradition and the understanding of confirmation developed in the report of the 1970 commission. It also is informed by recent liturgical scholarship on the ancient rite of Christian initiation.

The basic trajectory set in motion by the *LBW* and the 1970 study commission continues in the ELCA's most recent statement on confirmation, *The Confirmation Ministry Task Force Report*, adopted by the Church Wide Assembly in 1993.[52] The task force explicitly draws on the 1970 report's definition of confirmation and seeks to draw out further implications of this definition in light of new developments in church and society. The one change made in this definition is elimination of its reference to confirmation as a ministry to the "baptized child." This change makes it more open-ended as to who is involved in confirmation ministry, and it reflects the task force's special interest in adolescence.[53]

Building on the 1970 report's understanding of confirmation, the task force places great emphasis on the important role people beyond the pastor have in this ministry. Catechists, lay persons, parents, and youth all are portrayed as playing a vital part. Little is said about traditional catechetical instruction or the need to teach Luther's *Small Catechism*.[54] It is not possible to tell whether this is assumed by the report or marks a turn away from the catechism. In light of the widespread realities of theological illiteracy and denominational switching, this omission is surprising.

The report offers two particularly important contributions to the recent discussion of confirmation. First, it draws special attention to the relationship between confirmation and adolescence. One of its guiding, focal questions is: "What is the role of the congregation in affirming youth in Christian faithfulness with an emphasis on lifelong learning and discipleship?"[55] The 1970 report had recommended that tenth grade serve as the time for fulfilling confirmation ministry. It described this age in developmental terms that bordered on sentimentalism at points. The average tenth-grader was described as having "a degree of wholesome self-confidence," as possessing "a feeling of greater ease with the opposite sex," as "conscious of his own responsibility in handling emotions," and as "interested in achieving a personal religion."[56] It is clear that such a characterization of adolescents was formed prior to the massive cultural shift that has taken place over the past thirty years. Teen pregnancy, widespread drug use, adolescent suicide, and nihilistic strands of youth culture are realities in contemporary America. The 1993 task force rightly draws attention to the at-risk behavior of contemporary youth and casts many of its practical concerns toward this sector of the population.[57] Confirmation is portrayed as paying special attention to the needs and potentialities of adolescence. This is a theme that the ELCA and mainline Protestantism in general would do well to take seriously.[58]

The second major contribution this report makes is its attention to the close relationship between the "lifelong return to baptism" and the lifelong need to learn and grow through participation in the church's educational ministry. The theological and practical potential of this theme is great. Keying off the rites of Affirmation of Baptism, the report makes the important point that confirmation is not a graduation from the educational ministry but a culminating point of a process that should continue through life. Drawing on Luther's theology, it argues that a "lifelong return to baptism" stands at the heart of the Christian life, for the pattern of rising and dying with Christ is not something Christians ever outgrow. This represents a viable theological critique of the widespread pattern among Lutheran youth of dropping out of the educational program as soon as confirmation is completed, a pattern pointed to in the Introduction of this book.[59] It also represents a potent theological rationale for adult participation in the educational ministry.

From the 1970 study commission report to the present, then, the Lutheran Church has maintained a practice that stands in continuity with the older Reformation paradigm, although altering it in significant ways. Confirmation has been separated from admission to the Lord's Supper. Catechetical instruction is one of several objectives viewed as important to the confirmation program as a whole. Broadly speaking, however, the defining focus of confirmation remains *catechetical:* providing nurture and care that allows youth to confess the faith of the church and more fully take up the responsibilities of the Christian life. Although there are both *professional* and *catechumenal* elements in the new understanding of confirmation, both are subordinated to its catechetical purpose. The way the Lutheran Church has integrated all of these elements in its educational, theological, and liturgical work on confirmation over the past three decades represents an important contribution to the continuing ecumenical discussion.

The Anglican-Episcopal Tradition

The reform of the Church of England took a unique course between the churches of the continental Reformation and the Roman Catholic Church. While the English reformers were deeply influenced by Bucer, Calvin, and other reformers of the continent, this did not result in a wholesale sweeping away of all older church traditions, especially in the area of liturgy. As a result, two distinct patterns of confirmation came to be present in the prayer book tradition. One is *sacramental* and the other, *professional.*

The first maintains continuity with medieval theology and the practice of the Roman Catholic Church. It views confirmation *sacramentally,* although a sacrament based on tradition and not of equal status to the two "gospel sacraments." In this pattern, initiation into the church is not seen as complete until a bishop, standing in apostolic succession, confirms persons who have been baptized by performing certain sacramental acts. In some cases, this follows Baptism immediately; in others, it takes place at a later point in conjunction with an individual's profession of faith. In either case, confirmation is identified with the bishop's sacramental act.

The second pattern maintains continuity with the continental reformation and views confirmation along *professional* lines as the individual's ratification of the baptismal covenant. This pattern includes a strong *catechetical* subelement, however. Historically, the Anglican-Episcopal tradition has linked study of the catechism and confirmation quite closely. Moreover, its confirmation service often has included confession of the Apostles' Creed as an act in which the confirmand joins the church universal in confessing the one faith. The present confirmation service, for example, uses the Apostles' Creed in interrogatory form. For the most part, however, this catechetical element remains subordinate to the *professional* purpose of confirmation: ratification of the baptismal covenant. In this pattern, the bishop plays a representative and symbolic function, not a sacramental one, receiving the confirmands' professions on behalf of the whole church and praying that the Spirit will continue to strengthen them on a lifelong journey of faith.

The tension between the *sacramental* and *professional* patterns of confirmation has characterized the Anglican-Episcopal tradition from the beginning and is present in the most recent edition of the American Episcopal Church's *Book of Common Prayer (BCP* [1979]). We gain perspective on the present understanding of confirmation in this tradition by examining the earliest stages of the prayer book tradition.

The Early Period of Reform

Much of the early reform of confirmation in the Church of England was influenced by the work of Thomas Cranmer, the archbishop of Canterbury under Henry VIII and Edward VI.[60] It is helpful to place Cranmer's reforms in context. On the eve of the Reformation in England, the most widely used rite of Baptism was that of the *Sarum Manual,* which employed a "two-stage" pattern of initiation.[61] The water-washing of Baptism could be carried out by a minister but the postbaptismal anointing, representing the sacrament of confirmation, could only be performed by the bishop. This meant that confirmation frequently was separated from the water-washing and administered at a later time.

Cranmer was well aware of the critique of confirmation being formulated by the continental reformers and was especially open to Bucer's influence. He invited Bucer to come to England in 1548 and asked him to comment extensively on the first *BCP,* comments subsequently published as the *Censura.*[62] Like the Reformers, Cranmer viewed confirmation as standing in a close relationship to catechetical instruction. In the "Introduction" of his catechism of 1548, he portrayed confirmation as an examination of those who have been instructed in the articles and commandments of the faith and are ready to make a profession of the promises made on their behalf at Baptism.[63] At the same time, he continued to portray confirmation as a "sacramental ceremony," differentiating the two "sacraments ordained by Christ" (Baptism and the Lord's Supper) and the five arising out of apostolic practice, including confirmation.[64] It is no accident, then, that *sacramental* and *professional* forms of confirmation came to be present in the *BCP.* It was under Cranmer's guidance that the earliest prayer books were formed, passing through several editions.

The first *BCP* was published in 1549. For the most part, it maintains close continuity with the Latin rites of the medieval *Sarum Manual* in its baptismal service. Two changes are important, however. First, following the Baptism, the parents and godparents are charged to teach the ones baptized, "so soon as they shall be able to learn, what a solemn vow, promise and profession they have made by you."[65] They are told specifically that the child is to learn the Creed, Lord's Prayer, and Ten Commandments in English. This reflects the Reformers' increased

emphasis on catechetical instruction. Second, the prayer offered in conjunction
with the post-baptismal anointing is altered in a subtle, but important, way. Where
the *Sarum* had "anoint thee with the chrism of salvation," the *BCP* has "anoint
thee with the unction of his Holy Spirit."[66] This phrase was commonly used by
medieval theologians to refer to confirmation.[67] As Leonel Mitchell points out,
Cranmer may be attempting to reunify the rite of initiation, returning the anointing associated with confirmation to its original position within the baptismal rite
and making it the prerogative of the priest.[68]

The Prayer Book also contains a service of confirmation. It too combines reformed and medieval impulses.[69] It picks up the *catechetical* note in the first
rubric: ". . . none hereafter shall be confirmed but such as can say in their mother
tongue the articles of the faith, the Lord's prayer and the Ten Commandments,
and can also answer to such questions of this short catechism as the bishop . . .
shall by his discretion appose them in."[70] The next paragraph is strongly *professional*. It states that children, upon reaching the years of discretion and studying
the faith confessed on their behalf in Baptism, should "ratify and confess the
same" with "their own mouth" and "consent" before the church. A gap exists between this stated intent and its fulfillment in the actual service. At no point are the
confirmands asked to ratify the vows of the covenant in the service. This is not introduced into the confirmation service until the 1662 Prayer Book. Indeed, the service closely follows the *sacramental* pattern of the *Sarum Manual,* focusing on
the bishop's laying on of hands and consignation of the candidates in conjunction
with prayer for the Holy Spirit. The *Sarum's* prayer for the sevenfold gifts of the
Spirit goes all the way back to the *Gelasian Sacramentary* of the sixth century.[71]

Whereas the 1552 edition of the *BCP* introduced further elements of the continental reformation, it continued to combine them with older traditions. Baptism
was shortened and simplified.[72] The service at the door of the church and the exorcism were abandoned. The postbaptismal anointing was eliminated, but the
consignation was retained. The words spoken in conjunction with the consignation now recall imagery of the medieval confirmation service, describing the one
being baptized as a soldier equipped to do battle against sin and the devil. Like
the first prayer book, this service too can be interpreted as attempting to restore
confirmation to its original place in the baptismal service.[73]

A second confirmation service, however, still remains. It combines medieval
and Reformation impulses, although it clearly is moving farther away from medieval practice.[74] The introductory rubrics stressing the catechetical context are
retained, although there still is no place in the service for the ratification of the
baptismal covenant. A significant change takes place in the midst of the prayer for
the sevenfold gifts of the Spirit. Where God had been asked in the first prayer book
to "send down from heaven . . . upon them thy Holy Ghost," God now is asked to
"*strengthen them* . . . with the Holy Ghost, the Comforter, and *daily increase* in
them thy manifold gifts of grace" (emphasis added). This reads much less like a
direct bestowal of the Holy Spirit through the bishop's action and more like a stir-
ring up of a gift that has been given already.[75] Moreover, the consignation is
dropped and only the laying on of hands retained, the sign preferred by the conti-

nental reformers. God is no longer asked to "sign" the confirmands in conjunction with this act nor does the bishop use the first prayer book's more performative language: "I sign thee with the sign of the cross and lay my hand upon thee . . . " Rather, the prayer reads: "Defend, O Lord this child with thy heavenly grace, that he may continue thine for ever, and *daily increase* in thy Holy Spirit more and more, until he come unto thy everlasting kingdom. Amen" (emphasis added). The language of daily increase seems to come from Bucer's baptismal and confirmation services. It fits quite nicely with the second prayer book's efforts to make it clear that Baptism involves full initiation into the church, including the gift of the Spirit.[76] Confirmation involves prayer for the "daily increase" of a gift already given.

From the outset, then, the prayer books of the Church of England continued to hold together *sacramental* and *professional* understandings of confirmation, with the latter containing a strong *catechetical* element of study and confession. Although Baptism was viewed as the sole rite of initiation, it was combined with ancient elements of anointing, consignation, and prayer that had been long associated with the sacrament of confirmation. At the same time, a special service of confirmation was a part of the prayer book tradition, closely related to catechetical instruction and a personal profession of faith. In the 1662 edition of the *BCP*, the *professional* element was strengthened when explicit confirmation vows were added to the service. The basic patterns of Anglican-Episcopal confirmation were now in place. From the beginning, a tension has existed between these patterns. Is confirmation one moment in an integrated process of initiation? Is it a special episcopal act with sacramental status? Is it the individual's confirmation of the vows made on his or her behalf in Baptism? Is it the individual's confession of the church's faith? Or is it a combination of all these things?

Each of these questions have been answered in the affirmative at some point in the Anglican-Episcopal tradition. Jeremey Taylor, for example, granted confirmation *sacramental* status, writing: "the holy rite of confirmation is a divine ordinance, and it produces divine effects, and is ministered by divine persons, that is, by those whom God both sanctified and separated to this ministration."[77] Others vigorously opposed this position. For many years, Nowell's catechism undergirded a *catechetical* understanding of confirmation. The widespread influence of the covenant theology throughout the British Isles supported a *professional* interpretation of the vows made in confirmation. As in the Lutheran Church, a range of understandings thus began to surround confirmation in the Anglican-Episcopal tradition, making it impossible to describe a single unfolding trajectory.

To the Present

One of the most important results of the use of the first two prayer books was the spread of Christian education throughout England. The services of Baptism and confirmation both enjoined catechetical instruction, and this practice now came to be firmly implanted in English life. The general pattern was that found throughout continental Protestantism. Catechisms were written and taught in various institutional settings: the home, school, and congregation.[78] No official catechisms were published during the reign of Henry VIII, although a number of unofficial ones were used during this period.[79] Cranmer published his own catechism in 1548, based on a translation and revision of Justus Jonas's Lutheran catechism.[80] This was followed by the catechism of the 1549 *Prayer Book,* which reappeared in later editions. Both covered the traditional catechetical material. Neither gained the widespread popularity of Alexander Nowell's *A Catechism* or first instruction and learning of Christian religion, published in 1570.[81] Nowell's catechism came to be widely used in schools and congregations, and simpler catechisms for children frequently were used in the home.

As the initial zeal of the early reformers passed and the Church of England became an established church, the importance of creating a theologically informed laity through catechetical instruction gradually began to fade. The rote memorization and harsh drilling that sometimes were used in this instruction did not lead to a deep appreciation of this practice. As catechetical instruction declined, confirmation began to receive less emphasis as well. The difficulty of travel and the large number of people baptized as infants made it hard for bishops to carry out their confirmation responsibilities on a regular basis. Research about English religious life in the first part of the eighteenth century reveals hundreds of people confirmed simultaneously by a single prayer with no laying on of hands, and thousands were not confirmed at all.[82] Catechesis and confirmation fell on hard times in the seventeenth and eighteenth centuries.

An important period of renewal took place in conjunction with the evangelical movement in the Anglican Church during the mid-eighteenth century. A group of bishops, stressing teaching and personal piety, began to take their confirmation responsibilities seriously. Although preceding his episcopacy (1845 to 1873), Samuel Wilberforce is generally considered the leading figure of this movement.[83] He and the movement as a whole emphasized four things: (1) annual confirmation at many centers, instead of less frequent visits; (2) emphasis on the instruction and general preparation of confirmation candidates at the parish level; (3) services conducted with the dignity and solemnity appropriate to the importance of the occasion; and (4) placement of confirmation within the context of a broader service, including preaching and hymns.[84]

Confirmation in the American Episcopal Church during this period retained the theology of its English progenitor but not its practice. During the colonial period there were no bishops present to confirm those who had been baptized. This led to the admission of baptized members to Communion without confirmation. Even when bishops began to be present, they were responsible for dioceses that frequently included entire states. The same difficulties experienced in England were multiplied under these circumstances. Confirmation was infrequent and catechetical instruction spotty. This pattern was broken in a manner that was to exert a long-term effect on the Episcopal Church during the episcopacy of John Henry Hobert, Bishop of New York (ca. 1811). Hobert made frequent visits to different parishes to confirm young people and new members. He insisted that non-

Episcopalians receive an episcopal blessing on joining the church. This had the effect of making confirmation stand out as a distinctive emphasis of the Episcopal Church among American Protestantism.[85]

Influencing the discussion of confirmation in both England and the United States has been the liturgical renewal movement of the twentieth century. Among many things, it led to a renewed interest in the rite of Christian initiation in the ancient church. The recovery of ancient texts and new historical research allowed scholars to reach behind both the medieval and Reformation understandings of confirmation and Baptism to the patristic pattern of initiation. This scholarly renewal of interest in confirmation began in the 1890s with F. W. Puller's book *What Is the Distinctive Grace of Confirmation?* and A. J. Mason's *The Relation of Baptism to Confirmation.*[86] Both made a compelling case for a "two stage" theory of initiation. The water-washing was viewed as involving both the cleansing of sin and incorporation of persons into the church; the laying on of hands by a bishop was viewed as conveying the Holy Spirit. Both were portrayed as necessary parts of initiation and as having sacramental status.

Soon other scholars began to undertake research on early Christian initiation, making a similar argument that Baptism-confirmation-Eucharist were originally one integrated act of initiation that later disintegrated in the West. The works of Dom Gregory Dix on Hippolytus and J.D.C. Fisher on medieval developments were particularly influential in the Anglican-Episcopal tradition.[87] Others built on their scholarship and argued vigorously that Christian initiation was not complete until confirmation occurred.[88] This was typically viewed along sacramental lines and gradually began to lead to certain exclusionary policies. Persons from communions without "apostolic" episcopal confirmation sometimes were not allowed to commune in Anglican or Episcopal churches, for example.[89]

This view did not go unopposed. It received, among others, a significant reply in G. W. Lampe's *The Seal of the Spirit,* which challenged the biblical and patristic foundations of the belief that the Spirit was conveyed exclusively through the postbaptismal "sealing" by the bishop in the early church.[90] J.D.G. Dunn's *Baptism in the Holy Spirit* also offered an influential critique of the two-stage theory of initiation.[91] Building on these insights, Aidan Kavanagh pointed out that, according to scripture, the Spirit is present before, during, and after Baptism and cannot be limited to a single moment or liturgical act.[92] Exploration of the variety of postbaptismal acts in both the East and the West also undercut the two-stage position.[93]

Perhaps even more damaging to the two-stage position was the separation of confirmation and First Communion that began to take place during the second half of the twentieth century. Following the standard Reformation pattern, Anglican and Episcopal churches traditionally had admitted persons to Communion only after catechetical instruction and confirmation. This process has been altered in recent years in the Anglican-Episcopal churches of New Zealand, the United States, Canada, and England.[94] Nothing could make the noninitiatory status of adolescent-adult confirmation clearer. Children at Baptism are viewed as fully initiated into the church and as possessing all of the benefits and rights this bestows, including participation in the Lord's Supper.

The Contemporary Episcopal Discussion

The most important discussions of confirmation in the American Episcopal Church have focused on the revision of the 1928 *BCP,* which culminated in the 1979 edition. As Charles Price points out, these revisions can be seen as the natural outgrowth of the processes involved in the earlier revision of the prayer book that the 1928 edition represented.[95] Edward Parsons, one of the strongest advocates of prayer book reform at that time, puts it: "Further change is inevitable."[96] The Standing Liturgical Commission was established in recognition of this inevitability. This Commission began a complete review of the 1928 *Book of Common Prayer* in 1950, resulting in a series of "Prayer Book Studies." By and large, the changes envisioned by these studies were relatively small, and Elizabethan English was maintained throughout.[97]

We have pointed out already the renewal of interest in confirmation in the Anglican-Episcopal tradition that began to occur in the last decade of the nineteenth century. This was intensified by three new forces: (1) the liturgical movement, coming into its own after World War I and sparking a new wave of scholarship on patristic worship and practice; (2) new biblical scholarship, employing form and redaction criticism to investigate the ways biblical material was shaped by its use in the early church, especially its worship; and (3) the ecumenical discussion sponsored by the World Council of Churches (WCC) and beyond, leading to an examination of the common ministries of different Christian traditions. *Baptism, Eucharist, and Ministry,* produced under the auspices of the WCC in 1982, proved to be a landmark of ecumenical cooperation.[98]

These three trends led to a period of liturgical examination and renewal in a wide range of Protestant traditions. By the time the Standing Liturgical Commission finished the first series of "Prayer Book Studies" in 1963, forces were in motion that would support more sweeping changes. This Commission initiated a new series of "Prayer Book Studies" that were authorized for trial use in 1970. The language of the proposed liturgies was modernized. Material and insights emerging from the new wave of biblical and liturgical scholarship were used. Items that go beyond the scope of the present discussion also emerged out of this period of renewal. The establishment of a catechumenate for unbaptized adults is only one example.[99]

Revision of Baptism and confirmation initially was undertaken in *Holy Baptism with the Laying-on-of-Hands,* one of the new "Prayer Book Studies" series.[100] The study called for a major break with the prayer book tradition, abolishing the *professional* understanding of confirmation, allowing all baptized persons to commune, and "reunifying" Baptism-confirmation-Eucharist.[101] The report called for bishops to play the role of lead officiant in the rite of initiation yet allowed them to delegate the administration of all parts of the service to the priest, including the postbaptismal laying on of hands.[102] Many of these revisions were retained in the 1979 *BCP.*

One aspect of this study, however, ran into opposition: the suggestion that the profession of baptismal faith traditionally associated with confirmation be viewed as taking place regularly in a congregation's reaffirmation of its baptismal vows. The latter was now an important part of the normal baptismal liturgy.[103] The response to this proposal was twofold. First, regular renewal of the baptismal covenant was accepted as an important aspect of the baptismal liturgy. In the 1979 *BCP,* the entire congregation joins with those being baptized in affirming this covenant. Second, the proposal that the *professional* pattern of confirmation be eliminated was rejected. The need was reaffirmed for those baptized as infants to make a mature profession of faith and to voluntarily enter into the baptismal covenant.

Accordingly, *Prayer Book Study 26,* published in 1973, added a new service of confirmation.[104] Although the baptismal service continued to include the post-baptismal consignation, the term "confirmation" was now used to designate the service by which persons make a mature profession of faith.[105] It was viewed as one of several occasions on which individuals are given a chance to affirm their baptismal covenant as a sign of personal and corporate renewal. The 1979 *BCP* incorporated the recommendation of this study with some minor changes. It gave greater specificity to the occasions for which the Reaffirmation of Baptism liturgy was appropriate, designating three: the individual's mature profession of faith, the reception of new members, and the restoration of lapsed members. Confirmation was used exclusively to designate the first of these.

There are several important things to note about the Baptism and confirmation services as finally adopted in the 1979 *BCP.* An attempt has been made to restore the integrity of Baptism as found in the patristic period. This is accomplished in several ways. First, the *BCP* states unequivocally that "Holy Baptism is full initiation by water and the Holy Spirit into Christ's Body the Church."[106] Second, it portrays Baptism as located normatively in the context of the Easter Vigil and the eucharistic service. This places it squarely in the central events of the dying and rising of Christ and restores the early church's connection between Baptism and Eucharist. The service continues the long-standing tradition of asking those being baptized to renounce Satan and profess their allegiance to Christ and to join with the entire congregation in affirming the faith of the church by rendering the Apostles' Creed in interrogatory form. This represents the making of the baptismal covenant. Congregational participation at this important point allows the service to serve as both a moment of initiation and a reaffirmation of this covenant.

In keeping with the desire to make it clear that Baptism involves complete initiation, the water-washing is both preceded and followed by prayers asking God to send the Holy Spirit on those being baptized. Before the water is administered, God is asked to "Fill them with your holy and life-giving Spirit." The water-washing is followed by the prayer for the sevenfold gifts of the Holy Spirit and the "sealing" of the one being baptized through the laying on of hands and consignation, which may be done with chrism if desired.

A separate service for confirmation also appears in the 1979 *BCP,* however. As noted above, it is one of three occasions at which persons may reaffirm their baptismal covenant. In keeping with the long-standing tension between *sacramental* and *professional* patterns of confirmation, it can be interpreted along two lines. Those advocating an interpretation along the lines of the latter argue that whereas Baptism is viewed as complete sacramentally and as unrepeatable, it represents "the beginning of a process of participation, growth, and response."[107] Daniel Stevick conveys nicely the theological relationship between Baptism and confirmation viewed in this way as follows:

> The motivation of Christian life is often expressed as "become what you are." The Baptism rite should say as much as possible about "what you are." It is a summation, at the start, of that which can only be fully apprehended at the end. But from the start, the "becoming" develops from the "is." To say much about "what you are" at the beginning, does not remove the urgency from the "becoming." Rather, it sets the process in perspective. From Baptism on, a Christian is always making response to the total, self-giving claim of God which is declared in the Word and signified in Baptism.[108]

Confirmation represents one of many moments in the Christian life when Christians' "becoming" intersects their "being." It represents that special moment when they are prepared for the first time "to make a mature public affirmation of their faith and commitment to the responsibilities of their Baptism," to use the words of the *BCP*.[109] This affirmation is received and confirmed by the church in various actions by the bishop and congregation.

Alongside this understanding of the confirmation service in the 1979 *Prayer Book,* a second line of interpretation is offered by others.[110] There, the consignation and laying on of hands coming immediately after the water-washing in the present baptismal service are viewed as comparable to the first anointing in the ancient rites of initiation. Confirmation is seen as taking place only when the bishop lays on hands and prays, "Defend, O Lord, this thy child with thy heavenly grace. . . ." This act and prayer are found solely in the confirmation service proper, not in the baptismal service. People coming from churches that do not practice apostolic, episcopal confirmation must be confirmed with this service. Those coming from Catholic or Orthodox churches need only be received.

Although the Anglican-Episcopal tradition offers one of the liturgically richest understandings of confirmation and, to a large extent, has led the way in the recent ecumenical liturgical renewal, deep ambiguity remains in its understanding of confirmation. The combination of Protestant and Catholic elements characterizing the prayer book tradition from the beginning continues to haunt its most recent formulation.

The United Methodist Tradition

The United Methodist Church has the shortest story to tell with regard to confirmation because it has only included a service of confirmation among its official worship publications since 1964. For much of its history, however, it has grappled with the tension between its theological commitment to infant Baptism and a "high" view of the sacraments, on the one hand, and its strong evangelical commitment to the making of "a personal commitment to Jesus Christ as Lord and Savior" and the assuming of adult responsibilities in the church, on the other hand.[111] John Wesley's ability to hold together an Anglican view of the sacraments and an evangelical spirit valuing conversion and scriptural holiness has not always been easy to maintain.

Wesley portrayed Baptism as having a regenerating function. As he put it: "By the water then, as a means, the water of baptism we are regenerated or born again; whence it is also called, by the Apostle, 'the washing of regeneration.' Our Church therefore ascribes no greater virtue to baptism than Christ himself has done."[112] He was clear that this regenerating power was as fully present in the baptism of infants as adults. Its efficacy had to do with the nature of the sacrament, not the subjective response of the participant. Although Wesley affirmed the objective quality of the grace communicated in Baptism, he went on to affirm the importance of the personal appropriation of that which has been communicated. He constantly reminded parents and pastors of the importance of their teaching and discipline as part of the church's role in helping its baptized members fulfill the promise of Baptism. The work begun in Baptism must issue in repentance, faith, and holiness, or its grace may be lost at a later point: "Say not then in your heart, 'I was once baptized, therefore I am now a child of God.' Alas the consequence will by no means hold. How many are the baptized gluttons and drunkards, the baptized liars and common swearers, the baptized railers and evilspeakers, the baptized whoremongers, thieves, extortioners? What think you? Are these now the children of God?"[113]

The tension between a "high" view of Baptism and the need for a subsequent fulfillment of its forgiveness, regeneration, and initiation into the church did not lead Wesley to advocate a rite or practice of confirmation. Indeed, he attacked the Roman Catholic *sacramental* understanding of confirmation in a manner quite similar to the continental reformers, calling it an "abuse" and arguing that it was not established by Christ.[114] Moreover, he did not include a service of confirmation in his book of worship for American Methodists, the *Sunday Service*.

Although this settled the matter of confirmation on one level until fairly recently, on another level it did not. Wesley's attitude toward confirmation set the terms of American Methodism until 1964, when a service of confirmation was first included in the *Methodist Hymnal*. Almost from the beginning of American Methodism, however, a tension between the importance of infant Baptism and that ascribed to a personal commitment to Jesus Christ can be observed in its theology and practice. It did not take long for Wesley's *sacramental* understanding of Baptism to disappear in most Methodist circles.[115] The early tension between a regenerating sacrament that incorporates children into the church and the need for a subsequent *profession* of faith shifted toward the second pole. As a tradition with a clear commitment to the evangelism of adults and the importance of conversion, Methodism often came to view the baptism of infants as a "dedication" by the parents that would only be fulfilled when the one baptized became a "full member" of the church, upon making a personal commitment to Christ.

This sort of distinction did not come into play in official church practice until

1864, when the Methodist Episcopal Church introduced a membership rite for the first time. The southern branch of the church followed suit six years later. While infant Baptism was maintained, all people—whether they had been baptized as an infant or not—had to go through a period of probation during which they met regularly with a class leader, who then recommended them to the minister for full membership and awarded them a token admitting them to the Lord's Supper, the class meeting, and the Love Feast.[116]

Eight years earlier, the Methodist Episcopal Church had included in its *Discipline* for the first time a section entitled "The Relation of Baptized Children to the Church," attempting to clarify the status of baptized children. All children were at that point portrayed as members of the kingdom of God, whether they were baptized or not, "by virtue of the unconditional benefits of the atonement." Baptism was portrayed as placing the infant "under the special care and supervision of the Church," but not as altering its status from a state of sin to one of regeneration. In 1912, the General Conference added the phrase "as probationers" to the end of this sentence, and in 1916, changed this to "preparatory members."[117] The same year, the church added a "Form for Receiving Children as Members of the Church." The introductory address is particularly interesting: "Dearly Beloved, these persons here present before you are baptized children of the Church, who, having arrived at the years of discretion, desire now to *confirm* the vows of their baptism and to enter upon the active duties and the full privileges of membership in the Church of Christ" (emphasis added).[118] This is one of the earliest examples of confirmation language being linked to an act of public profession in the Methodist tradition. It also points to the continuing tension in the church between the initiatory role of Baptism and the need for a subsequent profession of faith that moves young Christians out of a preparatory status. In 1928, this form was incorporated into a single rite used for receiving three types of people into full membership: preparatory members, persons coming from other churches, and persons joining the church on confession of faith. Those baptized in infancy thus were classified with those who joined the church as adults.

With the reunion of the northern and southern branches of Methodism in 1939, a new rite of Baptism was formulated with much the same theological stance as the 1856 *Discipline*. All people were portrayed as "heirs of life eternal," with neither an acknowledgment of Wesley's understanding of original sin nor his belief in the regenerating power of the baptismal rite. Baptized children, moreover, continued to be classified as preparatory members who were admitted to full membership on "evidence of understanding their Christian privileges and obligations and of their Christian faith and purpose." A special order for the reception of children and youth into the church was created alongside one for the reception of adults. Neither was referred to as confirmation, although the latter did use confirmation language to refer to the Spirit's action in strengthening the new members through the fellowship of the church.

Although the language of confirmation is largely absent, clearly the central issues surrounding this practice as it emerged out of the Reformation and was given expression in the Lutheran and Anglican-Episcopal traditions were present in

Methodism as well. Infant Baptism entailed the nurture and care of the church, leading to a personal *profession* of faith signified by a rite marking the shift from preparatory to full membership in the church. As early as the 1940s, this change in status was occasionally referred to in various Methodist journals and literature as confirmation.[119] Major Methodist theologians such as Carl Michalson also began to use this language in the fifties.[120]

It was not until 1960, in the *Proposed Revision of the Book of Worship,* that confirmation language was used in the official documents of the church.[121] This document included an "Order of Confirmation and Reception into the Church," which took the place of the form for the reception of persons into full membership. The introduction to this confirmation service portrayed its inclusion as an attempt to do two things: (1) to restore Baptism to its full sacramental status "as a sign and seal of inclusion in Christ's holy Church" and (2) to make it clear that the profession of faith rendered at a later age is an act by which "the person simply confirms the vows taken at the time of his baptism."[122] In other words, confirmation points back to Baptism as the moment of full initiation into the church and is a personal appropriation of the status it has bestowed already. This is a *professional* understanding of confirmation.

The proposed changes continued to be revised until 1964, when they were adopted by the General Conference. The introduction to the baptismal service clearly stated the rationale behind the proposed changes: "The revision here offered seeks to restore the rite of baptism to its original and historic meaning as a sacrament."[123] An attempt is being made to recapture the "high" view of the sacraments first found in Wesley. Confirmation is viewed as clarifying the importance of Baptism. In the form approved by the 1964 General Conference, it describes membership as something conferred in Baptism and reaffirmed in confirmation, on the basis of young persons' instruction in the doctrines and duties of the Christian faith and their readiness "to profess publicly the faith into which they were baptized."[124] The adoption of this *professional* understanding of confirmation, in conjunction with a sacramental understanding of Baptism, has remained the sole focus of confirmation in the Methodist Church to the present.

Following the union of the Methodist Church and the Evangelical United Brethren to form the United Methodist Church, a Commission on Worship was established to oversee the process of unification and ongoing liturgical revision. In 1976, this commission was incorporated into the General Board of Discipleship's Section on Worship. This section oversaw the production of a series of Supplemental Worship Resources, including *A Service of Baptism, Confirmation and Renewal,* in 1976. This material was used on a trial basis and was revised until its publication, along with other services, in 1980 in *We Gather Together.*[125] After further revision, these services were adopted by the 1984 General Conference and published as *The Book of Services,* in 1985. Further revision took place in 1988. Three Services of the Baptismal Covenant were offered. The rituals reclaim Wesley's "high" understanding of the sacraments and conjoin them with his equally strong affirmation of salvation as a process that must be worked out over the course of a person's entire life.[126] In the accompanying piece, *Companion to the*

Book of Services, this is portrayed in covenantal terms.[127] Baptism points to God's active grace on our behalf and its application to the one who is baptized. But it also points to our "active response to God."[128] This is nicely summarized in the following: "Baptism, therefore, is a covenant. In the biblical tradition, God binds himself to his people through a covenant promise; those who are bound to God respond by promising to be faithful. . . . Baptism is not a contract that God negotiates with each person separately . . . [It] is an affirmation of what God has done for all of us in Jesus Christ."[129] Within this covenantal framework, confirmation is described as pointing to three things: (1) God's confirmation of the divine promise made in Baptism, when the confirmands were too young to understand it; (2) the confirmands' confirmation of their personal commitment to the baptismal covenant in a public testimony; and (3) the congregation's confirmation of the commitment it made at Baptism to nurture the one now being confirmed.[130]

This understanding of confirmation rules out three things. First, there is no association of this rite with the bestowal of the Holy Spirit. Indeed, the new baptismal service explicitly includes the laying on of hands after the water-washing, to make it clear that the Spirit should be closely linked to the primary rite of initiation and not something added at a later point. Second, it eliminates the need for adults to be confirmed. Adults are not first baptized and then confirmed. Confirmation only makes sense in relation to the Baptism of infants. Third, it rules out the idea that the baptismal covenant is reaffirmed only once in a person's life. If salvation is a process that must be worked out over the course of a person's entire life, confirmation is an important moment in this process, but not an exclusive one. Individuals and congregations may reaffirm their baptismal covenant on numerous occasions. Indeed, they should do so every time the congregation baptizes one of its members.

These new baptismal and confirmation services added a strong covenantal framework to the earlier understanding. This was used to clarify the relationship between Baptism and confirmation: the latter takes up and reaffirms a reality already given in the former. This allows a *professional* understanding of confirmation to be affirmed, while clarifying the important difference between this act of profession and a decisional understanding of regeneration. Although the latter may characterize the Anabaptist tradition, it is not consistent with a Methodist understanding of confirmation.

In the 1989 *United Methodist Hymnal,* this understanding of the relationship between Baptism and confirmation remained normative. In the introduction to the baptismal services, this relationship is described as follows: "Those baptized before they are old enough to take the vows for themselves make their personal profession of faith in the service called confirmation."[131] The basic form of a single service is used for Baptism, Confirmation, Reaffirmation of Faith, Reception into the United Methodist Church, and Reception into a Local Congregation. Three somewhat different forms are offered, differentiating services for the baptism of infants from those who can answer for themselves. All of these services include the liturgical elements already found in the Lutheran and Episcopal traditions as a result of contemporary scholarship on the ancient rite of initiation: renunciation and profession of faith (including congregational participation in the rendering of the Apostles' Creed in interrogatory form), thanksgiving over the water, the water-washing, the laying on of hands in conjunction with prayer for the Holy Spirit (optional), and the Eucharist.

As noted above, confirmation is portrayed as the act by which the individual takes up and personally ratifies the baptismal covenant. It at this point also is viewed as the church's acknowledgment of this act, as well as the prevenient action of the Holy Spirit that has made this profession possible. Confirmands are invited, along with those being baptized and new members, to renounce Satan, to pledge their allegiance to Christ, and to confess the faith of the church by joining the rest of the congregation in rendering the Apostles' Creed. Water may be used symbolically to remind them of their Baptism. The minister lays hands on each confirmand, praying "(*Name*), the Holy Spirit work within you, that having been born through water and the Spirit, you may live as a faithful disciple of Jesus Christ."[132]

In conjunction with this understanding of confirmation, the United Methodist Church published a new confirmation series entitled *Follow Me*.[133] The material is organized around thirteen modules taught over thirteen weeks, twenty-six weeks, or two years. The material encourages the leaders and teachers of confirmation to tailor the program to their particular group, and it offers a rich array of creative learning activities that can be pieced together in a variety of ways. Taken as a whole, these activities are designed to help the confirmands form a clearer understanding of the church and what it means to be a disciple of Jesus Christ.

The United Methodist Church is currently studying several important proposals about Baptism, with implications for confirmation, in a denominational study document titled *By Water and the Spirit: A Study of the Proposed United Methodist Understanding of Baptism*.[134] This document continues recent efforts by the church to reclaim Wesley's understanding of the sacraments and to draw out the theological and practical implications of a truly sacramental view of infant Baptism. Drawing on recent liturgical developments in Methodism, and contemporary liturgical scholarship, it identifies the "ritual for baptism as 'the Baptismal Covenant.'"[135] It restores the laying on of hands to this service "in recognition that the work of the Holy Spirit is prevenient."[136] It does not view the Spirit as bestowed through Baptism, and certainly not confirmation, but as effectively represented and communicated through Baptism in recognition of the Spirit's work before, during, and after Baptism.

In light of this restoration of the laying on of hands to the baptismal service, *By Water and the Spirit* calls for an end to the denomination's use of the term "confirmation" and its replacement with a service titled "Profession of the Faith into Which We Were Baptized." As the document puts it: "With the restoration of confirmation to the baptism ritual as the laying on of hands, it should be emphasized the 'confirmation' is what the Holy Spirit does. It is through the confirming work of the Holy Spirit, promised in baptism, that we are led to a first profession of faith."[137] Although strongly affirming the importance of a personal response in faith by those baptized as infants, the report does not want to use the term "confirmation" to refer to this act. It ignores the way both the Lutheran and Anglican traditions restore the post-baptismal laying on of hands and anointing to the rite of Baptism, while retaining a special confirmation service within the context of repeatable rites for the reaffirmation of the baptismal covenant. It repeatedly draws on a two-stage theory of Christian initiation to make its case, for example, "when baptism and confirmation were a unified rite."[138] It also ignores the *catechetical* and *professional* understandings of confirmation emerging out of the Reformation, which have long histories in other Protestant traditions. In each of these lines of thinking, the report parallels developments recently found in the Presbyterian Church. It is to this tradition that we now turn.

6

American Presbyterian
Confirmation Practices

Of the four Protestant traditions we are examining, the Presbyterian tradition has been the least receptive to the rite of confirmation. Calvin rejected the medieval theology and practice of confirmation and did not use the term. He was, however, open to the "ancient" rite of confirmation: "We should like to see that rite everywhere restored by which the young are presented to God, after giving forth a confession of their faith. This would not be an unbecoming approval of their catechism."[1] In light of this mixed attitude of Calvin toward confirmation, it is not surprising that Presbyterians have been cautious about its use. This attitude was reinforced by the historical experience of the English Puritans and Scottish Presbyterians, the sources of American Presbyterianism.[2] Political factors led them to draw an increasingly sharp line between their liturgical and theological convictions and those of the Church of England. Their critique of confirmation was part of a broader rejection of the liturgical practices of the established church. It was this attitude toward liturgical worship that the Puritan settlers brought with them to the New World.[3]

In this chapter, the unfolding story of the American Presbyterian Church's attitude toward confirmation and catechetical instruction will be examined. To tell this story properly, we must focus on both liturgical and educational contexts, and, accordingly, we will move back and forth between these contexts throughout this chapter. We will find the American Presbyterian Church continuing through the nineteenth century the basic paradigm established during the Reformation period: infant Baptism, catechetical instruction, and admission to the Lord's Supper.[4] In this paradigm, great emphasis was placed on the practice of catechetical instruction. It was viewed as enabling the baptized children of the covenant community on reaching the age of discretion to confess the one faith of the church. Typically, this *catechetical* orientation was closely linked to a service of admission to the Lord's Supper. Until this century, Presbyterians did not connect this service of admission to a rite of confirmation. Almost from the beginning of American Presbyterianism, however, a *professional* understanding of admission existed alongside this *catechetical* understanding. Instruction and admission were viewed as focusing on the individual's ratification of the covenant, involving acts of personal profession and pledging. At times, these two understandings have led to sharp conflict. At other times, they have comingled, leading to a powerful combination of communal nurture and individual piety.

Over the course of the nineteenth and twentieth centuries, the standard Reformation paradigm of infant Baptism, catechetical instruction, and admission to the Lord's Supper gradually began to come apart under the influence of the Sunday school movement, the religious education movement, early admission of children to the Lord's Supper, and the decision to move away from exclusive reliance on the Westminster standards. The breakdown of this paradigm has led to a period of uncertainty in the Presbyterian Church about the new patterns of church life that might take its place. It was precisely in this context that confirmation language first began to appear in Presbyterian liturgical and educational material. Unfortunately, the church was not able to achieve any lasting consensus about the viability of this rubric within a new set of practices that could replace those characterizing the older Reformation paradigm. To this day, it remains confused about this topic. This period of uncertainty and confusion has occurred just as the church most needed to help its members become clearer about matters of Christian identity in the face of an emerging secular order.

Early Reformed Liturgical Traditions

As Leonard Trinterud has pointed out, Presbyterianism in the United States had its origins in two main sources, English Puritanism and Scottish Presbyterianism.[5] These two trajectories of the Reformed tradition were the major formative influences on the educational and liturgical practices surrounding Baptism, catechetical instruction, and admission to the Lord's Supper in the American Presbyterian Church. Especially important were the doctrinal and liturgical standards formulated by the Westminster Assembly. These served as the sole standards of the American Presbyterian Church until its recent adoption of the *Book of Confessions*.

We gain a vantage point on these trajectories of the Reformed tradition by comparing them with the thinking and practice of the early Reformers. In matters of catechetical instruction, a clear line of continuity can be discerned. English Puritans and Scottish Presbyterians were strong proponents of this practice and developed a tradition of instruction that flowed into the Westminster catechisms. In liturgical matters, however, the situation is more complicated. Attitudes toward confirmation were shaped by an antiliturgical bent that went beyond Calvin's attitudes toward liturgical forms.

The early Reformers agreed on the need to greatly simplify and prune the liturgical traditions inherited from the medieval church. They were not of one mind, however, on how far this should go. Luther was willing to include elements of the tradition that were not specifically condemned by scripture. Calvin, in contrast, wanted to exclude everything that was not specifically enjoined by scripture. Worship, in all its elements, was to rest on a biblical foundation. He was not rigid in his application of this principle, however, making allowances for a number of "human traditions" in worship whose elimination would have created great turmoil among the churches of the reform movement.[6]

Of special importance in this regard is Calvin's attitude toward liturgical forms. He first drew up a liturgy based on Bucer's work while a pastor of a French congregation in Strassburg.[7] This was to serve as the basis of his Genevan liturgy of 1542. As the reform movement was institutionalized in Geneva, Calvin became aware of problems that arose when each minister or congregation was allowed to design its own service of worship. He went so far as to call for a prescribed liturgy in his famous letter to Somerset: "I highly approve of it that there be a certain form, from which the ministers be not allowed to vary."[8]

The liturgy of Geneva included a number of set prayers to be used in Sunday worship. Pastors could read them word for word, if they chose. Calvin explicitly contrasted the use of set liturgical forms in Sunday worship with those used in weekday worship. In the latter, the minister was encouraged to use "such words in prayer as may seem to him good, suiting his prayer to the occasion, and the matter whereof he treats in preaching."[9] Calvin thus advocated a combination of set liturgical forms and ministerial freedom, prayers following a uniform pattern and those written for a particular occasion or offered extemporaneously.

Calvin's attitude toward liturgical forms was to exert an enormous influence on the Reformed churches of the continent.[10] The Genevan liturgy was used by the Reformed church in France. The Reformed churches of Holland and the Upper Rhine also were directly influenced by Calvin. Many of the English Puritans and Scottish Presbyterians shared Calvin's approach to worship in the early stages of their reform movement. In large part, it was mediated to them by a direct descendant of Calvin's liturgical practice, John Knox's *Genevan Service Book*.[11] This worship book was written while Knox was in exile and used in the English Church at Geneva, where it was scrutinized and approved by Calvin.[12] The liturgical portion contained a confession based on the Apostles' Creed, an order for public worship, an order of Baptism and the Lord's Supper, a form of marriage, a form for visitation of the sick, an order for ecclesiastical discipline, and a funeral service. It was published with a collection of psalms and an English translation of Calvin's *Genevan Catechism*. Appended to Calvin's catechism was a brief section titled "The Manner to examine Children, before they be admitted to the Supper of the Lord."

When a more favorable political climate made it possible for the members of the English Church at Geneva to return home, they took copies of the *Genevan Service Book* with them. Its influence in Scotland was immediate. There is evidence that some congregations were using it as early as 1560, the year Roman Catholicism officially gave way to the Scottish Reformed Church.[13] It was printed in Scotland in 1562, and its usage for the administration of the sacraments, marriage, and funerals ordered by the General Assembly the same year. Two years later, another edition was published that was formally "approved and received" by the Church of Scotland.[14] As McMillan notes, the *Genevan Service Book* functioned more as a prayer book in Scotland during this period than as a simple directory for worship.[15] Not only did it provide full liturgies and set prayers, but it also was viewed as setting the normative practice of the church. Accordingly, it was known as *The Book of Common Order*.

Use of this book among the English Puritans was more complex, reflecting the diversity of this movement.[16] Although the Puritans were united in their desire to take the English reformation one step further and "purify" its theology and practice, they were not of one mind as to what this meant.[17] This was especially true with regard to liturgical matters. Many Puritans were open to the blend of liturgical order, ministerial discretion, and extemporaneous prayer found in Calvin, especially the Presbyterian wing of the Puritan movement. Among those parties remaining close to Calvin's liturgical practice, use of Knox's *Genevan Service Book* was common.[18] In contrast, the Barrowist and Brownist separatist parties rejected set forms of worship altogether and sanctioned extemporaneous prayer alone.[19]

It was only gradually that those branches of the Puritan movement sharing Calvin's attitudes toward liturgical worship adopted a more negative stance in response to political events. The Act of Uniformity, passed by Parliament under Elizabeth I, mandated conformity to the *Book of Common Prayer* in 1564–65. This eliminated ministerial discretion in liturgical matters and led to the suspension of many of the leading Puritan ministers. As Puritans began to gather for worship in private homes and hold "prophesying" meetings to study scripture for preaching and teaching, Elizabeth I made these gatherings illegal, going so far as to suspend the archbishop and place him under house arrest when he refused to carry out her orders.[20] This in turn led to the arrest and torture of Puritan leaders such as Thomas Cartwright. Things got even worse under the Stuart kings, James I and Charles I and II. James demanded strict conformity to the established order of the church, leading to the imprisonment of many clergy. His policies were carried to new extremes under his son and the new archbishop of Canterbury, William Laud, a staunch Anglo-Catholic.

It is not difficult to see why such an atmosphere would have a polarizing effect. What initially had been a process of negotiation between Puritans desiring further reform of worship and representatives of the established church, became embroiled in a political power struggle. Ceremonies that were tolerated by Calvin in order to preserve the unity of the church came to be viewed as signs of loyalty to one side or the other. The more extreme, separatist, attitude toward worship began to dominate. Confirmation, along with many other "human traditions," was viewed as epitomizing the arrogance of those in power who at that point were viewed as setting themselves above God's Word.

Antecedents of the American Tradition:
The Westminster Assembly

This context was to become even more highly charged in response to the extreme policies of Archbishop Laud, leading to outright rebellion, in which opponents of the monarchy and established church were willing to die for their cause. In 1637, Laud demanded conformity to a form of worship that was far more Catholic than the *The Book of Common Prayer* and went so far as to prohibit extemporaneous prayer in public worship.[21] The Scots were outraged, leading them to enter into a "National Covenant" in which they pledged to defend the doctrine and discipline of the Church of Scotland. When the king sent his military forces to enforce Laud's decrees, he was forced to withdraw in the face of stiff opposition. He soon faced a Scottish "covenanting" army camped in northern England and an English Parliament unwilling to provide him with the money to oppose it.[22] He was obliged to call a new Parliament, commonly known as the "Long Parliament," which met from 1640 to 1652. It was this Parliament that convened the Westminster Assembly, charging it with the task of undertaking the "necessary reformation of the government and liturgy of the Church."[23] It included representatives of the Church of Scotland and all parties of the English Protestant church, except the followers of Laud. The Assembly got its name because it met in Westminster, England, from 1643 to 1652.

Reflecting a long history of catechetical instruction and doctrinal reflection in the British Isles, the Assembly achieved a high degree of consensus in its work on catechetical instruction. As we might expect, it defined the goods of this practice in *catechetical* terms, as enabling young Christians to make an intelligent confession of the church's faith upon reaching the age of discretion. In its deliberations on liturgical matters, the Assembly reflected the recent history of conflict between the Scots, Puritans, and established church. There it was forced to take a minimalist approach, avoiding issues that had been embroiled in recent ecclesiastical and political conflict. A decidedly negative attitude toward confirmation was expressed by many of the followers of Calvin, for this rite seemed to epitomize the very things that needed to be reformed in the established church: "human traditions" that had no grounding in scripture and were used to enhance ecclesiastical authority. This attitude reflected a broader undercurrent of antipathy toward liturgical worship in general, an attitude that proved to have a lasting impact on American Presbyterianism.

The Shorter and Larger Catechisms

What sort of background did the commissioners to the Assembly bring to their work? Both the Scottish Reformed and English Puritans had long been engaged in catechetical instruction. As soon as the Catholic church was ousted, the church of Scotland established the standard Reformation pattern of infant Baptism, catechetical instruction, and admission to the Lord's Supper.

Background

The *Book of Discipline* explicitly required catechizing of the young, and a second service was held on Sundays for this purpose. Initially, Calvin's *Genevan Catechism* was used for this purpose. This was superseded, first, by John Craig's larger catechism (1581), and later, under the auspices of the General Assembly, his smaller catechism, *Ane Forme of Examination before the Communion* (1592).[24] The latter remained in use until it was superseded by the *Westminster Shorter Catechism*.

The English Puritans also had a long tradition of catechetical instruction. Next to preaching, catechizing was the chief duty of Puritan pastors.[25] Between the publication of William Perkins's *Foundation of Christian Religion* in 1590 and the publication of the *Westminster Shorter Catechism* in 1647, an extraordinary number of Puritan catechisms were written.[26] Some focused on scripture; others, on doctrinal material.[27] Some included the Apostles' Creed; others did not.[28] The most common division, however, was between short, relatively simple catechisms for children, and longer, more complex ones for youth and adults.[29]

Catechetical practices in a wide range of contexts were developed. Parents were strongly encouraged to take their catechetical responsibilities seriously, and the mother came to play an increasingly important role in this practice.[30] Many Puritan ministers, moreover, served as schoolmasters and used catechisms reflecting a Puritan theological perspective.[31] Pastors were given advice by prominent Puritan ministers. In *The Reformed Pastor,* for example, Richard Baxter described his practice of catechetical instruction during home visitation, in which he would instruct each family member individually so he could tailor his teaching to their own level of understanding.[32]

One aspect of Puritan catechizing that was to prove important to the American scene was its emphasis on the close relationship between knowledge and piety. The Puritans firmly believed that God's Spirit uses catechizing to nourish the seed of faith planted in infancy and to bring baptized children to spiritual maturity. William Perkins aptly expressed the basic goal of all Puritan catechizing: To enable young persons to apply the material being studied "inwardly to your heart and conscience, and outwardly to your lives and conversation."[33] Transmission of knowledge was not enough. Study of the catechism was wedded to spiritual growth. This led the Puritans to emphasize constantly the importance of teaching for understanding. As Samuel Annesley put it: When you catechize, if you do not impart understanding, you invite the children of the church to "act the parrot" and thereby "profane" God.[34] Children should be taught, he went on to argue, according to their "capacity and measure."[35] The parent or pastor should, "like a discrete schoolmaster, not pour in his precepts all at once; for then, like water pour'd on narrow-mouthed vessels would mostly run over; but instill drop by drop."[36]

The Work of the Assembly

Both the English Puritans and the Scottish Reformed thus brought with them to their work in the Assembly well-developed traditions of catechetical instruction. This practice was seen as essential to the spiritual health of the church, affording young Christians with the opportunity to understand and confess the faith of the church. How could they participate responsibly in the Lord's Supper or any other facet of church life without the foundation of knowledge it provided? At least twelve members of the Assembly had written catechisms themselves, and virtually every member had received such instruction or practiced it as ministers.[37]

Just as important, the commissioners also brought with them a tradition of doctrinal reflection and development closely related to catechetical instruction. The best theologians of the English Puritans and Scotch Reformed had been engaged in a process of doctrinal development for over half a century that placed in creative tension the theologies of Calvin, Zwingli, Bullinger, and Reformed orthodoxy.[38] Doctrinal emphasis on the sovereignty of God, the absolute authority of scripture, and the eternal decrees were conjoined with emphasis on the experiential side of faith, the free exercise of conscience in moral deliberation, and the importance of the visible community of faith. The Puritans, in particular, placed great emphasis on the *experimental* side of covenant theology, portraying the Christian life as involving an inward appropriation of God's grace, often manifesting itself in struggle, self-examination, and, ultimately, a sense of assurance.

These rich doctrinal developments were reflected in the content of the catechisms, as Alexander Mitchell has documented extensively.[39] Indeed, many of these doctrinal developments were already found in catechisms written prior to the Assembly, and commissioners frequently incorporated their questions and answers directly into those they were writing.[40] It is no accident, then, that the Westminster catechisms reflect the rich blend of theological currents that had long been flowing in the British Isles. Although their conceptuality often is technical and reflects themes important to Protestant scholasticism, they enrich these with elements of the experiential side of the covenant theology tradition.

Of special importance to our work is the catechisms' and confession's description of the relationship between infant Baptism and a later profession of faith. Here we see a kind of self-portrait being offered, wherein the catechisms give expression to the theological framework in which they view themselves being used. Covenant theology provides the larger framework for their discussion of Baptism. God's covenant of works with Adam is portrayed as having been set aside by God's covenant of grace in and through Jesus Christ.[41] The benefits of this covenant are available to the elect, and God alone knows whom God has called. However, the church has the right and responsibility to apply the baptismal sign of the covenant of grace to all who qualify. For adults, qualification depends on a profession of faith. The infants of believers are considered "federally holy."[42] Just as the children of Israel were circumcised on the basis of God's promise of an everlasting covenant with Abraham and his seed (Gen. 17:1–14), so too the sign of the new covenant was to be administered to the children of the members of the visible church. The assumption is that birth into a family of believers is a visible sign of election, and the children should be considered as belonging to the elect unless there are indications that this is not the case.

This stance is generally referred to as the "judgment of charity." The children of believers are extended this judgment by birthright, and so are baptized into the covenant community. They were expected to accept this covenant themselves when they reached the age of discretion, however.[43] This is evident in the Westminster confessional standards in two ways. First, children were not to be admitted to the Lord's Supper "until they receive instruction, and manifest their reformation."[44] Second, those who have received this Sacrament are told that they must "improve their baptism," which included, among other things, "growing up to assurance of pardon and sin, and of all other blessings sealed to us in that sacrament."[45] Until they take up the covenant themselves, they are like citizens who are under age. They are legitimate members of the community, but they do not yet have access to all of the rights and responsibilities afforded those who have reached their majority.

The standard Reformation paradigm of infant Baptism, catechetical instruction, and First Communion is placed in a covenant framework. The two-covenant schemetization of Protestant orthodoxy is combined with the experiential and activistic elements of Puritanism. This covenantal framework proved to be a particularly powerful way of holding together both *catechetical* and *professional* understandings of catechetical instruction and admission. Children are viewed as members of the covenant community by virtue of God's electing work, signified by their Baptism. There is no need for some future decision on their part for their salvation or regeneration to occur. However, they are to "manifest their reformation" and "improve their baptism," to use the language cited above. This involves both a confession of the church's common faith on the basis of their study of the catechism and their personal ratification of the baptismal covenant. Elements of inner struggle and personal appropriation are placed within a context of communal nurture and responsibility. Both were grounded in God's prior electing work. When rightly appropriated, this was to prevent the church from falling into pietism, on the one hand, or orthodox formalism, on the other.

Was the Assembly able to articulate this theological vision liturgically? Was it able to devise forms giving expression to the church's covenantal nature and the individual's place within this community? Unfortunately, the Assembly was forced to adopt a minimalist approach in this area, reflecting both a lack of consensus among its members and the history of recent controversy.

The Directory for Worship

What liturgical practices could the commissioners of the Assembly assume? In the Church of Scotland, the practice of examining candidates and then admitting them in a special service to the Lord's Supper was widely established.[46] Calvin's service of admission initially was followed, although new liturgical helps were soon developed. This service of admission was not called confirmation and was viewed along *catechetical* lines as the culmination of catechetical instruction and the individual's confession of the church's faith.

Background

The situation among the English Puritans was more complex. In some instances, catechetical instruction was not concluded with a special service admitting persons to the Lord's Table. A simple examination was deemed sufficient. In other instances, Calvin's practice of admitting persons to the Lord's Table in conjunction with the candidates' public confession of the catechism was followed. In this case the parallels with Scottish practice are evident, reflecting a common reliance on Knox's *Genevan Service Book*. Both defined the rite of admission in *catechetical* terms. Richard Baxter, among others, represented still a third approach. In a manner reminiscent of Bucer and Melanchthon, yet reflecting the unique covenant theology perspective of the Presbyterian Puritans, he advocated a full-scale service of confirmation. This service had strong *professional* overtones, even as it maintained close ties with catechetical instruction. It is worth pausing to examine Baxter's work, for it represents a fully developed theology of confirmation, standing squarely in the Reformed tradition. Not all the Puritans rejected confirmation, especially those who were open to Calvin's liturgical heritage and were ecumenically minded.

Although Baxter did not publish his thoughts on confirmation until after the Assembly had completed its work, he drew on liturgical practices long-established in his church at Kidderminster in his writings. He offered his understanding of confirmation in two places: the Savoy liturgy and *Confirmation and Restauration, The necessary means of Reformation and Reconcilation; For the Healing of the Corruptions and Divisions of the Churches.*[47] In the former, Baxter offers the quintessential Presbyterian-Puritan understanding of admission to the Lord's Supper:

> Let none be admitted by the Minister to the sacrament of the Lord's supper, till they have at years of discretion understood the meaning of their Baptismal covenant, and with their own mouths, and their own consent openly before the church, ratified and *confirmed,* and also promised, that by the grace of God, they will evermore endeavor themselves faithfully to observe and keep such things as by their mouth and confession they have assented to; and so being instructed in the Christian religion, do openly make a credible profession of their own faith, and promise to be obedient to the will of God (emphasis added).[48]

Baxter's book on confirmation was put forward as an attempt to heal the divisions separating the Episcopal, Presbyterian, Congregational, and Erastian branches of the church.[49] Drawing heavily on Puritan covenant theology, he describes confirmation as something that is necessarily administered to those baptized as infants who now are ready to take up the responsibilities of adult membership in the covenant community. The condition making this possible is a personal profession of faith, involving a "solemn renewing of the covenant of grace between God and the Adult-covenanter".[50] This profession is to be based on the essential tenets of Christianity offered in catechetical instruction. But it must involve more than the memorization of the catechism. It must be a "credible profession," that is, it must involve understanding, be voluntary, and be reflected in the person's life.[51] Pastors are to "try, judge, and approve" these confessions before confirming a person. The actual confirmation rite is portrayed as a "corroborating ordinance" in which baptized Christians confirm or corroborate the covenant in which they already participate, and God, in turn, corroborates their public declaration, conferring on them the privileges and benefits of adult membership through the power of the Spirit. Baxter approved of the ministerial imposition of hands to signify this divine corroboration.

It is clear that the accent in Baxter's treatment of confirmation is *professional.* Placed within a covenantal framework, however, it does not degenerate into pietistic individualism or decisionism. Ratification of the covenant is a response to God's prior electing work in Christ. Moreover, it takes place in the context of communal nurture and responsibility. The individual's act of profession and pledging is not granted too much or too little. Confirmation is something expected of each Christian upon reaching the age of discretion, but it is only one element of the covenant life.

The Work of the Assembly

As rich as it may have been, it is not difficult to see why Baxter's understanding of confirmation would have been virtually impossible for the commissioners of the Assembly to adopt. It was far too close to the position of the Church of England. Alongside it were other options, however: use of the service of admission found in Calvin and Knox and a brief examination at the end of catechetical instruction unaccompanied by a service. The *Directory* adopted none of these options, although it did not rule them out. What it offered were a set of general guidelines for admission to the Lord's Supper that left ministers with a great deal of latitude. In the baptismal service, infants of believers are portrayed as being "federally holy" and, as such, worthy of the sign of the covenant. Parents are exhorted to "bring up the child in the knowledge of the grounds of the Christian Religion, and in the nurture and admonition of the Lord."[52] In the prayer following the water-washing, God is asked to "continue and daily *confirm*" the good work that this Baptism represents. The hope is expressed that when the child might "attain the years of discretion, that the Lord would so teach him by his Word and Spirit, and make his Baptisme effectuall to him."[53] This is all that is said. The guidelines for the Lord's Supper merely forbid its administration to the "Ignorant and the Scandalous," but no more. In its comments on keeping the sabbath, families are encouraged to use this time for catechizing, among other things.

This lack of specific guidance, much less liturgical forms, reflects the minimalist orientation of the *Directory* as a whole. This is a by-product of the lack of consensus among the participants of the Assembly about liturgical matters. Early in their deliberations, the members of the Assembly agreed to set aside the *Book of Common Prayer* and work to create a simple directory. In its Preface, the *Directory* states that it seeks to set forth rules of worship where they are clearly set forth in scripture but allow ministerial discretion and congregational variety in those matters where they are not. As such, it makes a clear distinction between matters that are prescribed, those that inherently demand the exercise of ministerial judgment in their application, and those that are permitted.[54]

The refusal to form a prayer book and to rest content with a simple directory represented something of a victory for those parts of the Puritan movement that opposed liturgical worship, especially set forms of prayer. Long after the bitter fights between an established church and an embattled minority were left behind, this attitude toward worship continued to shape significant portions of the Reformed tradition, including the American Presbyterian Church. A "directory" approach to worship with no explicit liturgies for marriage, funerals, Baptism, the Lord's Supper, or admission to the Lord's Supper was viewed as normative for the Reformed tradition, in spite of the rich liturgical heritage characterizing the earliest phases of this tradition. For all intents and purposes, this left Presbyterian ministers free to formulate their own liturgical forms for Baptism and admission to the Lord's Supper. As we shall see, this led to a situation in the American Presbyterian Church in which the meaning of the latter was viewed along two very different lines.

The American Appropriation of the Westminster Heritage: Two Models of the Christian Life in the Early Tradition

The Westminster heritage was mediated to American Presbyterians by English Puritans and Scotch-Irish who immigrated to the United States.[55] Both groups spent time in new cultural contexts prior to coming together to form the American Presbyterian Church. Their sojourn in these contexts began a process of development that continued as the new denomination was born. English Puritanism was mediated to the emergent Presbyterian Church through New England, where many Independent Puritans had gone when hopes of reforming the Church of England began to fade. Scottish Presbyterianism was mediated through Ireland, where many Scots immigrated after James I crushed the Irish rebellion and invited Scots and English to settle confiscated lands.[56] The native Irish, who were Roman Catholic, did not take kindly to these settlers, and many of the Scots eventually came to the American colonies.

These two streams of the Reformed tradition flowed together in the middle colonies, and it is here that the Presbyterian Church first took shape.[57] During this early, formative period, two different understandings of the Christian life began to emerge out of the Puritan and Scotch-Irish streams of the Reformed tradition.[58] Although the members of both groups subscribed to the Westminster standards adopted by the nascent denomination and drew heavily on covenant theology, these standards were interpreted along different lines. The Scotch-Irish stream came to embody what has been called Old School Presbyterianism, representing the *churchly traditions* of the Reformation. The stream of Puritanism flowing through New England and giving rise to the Great Awakening came to be known as New School Presbyterianism, representing a "middle way" among the various branches of Protestantism. Different understandings of the purpose of catechetical instruction and admission to the Lord's Supper emerged in each stream of early Presbyterianism.

The *churchly traditions* of the Scotch-Irish portrayed Christianity in a manner that did not focus primarily on the individual's experience of salvation but on "a body of truth articulated in more or less elaborate theology, expressed in formal liturgical worship, and proclaimed and enforced by a highly organized ecclesiastical body."[59] This branch of early Presbyterianism rejected the *gathered community* understanding of Christianity found among the Baptists, Mennonites, and Quakers that made an individual's spiritual awakening a condition of church membership. They advocated what can be called a *nurture/development* model of the Christian life.

In this pattern, social and objective elements are placed in the foreground— hence, *nurture* is the first term. The pattern of beliefs supporting this model went something like this: The mystery of God's election cannot be unlocked by examining one's own experience. Neither a dramatic conversion experience nor a sense of personal assurance are guarantees of salvation. In fact, Christians should not become preoccupied with their inner spiritual state. This leads them to turn away from the one true basis of salvation: God's sovereign, electing work in Jesus Christ. God's objective work in Christ and continuing work in the Spirit are mediated to individuals through the ecclesial community. Consequently, the liturgical, confessional, and ethical norms of the community should be taken very seriously. The Christian life depends heavily on the *nurture* provided by the ecclesial community, because *development* largely is a matter of understanding and appropriating the practices it offers with increasing depth. Participation in the ordinary means of grace allows the elect to recognize the inner witness of the Spirit and gradually grow into the covenantal responsibilities of a mature Christian life.

Standing alongside and often over against this understanding of the Christian life was a second model mediated to early Presbyterianism by the New England Puritans. This emerged out of the Independent wing of the English Puritan movement as given new shape during the Great Awakening. The New England Puritans represented a "middle way," combining elements of churchly and gathered community types of Christianity.[60] Like the latter, they held to the ideal of a regenerate membership and placed great emphasis on the inner spiritual life of the individual. Like the former, they found an important place for doctrinal standards, the ordinary means of grace, a professional ministry, and other elements of a more social and objective understanding of Christianity. They developed what can be called a *crisis/nurture* model of the Christian life. A crucial place was given to the experience of *crisis* and struggle in the Christian life, manifesting itself in conversion or a time of spiritual awakening. This crisis, however, was viewed as taking place in the context of a community providing ongoing *nurture*. Without this nurture, it was thought to be difficult, if not impossible, for the new life engendered by a period of crisis to grow and come to maturity. Moreover, a role was seen for Christian nurture in the home, school, and congregation prior to the crisis of spiritual awakening.

In large measure, this second stream of the Reformed tradition made its most important impact on early Presbyterianism through the influence of the First and Second Great Awakenings. It is important not to view the advocates of this understanding of the Christian life in terms of the revivalism of the nineteenth century.[61] Its best-known representatives, William Tennent, Sr., and his sons, Gilbert, John, and William, Jr., were all active ministers, committed to the Westminster standards, and they advocated catechetical instruction alongside convictional preaching.[62] Like Jonathan Edwards and other New England Puritans identified with the Great Awakening, the Tennents were influenced by the experiential side of English Puritanism.[63] While continuing to practice infant Baptism and to advocate childhood education, they placed emphasis on a state of "inner conviction" in their preaching and visitation. God was seen as awakening persons spiritually through the ordinary means of grace (preaching, the sacraments, Bible study, prayer, and church discipline), along with special preaching services for those outside the church. Nurture was seen as issuing in spiritual struggle, and spiritual struggle as entailing ongoing nurture.

Two models of the Christian life thus can be found in the formative stage of American Presbyterianism: the *nurture/development* model characteristic of Old School Presbyterianism and the *crisis/nurture* model characteristic of New School Presbyterianism. Although these terms are awkward, this may prove to be helpful, reminding us of the complexity of the positions being pointed to. It also makes it clear that the models overlap at significant points, in spite of their very real differences. These differences at times led to open warfare in the church. At other times they resulted in a creative tension that enriched the life of the church. One of the significant areas of church life where both of these results can be seen is in the practice of catechetical instruction and admission to the Lord's Supper. Here, in the interaction of New School and Old School Presbyterianism, the Westminster traditions began to take a uniquely American shape.

Admission to the Lord's Supper:
The Two Models in Practice

It is important to underscore the fact that both wings of the church supported the practice of catechetical instruction. They agreed that the teaching of the catechism should be the center of the church's educational ministry and should be carried on in three contexts: congregation, home, and school.[64]

In early American Presbyterianism, congregations offered it in a variety of ways. Ministers frequently offered it to children at the end of Sunday afternoon services. Instruction of young and old alike was a regular feature of home visitation. Some ministers organized their congregations into districts and periodically gathered the families of each district together for neighborhood catechetical classes. Others offered regular public lectures on the catechism in the church during the week. The home also was an important center of instruction. Journal accounts make it clear that parents took their baptismal promises seriously, guiding all of the members of the household—children, servants, and apprentices alike—in the study of the catechism. Schools, likewise, were important centers of catechetical instruction. One of the most widely used teaching resources during this period was *The New England Primer,* which placed the *Westminster Shorter Catechism,* the Apostles' Creed, the Lord's Prayer, the Ten Commandments, and other religious material alongside alphabet lessons and elementary phonetics. Teaching the catechism was a standard part of the curriculum in many schools.

In their support for the practice of catechetical instruction as carried on in these different settings, Old School and New School Presbyterians were of one mind. They adopted and adapted the standard European practice. They parted ways, however, in their understanding of the purpose of catechetical instruction. Each wing of the church viewed the primary goods it generated along very different lines. Old Schoolers advocated a *catechetical* understanding of this practice, New Schoolers, a *professional* understanding. This led them to view the service of admission along very different lines.

Old School Presbyterians viewed admission to the Lord's Supper as the outgrowth of a young Christian's participation in the church, a by-product of the nurture he or she had received over the years. They placed the accent on God's electing grace and on Baptism, the sign of this electing grace and the single point of initiation into the covenant community. The children of Christian parents were viewed as members of the covenant community by birthright and worthy of the sign of the covenant. The church's withholding of Communion until a later age was compared to the common distinction between minority and majority rights of citizens. In arriving at their majority, persons who are members of a community already receive new rights and responsibilities: the right to vote, to drive a car, or to serve in the military. So too the right to participate in the Lord's Supper was conferred on those who had reached the age of discretion and could "discern the Lord's body" in this sacrament. This was thought to depend on their participation in catechetical instruction that taught them the basic beliefs of the church. Admission to the Lord's Supper thus was viewed as having a *catechetical* purpose: allowing individuals to make a public confession of the church's faith. Emphasis was placed on understanding and acceptance of the church's confession, as represented by the catechism, not by their own spiritual experience.

New School Presbyterians viewed admission to the Lord's Supper quite differently. Although they practiced infant Baptism and strongly affirmed the role of catechetical instruction, this instruction was viewed as designed to bring about a spiritual awakening in young people. Children were under the care of the church, but when they reached the age of discretion, it was crucial that they personally acknowledge and ratify the covenant of grace. If the church made anything less than this personal declaration its goal, it would be fostering formalistic religion no better than that of the Church of England. Admission to the Lord's Supper thus was viewed along *professional* lines, representing a young person's heartfelt profession of faith and personal ratification of the covenant of grace. Baptism pointed to this covenant and entailed catechetical instruction. But it also included a subsequent act of personal appropriation. No one made vows on the infant's behalf at Baptism. These were to be offered at a later date by the one being baptized. The service of admission marked the rendering of these vows.

Both understandings of admission to the Lord's Supper have their roots in the Westminster heritage. Old School and New School Presbyterians, alike, could legitimately appeal to these confessional standards and to the traditions lying behind them. To warrant their *catechetical* position, Old Schoolers could appeal to the "high" Calvinism of Protestant scholasticism, especially its emphasis on God's sovereign, electing work. New Schoolers could argue for a *professional* interpretation by appealing to the experiential side of Puritan thought, especially its activistic interpretation of covenant theology. Moreover, the Westminster liturgical standards did not settle this matter, as we have seen, offering open-ended guidelines that left much room for ministerial discretion and variation in congregational practice. This was not rectified by the American directory.

The first General Assembly of the American Presbyterian Church adopted the *Westminster Directory for Worship,* rejecting an attempt to add a richer set of liturgical forms to its meager offerings.[65] One item it did add was a new chapter entirely absent in the original *Westminster Directory:* "Of the Admission of Persons to Sealing-Ordinances." This did little more than direct pastors to follow the standard practice of instructing baptized children and informing them upon reaching the age of discretion that it was their duty and privilege to come to the Lord's Supper. It did add one important new element. The criteria for admission were the candidates' "knowledge and piety." This reflects both sides of early Presbyterianism: knowledge, the Old School's catechetical understanding of admission as confession of the church's faith on the basis of catechetical instruction, and piety, the New School's professional understanding of admission as a moment of spiritual awakening and covenant ratification. The Presbyterian Church has fared best when both of these elements have been held in creative tension. It has fared worst when political and theological infighting have led to their bifurcation.

Admission to the Lord's Supper
in the Crisis/Nurture Trajectory:
From Profession of the Covenant
to Full-scale Conversion

New School Presbyterians, we noted earlier, took their bearings from the New England Puritans. This group had long experienced controversy in the area of assessing persons' "fitness" for admission to the Lord's Supper. As early as 1640, admission depended on persons' ability to offer a narrative account of God's saving grace in their lives. The Lord's Supper gradually became a Sacrament in which only a small number of persons participated. According to the records of South Church in Boston, for example, only 14 percent of its members took communion between 1669 and 1718.[66] Various attempts were made to liberalize the standards of admission, including the infamous Half-Way Covenant of 1662.

Narrative accounts of saving grace were never an official requirement of admission to the Lord's Supper in the Presbyterian Church. In practice, however, many New School Presbyterians viewed catechetical instruction and admission to the Lord's Supper as related to a young person's spiritual awakening. One of the most influential leaders of this school of thought was Gilbert Tennent, and his thinking on this matter is representative.[67] In *Twenty-three Sermons upon the Chief End of Man,* Gilbert Tennent argues repeatedly that the "chief end" that the catechism teaches is a changed heart.[68] As he puts it: "The heart is certainly the main spring of practical religion; when that is set right in its aims, then all the wheels of motion keep their proper distances and spheres, and answer a valuable end. But when the main spring is wrong set, all is wrong; the motion of the soul's power is irregular and vain, because it tends to a wrong mark."[69] The title of this collection of sermons, of course, keys off the first question of the *Westminster Shorter Catechism* (What is the chief end of man?), and Tennent makes it clear that the only appropriate answer is the spiritual worship of God, involving "experimental knowledge" that "affects and humbles us." Elsewhere, in perhaps his most famous sermon, "The Danger of an Unconverted Ministry," Tennent argues that education alone is not enough in the Christian life. Only experience of the saving grace of God can take the offerings of education and bring them to life. As he puts it in the sermon:

> The Doctrines of Original Sin, Justification by Faith alone, and the other Points of Calvinism, are very cross to the Grain of unrenew'd Nature. And tho' Men, by the Influence of a good Education, and Hopes of Preferment, may have the Edge of their natural Enmity against them blunted; yet it's far from being broken or removed: It's only the saving Grace of God, that can give us a true Relish for those Nature-humbling Doctrines; and so effectually secure us from being infected by the contrary.[70]

The doctrinal teachings pointed to here are precisely those covered in catechetical instruction. They run against the grain of ordinary human inclinations, Tennent argues, for humans do not naturally seek to humble themselves before God. Only a spiritual awakening can give persons a "relish" for these teachings, making them a matter of personal conviction and not merely intellectual knowledge or social convention. From this perspective, a spiritual awakening in which the signs of piety are present in a person's experience is the goal of catechetical instruction. Nurture alone is not enough. It must issue in a crisis by which individuals come to believe and profess as a matter of firsthand acquaintance all they have been taught by the church.

We can trace this trajectory through the Second Great Awakening and far into the nineteenth century. The decades immediately following the American revolution saw a general decline of church membership and a widespread feeling that the church was in a state of spiritual apathy. Less than 10 percent of the total population belonged to a church.[71] A second great period of revival began to take place in the 1790s. Although not a Presbyterian, Timothy Dwight was prominent in this movement, and his attitudes toward catechetical instruction influenced Presbyterians taking part in the awakening.[72]

Dwight argued that catechetical instruction served as one of the chief means of a child's conversion, and he pointed out that the church was largely composed of people who had received this instruction as children. Such instruction prepared their hearts for conversion at an appropriate time. As the Second Great Awakening gathered momentum, this view of catechetical instruction made inroads into the Presbyterian Church. The minutes of the General Assembly of 1814, for example, share in glowing terms the fact that the greatest number of young people converted in recent revivals had received catechetical instruction from their parents and pastors. Likewise, communicant manuals gained popularity during this period that emphasized the individual's spiritual awakening.[73] Thomas Haweis's *The Communicant's Spiritual Companion or An Evangelical Preparation for the Lord's Supper* and John Willison's *Young Communicant's Catechism,* both of which were written during the middle part of the eighteenth century, gained new prominence and were reprinted in this country.[74] Haweis describes the first, and most important, purpose informing his catechetical manual as follows: ". . . to open the conscience to a discovery of its guilt and misery, its great need of Jesus, and the salvation which is in him."[75]

The Second Great Awakening led to increased emphasis on special revival services alongside the regular worship and practices of the church. Among Presbyterians, this led to the blending together of American revivalism and an older practice originating in Scotland: the sacramental season.[76] In Scotland, the sacramental season initially was a highly charged occasion at which ministers who had been forced to leave the ministry for political reasons were still able to preach and serve communion. These services gradually evolved into tools of evangelism designed to attract large crowds by fostering a fair-like atmosphere. They were used in this way to evangelize the Scots who immigrated to Ireland and later to the American colonies. The sacramental season was well-established in colonial America but gained new import during the Second Great Awakening.

E. T. Thompson provides us with an outline of what these events were like in the South.[77] When notice was given that the Lord's Supper was going to be served, people traveled great distances to the appointed meeting place and camped out. Services lasted for several days, culminating in the Lord's Supper. Under the influence of revivalism, the fencing of the table and the invitation to the table became a kind of altar call. In one account, for example, the minister issued the invitation in the following manner: "Can you, will you any longer reject and trample on this precious blood, poured from the wounds of a dying Saviour? I call God and this great assembly to witness that it is offered you afresh this day. Again dare to spurn it from your lips, and the record will be written against you on high."[78] Other changes also were made. Examination no longer focused on knowledge of the catechism but the individual's religious experience. Baptized and unbaptized alike were to make a public profession of their conversion before they were admitted to the table.[79]

These developments posed a threat to the inherited paradigm of infant Baptism, catechetical instruction, and admission to the Lord's Supper. The close link between the crisis of spiritual awakening and nurture offered by the church was being sundered. Assessments of "fitness" to participate in the sacrament depended on narrative accounts of personal experience offered by the individual. The importance of theological or scriptural knowledge gained through a lengthy period of education and discipline in the church was giving way to an instantaneous view of Christian conversion. Moreover, baptized and unbaptized alike were supposed to make a public testimony. A real step away from profession of the baptismal covenant toward conversion was being taken. Earlier representatives of a *crisis/nurture* model, such as Gilbert Tennent, had always tempered their evangelicalism with deep appreciation of the Westminster standards and the English Puritan traditions surrounding them. Revivalism now threatened to turn Tennent's portrayal of catechetical instruction and admission as a time of spiritual awakening into a freestanding, full-scale conversion, independent of the nurture of the church.

A further step away in this direction was taken under the influence of Charles Finney. Finney grew up in the Presbyterian Church. After his conversion in 1821, he became a popular evangelist in western New York. What was new about Finney's work was not his evangelistic preaching but the fact that it was aimed squarely at church members and not at the unconverted on the frontier. He also self-consciously advocated the use of new revivalistic methods: lay preaching, protracted revival meetings, the anxious seat, women's prayer-meetings, and prayer for conversion by name.[80] Since the Bible provided "no particular system of measures to be employed and invariably adhered to in promoting religion," ministers were free to devise new measures for their own generation.[81] The sole criterion by which these measures were to be judged was their effectiveness in touching the hearts of their participants. Persons were portrayed as free to choose or reject God's offer of grace, leading Finney to portray preaching and worship as opportunities to induce people to make up their minds.

Even though Finney eventually left the Presbyterian Church, his revivalistic orientation influenced New School congregations and, indirectly, other parts of the church in three ways. First, Finney helped legitimate the inroads of the sabbath school in the church, describing it in glowing terms and praising its emphasis on conversion, not development.[82] Second, Finney's overwhelming emphasis on conversion influenced the way New School pastors and congregations viewed admission to the Lord's Supper. In some instances, it was assimilated to a conversionistic model and became the marker event of conversion, along the line of the sacramental season. In other cases, it was separated from conversion and thereby relegated to a secondary status. In both instances, the baptized children of the church were portrayed as candidates for conversion, not full members of the covenant community. A transformation of the *professional* understanding of admission, in which the children of the covenant personally ratify its meaning for their lives, gives way to a *conversionistic* understanding of admission. From the vantage point of the middle of the nineteenth century, Lyman Atwater described this development as follows:

> Many hold that they [the children of the church] are members only quasi . . . until they profess to have experienced that conscious change, which opens the door of full church privilege alike to the baptized and unbaptized. . . . in considerable portion of our evangelical Churches there is no recognition, no consciousness of any relation being held by baptized children, prior to conscious and professed conversion, other than that of outsiders to the Church, in common with the whole world lying in wickedness.[83]

This is closely related to a third result of Finney's influence on the church: the decline of infant Baptism. Drawing on statistical reports of the General Assembly between 1807 and 1856, Charles Hodge was able to document this decline, writing:

> Fifty years ago, there were about 200 children baptized for every thousand communicants; now but 50—only one-fourth as many. Fifty years ago, there was one child baptized for every five members; now but one for 20!
>
> In 1811 there were only 23,639 communicants, and yet there were 4,677 baptisms. And yet in 1856, with ten times as many members, we have only twice as many baptisms of children: showing . . . 34,328 children excluded from this holy ordinance within the past year, being almost three-fourths of the infant members of the Church![84]

Particularly telling was Hodge's comparison of church records on infant Baptism between 1839 to 1856 in the New School and Old School denominations that had been formed as a result of denominational infighting in 1837. He compared data from the two denominations.[85] The New School Presbyterian denomination reported only nineteen infant Baptisms for every thousand members in 1847, for example; the Old School denomination, fifty-two per thousand—nearly three times as many.

Thus by the middle of the nineteenth century, the *crisis/nurture* model of the Christian life, first emerging during the Great Awakening, gradually had become more focused on the crisis side of the equation and less on the nurture side. The inroads of the Sunday school movement and the decline of catechetical instruction, the identification of church membership with conversion that was sometimes signaled by admission to the Lord's Supper, and the decline of infant Baptism posed a serious threat to the older Reformation paradigm of infant Baptism, catechetical instruction, and admission to the Lord's Supper. This represented a departure from the original intentions of New School Presbyterians such as Gilbert Tennent, who had drawn on the evangelical and spiritual writings of the English Puritans to interpret the Westminster standards. As the creative impulse of these persons was swallowed up by revivalism, their legitimate insights about the place of crisis, inner struggle, and personal piety in the Christian life were turned into a formulaic understanding of conversion that frequently was anti-intellectual and manipulative. Advocates of a different understanding of the Westminster heritage began to make their case.

Admission to the Lord's Supper
in the Nurture/Development Trajectory:
Defense of the Reformation Paradigm

Political infighting between New School and Old School Presbyterians began with the very inception of the denomination, even leading to a temporary split into two ecclesiastical bodies. As New Schoolers came under the influence of revivalism, they drew heavy fire from advocates of the *nurture/development* model of the Christian life. Increasingly, the latter cast themselves as the true defenders of the Westminster heritage, portraying the evangelical wing of the church as importing theological beliefs and practices that were a departure from the Reformed tradition. To the extent that New School congregations viewed admission to the Lord's Supper as a marker of the individual's conversion and downplayed the importance of infant Baptism and catechetical instruction, it was easy to make this charge stick. Old School Presbyterianism countered with an understanding of admission that was clearly *catechetical*. Moreover, they were able to include a subordinate *professional* element on the basis of their use of covenant themes.

The *Minutes* of the General Assembly during the early decades of the nineteenth century are full of criticisms of revivalism's influence on the church.[86] However, the most comprehensive articulation of a *catechetical* interpretation of the Westminster standards during this period is found in the Romeyn Report, presented to the General Assembly in 1812.[87] Titled, "The Duty of the Church in the Instruction and Discipline of Her Baptized Children," the report was prompted by questions raised in a number of presbyteries about the church's role in nurturing and disciplining children who had been baptized but not yet admitted to the Lord's Supper. The report appeals repeatedly to the Westminster standards and other confessional documents of the Reformed tradition. It begins by affirming the practice of infant Baptism, describing it as a seal of the covenant promised by God to the members of the church and their children (Genesis 17). It then points out the implications of this position: "On the ground of the promise, therefore, the children of those who profess faith in Christ, and obedience to his commandments, *are considered as members of the church*" (emphasis added).[88] As members of the church, baptized children are subject to its discipline.[89] This is described as being of a twofold nature: preventive and corrective.[90]

Preventive discipline is portrayed exclusively in terms of instruction. Whereas the teaching of doctrinal and biblical content clearly is held up as important, this is balanced by equal attention to the effect this teaching has on children. As the report puts it, such teaching "must first convince the understanding, and then excite the affections."[91] Memorization is not enough, for children's "judgment" also is to be shaped: their ability to understand and use what they are learning.[92] The larger goal of instruction is described as breaking the dominion of sin in the hearts of believers and helping them set their hearts on those things that bring true peace, comfort, and happiness. The report goes on to affirm the importance of this kind of teaching in the traditional ecology of Reformed education: the home, the school, and the congregation. The importance of catechetical instruction in each of these contexts is emphasized.[93] The following passage, describing the important role of parents in this regard, is representative:

> They must, moreover, teach them their Catechism. . . . Their relation to the Church, as baptized children ought to be sedulously impressed upon their minds, as also their consequent obligation to walk in newness of life, and their subjection to the spiritual authority which Christ hath established in his Church. From the first dawnings of reason, they ought to be taught to consider themselves as the Lord's children, solemnly dedicated to him, and bound to glorify him in soul and body.[94]

The difference between this orientation and that of revivalism is apparent. Although children are portrayed as struggling against sin, they also are seen as belonging to Christ and as members of the church. As they grow, they are to assume the obligation "to walk in newness of life" in conjunction with learning the catechism.

The place of admission to the Lord's Supper is discussed in relation to the second, "corrective" form of discipline covered by the report. In general, this form of discipline receives much less attention. A variety of corrective measures are described, each of which takes the age and circumstances of the recipient into account. Participation in the Lord's Supper is viewed as one of the duties incumbent upon the baptized members of the church when they have "arrived to years of maturity." It is to be accompanied by a profession of faith.[95]

A more eloquent defense of the *nurture/development* trajectory of the Presbyterian tradition during this period cannot be found. Baptism of the children of believers entails their instruction, creating the possibility of their self-conscious acceptance of the covenant of grace in which they already participate. This involves more than head knowledge. It is a matter of the heart, and it involves the gradual recognition of what it means to walk in newness of life. Knowledge and piety, long the church's two criteria of admission to the Lord's Supper, are held together, not played off against one another, as they tended to be in revivalistic circles.[96]

In addition to the Romeyn Report, there are numerous journal accounts of Presbyterians living during this period whose experience was not shaped by revivalism but by the marker events of Baptism, catechetical instruction, and admission to the Lord's Supper.[97] The nurture of the church shaped their development in faith. This did not preclude the importance of a heartfelt, personal profession when they reached the age of discretion. At its best, the catechetical instruction they received addressed matters of knowledge and piety. It attempted to foster simultaneously the most important goods long associated with this practice: understanding of the basic beliefs of the church, judgment in applying these beliefs and accompanying moral principles to their lives, identification with the covenant community, and cultivation of a relationship of trust in the sovereign God.

The Breakup of the Reformation Paradigm

To this point, little mention has been made of confirmation in the American Presbyterian Church. The Westminster standards and the Scottish and Puritan traditions shaping early Presbyterianism did not view admission to the Lord's Supper as a confirmation service. Indeed, these traditions often were hostile to confirmation in particular and liturgical worship in general, an outgrowth of their conflicts with the Church of England. Presbyterian attitudes toward confirmation began to change during the middle of the nineteenth century. In large part, this was due to a recovery of the pre-Puritan, liturgical heritage of the Reformed tradition, allowing the church to enter into dialogue with new scholarship on Christian initiation and with liturgical developments taking place in other denominations.

This newfound interest in confirmation came precisely at a time when the older Reformation paradigm of infant Baptism, catechetical instruction, and admission to the Lord's Supper was beginning to break up. Without a theological tradition specifying the meaning of a Reformed understanding of confirmation, it has been swept up in the confusion surrounding the collapse of the older pattern. At times, confirmation language has appeared in denominational educational material, just as it was being explicitly rejected by the liturgical standards of the church. During other periods, the exact opposite has occurred. Before tracing these bewildering developments, it may be helpful to have an overview of the confusion characterizing the church during this period. Historical developments traced in the remainder of this chapter are outlined in table 1.

The collapse of the classical Reformation paradigm and ensuing period of confusion can be followed by tracing three trends: (1) the decline of catechetical

Table 1. CONFIRMATION LANGUAGE IN PCUSA (NORTHERN)
AND PCUS (SOUTHERN) CHURCHES

Liturgical Documents	Instructional Documents
1789 *Directory for Worship* adopted Admission to Sealing Ordinances No service for confirmation	1789 Westminster Confession and Catechisms adopted
1861 Adoption of the Westminster standards by PCUS (southern church)	
Manuals for Worship compiled by individuals using confirmation language 1857 C. Baird, *Eutaxia* 1882 A. A. Hodge, *Manual of Forms* 1900 H. Johnson, *Forms*	1892 Peak sales of *Shorter Catechism*
1894 Revised *Directory for Worship* (PCUS), includes optional questions for Baptism and admission to the Lord's Supper; profession, not confirmation language	1902 Brief Statement of Faith (PCUSA)
1906 *Book of Common Worship* (PCUSA) includes confirmation service	Communicant's Class Manuals using profession, not confirmation language **1905 Miller, *Manual for Communicants' Classes* 1912 Erdman, *Coming to Communion* 1915 Lukens, *A Pastor's Instruction Class*** **1912 *Intermediate Catechism* (PCUSA)** **1920 Kerr, *My First Communion*, confirmation language**
1929 Revised *Directory for Worship* (PCUS), questions for Baptism and admission to the Lord's Supper; profession, not confirmation language	
1932 Revised *Book of Common Worship* (PCUSA) confirmation language removed	

(Table continues.)

Table 1 *(continued.)*

Liturgical Documents	Instructional Documents
	1937 Kerr, *Manual for Faith and Life*, based on *Intermediate Catechism*, confirmation language; catechetical purpose
	1938 Moody, *Teacher's Guide for Faith and Life*, diminished use of confirmation language
	1943 Sherrills, *Becoming a Christian,* strong use of profession, not confirmation language
1946 Revised *Book of Common Worship* (PCUSA) confirmation service	1947 *Outline of Christian Faith* based on *Intermediate Catechism,* catechetical purpose
	1957 *This Is My Church*, confirmation language
1960 Revised *Directory for Worship* (PCUSA) confirmation service	
1963 Revised *Directory for Worship and Work* (PCUS), questions for Baptism and admission kept (addition: church as sponsor); profession, not confirmation language	
1970 *The Worship Book* (PCUSA), confirmation one of two commissioning services; confirmation and profession language greatly diminished	
1971 Admission of children to the Lord's Supper prior to confirmation (PCUSA)	**1973 *Context for Choice* (UPCUSA), confirmation and commissioning language**

(Table continues.)

Table 1 *(continued.)*

Liturgical Documents	Instructional Documents
	1977 Turnages, *Explorations into Faith,* **confirmation and commissioning language (both denominations)**
1981 Committee to write New *Directory for Worship* of the reuniting denominations	
1982 Admission of children to the Lord's Supper prior to confirmation or profession (PCUS)	
1983 Reunion of PCUSA and PCUS	
1985 *Supplemental Liturgical Resource 2: Holy Baptism and Services for the Renewal of Baptism,* no confirmation language; a service of public profession of faith located amid services for the reaffirmation of the baptismal covenant	
	1990 *Journeys of Faith,* **confirmation and commissioning language**
1993 New *Directory for Worship,* **confirmation and commissioning language W-4.2003**	
1993 *Book of Common Worship,* no confirmation language; a service for Reaffirmation of the Baptismal Covenant for Those Making a Public Profession	

Note: Bold type indicates use of confirmation language.

instruction in the church and the emergence of communicant or confirmation curriculums based on modern educational pedagogy; (2) the emergence of a liturgical renewal movement in the church, leading to the formation of the first Presbyterian *Book of Common Worship* and revisions of the *Directory for Worship;* and (3) the admission of children to the Lord's Supper prior to confirmation. These trends can be discerned in both the southern branch of the Presbyterian Church—the Presbyterian Church in the United States—and the northern branch—the Presbyterian Church of the United States of America, later called the United Presbyterian Church in the U.S.A. after joining with the United Presbyterian Church of North America. The southern and northern branches of the

Presbyterian Church were formed during the Civil War and were reunited only in 1983.

These three trends will be traced in both denominations during two distinct periods: (1) the post-Civil War period through the 1930s; and (2) the 1940s to the present. The first period represents the decline of catechetical instruction, the transition to modern communicants or confirmation curriculum, and renewed interest in Reformed worship in the American Presbyterian Church. During this period, confirmation language appeared in the Presbyterian Church on a wide scale for the first time. It was used to hold on to professional and catechetical elements of admission, even as the practice of catechetical instruction began to decline. Slowly but surely during this period, the balance begins to tip toward a *professional* understanding of confirmation.

The second period represents a time of rapid but bewildering innovation. Confirmation language is mingled with commissioning language. The *Directory for Worship* and *Book of Common Worship* are altered several times. Children are admitted to the Lord's Table with little provision for their education. Confirmation curriculums are produced that self-consciously break all ties with the older practice of catechetical instruction. Long under pressure, the classical Reformation paradigm collapses. Confirmation and commissioning language during this period is used to refer to both educational programs and specific rites. The older practice of catechetical instruction gives way to a new confirmation practice that culminates in a confirmation (and commissioning) service. The goods generated by this program vary considerably. In some instances, an attempt is made to hold on to the older goods of profession and confession. In other cases, a new *developmental* understanding of confirmation begins to emerge. In this approach, the primary goods fostered by the confirmation program are defined psychologically and focus on support of the young person's faith exploration and discovery.

In making these generalizations, several qualifications must be made with regard to important differences between the northern and southern branches of the church. On the whole, the southern church was far more conservative doctrinally than its northern counterpart. As early as 1884, the southern church made it more difficult to change its doctrinal standards, requiring the approval of three-fourths of the presbyteries for ratification, not the two-thirds necessary in the northern church. While the northern church would make significant changes in the Westminster Confession during the first part of the twentieth century, the southern church consistently would resist attempts at doctrinal revision.[98] A concomitant of this doctrinal conservatism was the continuation of catechetical instruction through the middle part of the twentieth century. As late as the 1950s, the General Assembly of the southern church was still calling on its presbyteries and denominational agencies to support catechetical instruction in the home, Sunday school, and communicant's class.

On the surface, then, it might seem surprising that the southern church moved to revise the *Directory for Worship* at a much earlier point than its northern counterpart. This included important revisions in its directives for the baptism of infants and admission to the Lord's Supper. The fact that the southern church was composed almost entirely of Old School Presbyterians, however, made it far more willing to regulate the worship of its congregations than was the PCUSA. The presence of a large number of New School Presbyterians in the northern church, who were of an anti-liturgical bent, posed major difficulties for the enactment of liturgical reform in this branch of the church.

Although there were significant differences between the northern and southern branches of the Presbyterian Church, there also was significant cross-fertilization. The General Assembly of the southern church, for example, consistently authorized use of the various editions of the *Book of Common Worship,* produced by the northern church.[99] Moreover, the two denominations collaborated on various educational and liturgical projects. Although the differences between the two branches of the church must be kept in mind, the cross-fertilization at both official and informal levels created a number of commonalities.

From the Civil War to the 1930s

The period immediately after the Civil War was an important time of transition for both the northern and southern branches of the Presbyterian Church. It is during this period that the church created the *Book of Common Worship* and began to revise its directory for worship. It also began to introduce confirmation language into its liturgical and educational material for the first time. The story being told in this chapter takes a significant turn during this period.

Liturgical Renewal and the Emergence of Confirmation in the Presbyterian Church

The central context in which the language of confirmation was first introduced into the American Presbyterian Church was liturgical. Beginning in the middle of the nineteenth century, a number of scholars, ministers, and laypersons began to take a new interest in the pre-Puritan Reformed liturgical heritage. Calvin's and Knox's approaches to liturgical worship and the "high church" elements of English Presbyterian Puritanism (represented by individuals such as Richard Baxter) received a new hearing. Liturgical renewal in other branches of the Reformed tradition, especially the Church of Scotland, also exerted some influence during this period, as did liturgical reforms taking place in other denominations. This liturgical renewal culminated in the revision of the *Directory for Worship* in the southern church and the creation of American Presbyterianism's first *Book of Common Worship* in the northern church. It was in this context that the language of confirmation first began to be used on a wide scale in the Presbyterian Church.

Confirmation and the First *Book of Common Worship* in the Northern Presbyterian Church

One of the most important dynamics during this period was the very different attitude held by New School and Old School Presbyterianism toward liturgical reform. New Schoolers were solidly against liturgical reform. In some ways, this harked back to the fears of formalism in worship held by the Puritans, but it also reflected the more recent antiliturgical bent of revivalism. Many New Schoolers shared Charles Finney's attitude toward worship: It should be governed by what is effective in touching the hearts of those who are worshiping, something that cannot be determined by the imposition of generic liturgical forms. Repeatedly, the New School wing of the church blocked attempts at liturgical reform in the church and were highly critical of liturgical developments in other denominations. Albert Barnes's characterization of liturgical renewal as a contemporary form of Pharisaic Judaism and medieval Catholicism was typical.[100] Old School Presbyterians in both branches of the church were far more interested in reclaiming the pre-Puritan liturgical heritage and engaging the liturgical scholarship that was beginning to emerge. Ironically, no less a defender of the Westminster standards than Charles Hodge articulated the first theological rationale for a Reformed understanding of confirmation in the American Presbyterian Church. Hodge did so in an article written around the middle of the century called "Presbyterian Liturgies," in which he responded to the charges being made by persons such as Barnes.[101]

In the context of both affirming the richness of the early Reformed liturgical tradition and the American church's long-standing resistance to compulsory liturgies, Hodge set forth a brief theological and historical defense of confirmation, arguing: "It is a great mistake, therefore, to represent confirmation as a prelatical service. In one form or another, it is the necessary sequence of infant baptism, and must be adopted wherever pedo-baptism prevails."[102] In its Protestant form, he pointed out, confirmation always has been administered to the baptized children of the church following an examination of their knowledge and piety. They are confirmed when they are deemed ready to "assume for themselves their baptismal vows, and are recognized as members of the church in full communion."[103] He pointed out that the Presbyterian Churches of Great Britain, Ireland, and the United States, have consistently asked for something more than knowledge, confirming persons only when "they are prepared to make a credible profession of a change of heart."[104] This heartfelt confession of faith is the real focus of confirmation, he argues. It represents a person's confirmation of his or her baptismal vows and is acknowledged by the prayers and blessing of the church. No one could ever accuse Charles Hodge of being uninterested in the teaching of the Westminster catechisms, but at this point he is clearly offering a *professional* interpretation of confirmation. It is based on study of the catechism, but goes beyond that.

Hodge's reflections were prompted, in part, by the work of a young Presbyterian minister, Charles Baird, who collected and translated a number of early Reformed liturgies, compiling them into two books, *Eutaxia, or the Presbyterian Liturgies: Historical Sketches* and *A Book of Public Prayer*.[105] Baird's work stimulated renewed interest in the pre-Puritan Reformed liturgical tradition, pointing to a middle way between compulsory liturgies and complete ministerial freedom. Among the items Baird translated was the Waldensian Liturgy for "The Admission of Baptized Persons to the Table of the Lord," a liturgy that had been influential among continental Reformed churches.[106] In the liturgy's initial address to the members of the congregation, the service is described as allowing the young people who stand before them to "publicly ratify in your hearing the engagements of their Baptism, and be received to the full participation of the benefits of the Covenant of Grace," a theme that is reiterated in the prayer that immediately follows.[107] In the questions asked of those seeking admission, the following appears: "Do you then sincerely and with your whole hearts confirm and ratify the vows of your Baptism . . . ?"[108] Similarly, the prayer offered over the kneeling candidates describes them as coming "now to confirm the vows of obedience that were taken for them."[109]

It is noteworthy that Hodge and Baird's Waldensian liturgy both identify confirmation with the individual's personal profession of faith and ratification of the covenant. While these are based on the knowledge gained in catechetical instruction, they go beyond it. This trend toward a *professional* understanding of confirmation continued in the next step by which it was introduced into the church: the introduction of worship manuals. In large measure, these manuals were prompted by the Civil War. Without a standard book of worship, Presbyterian soldiers were left to their own devices when no minister was present to conduct worship services and funerals. Scholars and ministers alike came to believe that the *Directory for Worship* needed to be supplemented with worship manuals that provided liturgies for various occasions. A number of unofficial manuals were published by the denominational publishing house. It was in the context of these manuals that actual confirmation/admission services first appeared. One of the most important of these was produced by Charles Hodge's son, Archibald Alexander Hodge, in 1882, *A Manual of Forms*.[110]

This manual includes an "Order for the Public Reception into Full or Confirmed Communion of Those Who Have Been Baptized in Infancy."[111] The service presupposes the classical Reformation pattern: Young people, having reached the age of discretion, been instructed in the faith, and examined by the session were to be admitted to the Lord's Supper. What is new is the use of confirmation language to describe the act by which the young person comes to "renew and publicly ratify the covenant of discipleship" in which they were "sealed" in their baptism.[112] Hodge even includes the ancient prayer for the sevenfold gifts of the Holy Spirit, traditionally associated with the postbaptismal anointing and, later, with confirmation itself.[113]

Hodge was not alone in his use of confirmation language in manuals of this type.[114] They represented the first step of a broadly based movement of liturgical renewal in the northern church that culminated in 1906 in the creation of the *Book of Common Worship*. This book, the first officially sponsored book of common worship in the Presbyterian Church, included "An Order for the Confirmation of Baptismal Vows and Reception to the Lord's Supper." The very idea of a service book with set liturgical forms proved to be quite threatening to many in the church, especially the New School wing of the church.[115] The initial draft was sent back to committee for additional revisions and only passed a year later with a weakened endorsement.[116]

Nonetheless, the Presbyterian Church had its first *Book of Common Worship,* and it included a confirmation service.[117] The title of the service ("The Order for the Confirmation of Baptismal Vows") made it clear that confirmation had a *professional* orientation, representing the individual's personal profession of faith and ratification of the baptismal covenant. This is signalled in the baptismal service for infants, in which God is asked in prayer *to confirm* the promises being made that the infant at a later point in life might "not be ashamed to confess the faith of Christ crucified."[118] In the confirmation service itself, the baptisms of the candidates are recalled and their participation in the present service is portrayed as the outgrowth of their "desire to confirm the covenant then made in your behalf." [119] They are asked a series of questions, including the following: "Do you ratify and confirm the vows of your baptism, and promise with God's help to serve the Lord, and keep His commandments all the days of your life?" The minister then is "permitted" to lay hands on the confirmands, offering the traditional confirmation "Defend" prayer, found in the 1552 edition of the Church of England's *Book of Common Prayer.* The service concludes by asking God to protect the confirmands that they might be able to keep the covenant.

For the first time in American Presbyterianism, the church had a book of set liturgical forms. Although controversy surrounded the adoption of this book, the attitude of the church was to become much more positive toward liturgical worship in the ensuing decades. Only twenty-two years later, when the General Assembly appointed a committee to revise the worship book, its recommendation met almost no opposition. The revised edition, adopted in 1932, made few significant changes to the 1906 edition, although it included much new material.

It is significant that one of the few major points of revision in the new *Book of Common Worship* was the service of confirmation. Every usage of the term "confirmation" was deleted. A side-by-side comparison of the original book and the 1932 edition is startling.[120] (See table 2.)

The only place where confirmation language is used in the new edition is in the service for infant Baptism, which asks God, in prayer, "to confirm Thy favor more and more toward us, and to take into Thy tuition and defense this child . . . "[121] Whereas it is clear that the new edition of the *Book of Common Worship* still views this service as focusing on the individual's profession of faith and covenant ratification, it has drawn back from the use of the term "confirmation" to refer to this act. This was the beginning of a bewildering series of changes in the definition of confirmation in the liturgical standards of the northern church. This confusion was compounded by an equal lack of consistency in the educational material produced for communicants' classes during this same period.

Revision of the *Directory for Worship* in the Southern Church: Strengthening the Liturgical Link between Baptism and First Communion

Throughout this period, the southern Presbyterian Church also was engaged in liturgical revision. Its focus was not on the creation of a book of common worship

Table 2. COMPARISON OF TWO EDITIONS OF BOOK OF COMMON WORSHIP

1906 Edition	1932 Edition
"The Order for the Confirmation of Baptismal Vows and Reception to the Lord's Supper"	"Reception to the Lord's Supper"
Initial charge: And foreasmuch as you now desire to confirm the covenant then made in your behalf, and to obey His commandment by confessing Him before men . . .	Forasmuch as you now desire to obey His commandment by confessing Him before men
*Q*2: Do you ratify and confirm the vows of your Baptism . . . ?	Do you promise with God's help to serve the Lord?

but on revision of the *Directory for Worship,* initially adopted when it split off from the northern church. As early as 1867, it began a tortuous process of revision that finally resulted in adoption of a revised *Directory* in 1894.[122] This new directory did not include a confirmation service or even confirmation language. What it did was to strengthen the link between infant Baptism and admission to the Lord's Supper, while maintaining the traditional emphasis on catechetical instruction.

This is evident in the new directory's sections on Baptism and admission. Both now included questions that could be asked directly of participants. Although these questions were presented as entirely optional, they were widely used in the southern church. The section on Baptism continues the Reformed tradition's emphasis on the parents' confession of their own faith and their promise to bring their child up in the "nurture and admonition of the Lord," including instruction in the "doctrines of our holy religion."[123] In the section on Admission to Sealing Ordinances, emphasis is placed on the candidate's personal confession. The new *Directory* describes what is at stake in admission as follows: "And when they come to years of discretion, they ought to be urgently reminded that they are members of the church by birthright, and that it is their duty and privilege personally to accept Christ, confess him before men, and seek admission to the Lord's supper."[124] This *professional* element is the primary focus of the questions asked of the candidates. In the minister's charge immediately before these questions, they are told that they are about to make a "public profession of faith" by which they "enter into a solemn covenant with God and his church."[125] The following questions then are asked:

1. Do you acknowledge yourselves to be sinners in the sight of God, justly deserving his displeasure, and without hope save in his sovereign mercy?
2. Do you believe in the Lord Jesus Christ as the Son of God, and Saviour of sinners, and do you receive and rest upon him alone for salvation as he is offered in the gospel?

3. Do you now resolve and promise, in humble reliance upon the grace of the Holy Spirit, that you will endeavor to walk as becometh the followers of Christ, forsaking all sin, and conforming your life to his teaching and example?

4. Do you submit yourselves to the government and discipline of the church, and promise to study its purity and peace?[126]

Nowhere in these revisions does the language of confirmation appear. A closer link between Baptism and admission to the Lord's Supper, however, could hardly be made. Baptism is portrayed as entailing and looking forward to the infant's personal profession of faith upon reaching the age of discretion. The service of admission involves just this profession. This close link between Baptism and admission to sealing ordinances is maintained in each of the successive revisions of the *Directory for Worship* in the southern church, the next of which took place in 1929.[127]

The Decline of Catechetical Instruction

During the period following the Civil War and the first three decades of the twentieth century, liturgical reforms were slowly leading to the introduction of confirmation language and services in a variety of resources. In large measure, confirmation language gave pride of place to the element of profession, although it continued to be linked with catechetical purposes as well. Parents were supposed to teach, and confirmands were supposed to understand the traditional catechetical material. What was actually going on in the church educationally during this period? Catechetical instruction was in a period of decline. This was to represent the first major blow to the inherited paradigm of infant Baptism, catechetical instruction, and admission to the Lord's Table.

The Sunday school movement had been making inroads into congregational education since the beginning of the nineteenth century. This continued after the Civil War. While there is evidence that the catechism continued to be taught in the home and church and that special pastor's classes still were offered, it is clear that the Sunday school had become the dominant form of Christian education in both branches of the Presbyterian Church. The Sunday school movement was a nondenominational, lay-led movement that had no interest in teaching confessional documents such as the catechism. As Sunday school's influence became greater, catechetical instruction continued to decline. The Presbyterian Church took various steps to shore up this practice.

An important attempt to adapt the catechism to the Sunday school format was the publication of *The Westminster Question Book: International Series,* from 1875 to 1898.[128] This included several questions from the catechism in every Sunday school lesson, covering the entire catechism in a two-year period. The church also began using very brief and simple catechisms for young children, two of the most popular of which were Joseph Engels's *Catechism for Young Children: An Introduction to the Shorter Catechism* and Frances Platt's *A Catechism for Little Children.*[129] Various attempts also were made to revise the language of the

Westminster Shorter Catechism, making it easier for contemporary children to use it. Reflecting a sense of uneasiness with the Westminster standards, however, the General Assembly of the northern church appointed a committee in 1908 to write an *Intermediate Catechism,* designed to take the place of the *Westminster Shorter Catechism.*[130] During this period, a "Brief Statement of the Reformed Faith" (1902) was written, a document that was to figure prominently in confirmation material written in the 1930s.[131]

None of these steps prevented the continuing decline of catechetical instruction, however. Yearly sales of the *Shorter Catechism* peaked in 1892 at 130,000.[132] By 1900, this had declined to 53,000 and leveled off at around 50,000 through 1938, even though church membership and Sunday school enrollment increased dramatically during this period. Although the General Assemblies of both branches of the church continued to sound the warning against allowing the Sunday school to completely supplant catechetical instruction, it was to no avail.[133] The Sunday school movement had deeply infiltrated the church and become the dominant pattern of the church's educational ministry. It was the rise of the religious education movement during the first part of the twentieth century, however, that would lead to its demise. This movement paralleled the rise of progressive education and reflected the differentiation of secular and religious educational systems that had taken place over the course of the nineteenth century in the United States. Drawing heavily on social gospel and liberal theologies, and the newly emerging social sciences, the leaders of the religious education movement attempted to project an entirely new vision of the church's teaching ministry.[134] They consistently portrayed catechetical instruction as epitomizing everything that was wrong with the inherited approach to education. George Albert Coe, for example, described it as producing "pseudo-knowledge" and its reliance on "particular words" as fostering "a verbal mental habit that prevents thinking."[135] Harrison Elliott similarly characterized catechetical instruction as an "authoritarian tradition which developed in the Reformation and which was prominent in the colonial period in the United States."[136]

In many ways, the influence of this movement on the church was positive. It helped support the use of modern educational approaches and led to the emergence of a new genre of educational material that was sensitive to students' developmental differences and included instructions to teachers about how the material might be used.[137] It went far beyond this, however, beginning to question the basic theological assumptions of the classical Reformation understanding of the teaching office: the authority of scripture, the importance of confessional traditions, and the significance of communal forms of Christian identity. A transformation of the *nurture/development* model of the Christian life was beginning to take place.

In the older model, grounded in the basic theological convictions of the Reformation as mediated by the Westminster Assembly, childhood nurture, especially catechetical instruction, was viewed as entailed by Baptism and as culminating in admission to the Lord's Supper. The ordinary means of grace offered by the community were seen as the key context through which the Word and Spirit work to bring persons to faith and help them grow in their covenant with God and one another. Development, as such, was inherently social, ethical, and spiritual. It had to do with the acquisition of the knowledge and skills necessary to participate with greater maturity in the practices of the covenant community and to live out one's vocation in the world. Development presupposed Christian nurture, for it depended on the internalization of the beliefs and practices of the covenant community.

The religious education movement's critique of catechetical instruction was only one small part of its overall rejection of this basic vision of the Christian life. Its deep ambivalence about the central theological tenets of the Reformation led it to ground its vision of the church in ethics, particularly social ethics, rather than in the central doctrines of the church: Christology, justification, election, and eschatology.[138] Without a guiding theological framework, the social sciences, particularly psychology, gradually came to dominate its understanding of education. Long after the influence of the religious education movement had declined, this psychological focus continued to dominate educational material. The long-term effect was to reverse the traditional *nurture/development* model of the Christian life to a *development/nurture* pattern. The individual's psychological growth was moved into the foreground and substantive theological definitions of the church moved into the background. Frequently, the church was portrayed as little more than a predicate of the psychological subject.

Nowhere are these trends more evident than in the new material beginning to be used alongside of or in place of the catechism. Over time, the curriculums for what was then called communicants' or confirmation classes came to be dominated by a *developmental* understanding of confirmation, placing emphasis on the individual's psychological growth. Journey language and themes became prominent. Pedagogics allowing "faith exploration" were widely used. What was lost was the theological vision of the church as a covenant community and the acquisition of the knowledge and skills it offers through participation in its practices.

The first three decades of the twentieth century were a transitional period. Three trends can be identified that would lead to the emergence of a *developmental* understanding of confirmation. First, the catechism, taught in the home, school, and family over a long period of time, is replaced or supplemented by communicants' or confirmation curriculums that can be taught in relatively short classes led by ministers. This material continues to see its role as catechetical, that is, as providing a "short course" on the basic beliefs of the church. Second, these new curriculums begin to pay explicit attention to the social sciences, drawing on education to provide instructions for teachers and on psychology to offer insights into the developmental dynamics of students. Third, the purpose of confirmation or first communion becomes deeply confused. A number of purposes are advocated in different curriculums. These frequently are not integrated with the purposes described in *The Book of Common Worship*. As the classical Reformation paradigm of infant Baptism, catechetical instruction, and admission to the Lord's Supper breaks up, the church moves into a period of uncertainty about what will take its place.

Several widely used curriculums are illustrative of these trends. In 1904, the General Assembly of the northern church was urged to prepare a curriculum that could be used by ministers in communicants' classes. The following year, J. R. Miller, the Editorial Superintendent of the Board of Publication and Sabbath-school Work, wrote *Manual for Communicants' Classes,* which was revised the following year by Gerrit Verkuyl.[139] The manual does not yet include explicit teaching instructions or draw on developmental psychology. It is written for the class participants and attempts to address them personally. Whereas the manual moves completely away from the *Shorter Catechism,* it attempts to cover the basic beliefs of the church in a relatively short period of time. Its defining purpose is *professional*—the task of enabling young people to make a personal confession of faith in conjunction with admission to the Lord's Supper. This is described as both an act of "uniting with the Church" and as entry into a self-conscious relationship with Jesus Christ.[140] Although a catechetical interest is still present in the manual's attempt to cover some basic doctrinal material, it is clearly in a subordinate role. This same trend is found in other communicant's class manuals written during this same period: Erdman's *Coming to the Communion: A Manual of Instruction for Preparatory Classes and Private Study* and Lukens's *A Pastor's Instruction Class for Children.*[141]

Hugh Kerr's *My First Communion* (1920) was the first educational piece in the church to explicitly use the language of confirmation.[142] Kerr included the entire confirmation service in his manual and used the conceptuality of confirmation to frame the purpose of the course being offered:

> The first Communion is a sacred time in the life of the Christian. It marks a definite step in life. It is an act of faith in which the Christian gives himself to the Saviour and in which the Saviour gives himself to the Christian. . . .
>
> Those who have been baptized in infancy are already members of the Church and the Communion service is for them the *confirmation* of the vows which were undertaken for them by their parents at the time of their baptism. . . .
>
> It is the happy privilege of the pastor to seek and to find those who wish to *confess and confirm* their faith in the Lord Jesus, by participating in the Holy Communion, and it is his joy to prepare them for their first Communion, and to instruct them concerning the Christian life (emphasis added).[143]

Clearly, a *professional* understanding of confirmation is dominant here as well. The goal of the material is to allow individuals to confirm the baptismal covenant. Whereas a catechetical purpose remained, it appears in a subordinate role. Like Miller's manual, Kerr's is not so much a modern curriculum piece, with instructions for teachers, as a manual for class participants, inviting them to take the important step of confirming their faith.

Kerr's manual proved to be so popular that he was asked to write a new communicant's manual on behalf of the General Assembly of the northern church, in 1932. He presented his work to the General Assembly in 1937, *A Manual of Faith and Life: A Guide for Individual Christians or Communicant Classes.*[144] This focused on a "Brief Statement of the Reformed Faith" (1902), which was an attempt to offer a fresh statement of the church's faith, moving away from the Westminster standards. Although the format was somewhat catechetical, focusing on the sixteen articles of the "Brief Statement," confirmation conceptuality is used to frame the goal of the course. As Kerr puts it in his discussion of the sacraments:

> The sacrament of baptism is the ordinance of admission to membership in the Church. . . . It is administered only to believing Christians and their infant children. . . . When they come to years of understanding and know the meaning of the sacrament they are "*confirmed*" in the faith in which they were baptized and admitted to the holy Communion. They do not "join the Church" but are *confirmed* in their Christian faith on their own confession. They take upon themselves the vows their parents took for them (emphasis added).[145]

The "Foreword" signaled that a teacher's guide would soon follow.[146] The publication of this guide, written by Winfred Moody the following year, represented a major development in the trends we have been following. Not only does it address teachers directly, including explicit guidelines for each session, and adopt a developmental framework, but it also offered a qualitatively new understanding of the purpose of communicant's classes.[147] Indeed, this purpose stood in stark contrast with that informing Kerr's book, ostensibly the one on which the teacher's guide was based. Kerr's manual now was portrayed as a resource for the teacher's own preparation and not as material to be studied by students.

Although Moody makes passing reference to confirmation in the opening sentences of her manual, it is clear that she thinks of the step young people are about to make as joining the church. The class for which the curriculum is written is referred to as the "Church Membership Class," and this rubric is used repeatedly throughout the material.[148] Moreover, she diminishes both catechetical and professional elements of the course, going so far as to write in the Introduction that ". . . too great emphasis on the subjective realities of repentance and the new birth may even result in morbid fears and a sense of spiritual failure."[149] She advocates a purpose informed by modern educational theory. Students are to "discover" the truth of the Bible and Christian tradition for themselves.[150] The "Introduction" encourages teachers to consider organizing the lessons inductively around the "interests" of the students, "discovering the questions and issues of which the young people are aware, then listing these in an order of preference indicated by the class, and basing the development of the course upon this order."[151]

The "interest" approach being advocated by Moody was an outgrowth of the progressive education movement and had long been championed in the field of religious education by persons like George Albert Coe, under the influence of John Dewey. The shift from the older pattern of catechetical instruction and humanistic education could hardly be more apparent. The experience of students, not classic texts, was now the center of the curriculum. Students' questions, not those of the catechism, were to set the agenda for the lessons. The transition from catechism to modern curriculum was now complete.

Moody's piece marked the entry of a *development/nurture* model of the Christian life into confirmation material, undergirding a *developmental* understanding of confirmation. Henceforth, there was a strong tendency in much of this material to allow understandings of the individual's psychological growth, correlated with a description of the Christian life as a journey, to frame its purpose and process. Just as the older *crisis/nurture* model had gradually given way, under the influence of revivalism, to one focusing on the moment of crisis, so too, the *nurture/development* model was being reduced to one focusing on development, under the influence of liberal theology and modern educational theory. This approach represented a major break with the older catechetical and professional purposes of confirmation and admission. The classical Reformation paradigm of infant Baptism, catechetical instruction, and admission to the Lord's Supper was beginning to break up. Its final collapse was to take place in conjunction with liturgical innovations during the period that followed. The church was entering a time of innovation and confusion as it struggled to determine what would take the place of the inherited pattern of church life.

From the 1940s to the Present

The most important liturgical innovation taking place since 1940 was the decision to admit children to the Lord's Table at an early age. The marker event of the classical Reformation paradigm—admission to the Lord's Supper—was eliminated. This took place in the United Presbyterian Church in 1971 and in the Presbyterian Church (US) in 1982.[152]

Further Liturgical Revision

What led the church to make this important innovation of admitting children to the Lord's Table? The report of the special committee of the United Presbyterian Church in the U.S.A. (UPCUSA) recommending this change gave the following rationale:

> Three reasons in our day argue strongly for admission by the United Presbyterian Church of baptized children to the Lord's Supper at an early age, which would be previous to examination by the session. (1) The Reformed creeds and confessions make it very clear that all who are baptized enjoy full membership in the covenant. (2) The United Presbyterian Church's *Book of Order* sets forth a large conception of the meaning of the Lord's Supper and offers an inclusive invitation to commune. (3) The present day has a less exclusively intellectual conception of Christian instruction and growth than did the Reformation era, and has a much deeper awareness of the function of rites and ceremonies in communicating understanding and evoking inner response.[153]

The report went on to unpack the third of these in terms of developmental psychology, arguing that it shows us that knowledge and experience come to young children, "not only through words and statements, but often much more through experiences, symbols, and various forms of association with others."[154] Accordingly, children need to be nurtured, not only by "instruction and command, but also, by participation and involvement."[155]

There are two sides to this rationale. The first is the argument that Baptism is the point of admission to full membership into the covenant community. Accordingly, it should constitute the real point of admission to the Lord's Supper, even if the exercise of this right is temporarily postponed until the child is old enough to understand what is being done and receives elementary education about the meaning of this Sacrament. The second is the argument that childhood nurture should not be viewed in exclusively cognitive terms but as including the dynamics of identification with significant others and communities.

Within the context of this important alteration in the practices of the church, an important change is made. The *catechetical* and *professional* goods long associated with the practice of catechetical instruction/admission are now attached to confirmation. Confirmation is no longer a rite within a catechetical practice, it is the name used for the practice itself. The report describes confirmation as serving two purposes: "(a) an indication of appropriation of the church's faith as one's own; (b) an admission to the ranks of those who make decisions for the group and bear responsibility. We urge that confirmation focus on commissioning for ministry."[156]

It was confirmation, not admission to the Lord's Supper, that was to serve as the key marker event of personal confession, instruction in the church's faith, and entry into new rights and responsibilities of the covenant community. The latter was signaled by the use of the term "commissioning." When confirmed, young people were "commissioned" to ministry, signaling the taking up of their vocation as Christians and their active participation in the governance of the church.

How did the church come to the point where it decided to make participation in the Lord's Supper the prerogative of children and make participation in a confirmation practice, culminating in a special service, the marker event of ratification of the baptismal covenant and confession of the church's faith? We saw important movement in this direction in the previous period with the introduction of confirmation language into both liturgical and educational contexts and the movement away from catechetical instruction to new forms of education with a professional orientation (for example, Miller and Kerr). The final steps taking place after the 1930s can be summarized briefly.

The language of confirmation, we recall, was dropped from the second, 1932 edition, of the northern church's *Book of Common Worship,* even though it had been central to the 1906 edition and had begun to appear in influential educational pieces such as Hugh Kerr's *My First Communion* and *A Manual of Faith and Life.* It reappeared in the 1946 edition of *The Book of Common Worship.* This third edition included a service of confirmation, reverting to the same title used in the 1906 version: "Order for the Confirmation of Baptismal Vows and Admission to the Lord's Supper." The service, however, was quite different, relying heavily on that of the Church of Scotland's 1940 *Book of Common Order.*[157] Confirmation, however, continued to be defined in a manner consistent with the trajectory emerging in American Presbyterianism from the middle of the nineteenth century forward. It was portrayed as having primarily a *professional* purpose of personal covenant ratification that was closely linked to a *catechetical* purpose of confession of the church's faith. The latter is found in the first question asked of the confirmands, which reflects the Trinitarian structure of the Apostles' Creed. Covenant terminology is used throughout the service and the confirmands are called on to "acknowledge" and "confirm" the covenant made when they were baptized.[158] The church is portrayed as praying for and blessing those confirming their faith, symbolized by laying on of hands and prayer for the Holy Spirit. Two traditional confirmation prayers are used: The "Defend Prayer" and the prayer for the sevenfold gifts of the Holy Spirit, both of which ask God to increase the Spirit already active in the confirmands' lives.

This understanding of the practice of confirmation was maintained through the next stage of liturgical revision found in alterations of *The Directory for Worship* in 1961 in conjunction with the union of the Presbyterian Church (USA) and the United Presbyterian Church of North America to form the United Presbyterian Church in the U.S.A. (UPCUSA). In preparation for this merger and exploration of possible reunion with the southern church as well, a "Joint Committee on Worship" was formed, composed of representatives of all three denominations. The new *Directory* growing out of the work of this committee continued to define confirmation along the lines that had been emerging since the middle of the nineteenth century:

> Section 3. Reception into communicant membership, or confirmation, is an act whereby the Church recognizes the *personal encounter with Jesus* Christ as Lord and Savior of those who were baptized in infancy, and having now attained unto years of discretion, desire to *profess their faith in him.* Confirmation does not signify the completion of something left incomplete by the initial act of baptism, for in baptism God's continued claim upon the child was made manifest once for all. But at the time of confirmation, the Church calls the individual to make a *personal response to the grace of God,* which has been continually at work in his life, and which was shown forth by his baptism in infancy (emphasis added).[159]

Although the southern church did not opt for reunion at this time, it too began revising its *Directory for Worship* in 1963, renaming it the *Directory for the Worship and Work of the Church.*[160] Especially important for our purposes is its depiction of admission to sealing ordinances. On the basis of catechetical instruction, still strongly encouraged in the parent's baptismal promises, young persons were to make a "profession of their faith and purpose of obedience" before the congregation, representing a "solemn covenant with God and his Church."[161] While the southern church does not use the term "confirmation" to refer to this profession, its understanding of what was at stake in admission to the Lord's Supper was virtually identical to that of the northern church. In both the southern and northern churches, thus, confirmation/admission was defined primarily in terms of *professional* goods that included a strong *catechetical* component.

With this common understanding now present in the constitutional standards of both branches of the church, it is somewhat surprising that the northern church engaged in still another liturgical innovation: the introduction of commissioning language. This first took place with the publication of *The Worshipbook: Services,* in 1970.[162] This was the creation of the Joint Committee on Worship's revision of the *Book of Common Worship*. Confirmation now was portrayed as one of two services for "The Commissioning of Baptized Members." The other commissioning service was a service for the reception of new members. The new confirmation service was a striking departure from that of both the 1906 and 1946 editions of the *Book of Common Worship*. The language was completely contemporary, and every part of the service was new. Notably absent was any mention of the individual's confirmation of the baptismal covenant. Indeed, the language of confirmation was absent altogether except in the title of the service. The element of personal confession, moreover, was diminished. The service became one of commissioning young people to the ministries of the church. Totally new phrases placing the accent on active involvement in the ministry of Jesus Christ appear again and again: "in the service of Jesus Christ," "go and bear fruit," "go out to serve him as faithful disciples," "be his disciple . . . obey his word . . . show his love," and "he has commissioned you . . . live his love and serve him."

The *Worshipbook* represented a marked shift from the understanding of confirmation that had been developing for over a century in the church and had finally made its way into the *Directory for Worship* of the northern church. It seems to reflect the activistic ecclesiology of the Confession of 1967 and Max Thurian's portrayal of confirmation as the act by which the church commissions Christians to the ministry of the laity.[163] When the UPCUSA decided to admit children to the Lord's Table, the year after the publication of *The Worshipbook*, this understanding of commissioning was linked to the more traditional purposes of instruction, confession, and covenant ratification.

A commissioning purpose was given a position of dominance, however, in two important studies commissioned by the General Assembly of the UPCUSA in the early 1970s: a report on Baptism (1970–72) and one on church membership (1971–74).[164] In both reports, commissioning conceptuality virtually replaced that of confirmation. As the report on Baptism put it: "Commissioning of Baptized Members, rather than Confirmation, is the service of admission of persons . . . into the governing rights and witnessing responsibility of the Church."[165] These reports also introduced a motif that proved to be an important conceptual link between liturgical and educational contexts: Christian life as journey. Both reports gave strong play to journey themes in their description of Baptism, commissioning, and the Christian life in general. The new confirmation-commissioning educational material beginning to appear during this period would correlate this motif with psychological understandings of the self to portray adolescence as an important period in a lifelong journey of faith, largely framed in terms of developmental psychology.

Confirmation-Commissioning Instructional Material

What effect did these liturgical revisions have on confirmation instructional material? They had quite a bit of influence. This period saw much greater integration of the educational and liturgical endeavors of the denomination. When the

Book of Common Worship came under the official supervision of the General Assembly of the northern church in 1941, the national structure of the church was increasingly adopting rationalized procedures, including integrated planning and implementation by its various agencies. Each of the liturgical revisions described in the previous section were reflected in the new educational material produced by the denomination.

At the same time, however, material continued to be produced that reflected older understandings of catechetical instruction and admission to the Lord's Supper. At the congregational level, the church did not seem to have made up its mind about how it wanted to view these things. The *catechetical* purpose of this instruction, for example, continued to be upheld by both General Assemblies. As late as the 1950s, the General Assembly of the southern church continued to receive and approve overtures encouraging parents, Sunday school teachers, and the Board of Christian Education to teach the catechism.[166] In 1939, Eric Haden surveyed Presbyterian pastors in the northern church about their use of the *Shorter Catechism* and found that approximately 66 percent were still using it in their communicants' classes, even if in a diminished form.[167] In 1944, the General Assembly of the northern church appointed a committee to revise the *Intermediate Catechism* and prepare a commentary useful for teaching in the church.[168] The result was *An Outline of the Christian Faith in Question and Answer Form for Use in Communicants' Classes, in the Church School, and in the Home, with A Commentary on the Outline.*[169] As late as the sixties and seventies, George Kluber's *On Holy Ground* was widely used by Presbyterian pastors, being reprinted more than twelve times.[170] It focused on teaching children basic biblical and doctrinal material.

Nor did the church completely abandon the *professional* purpose of confirmation/admission. As we have seen, this remained the focus of admission to the Lord's Supper in the southern church's various directories for worship throughout this period. One of the most popular manuals used in the south that reflects this professional focus was written by Lewis and Helen Sherrill in 1943, *Becoming a Christian: A Manual for Communicant Classes.*[171] This book viewed its basic purpose as providing class members with a chance to consider becoming followers of Jesus Christ. It was still widely used as recently as the 1970s.

A wide range of purposes thus continued to be present in educational material used throughout the church. Of particular interest to our story, however, is the confirmation material produced under the auspices of denominational publishing houses. This material was closely related to the liturgical revisions pointed to in the previous section. It both drew on these revisions and, simultaneously, transformed them, serving as one of the gateways to the introduction of a *development/nurture* model of the Christian life into the church. Psychological understandings of the self, conjoined to a journey motif, were used to frame a *developmental* understanding of the purpose and process of confirmation-commissioning. Trends first appearing in Moody's teacher's guide for a *Manual for Faith and Life* now became more prominent.

The first new churchwide communicant's class material in the northern church following the 1946 revision of the *Book of Common Worship* was part of the *Christian Faith and Life* curriculum: *This Is My Church* (student book) and *The Pastor's Guide for the Training of Church Members*.[172] These books were published in 1957 and revised in 1959 after the UPCUSA came into being. It was during this period that the new denomination was in the process of revising its *Directory for Worship,* incorporating the understanding of confirmation offered in the 1946 edition of the *Book of Worship*. This is precisely the understanding of confirmation that informs the material. In its discussion of Baptism, the student guide reaffirms infant Baptism as a sign that the children of believing parents are included in the household of God.[173] It then describes confirmation as follows:

> Later when this child becomes a young person or adult, he must make his own confession of his faith. At this later time he acknowledges before all the congregation what Christ has done for him, of which his baptism was a sign. His acceptance by Christ into his church at baptism is confirmed at this later time. The vows taken by parents when their child is baptized are "confirmed" by the young person or adult when he becomes a communicant member. . . . This is why we sometimes call the communicant's class a class preparing for confirmation of vows, or a confirmation class.[174]

Accordingly, the student book pays a minimal amount of attention to doctrinal material, spending seven of ten chapters on topics germane to the Christian's present involvement in the church. The material assumes that the class participant has been learning the Bible and church doctrine through the curriculum used in the church school.[175]

In 1971, the northern church made the decision to admit children to the Lord's Supper prior to confirmation and began to introduce commissioning language into its discussions of confirmation. As early as 1970, the planning guide for the denominational curriculum, *Christian Faith in Action, 7–10,* advocated the use of both confirmation and commissioning language.[176] Confirmation, it is argued, looks backward to an individual's Baptism and marks the responsible decision by which he or she "personally confirms what was earlier done for him."[177] Commissioning looks to the future and focuses on the process by which "one becomes a fully responsible member of the church."[178] It is a public act of commissioning to ministry, something that can happen many other times in a person's life.

This understanding of confirmation-commissioning was to inform the two major curricular pieces sponsored by the denomination prior to reunion of the church. These pieces represent the major avenue for entry of a *developmental* understanding of confirmation practice into the church. The first was *Context for Choice: A Confirmation-Commissioning Manual,* published in 1973.[179] David Ng, who later was to be the project director of the confirmation-commissioning material for the reunited church, was involved in the creation of this manual. It unabashedly acknowledged the state of flux the church currently was in on these issues and described five different models of confirmation currently being used in Presbyterian congregations.[180] Its clear preference, however, was for a confirmation-commissioning model that focused on the various social and educational

processes by which the children and youth of the church form a sense of Christian identity. This was explicitly portrayed as standing over against catechetical
and confessional approaches to confirmation: "This dynamic process is just the
opposite of much that passes for confirmation-commissioning. All too often it is
a cram course designed to enable the young people to parrot the correct answers
back to a questioning session. And if there is anything dynamic taking place, it is
the pressure to make the young person commit himself to Christ and the church
before he eludes us forever."[181]

The manual relied heavily on psychological understandings of adolescence for
the framework by which confirmation-commissioning is understood, devoting an
entire chapter to adolescent psychology. This is correlated with a description of
the Christian life in terms of the journey motif. As a stage of life involving search-
ing and questioning, adolescence is portrayed as best met by a confirmation
process that is participatory and nondidactic. Its purpose is not to teach the basic
elements of the faith or to allow an individual's profession of faith but to further
the process of Christian identity formation. The decisions formed during this stage
of life will be reexamined in future stages of the person's journey. Confirmation,
consequently, is not best viewed as a key moment in which the young person
claims the covenant into which he or she was baptized as an infant through an act
of personal confession and pledge of obedience or confesses the faith of the
church. It is one step on an unfolding journey of faith.

This *developmental* understanding of confirmation-commissioning was explicitly adopted by the most popular curriculum in the late seventies and eighties,
written by Mac and Anne Turnage: *Explorations into Faith: A Course for Youth
Preparing to Be Confirmed/Commissioned.*[182] The material was written for both
the southern and northern branches of the Presbyterian Church.[183] Although recognizing the diversity of purposes informing the church's understanding of this
class, it makes the confirmation-commissioning purpose normative: "In offering
a confirmation/commissioning class the church provides an opportunity for the
young person to explore the basic meanings of the Christian faith and to be commissioned to live out that faith in the world."[184] Statements such as the following
are representative of how this is construed by the Turnages:

> As youth move from childhood to adulthood, they move from unexamined faith
> that has been inherited to faith that is deliberately developed, or from no faith
> to some new commitments in faith. The church can use this movement as an op-
> portunity to strengthen and inform, to confirm and to commission these persons
> as they move along their journey into faith.[185]

> This course, therefore, becomes a part of the process by which the church rec-
> ognizes and nurtures the growth and the commitment of these persons.[186]

We see here a *developmental* model at work. Psychological understandings of
growth set the primary terms for the church's understanding of confirmation-commissioning. These are placed within a journey framework, which is used as the
dominant metaphor for the class. The teacher's role in each session is described

as that of a guide on a journey, and the participants are portrayed as deciding at the end of the program whether "to continue the journey" by being commissioned.[187] This dovetails quite nicely with the experiential educational methodology used throughout. The accent is on helping students discover meanings and on faith exploration.

The Reunited Church

A straight line runs from *Context for Choice* through *Explorations into Faith* to the present confirmation-commissioning material of the reunited church: *Journeys of Faith.* This is no accident, because David Ng, involved in the writing of *Context for Choice,* served as the director of the team writing the new material. The new curriculum includes a *Sessions Notebook* and several accompanying pamphlets. In the introductory pamphlet describing the nature of confirmation, two somewhat different understandings of confirmation appear. One describes the church as the agent of confirmation: "The church confirms and the church commissions. . . . In confirmation the community affirms the vows of commitment."[188] The other focuses on the individual's profession of faith, linking it closely with Baptism: "Using their knowledge and experience as a foundation, they need to decide for themselves to publicly affirm the vows taken on their behalf in baptism . . . "[189] It is the second of these that informs the *Sessions Notebook.* There, confirmation is defined as follows: "Confirmation: a personal affirmation of the vows made on behalf of persons by their parents or caregivers and the church; a personal profession of faith in Jesus Christ."[190] The difference is significant. Is it the church that is confirming the individual or the individual who is confirming his or her faith through an act of profession? Or is it both? Equally important in this program is the concept of commissioning. This concept is used with a great deal of precision and consistency throughout the material. It is clear that it is the church that commissions the participants, preparing them and sending them forth "to minister in the name of Christ, through the church and in the world."[191]

Perhaps more important to this program than either of these definitions is the journey motif. It is the single most important organizing principle for both the theology and educational process of the program. Theologically, the normative view of the Christian life assumed by the material is that of an unfolding journey. Confirmation-commissioning is portrayed as a significant step on this journey, but it is only one step. It pulls together earlier learnings and experiences and launches its participants into an ongoing life of growth and service. In terms of process, this leads the material to place an enormous emphasis on educational approaches supporting "discovery" and "exploration." Each person and each group is on a unique journey and can grasp the meaning of God and their calling to partnership with God in terms of the particular circumstances of their life situations. As the introductory pamphlet puts it: "Confirmation-commissioning relates to experiential exploration and personal discovery."[192]

Accordingly, the material in the *Sessions Notebook* offers a wide range of creative activities designed to facilitate the exploration and personal discoveries of its participants. Obviously, this can only be done if the program is organized in a manner that is highly sensitive to the interests, needs, and capacities of those who are involved. This sort of *interest-based* educational format goes all the way back to Moody's 1938 teacher's guide for the *Faith and Life* confirmation material, which reflected the influence of the religious education movement. *Journeys of Faith* continues to explicitly set this approach over against catechetical instruction. In the short, introductory pamphlet, only twenty pages long, this is done no less than four times:

> The church does not teach faith solely to ensure that young persons are properly indoctrinated and can talk accurately about faith.
>
> Confirmation-commissioning involves more than indoctrinating people with right information or testing them for proper practice.
>
> The work of confirmation-commissioning should not be visualized as filling containers that will hold or preserve a set of facts or truths.
>
> Their statements should be an expression of their own faith rather than an unreflective repetition of what they have been taught to say.[193]

These statements represent a caricature of catechetical instruction which, at its best, sought to enhance students' understanding of the catechism, allowing them to make an intelligent confession of the church's faith.

Moreover, the *Journeys* material also casts the element of personal profession and covenant ratification in terms of the journey motif as it emerged in the 1960s and 70s. Profession is viewed organically, as a process of growth and maturation. The material's brief discussion of the Holy Spirit, for example, describes it in organic terms: "Confirmation-commissioning is an opportunity to recognize the presence and power of the Spirit in maturing lives."[194] What is missing are elements of discontinuity and transformation, long a part of the *crisis/nurture* model of the Christian life. The permanent crisis in which all Christians stand, as those created for covenant relationship with God but violating that relationship through the worship and service of other gods, is not a dominant theme. Descriptions of the Christian life as a crisis, an existential leap, or a difficult struggle against the lure of sin are transmuted into the kinds of struggles and doubts that are age-appropriate, developmental tasks on an unfolding journey of faith.

Clearly, *Journeys of Faith* represents the culmination of trends present in confirmation-commissioning material since *Context for Choice* and the full use of a *development/nurture* model of the Christian life to structure a *developmental* understanding of the purpose and process of confirmation-commissioning. The dominance of developmentally oriented journey themes at the expense of the existential dimensions of the faith, the centrality of experience-centered education coupled with an undercurrent of hostility toward catechetical instruction, and the concern with individualization and contextualization to the exclusion of the internalization of knowledge and skills acquired through participation in common ecclesial practices are defining characteristics of this material. Missing are many of the most important elements of confirmation and admission to the Lord's Supper when construed as *professional* or *catechetical* practices.

To a large extent, the approach represented by *Journeys of Faith* stands in tension with the liturgical revisions found in the *Book of Common Worship* created when the UPCUSA and southern church reunited to form the Presbyterian Church of the United States of America (PCUSA). The antecedent denominations of the PCUSA began a process in 1980 by which a series of liturgical resources were written for trial use.[195] For our purposes, the most important of these was *Supplemental Liturgical Resource 2: Holy Baptism and Services for the Renewal of Baptism.*[196] This included the text of services for the reunited denomination, along with commentary on their meaning. With some minor modifications, the proposed services of this resource were incorporated into the *Book of Common Worship* published in 1993.[197]

The service of Baptism is deeply informed by the mainstream of ecumenical liturgical scholarship and practice.[198] As the *Book of Common Worship* puts it in its introductory comments: "We are beginning to recognize that our true unity begins at the baptismal font."[199] Especially important was the decision to follow those scholars arguing for a return to an integrated practice of initiation in which Baptism, confirmation, and Eucharist were part of a single act. As *SLR 2* puts it: "Thus Christian initiation has traditionally included three actions: washing with water, anointing with oil, and celebration of the Eucharist."[200] What had been broken apart in the West and kept intact in the East was to be restored in the baptismal service. Accordingly, *SLR 2* and the *Book of Common Worship* avoid either "confirmation" or "confirmation-commissioning," replacing them with a service titled "Reaffirmation of the Baptismal Covenant for Those Making a Public Profession of Faith." This is one of several repeatable rites by which individuals and congregations may reaffirm their baptismal covenant at significant turning points.[201] It also places in the baptismal service, immediately after the water-washing, liturgical actions traditionally associated with the bestowal of the Holy Spirit. Originally, of course, these were the precursor of confirmation as an independent rite.

The baptismal service is divided into six parts.[202] It begins with the *Presentation,* in which candidates are presented by a representative of the session. Scripture passages recalling God's promises in Baptism are read. Particularly important is the declaration that in Baptism God claims and seals us, freeing us from sin and death by uniting us with Jesus Christ in his death and resurrection and incorporating us into his body. Parents and sponsors promise to teach the faith to the one being baptized and to support him or her through prayer and example. This is followed by the *Renunciation and Affirmation.* In this part of the service, the ancient practice of inviting the baptismal candidates to turn away from sin and toward Christ in a series of brief questions and answers is used. This can be traced all the way back to *The Apostolic Tradition* of Hippolytus, the earliest extant baptismal liturgy. Covenant language is used to frame these interrogatories: "Through baptism we enter the covenant God has established. Within this covenant God gives us new life, guards us from evil, and nurtures us in love. In embracing that covenant, we choose whom we will serve by turning from evil and turning to Jesus Christ."[203]

This represents something of a departure from the Westminster tradition, in which the children of believers are viewed as members of the covenant of grace by birthright, not by the baptismal action itself.

Next comes the *Thanksgiving over Water,* in which key moments of salvation history are rehearsed, providing the context for the central action of the service: the water-washing. The minister "may" touch the water, implying no more than the symbolic import afforded the lifting of the chalice and bread during the prayer of thanksgiving in the Lord's Supper. This is followed by the *Act of Baptizing.* In the commentary of the *SLR 2,* ministers are encouraged to use enough water to represent dramatically what is taking place: a washing away of sin, immersion in the waters of chaos and death, and refreshment making new life possible.[204] It defends use of the traditional Trinitarian formula employing Father language as one of the essential elements of a valid Baptism and a mark of "the one baptism" that unites all Christians in one holy and catholic church.[205]

The water-washing is followed by the *Blessing,* which includes the laying on of hands in conjunction with prayer for the Holy Spirit, using either of two traditional prayers (the Defend Prayer or Sevenfold Gifts of the Spirit Prayer). This "may" be followed by the signing of the one who is being baptized, including the optional use of oil. The commentary of the *SLR 2* makes a strong connection between this portion of the service and the gift of the Holy Spirit, arguing that these traditional acts should be restored to their proper place in an integrated practice of initiation. It points to the richness and biblical foundations of laying on of hands and anointing, arguing that they, along "with the prayer and the washing, express the fullness of the biblical teaching about baptism."[206] The final portion of the service is the *Welcome.* This involves the congregation's acknowledgment of its responsibility to include those who are newly baptized into the ministry of the church, making it clear that they are full members of the church.

The basic pattern of the baptismal service is used in the services for the reaffirmation of the baptismal covenant. It combines both *professional* and *catechetical* purposes. For the reasons noted above, however, neither *SLR 2* nor *BCW* use the language of confirmation. Their argument is clear: What became confirmation in the West has now been restored to its rightful place in an integrated practice of initiation. The term "confirmation" is confusing and, perhaps, even irretrievably bankrupt. Using the rubric "reaffirmation of the baptismal covenant" instead of confirmation makes it clear that what is going on in a profession of faith is a claiming of an identity and covenant relationship that has been bestowed already in Baptism. The parallel structure of the services of reaffirmation and Baptism make this link unmistakably clear. Use of the rubric "reaffirmation" also points to the fact that a public profession of faith is only one of many moments in Christians' lives when they will reaffirm their baptismal covenant as individuals and as members of a congregation. Baptism entails a lifelong process of repentance and conversion.

Conclusion

This examination of the confirmation-commissioning curriculum and *Book of Common Worship* of the reunited Presbyterian Church has found it to be no more united in its understanding of this practice than it has been throughout this century. While denominational education material employs the language of confirmation-commissioning, first used in the northern church during the late 1960s and early 1970s, its liturgical standards self-consciously avoid the use of this term or that of confirmation. The differences go even deeper. *Journeys of Faith* represents the culmination of trends that have been unfolding for several decades. It draws on a *development/nurture* model of the Christian life to portray the practice of confirmation-commissioning in *developmental* terms. It takes very seriously the importance of tailoring the program to the needs and interests of those individuals who are participating in the program and portrays the exploration, discovery, and decisions made by the participants as a significant step on an unfolding journey of faith.

In contrast, the services of Baptism and reaffirmation of the baptismal covenant in the *Book of Common Worship* can be viewed as standing in continuity with the *catechetical* and *professional* purposes of confirmation/admission as found in both the *nurture/development* model of Old School Presbyterianism and the *crisis/nurture* model of New School Presbyterianism. This is not immediately apparent because the new services are deeply influenced by recent ecumenical scholarship and hark back to themes that emerged as early as the patristic period. Like the "churchly traditions" of Old School Presbyterianism, however, they continue the trend toward the use of common liturgical resources to order the life of the church. As we have seen, the interest in reclaiming the pre-Puritan, Reformed liturgical heritage began as early as the middle of the nineteenth century in American Presbyterianism, culminating in the first *Book of Common Worship* in 1906. The current efforts to broaden the scope of ecumenical scholarship on which Presbyterian worship is based can be viewed as a continuation of this trend, even if debate on how far the church legitimately can go in this direction is likely to continue.

What is at stake is an affirmation of the importance of social and objective dimensions of the Christian life. Participation in patterns of worship form the inner life of Christians along certain lines. Marker events such as Baptism and profession of faith, marriage, and burial of the dead provide corporate patterns that shape the thinking, feeling, and acting of the members of the church. The *nurture* provided by these patterns influences the *development* of its members. In the following chapter, I will argue that the *Book of Common Worship* does not make a compelling case for its elimination of confirmation language, and I will try to provide a theological rationale for its reincorporation into Presbyterian liturgical standards. In no way, however, does this critique extend to the role of corporate, ecclesial patterns in shaping the life of the individual. The older Reformation paradigm of infant Baptism, catechetical instruction, and admission to the Lord's Supper has broken apart. What new corporate patterns will take its place? The *Book of Common Worship* makes an enormous contribution in helping us begin to discern the common patterns that have begun to emerge on a broad, ecumenical basis.

It is consistent with this move, I believe, to attend equally to the internalization of the basic beliefs of the church and narrative patterns of scripture, shaping the language and interpretive schemas of contemporary Presbyterians. The danger of a *developmental* understanding of confirmation-commissioning practice along the lines of *Journeys of Faith* is neglect of the important role of corporate life. By so focusing on the individual and on congregational contextualization, it attends insufficiently to the church's role in providing its members with a common theological language in terms of which they can participate in its work and pursue their vocations in the world. In contrast, the use of the Apostles' Creed in the baptismal and reaffirmation services of the *Book of Common Worship* seems to point in the direction of a kind of catechetical instruction that helps persons understand the traditional catechetical pieces (Apostles' Creed, Lord's Prayer, Ten Commandments), uniting us as a church and with other denominations.

Odd as it might seem at first glance, the *Book of Common Worship* also can be seen as including *professional* elements consistent with a *crisis/nurture* model of the Christian life. As we have seen, the personal elements of profession and covenant ratification have long been a part of the Reformed understanding of admission to the Lord's Supper. As early as Bucer and Baxter, this element was distinguished from the act of confessing the church's faith on the basis of studying the catechism. It can be discerned in the renunciation and profession of the baptismal and reaffirmation services of the *Book of Common Worship,* where each individual is addressed and asked to make a choice: Will you "turn from the ways of sin and renounce evil" and toward "Jesus Christ and accept him as your Lord and Savior?" The covenant language surrounding this act links it to long-standing theological themes in the Reformed tradition and to the covenant-making language of the Bible itself: "Choose this day whom you will serve" (Judg. 24:14). I believe this *professional* element should be clarified and made more prominent in a comprehensive confirmation practice. It is to the projection of such a practice that we turn in Part 3.

Part 3

A Contemporary Proposal for Confirmation

Introduction to Part 3

7. A Theology of Confirmation

Confirmation: A Contemporary Theological Proposal
Confirmation: Choosing to Become Who You Already Are
Confirmation and the Sacraments
Confirmation and Baptism
Confirmation and the Lord's Supper
Confirmation and Catechetical Instruction

8. A Fitting Practice of Confirmation

Confirmation in Congregational Context
Enrollment
Spiritual Mentoring
Vocational Discernment
Catechetical Instruction
The Confirmation Service
After Confirmation

Introduction to Part 3

As we turn to the final part of this book, it may be helpful to begin by tracing the various strands of the story that has been told to this point. Together they constitute different parts of an integrated argument that lies behind the constructive proposal offered in the chapters that remain. While this proposal is addressed most directly to the American Presbyterian Church, it also seeks to engage a broader ecumenical conversation. This ecumenical thrust is an inherent part of Reformed theology, which, at its best, has sought to represent Christianity in its catholicity. A spirit of openness is balanced by a commitment to speak the truth in love.[1] A recent study document of the Presbyterian Church aptly describes Presbyterian churches at their best: "They have not claimed to be the only true church, with a monopoly on Christian faith and life, but have always been open to learn from other churches and traditions and eager to participate in conversations with them that could lead to mutual correction and reconciliation."[2]

It is in this twofold ecumenical spirit of openness and honest exchange that the story of confirmation in the church has been told. The past and present history of this practice is *our* past and present, not merely that of another church that can be easily dismissed. How do the various parts of this story hang together? What is the larger argument that is being made?

We began by considering what might be called the *modernization argument* in the first part of this book. There the claim was made that the contemporary practice of confirmation is in serious difficulty. Empirical data from the Presbyterian, Episcopal, and Lutheran churches was used to describe the widespread departure of youth from the church during late adolescence and young adulthood. Confirmation no longer seems to have a lasting impact on its participants. While programs internal to the life of the contemporary church have something to do with this, in large part the inadequacy of these programs is due to their inability to address certain conditions that have been created by the processes of modernization. Features of modernity such as institutional and cultural differentiation, rapid social change, and technological innovation have made it very difficult for the older practice of catechetical instruction and confirmation to work. Of special importance in this regard has been the advent of adolescence, a whole new stage in the life cycle. This stage of life mediates the individualizing features of contemporary social life and the psychological demands of individuation that accompany the work of identity formation. By locating confirmation prior to the psychosocial work of adolescence, contemporary churches, for all intents and purposes, define it as an aspect of childhood or early adolescent faith and not as an act of Christian maturity. Not only has this proven to be ineffective at a practical level, but it is questionable theologically as well.

This assessment of the current state of confirmation in Protestant churches opened out to the *historical* argument of Part 2 of the book. There we explored the history of confirmation, arguing that its origin is not to be found in the New Testament church but much later, in the liturgical elaboration of the baptismal service, which took place between the second and fifth centuries. During this period, many parts of the church began to include liturgical acts such as consignation, laying on of hands, and anointing after the water-washing that served as the symbolic center of the Holy Spirit's participation in the Christian life. This liturgical moment was part of a practice that primarily was *catechumenal* in nature, a process of formation in which teaching, worship, and spiritual guidance worked in concert to create new habits of thought, feeling, and action in those being initiated into the church.

Gradually, for a variety of reasons, the various postbaptismal acts that developed during this period were separated from the water-washing, and by the time of the high Middle Ages were officially recognized as having a *sacramental* purpose. Aquinas and other medieval theologians portrayed this Sacrament as communicating the grace to take up the struggle of the mature Christian life, withstanding temptation and fighting evil. The Reformers were not convinced by this understanding of confirmation, viewing its medieval theology and practice as detracting from the centrality of Baptism. In its place, they constructed a new practice that attempted to integrate the theological meaning of infant Baptism, catechetical instruction, and admission to the Lord's Supper. Some denominations called the service standing at the end of catechetical instruction and the beginning of participation in the Lord's Supper, confirmation. Others did not. In either case, it was viewed as the culmination of a *catechetical* educational program enabling individuals to make a confession of the church's faith on the basis of their study of the catechism. Emerging during this same period was a *professional* understanding of confirmation, focusing on the individual's ratification of the baptismal covenant through a personal profession of faith and pledge of obedience. Although this approach took exaggerated form among the continental pietists and certain wings of Puritanism, it was located by persons like Bucer and Baxter in a covenantal framework balancing personal profession or pledging and congregational nurture and care.

In the American Presbyterian Church, *catechetical* and *professional* understandings of confirmation/admission have coexisted. At times, they have come together to form a practice combining the elements of communal nurture and teaching with highly personal dimensions of spiritual struggle and growth. At its best, catechetical instruction offered in the home, school, and congregation allowed young Presbyterians to confess the faith of the church on the basis of the catechism and, simultaneously, to ratify personally the covenant of grace signified by their Baptism as infants.

As the story of confirmation in the Presbyterian Church moved closer to the present, it began to speak of increased confusion and change. The inherited paradigm of infant Baptism, catechetical instruction, and admission to the Lord's Supper in which *catechetical* and *professional* understandings of confirmation cohered began to break up. Catechetical instruction was the first piece to decline under the impact of the Sunday school movement in the nineteenth century and the religious education movement in the twentieth century. The decision of the church to admit children to the Lord's Table prior to catechetical instruction or confirmation, in the 1970s and 1980s, represented the final blow. Gradually, a confirmation practice came to take the place of the older catechetical practice. Initially, it held in tension traditional professional and catechetical goods. Gradually, a *developmental* understanding of confirmation-commissioning began to appear, portraying this practice as a special moment of faith exploration and discovery on an unfolding journey.

At this point, the *historical* and *modernization* arguments began to overlap. Just as the pressures of modernization became greatest, the inherited theology and practice of confirmation became less viable. The Presbyterian Church, along with other denominations, has been in a period of confusion about this practice for much of this century. Sometimes it has included the rubric "confirmation" in liturgical standards and educational material and other times, it has eliminated it or called it something new (that is, confirmation-commissioning, commissioning, or reaffirmation of the baptismal covenant). Confused within and under pressure from the outside, the church was unable to offer a confirmation practice that communicated a compelling vision of the Christian life to its younger members.

Has a new paradigm begun to take the place of the old? The answer to this question started to emerge in our discussion of recent liturgical developments. This can be called the *ecumenical* argument. To a large extent, we must pull the various strands of this line of thinking together and clarify the claims being made. In all four denominations examined, important changes have taken place in recent years in their services of Baptism and confirmation. In large measure, these changes were driven by contemporary liturgical scholarship and ecumenical discussion. All four denominations have begun to reach back to patterns of initiation found in the first centuries of the church's life. A remarkable degree of consensus can be seen in the baptismal services of these denominations, outlined in the following chart. While these elements do not appear in identical order in each service, they are present at some point in the services for adult and infant Baptism in all four denominations (see table 3).

This consensus has important implications for the practice of confirmation. All four denominations have made it clear that Baptism is the one Sacrament of initiation. Membership does not come later; nor is the Holy Spirit conferred at a later point. Accordingly, all four attempt to include in the baptismal service liturgical acts in conjunction with prayer for the Holy Spirit to make it absolutely clear that confirmation cannot be identified with medieval developments in which the acts of episcopal anointing, laying on of hands, or consignation became an independent sacrament of the church. All four denominations, however, are equally clear that some further "confirming" act must be offered by those baptized as infants. Accordingly, the Lutheran, Episcopal, and United Methodist denominations have special confirmation services. Although the Presbyterian Church currently does not use the term "confirmation" for its equivalent service, it too has a special service of profession.

In all four denominations, an extremely close relationship now exists between the baptismal service and the confirmation or profession service. The basic structure of the baptismal service is repeated. Those baptized as infants affirm the bap-

---

TABLE 3. ADULT AND INFANT BAPTISMAL RITES

Presentation of Candidates
[Promise by Parents/Sponsors to Nurture and Teach Infants]*
The Baptismal Covenant
  Renunciation
  Profession
  Common Confession Using the Apostles' Creed in Interrogatory Form
Thanksgiving over the Water
Water-washing
Postbaptismal Acts
  Laying on of hands and Prayer for the Holy Spirit (Episcopal service can be
    interpreted as including only the latter)
  Consignation in Conjunction with Sealing Language or Prayer for the Holy
    Spirit (optional in Presbyterian Church; not present in United Methodist
    Church)
Welcome of New Members
Eucharist

Brackets [ ] indicate infant Baptism only.

tismal covenant in which they have long participated. This has both *catechetical* and *professional* dimensions. On the one hand, confession of the church's faith is signified by common rendering of the Apostles' Creed in interrogatory form. On the other hand, personal ratification of the covenant is signified by the renunciation and profession. Moreover, all four denominations now place their confirmation or profession services in the context of several repeatable services in which persons can reaffirm the baptismal covenant over the course of their lives. In a sense, they pick up on the journey element of the *developmental* understanding of confirmation.

This remarkable degree of consensus does not eliminate residual ambiguities and differences, however. One influential line of thinking argues that confirmation has now been restored to its original location in the baptismal service and should no longer be used to refer to the mature affirmation of the baptismal covenant taking place when youth reach the age of discretion. From this perspective, the ecumenical pattern of Baptism described above is viewed as reuniting three distinguishable moments of the ancient rite of initiation: Baptism, confirmation, and Eucharist. The Presbyterian Church, *Supplemental Liturgical Resource 2,* argued along these lines, as did the United Methodist's recent study document, *By Water and Spirit* and Pfatteicher's *Commentary on the Lutheran Book of Worship.*

There are others, myself included, who would argue somewhat differently.[3] The current practice of Lutherans, Episcopalians, and United Methodists continues to view confirmation as something other than the postbaptismal acts now restored to the baptismal service. It is represented in the special service by which the mature individual confesses the faith of the church and personally ratifies the baptismal covenant. My criticisms, at this point, are directed against my own tradition, but they have ecumenical implications as well.

It is anachronistic to argue, as *Supplemental Liturgical Resource 2* does, that confirmation can be identified as a clearly distinguishable moment in the liturgies of the early church.[4] This is problematic on both historical and theological grounds. In Chapter 3 of this book, historical investigation revealed a wide variety of baptismal practices throughout the second through the fifth century. Some of these included postbaptismal laying on of hands, consignation, or anointing, and some did not. It is an idealization and an over-generalization of relatively sparse sources to claim the authority of a uniform practice in which confirmation existed as a clearly defined moment in initiation.

Arguing along these lines leads the authors of *SLR 2* to lose contact with the *catechetical* and *professional* understandings of confirmation emerging out of the Reformation. Although there is some ambiguity across denominational lines, the Presbyterian Church would do well to adopt the term "confirmation" to refer to this rite, along with the practice of which it is a part. Not only do the Episcopal, United Methodist, and Lutheran churches currently use this term, but the Presbyterian Church itself has employed it in its liturgical standards and educational material at various points since the middle of the nineteenth century. In many ways, use of this rubric would not represent a major change in the *Book of*

Common Worship, for it already includes a special service for reaffirmation of the baptismal covenant for "Those Making a Public Profession of Faith." The appropriate term for this act is *confirmation,* understood in both catechetical and professional senses. Indeed, both elements are pointed to already in the common pattern of Baptism and reaffirmation emerging across ecumenical lines.

At this point, the various arguments of this book begin to converge. The need for an accentuation of the act of covenant ratification is especially pressing in light of modernization and the emergence of adolescence as a new stage in the life cycle. There are no compelling historical reasons not to claim the term *confirmation* to describe this practice and to redefine it along appropriate theological lines. This has been done since the time of Bucer and Baxter and has received new attention over the course of this century. The constructive proposal offered in the final chapters of this book is an attempt to develop a contemporary theology and practice of confirmation suitable to American Protestantism today. Although directed to the Presbyterian Church, it has been deeply informed by conversation with other denominational traditions. Its perspective is decidedly Reformed, but its intent is deeply ecumenical.

7

A Theology of Confirmation

In this chapter we will argue that the contemporary practice of confirmation should focus on both the individual's confession of the church's faith and an act of covenant ratification by which he or she personally professes the faith and pledges obedience to the Triune God. This understanding of confirmation stands in continuity with the way this practice has been understood since the Reformation and has been developed in the American Presbyterian tradition. It harks back to Calvin's emphasis on the individual's internalization of the beliefs of the church, allowing her or him to confess to the faith of the church in an intelligent manner. But it also includes Bucer's accent on the personal character of confirmation. Confirmation is a personal act of covenant ratification involving heartfelt profession and pledging. Both of these elements have made their way into the American Presbyterian tradition. *Nurture/development* models of the Christian life, found in Old School Presbyterianism, have long viewed admission to the Lord's Supper as the individual's confession of the church's faith. *Crisis/nurture* models have placed the accent on the individual's personal act of covenant ratification. Over the years, these elements comingled in Presbyterian services of admission and confirmation.

Confirmation: A Contemporary Theological Proposal

The proposal offered in this chapter thus attempts to maintain both *catechetical* and *professional* elements in its depiction of the meaning of confirmation. It does so, however, in a new context. The older Reformation paradigm of infant Baptism, catechetical instruction, and admission to the Lord's Supper is no longer in place. Although an ecumenical consensus has begun to emerge about the shape of Baptism in recent years, this has not yet resulted in a common pattern of confirmation practice across denominational lines. As yet, only the bare outline of a new paradigm can be discerned, with many areas still in need of discussion and debate.

In the emerging paradigm, infant Baptism continues to be the normative practice for the children of church members, although there is some debate of this point among those influenced by Barth, on the one hand, and the Rites of the Christian Initiation of Adults, on the other. The practice of mainline Protestantism and the official documents of the churches examined in this book overwhelmingly support the continuing normativity of infant Baptism for the children of believers.[1] This, in itself, is not new. What is new is the consensus about what this means. Baptism not only entails nurture and instruction by the congregation but, as the moment of full sacramental initiation, admits children to the Lord's Supper. Some denominations continue to wait until children are old enough to understand what they are doing and have received elementary instruction in the sacraments. No rite or act of admission coming after Baptism, however, confers this right. It comes with Baptism itself. This means two things in the emerging paradigm. First, most children already will have participated in the Lord's Supper for a long time prior to confirmation. Second, confirmation now represents the marker event by which those baptized as infants and participating in the Lord's Supper as children can claim the covenant in which they already participate. The implications of these things for confirmation have not always been recognized.

The second, perhaps, is more obvious. The older logic informing Reformed practice that linked the individual's confession of the church's faith and personal ratification of the covenant to admission to the Lord's Supper has broken apart. The church is in need of a clear liturgical and educational practice that will mark the individual's corporate confession and personal claiming of the covenant. This practice should be confirmation. This is true, not only for Presbyterian churches, but Episcopal, United Methodist, and Lutheran churches as well. The advent of adolescence, the disestablishment of the Protestant church in an increasingly pluralistic culture, and the high mobility of Americans make it imperative that every baptized and communed child of the church be given the opportunity to make a clear profession of faith and pledge of obedience. In the emerging paradigm, the singular importance of confirmation should be held up, not dissolved into one more repeatable rite. In its irrepeatability, confirmation reflects the nature of Baptism, something explored below.

Equally important, however, is the relation of confirmation to the Lord's Supper. This has not received a great deal of attention in the recent ecumenical discussion, even though participation of children in this Sacrament now takes place prior to confirmation. What are the implications of this shift for our understanding of confirmation? Does confirmation not only take up and reflect Baptism but also the Lord's Supper? I believe it does. It is here that the open-ended nature of confirmation becomes most apparent. Baptism is not repeated; the Lord's Supper is. Confirmation is a distinctive moment on an unfolding journey. Central to the proposal offered here, then, is attention to confirmation's relationship to both Sacraments of the church. In the emerging paradigm, it is not enough to attend to its relationship to Baptism alone, for those who are confirmed have long participated in the Lord's Supper.

A final issue, also, must be addressed. In the emerging paradigm, what is the relationship of confirmation to catechetical instruction or confirmation education? In the old paradigm, admission and confirmation represented the culmination of catechetical instruction. With the decline of this instruction, confirmation education programs have taken its place. Are these adequate? What should such education cover? When should it be offered? Does an age-related program do justice to the free and personal nature of covenant ratification that confirmation should represent? These questions will be addressed briefly in the final part of this chapter and given fuller attention in the one that follows.

Confirmation: Choosing to Become Who
You Already Are

Throughout this chapter, a covenantal interpretation of confirmation will be developed, going back to the covenantal interpretation of Baptism and the Lord's Supper offered by many of the early Reformers, which was developed in the theology of the English Puritans and Reformed Scotch-Irish. In fundamental ways, however, the understanding of the covenant developed here has been influenced by Karl Barth. Here I move away from an attempt to identify an emerging ecumenical consensus and bring a voice that is distinctly Reformed to the conversation. Like Thomas Aquinas, Barth has been relatively neglected by the generations that have immediately followed him. Probably Barth's theology (again, like that of Aquinas) will receive the kind of sustained attention it deserves in the next century.[2] Barth remains the greatest Protestant theologian of this era. In my view, the primary failing of his theology was not dogmatic but an inability to generate the kind of practical theology necessary to reform the modern church along the lines he envisioned. Although critical of Barth at points, the present proposal represents an attempt to build on his insights, constructing a contemporary practical theology of confirmation.

No modern theologian has explored more fully and brilliantly the covenantal dimensions of the Christian message than Karl Barth. It is somewhat ironic then that few modern theologians have been more critical than Barth of the Christian tradition's understanding of the sacraments, including the covenantal interpretation of the Reformers. Whereas the broad contours of Barth's understanding of the covenant are employed throughout this chapter, his understanding of the sacraments is explicitly rejected.[3] Broadly speaking, his position is Zwinglian; the one offered here is Calvinist and seeks to maintain continuity with the Reformed confessional tradition.[4]

Briefly put, Barth viewed Jesus Christ as the one Sacrament of God, leading him to reject the ascription of sacramental status to Baptism and the Lord's Supper.[5] If the term "sacrament" refers to the mystery of God's coming to humanity, he argued, then it should be understood to point first to the history of Jesus Christ: Emmanuel, God-with-us. Even individuals' appropriation of this history must point to God's action in the work of the Holy Spirit, what Barth calls their "baptism in the Spirit."[6] As he puts it: "Baptism with the Spirit is effective, causative, even creative action on man and in man. . . . Here if anywhere, one might speak of a sacramental happening in the current sense of the term."[7] Baptism with water, in contrast, is not to be closely identified with God's action. It represents *human action* in response to God's prior activity. It is the first step of obedience by which a person says yes to God.[8] As Barth puts it, referring here to water baptism: "It is not itself . . . the bearer, means, or instrument of grace."[9]

In this statement, Barth is explicitly defining his position over against that of

Calvin, who described the sacraments as means of grace, a position taken up by many of the major Reformed confessions.[10] Calvin's position does indeed stand in sharp contrast to the more Zwinglian perspective of Barth.[11] When Calvin referred to the sacraments as means of grace, he had three things in mind: (1) the sacraments were explicitly instituted by Christ; (2) they are visible forms of the Word, serving as signs of God's covenant of grace; and (3) the Holy Spirit uses them as instruments by which to effect union with Christ, generating and strengthening the faith of individuals.

Calvin developed his understanding of the sacraments as means of grace in explicit opposition to Zwingli's position, and recalling his differences with Zwingli can help show what is at stake in my acceptance of Calvin's position instead of Barth's.[12] For Zwingli, the sacraments were memorials of Christ's action and means of making a public profession of allegiance to Christ. They were, first and foremost, *human actions* and were to be sharply distinguished from the inner work of the Spirit. In contrast, Calvin argued that the sacraments, as means of grace, *cause and communicate* that which they signify.[13] Although they must be clearly distinguished from the free activity of God in Christ and the continuing work of the Holy Spirit, they stand in a special relation to these realities. They have been established by Christ to stand alongside the proclamation of the Word as means of divine self-communication.[14] They are used by the Holy Spirit to unite the elect with Christ and to bestow on them the benefits of salvation. Only in a very secondary and derivative sense do they also function as human acts of profession.[15]

In the constructive proposal developed in this chapter, Calvin's understanding of the sacraments as means of grace is retained. It is placed in a somewhat different theological framework than Calvin offered, however. Indeed, the broader contours of Barth's theology of the covenant of grace is used to redefine Calvin's understanding of the sacraments' content and instrumentality. Of special importance in this regard is Barth's reinterpretation of Calvin's doctrine of election. While this will be discussed in greater detail below, enough can be said at this point to indicate how this influences the understanding of the sacraments developed here.

Although the doctrine of election always lurked in the background of Calvin's discussion of the sacraments, it did not come to the fore in his explication of their theological content. Why? Because election remained a "terrible doctrine" for Calvin, an affirmation of God's unknowable determination of salvation and damnation in eternity. In contrast, Barth reinterpreted election as an affirmation of God's decision to be for humanity in Christ in eternity. It became the first step in the history of God's covenant love, a history continued in creation and reconciliation and consummated in the cosmic renewal of the world, taking place when Christ returns. When viewed along these lines, election becomes part of the gospel witness of Baptism and the Lord's Supper. It is a key aspect of their content.

Perhaps even more important, Barth's reinterpretation of this doctrine opens up a new way of thinking about the instrumentality of the sacraments as means of grace. Here, of course, we must travel in a direction somewhat different than did Barth himself. The sacraments are viewed as signs by which God communicates to persons who they already are in Christ. What does this mean?

It means the sacraments point beyond themselves to the divine history in which the covenant of grace is established and fulfilled in Christ. In his reinterpretation of the doctrine of election, Barth repeatedly emphasizes that all persons are elected in eternity to covenant fellowship in and through Christ. Christ's history is representative history. It is undertaken on humanity's behalf and in its stead. This strongly Christocentric way of construing humanity goes beyond the doctrine of election and embraces every aspect of Barth's thought. All persons also are represented in Christ's work of reconciliation and his redemption from death. Christ is the true covenant partner who responds in faith and obedience to the covenant love characterizing God's relationship with humanity.

In Baptism and the Lord's Supper, this representative history is re-presented in a manner that places the participants squarely within it. It is no longer an abstract "we" or "they" who are represented in this history but a concrete "you." You, who are being baptized now, you were there with Christ when John baptized him and when he was baptized unto death. You, who are now eating the bread and drinking the wine, you were there when he reinterpreted the Passover meal on the night of his betrayal and when his body was broken and his blood was shed.

This is more than an act of human recollection. It is a divine declaration. God is declaring to this concrete infant or that particular adult: "This is who you are already in Christ." It is a declaration that constitutes their very identity, marking the transition from their participation in Christ's history as a member of humanity to participation as a concrete individual and member of the covenant community. Henceforth, the unfolding course of their lives in all their concreteness is lived under the signs of Baptism and Eucharist. They have been washed and fed. These are indelible marks on their history. They may resist them at a later point or even misunderstand them. They may fail to heed the claims they make. But no inadequacy of human response can take away the reality of the declaration that has occurred and continues to occur as long as they partake of the means of grace. Their history in all its concreteness has been set within the history of God's covenanting activity in Christ. Who they are *in principle,* they are on their way to becoming *in fact.*

In this understanding of the instrumentality of the sacraments, the accent falls on the divine actor. It is God's past and present covenanting activity that is primary. The sacraments, as such, are means of grace, instruments used by God to communicate and conjoin the history of God's electing, reconciling, and redeeming work in Christ to the unfolding history of particular individuals and communities. What happens to the element of human response, so central to Zwingli's and Barth's understandings of the sacraments? Following Calvin, it is placed in an important, but secondary, position. This role is evident in adult Baptism and the Lord's Supper, where elements of understanding, self-examination, and profession are important. Even there, however, they remain subordinate to God's past and present action communicated through the sacramental signs. *In confirmation, however, the element of human response is primary,* placed squarely on individuals' self-conscious and free acceptance of the covenantal realities in which they already participate.

The need for this sort of free, human response has long been recognized in the Christian tradition. In the various streams emerging out of the center of the Reformation, however, it has never been allowed to dominate the Christian life. Human freedom and obligation are always viewed within the broader context of the covenanting activity initiated and sustained by God. For this reason, confirmation is described in a manner that subordinates it to the sacraments, which in turn depend on the Word. Confirmation, as a free, human response, takes up and gives answer to God's covenanting activity of which the sacraments are effective signs. In both its theological content and its form, it is viewed here as derived from Baptism and the Lord's Supper. This is not to deny the significance of the freedom confirmation represents. It is to put it in its proper place. Indeed, the present proposal accentuates this freedom by altering the way confirmation and catechetical instruction typically have been linked since the Reformation, taking up Bucer's proposal.

In the early stages of the Reformation, there was a widespread tendency to link closely personal profession of faith and the appropriation of the church's catechism. The heart of catechetical instruction was the individual's cognitive mastery of the traditional catechetical pieces (the Lord's Prayer, Apostles' Creed, and Ten Commandments), ordered theologically and divided into a question and answer format. Personal profession of the faith was viewed primarily as a matter of internalizing the catechism. Contrary to later caricatures of this process, the best catechetical instruction sought to ensure that its participants went beyond mere recitation of the catechism and both understood and personally believed the doctrines it articulated. It enabled the individual to make an intelligent confession of the church's faith.

Even when explicit efforts were made to include or even accentuate the individual's ratification of the covenant through an act of personal profession and pledging, the close link between catechetical instruction and confirmation and admission tended to diminish the personal element. Entry upon reaching a certain age into a special catechetical class taught by the pastor linked the educational process so closely to the confirmation service that it was very difficult for young participants to gain a sense that their confession was both an act of identification with the church's faith and a personal ratification of the covenant. Theologically, both elements have long been affirmed in American Presbyterianism, but the latter has been very difficult to maintain. This pattern has continued until the present, long after the common catechism was replaced by denominational confirmation curriculums based on modern educational theory. Despite frequent disclaimers, confirmation still remains primarily the culmination of an educational program and not a freely given personal profession of faith and pledge of obedience. Unfortunately, recent confirmation material pays so little attention to the church's basic beliefs that it is even difficult for confirmands to make an intelligent confession of the church's faith.

The massive failure of mainline Protestantism to communicate a compelling vision of the Christian life to its young people, manifested in their exodus from the church during late adolescence and young adulthood, would be enough in its own right to raise serious questions about the efficacy of this understanding of confirmation today. Even more important, however, are theological issues about confirmation's meaning that remain unresolved. It is ironic that Karl Barth, who rejected confirmation along with infant Baptism, saw so clearly what is at stake in the continued definition of personal profession in terms of participation in a confirmation educational program:

> The familiar modern interpretations of confirmation which expound it as simply the climax of ecclesiastical instruction, admission to the Lord's Supper, or a kind of dedication of Christian youth, obscure its content. What if even in confirmation . . . there is again no express desire or confession on the part of the supposedly Christian young person. . . . What is the point of a subsequent act of confession and dedication when its freedom and sincerity are compromised already by the fact that it is not spontaneously desired by those who perform it but automatically falls due at a specific age or stage, when . . . it is simply the fulfillment of a general custom.[16]

Barth's point is on target, whether the confirmation program represents the best of catechetical instruction or creative modern education. As long as confirmation is the culmination of an educational program that youth enter upon reaching a certain age, the personal elements of profession and pledging will be extremely difficult to maintain. In the present proposal, they are separated, something that is taken up in the last part of this chapter. This does not mean that an equal concern for understanding the basic beliefs of the church has been abandoned. The present proposal calls for a return to catechetical instruction based on the ecumenical center of church confession: the Apostles' Creed, Lord's Prayer, and Ten Commandments. This affords confirmands the opportunity to confess the church's faith, a faith that crosses denominational boundaries and differences. Such instruction, however, is not offered in a way that prestructures the individual's choice to be confirmed. Rather, it deepens a process that has been entered already.

Confirmation and the Sacraments

In the classical Reformation pattern, confirmation or catechetical instruction was located *between* Baptism and First Communion. The present proposal breaks with this pattern. It argues that there are good theological reasons for allowing participation in the Lord's Supper *before* confirmation, a practice already established in contemporary Protestantism. The reasons for this shift in the location of First Communion will be taken up in greater detail below in our discussion of the relationship of confirmation to the Lord's Supper. There is a sense, however, in which the present proposal continues to hold to the theological intent of the older Reformation pattern. It locates confirmation between Baptism and the Lord's Supper theologically, if not in practice. What does this mean?

Between Baptism and the Lord's Supper

In the New Testament, Baptism and the Lord's Supper derive their meaning from identical gospel content with strong covenantal overtones.[17] Both Sacraments give witness to the saving significance of Jesus' death in reconciling a sinful humanity to God, to the future work of redemption, to the Spirit's anticipatory actualization of that redemption in the present, and to God's preexistent desire for a relationship of covenant love with creation. In terms of the theological content of Baptism and the Lord's Supper, there is virtual identity. Their central themes are the essential elements of the gospel. In terms of the role each Sacrament plays in communicating these theological themes, however, there are important differences.

Fundamentally, the temporal nature of each Sacrament is different. Baptism is a once-and-for-all event; the Lord's Supper is cyclical. Baptism marks initiation into the covenant community and the application of the sign of the covenant of grace to the life of a concrete individual. The Lord's Supper is a service of covenant renewal, repeatedly bringing individuals and the community before God to renew their covenant bonds. Jürgen Moltmann has captured well the different temporal orientation of each sacrament: "Just as baptism is the eschatological *sign of starting out,* valid once and for all, so the regular and constant fellowship at the Table of the Lord is the eschatological *sign of being on the way.*"[18] Confirmation takes up the meaning of both of these Sacraments. Theologically it is located between them.

On the one hand, the temporal singularity of Baptism is reflected in the temporal singularity of confirmation. Confirmation is that unique and irrepeatable moment in a Christian's life when he or she stands before the church and the world to make a personal profession of faith and pledge of obedience, taking up and self-consciously affirming the vows of the baptismal covenant. On the other hand, confirmation also takes up and reflects the cyclical nature of the Lord's Supper. Confirmation is not the moment when a person is "saved," for this is something that God has accomplished already in Christ. It is one of many times when a person will hear God's Word anew and respond in trust and obedience.

Thus, theologically, confirmation is located between Baptism and the Lord's Supper. It marks both a turning point in an individual's life and her or his participation in an ongoing process of repentance and conversion. If either side of this tension is lost, confirmation loses its character as a Reformed evangelical rite. If its orientation to Baptism is lost, it becomes little more than a rite of passage, the quasi-automatic transition to a new status bestowed by the community when a person reaches a certain age. If its orientation to the Lord's Supper is lost, it becomes little more than a form of decisional regeneration, closer to the Anabaptist tradition than evangelical Reformed theology. Confirmation must remain situated between Baptism and the Lord's Supper theologically, if not in practice. In the discussion of each sacrament that follows, we will unpack what is at stake in maintaining this perspective.

Confirmation and Baptism

Baptism marks the initiation of a person into the covenant community. It is an unrepeatable sign of his or her participation in the covenant of grace by which the church is established. The unrepeatability of Baptism, however, does not rule out the need for an additional, corresponding response, a yes or amen at God's declaration in Baptism.

The need for this kind of response to the act of baptismal initiation has been recognized in a variety of ways in the Christian tradition. Historically, it has been evident in the vows made during infant Baptism. Whether these are viewed as made on the infant's behalf, as in the Lutheran and Episcopal traditions, or focus exclusively on the parents' and congregation's responsibilities in providing Christian education for the infant, as in the Reformed tradition, it is clear that the person being baptized is expected to take up and affirm the vows of the covenant at a later point in life. Traditionally, this has been seen as taking place at the "age of discretion," the period of life when an individual has developed the capacities to weigh alternatives rationally and to exercise moral agency.

This way of framing the relationship of confirmation and Baptism obviously has the situation of persons baptized as infants in mind. Does this mean that infant Baptism should be normative for the church? The answer is yes and no! Both infant and adult Baptism have equally legitimate roles in the church. They address two different situations, however. Adult Baptism addresses the situation of persons raised outside of the church or marginally related to it who are converted later in life. The church can never abandon this because that would be tantamount to abandoning its calling as a missionary community with the task of proclaiming the gospel to an unbelieving world. Adult conversion and Baptism should be a normal occurrence in the church, an outgrowth of its evangelical witness.

Infant Baptism, in contrast, addresses the situation of the children of believers. Although the baptism of children is neither expressly commanded nor forbidden in the New Testament, there is enough evidence to indicate that it probably was practiced in the New Testament church.[19] Jesus' attitude of acceptance toward children (cf. Matt. 19:13–15), the widespread practice of household baptism (Acts 10:44–48, 16:14–15, 33, and 1 Cor. 1:16), Paul's comments about the sanctity of the children of believers (1 Cor. 7:14), various epistles' admonitions to children that seem to address them as if they were already members of the Christian community (Eph. 6:1; Col. 3:20; 1 John 2:13–14), the precedence of circumcising infants as a sign of membership in Israel, and Peter's clear reference to the continuance of this covenantal understanding of God's work in the early church ("For the promise is for you, for your children, and for all who are far away, everyone whom the Lord our God calls to him" [Acts 2:39]), all point to the likelihood that infant Baptism was a regular part of the early church. There is no question that it was well-established by the end of the second century and beginning of the third.[20]

Infant Baptism is a powerful witness to the fundamental logic of the gospel: Become who you already are in Christ! Long before they can understand or respond to what is happening, the infants of believers are marked with the sign of the covenant, a witness to the priority and prevenience of God's activity in establishing the covenant of grace. They are expected to respond personally to this covenant at a later point, ratifying the baptismal covenant and confessing the corporate faith it represents. For this reason it is important not to diminish the singular importance of confirmation by dissolving it into a series of repeatable acts. The confirmation service should retain its unique identity and purpose, as it currently does in the Episcopal, United Methodist, and Lutheran churches.

But what of the situation of adult Baptism? The theological pattern we have been describing seems to break down here, for the elements of profession and pledging are a part of the Baptism itself. Even here, however, we can discern a theological distinction comparable to one we have just found in infant Baptism: the distinction between the covenanting activity of God and a corresponding human response. It is the former that continues to have priority. This is clearly signaled in the Thanksgiving Over the Water, preceding the Baptism. There God's mighty acts are rehearsed. In the baptism of adults, just as surely as in the baptism of infants, the primary actor is God, not the human participant. Acts of profession included in the adult baptismal service represent the confirmation of God's prevenient covenanting activity. They stand theologically in a subordinate position to the divine initiative.

The practice of confirmation, then, is largely directed to the situation of persons who were baptized as infants and need to take up and affirm for themselves the vows of the covenant, pointing to when they were initiated into the Christian community. Greater specificity can be given to the theological content of these vows by explicating the way confirmation takes up each dimension of the trinitarian formulae uttered at their Baptism. Historically, this refers to Matthew 28:19: "Go therefore and make disciples of all nations, baptizing them in the name of the Father and of the Son and of the Holy Spirit." It is the covenanting activity of the triune God that is declared and applied in Baptism. Whereas each person of the trinity is involved in the entire economy of salvation, for convenience's sake we will unfold what is signified in this baptismal formula by describing the work of the Father as the election to covenant fellowship, that of the Son as reconciliation, and that of the Spirit as redemption. Baptism is an effective sign of the electing, reconciling, and redeeming work of God. Each of these can be described in terms of what we already are "in Christ," an identity that is applied to the life of the individual in Baptism and freely chosen by him or her in confirmation.

In the Name of the Father:
The Work of Election

The use of Father language to refer to God in the baptismal formula is something that many would choose to avoid for good reasons.[21] The decision to hold on to the scriptural baptismal formula thus warrants explanation. One of the most important arguments for doing so has recently been made by Cynthia Campbell who points out: "Baptism with water in the name of the Triune God . . . is perhaps the most widely held practice across the Christian family. It is probably the worship practice of longest standing about which there is the greatest consensus."[22] Like the great ecumenical creeds of the church, baptism with water in the name of the Father, Son, and Holy Spirit represents an important point of visible unity among church traditions that all-too-often are divided in their witness. Many who care about the visible relatedness of the church are cautious about abandoning this point of convergence in its sacramental life, even as they encourage the inclusion of a range of scriptural images for God in other parts of the service.

Much can be learned from the contemporary discussion of these issues. Jürgen Moltmann has offered a compelling interpretation of the Trinitarian formula in relation to issues of patriarchy.[23] At the heart of New Testament usage of Father language is Jesus' reference to God as "Abba," a term that reflects Jesus' unique relationship of intimacy to God as the Son and presupposes an inner-Trinitarian relationship of perichoresis characterized by radical mutuality and self-giving. Those who follow Jesus are invited to address God as Abba and to participate in a new community characterized by mutuality and self-giving, not hierarchy, domination, or inequality. As a rule, we do well to heed John 14:9: "Whoever has seen me has seen the Father." Our understanding of who this God is is not shaped by generalized human experience but by the practice of love and freedom carried out by the Son. We are not being called to worship a god who legitimates patriarchy, but the One to whom Jesus prayed and for whose kingdom messianic acts of healing, forgiveness, and liberation were undertaken.

Nowhere is this more important than in our understanding of the doctrine of election, the focal point of our understanding of the Father's work. The classical pattern of the early Reformers in which infant Baptism, catechetical instruction, and admission to the Lord's Supper cohered, assumed a doctrine of election in which double predestination figured prominently. Calvin, in particular, struggled with this doctrine, locating it first in one place and then in another in the *Institutes*.[24] His beginning point was a simple fact of experience: Some people respond to the message of the gospel and others do not. How can this be explained in a manner that preserves the freedom and sovereignty of God? Calvin believed that scripture itself provides the answer to this question in the doctrine of double predestination. In eternity, God elects some to salvation and others to eternal damnation. It was within this theological framework that Calvin developed his understanding of infant Baptism. Following the precedent of Israel and God's covenant with Abraham to extend his covenant to him and "his offspring" (Gen. 17:1–14), the church should assume that the children of believers are among the elect and mark them with the sign of entry into the covenant community.

No modern theologian has penetrated more deeply into Calvin's understanding of election than Karl Barth, and none has been more critical. Barth argued that the fundamental mistake made by the Reformers in general and Calvin in particular was to construct a doctrine of election apart from the God disclosed in Jesus Christ. It was this mistake that led Calvin to posit an arbitrary, inscrutable God to account for the fact that some respond to the gospel and others do not. Is the God revealed in Jesus Christ a God of absolute decrees, arbitrarily electing some and rejecting others? Barth's resounding no! led him to reconstruct the doctrine of election along lines quite different from anything previously found in Christian theology.[25]

The pivotal insight in Barth's reinterpretation was his recognition that the covenantal love disclosed in Jesus Christ is consistent with the covenantal nature of God's inner being. In formulating the doctrine of election, Christian theology does not have to speculate about God's decisions in eternity. It can be confident that the God disclosed in Jesus Christ is the same God who existed prior to the foundation of the world.

Indeed, Barth viewed election as the Father's election of Jesus Christ, the Son, in eternity. In choosing to be in fellowship with the Son, the Father makes a decision that reverberates throughout his dealings with creation: God will be gracious in dealing with all that is other. Typically, Barth uses covenantal language to describe this relationship. The covenant fellowship between the Father and Son is one in which each loves the other freely. It is this kind of relationship that the Father chooses to have with the rest of creation.

The inner-Trinitarian covenant love between the Father and Son is the presupposition of creation and the basis of God's future covenanting activity with Israel and the church. All that is created by God is created out of love and for the purpose of returning that love. God realizes in eternity, however, that humanity will not fulfill this intention for creation. Though it is elected to covenant fellowship, it will rebel against this relationship. This makes God's decision to be *for* humanity all the more amazing. It is this fallen, sinful humanity that God elects to love in Christ before the foundation of the world.[26]

Like Calvin and the other Reformers, Barth views election as having to do with God's decisions in eternity. He alters radically, however, what this decision involves. It focuses first on the Father's relationship with the Son and second on God's relationship with the whole of humanity in and through Christ.[27] The circle of those who are elected in Christ is as broad as humanity itself.[28] Barth goes on to describe two circles within this all-inclusive circle: the church and the individual. The church is the sphere in which God's election of humanity to covenant fellowship is self-consciously recognized and affirmed. It is the task of this community to give witness to God's decision to be *for* humanity in Jesus Christ.[29]

The community, however, is not the telos of election. It is the midpoint between God's election of humanity in Jesus Christ and concrete individuals whose lives are determined by their election in Christ.[30] Barth underscores the transition from a person's election in principle as a member of humanity to his or her election in fact as a concrete individual. In the following passage, he discusses this in terms of the contrast between "being" and "life": "Between the being of the elect and his life as such there lies the event and the decision of the reception of the promise. It is not for his being but for his life as elect that he needs to hear and believe the promise. Not every one who is elected lives as an elect man."[31] The individual represents the innermost circle in election. While all persons are elect in Christ, this remains to be taken up by each one concretely. The church's witness to election, ultimately, must take the form of an "address to a subject," one who is capable of saying yes or no, who can determine her or his life on the basis of God's prior determination.

It is this act of choosing to become who they are elected to be in Christ that is the focal point of confirmation. When the church marks its members with the sign of God's covenant in Baptism and says to them: "I baptize you in the name of the Father," it is telling its members that God's supreme and eternal purpose for humanity is covenant fellowship.[32] It is initiating them into the circle of the church, the community of those who know that God has chosen to be *for* humanity in Christ. It remains for those who have been baptized to step into the innermost circle, to recognize and acknowledge as individuals who they already are in Christ. This is what is brought into focus by confirmation. It represents that moment when individuals freely acknowledge their election in Christ by coming before the church and saying, in effect, "I accept my chosenness. I make a decision that corresponds to God's prior decision. Just as God has chosen to be for me, I choose to be for God."

In the Name of the Son:
The Work of Reconciliation

Baptism in the name of the Son points to the reconciling work of Christ. If the electing work of the Father points to God's decision in eternity to be for all that is other, the work of reconciliation is the actualization in history of this fundamental intentionality.[33] Reconciliation stands in continuity with the graciousness characterizing God's covenanting activity from the beginning. It is undertaken, however, in the face of the history of humanity's relationship with God. More particularly, it is undertaken in the face of humanity's rejection of its calling to covenant fellowship with God. Accordingly, it can be defined as follows:

> "Reconciliation" is the restitution, the resumption of a fellowship which once existed but was then threatened by dissolution. It is the maintaining, restoring and upholding of that fellowship in the face of an element which disturbs and disrupts and breaks it. It is the realization of the original purpose which underlay and controlled it in defiance and by the removal of this obstruction. The fellowship which originally existed between God and man, which was then disturbed and jeopardized, the purpose of which is now fulfilled in Jesus Christ and in the work of reconciliation, we describe as the covenant.[34]

The theological logic we have been following throughout this chapter once again appears in relation to the work of reconciliation: Become who you already are in Christ! The history of Christ's reconciling work is representative, for "in him" the true covenant partner is found and the original intention of God for creation is fulfilled. This can be described as involving two distinct, but inseparable, activities: justification and sanctification. The former describes Christ's reconciling work as God; the latter, his work as human. Each is an important part of the witness of Baptism and, consequently, is taken up in confirmation.

Responding to the Justifying Work of Christ

Justification points to the downward movement of God toward a sinful humanity. In an obedient act of divine condescension, Christ entered into creation, submitting to its limitations and exigencies and accepting solidarity with humanity. Justification is a legal term that points to the acquittal of a person, the declaration of innocence in the face of a charge brought by another. Accordingly, it involves two dimensions.

First, justification points to God's judgment in the face of humanity's rebellion against the offer of covenant fellowship. The effect of humanity's rebellion is a fundamental disordering of its place in creation, a magnification of its own role in pride and its diminishment in sloth. Second, justification points to the fact that this judgment does not fall where it should, on humanity, but rather, falls on Christ. As Barth puts it: "The judge is judged in our place."[35] A real exchange takes place in which the suffering and death of the One who is innocent takes the place of the judgment that should fall on the many.

Both of these themes are closely associated with Baptism in the New Testament. Christ's submission to John's baptism of repentance represents an act of solidarity with sinful humanity. Likewise, an individual's passage under the baptismal waters represents participation in Christ's justifying death and the washing away of sins that it makes possible. Confirmation takes up these themes by inviting baptized Christians to confess their complicity in sin and to acknowledge their utter reliance on God's declaration of forgiveness in Christ.

The reality of sin is rarely discussed in mainline Protestantism today, especially in teaching children and adolescents. Ministers and teachers are so afraid they might inadvertently portray Christianity as a "guilt trip" that they avoid this topic altogether.[36] The result is a Christ without a cross and a church without a message that can address the depths of human existence. If it is faithful to the baptismal witness to justification, however, confirmation cannot avoid this topic. It must include an individual's acknowledgment that he or she concretely participates in the forces of evil. Sin, in this case, is not merely personal sin, although it includes this. It is an ontological reality, a cosmic force that incarnates itself in social systems and natural processes, as well as in an individual's character and personal choices. Confirmation invites us to confess our participation in sin, not particular sins.

In the current Baptism and reaffirmation services of the *Book of Common Worship,* candidates are asked: "Do you turn from the ways of sin and renounce evil and its power in the world?" It must be clear to confirmands that something highly personal is at stake in this renunciation. They are confessing something similar to the following: "I too participate in the reality of sin by which the world is disrupted at every level of life. I give my allegiance to evil structures and forces without even realizing it, participating in patterns of life that do great harm to others and, ultimately, to myself." If confirmation is to take up Baptism's witness to Christ's justifying work, then it cannot avoid making it clear what is at stake in this act of renunciation.

But it also must include the second dimension of justification: God's forgiveness in Christ. The renunciation is followed by a second question: "Do you turn to Jesus Christ and accept him as your Lord and Savior, trusting in his grace and love?" This is not a general profession of trust. It is a deeply personal acceptance of what God has done in Christ on the confirmand's behalf. Accordingly, the confirmand must realize that he or she is affirming something such as the following: "I recognize that the Son has borne the judgment of my participation in these sinful forces, freeing me from a need to make restitution. I thereby give thanks to God and will attempt to live on the basis of the forgiveness offered in Christ."

Forgiveness, in this sense, is not primarily a psychological reality. It is not merely a psychic release from inner guilt. Rather, it is entry into a new state of being, especially a new relationship with God, on the basis of God's declaration of forgiveness. It is analogous to the acceptance of the conditions of a peace treaty. The war is over and peace has been declared. The very One who is victorious has promulgated an unconditional amnesty to the members of the opposition. There is no longer any reason for them to engage in combat or maintain battle readiness. All they must do is lay down their arms and enter into the new state of things that has already been declared.

Responding to the justifying work of Christ in confirmation is a public declaration of acceptance of the new state of reconciliation that God has made possible. Each confirmand stands alone in this regard. He or she stands within the circles of humanity and the church, to be sure, but at this moment of profession, stands as a particular individual. This single, concrete person tells the world that she or he is ready to accept the declaration of forgiveness that has been promulgated in Christ. Henceforth, that person will attempt to live as a forgiven sinner. This is what it means to respond to the justifying work of Christ.

Responding to the Sanctifying Work of Christ

Sanctification points to the exaltation of humanity in Christ's reconciling work. Christ is the faithful and obedient covenant partner that humans were created to be. He represents the fulfillment of all righteousness, both the obligations of the law and the "higher righteousness" of discipleship. Once again, the logic of the gospel we have been following holds true: Become who you already are in Christ! Christ is our sanctification. His fulfillment of the covenant promises and obligations are done in our stead and on our behalf. This does not rule out a corresponding response by human subjects, however. Indeed, Christ's sanctifying work is truly recognized and appropriated only when it elicits a corresponding sanctification of the individual in the concrete circumstances of life.[37]

Again, the baptismal texts of the New Testament point to a close relationship between sanctification and Baptism. Jesus' baptism by John was a commissioning to the ministry of suffering love, as the allusion to the suffering servant passage of Isaiah 42 in the divine declaration makes clear: "This is my Son, the Beloved, with whom I am well pleased" (Matt. 3:17).[38] Similarly, Paul reminds his readers that in baptism they not only have died with Christ, but also will rise with him (Rom. 6:1–11). Although his comments point to the future, implicitly critiquing those who would claim to live the resurrected life fully already, they have important implications for life in the present. Within the context of Paul's letter to the Romans, they serve as a transition to the ethical admonitions that follow. Christians are to live as those who have been freed from the dominion of death so that they might be alive to God in Christ Jesus. This is why the Christian tradition frequently has described sanctification as a twofold process of mortification and liberation. Different theologians have placed the accent on one or the other of these dimensions.

Calvin, for example, places primary emphasis on mortification, accenting the struggle to break with the old self that following Christ entails. This involves dying to old patterns and allegiances by which the self is defined. Although acknowledging this side of sanctification, Barth places his primary accent on the liberation that Christ's sanctifying work makes possible.[39] It is not just a turning away from the old, a letting go and a dying, but, even more, it is a turning to, an awakening and a renewing. It is a turning to the possibilities of covenant love toward God and the neighbor.

This possibility must be acknowledged and taken up in confirmation. Those who participate in Christ's reconciling work must follow Jesus concretely. They must take concrete steps to break with their old ways of life and enter into the way of covenant love. Confirmation must emphasize both sides of this process. It must invite its participants to count the cost of following Jesus, making it clear that this sets them in a struggle to break with the forces of sin and evil. Real, tangible steps must be taken and decisions must be made reflecting this break. A dying, a letting go, a turning away is involved.

Even more, however, confirmation must invite its participants to enter the way of covenant love. This is a liberation, a freedom. It is crucial that the liberating character of sanctification be held up. Whereas the moral teachings of the Bible, for example, provide the broad outlines of the direction love should take, they should not be turned into a set of rules that replace a dynamic relationship with the living God. The freedom of God's Word to address the confirmand in the concreteness of daily life must be held up, eliciting a free and spontaneous response. One of the most difficult, but most important, tasks of confirmation is teaching people how to use the Bible as an authoritative source of guidance in a way that avoids the trap of legalism. This involves teaching confirmands how to enter into a process of *discernment* by which they actively seek to hear and obey God's living voice. The disciplines of Bible study, prayer, and moral reflection are involved.

In the Name of the Spirit

Baptism in the name of the Spirit points to the work of redemption. By redemption is meant the transformation of the world that will occur fully when Christ returns, a future that breaks into the present in the work of the Spirit.[40] The Spirit's presence in Christ's ministry is a sign that the future kingdom has broken into the present already: "But if it is by the Spirit of God that I cast out demons, then the kingdom of God has come to you" (Matt. 12:28). The New Testament describes the work of the Spirit as confined exclusively to Jesus prior to Easter. The Spirit empowers Jesus' preaching and mighty deeds and is even described by Paul as the power by which he is raised from the dead (Rom. 8:11). It was only after Jesus' resurrection that the Spirit was poured out on "all flesh," gathering together a community of the new covenant and empowering the disciples to carry out their ministries in ways that anticipated the coming redemption (Acts 2; cf. John 7:39, 20:22).

Paul expresses well the anticipatory nature of the Spirit's work in the church by describing it as a "first installment" of the coming kingdom (2 Cor. 1:22, 5:5;

Eph. 1:14). The image is based on the common practice of depositing money after a bargain has been made, money that will be forfeited if the deal is not carried out. This first installment serves not only as a pledge and guarantee, but it also indicates that the amount of money will be paid in full in the future.[41] In using this image to describe the work of the Spirit, Paul is emphasizing the anticipatory nature of the Spirit's work. It is God's first installment of the coming kingdom. It serves as a pledge of the covenant fellowship that will be fully established when Christ returns.

The work of the Spirit does not replace or surpass that of the Son, although the Spirit has its own work as well. It illumines and instructs people in the revelation that has already taken place in Christ (John 15:26) and begins the glorification of God through the new creation's praise and testimony. It carries out the subjective side of revelation, allowing persons to appropriate the justifying work of Christ in faith and his sanctifying work in obedience.[42] Scripture repeatedly describes the Spirit as giving birth to those capacities that allow persons to recognize Jesus as the Christ in whom the kingdom is inaugurated (for example, John 1:12–13; 3:3f) and making persons children of God (see Rom. 8:14–17). It also points to the Spirit's role in the moral transformation associated with sanctification. Believers are encouraged to live by the Spirit (Gal. 5:16, 25), and the Spirit is described as producing fruits in those whom it leads (Gal. 5:22–23). This moral transformation, however, is best viewed as part of the Spirit's primary redemptive work: the glorification of God in and through the new creation.

What distinguishes the work of the Spirit from the work of the Son? It is the future orientation of the Spirit's activity. The Spirit is a first installment of the cosmic renewal that is yet to occur. Whereas reconciliation has taken place already, redemption and glorification are still to come. The futurity of the Spirit's work points to the time when the covenanting activity of God in election and reconciliation come to full fruition and God will be in all and through all.

As we have seen, the Spirit's relation to Baptism has been the focus of much theological reflection across church history. The position taken here is one in which the Spirit is not viewed as bestowed solely through the baptismal service. The Spirit blows where it chooses (John 3:8), and as the book of Acts makes clear, the Spirit carries out the work of renewal before, during, and after Baptism. The attempt to limit the Spirit's work to sacramental acts or to parcel out its work between Baptism and confirmation places limits on God's free and sovereign activity.

The theological logic followed here is the same used throughout this section. Baptism in the name of the Spirit points to who we are already in Christ. In Christ, the Spirit of the future renewal of the cosmos already has broken into history. Those who belong to Christ belong to that future. With Christ's ascension, the Spirit's task is the continuing actualization of that future in the period between Christ's first and second comings. Baptism in the name of the Spirit, thus, is Baptism into the future that belongs to the resurrected Lord.

Confirmation represents that moment in a baptized Christian's life when he or she chooses to walk in the Spirit. The path has been blazed already, the signposts set, and provisions for the journey provided. The individual has traveled far down the path already. There is a point, however, when a decision must be made to journey on. The path is spread out ahead, but there are other paths that might be taken. Confirmation represents the point along the way when the individual who has already started out decides to move toward the future, to continue the journey toward a destination that will not be reached in this world.

What does this involve? Much of what we have pointed to already in our discussion of sanctification could be reiterated here. Every act of liberation to covenant love is also a sign of the coming kingdom and the work of the Spirit. It is a foretaste, a first installment of the full work of redemption that will occur when Christ returns. Two aspects of the Spirit's work, however, must be lifted up for special consideration in our description of the relationship between Baptism and confirmation: (1) the creation of hope in those whom the Spirit touches; and (2) the Spirit's creation of parables of the kingdom.

The Spirit's Work in Creating Hope

Baptism in the name of the Holy Spirit is Baptism into a life of hope. Even before an infant can acknowledge this hope, she or he lives between the certainty of God's reconciling work in Christ and the full work of redemption at the end of time. It is the task of the Holy Spirit to make this hope real and efficacious in the life of those who believe. Faith and hope go hand in hand. As Calvin puts it:

> Hope is nothing else than the expectation of those things which faith has believed to have been truly promised by God. Thus, faith believes God to be true, hope awaits the time when this truth shall be manifested; faith believes that he is our Father, hope anticipates that he will ever show himself to be a Father toward us; faith believes that eternal life has been given to us, hope anticipates that it will some time be revealed; faith is the foundation upon which hope rests, hope nourishes and sustains faith.[43]

Faith provides hope with the substance of what it longs for. But hope is the animating force of faith. Without hope, faith is dead, because hope is the expectation of those things that faith believes. Hope is both confidence in and longing for the promised future revealed in Christ's past. It is the role of the Holy Spirit to kindle hope in the minds and hearts of those who believe.

The importance of Christian hope is especially evident when the tragic quality of historical existence is faced.[44] Human consciousness does much to protect itself from the tragic character of life. It tries to shield itself from the crushing cycles of death and destruction so characteristic of history. It turns away from the reality that even the noblest of human achievements participate in these cycles and cannot actualize good in an unambiguous fashion. This tragic quality of life is too much for humans to bear directly, and many aspects of culture are an attempt to cover it or justify it. Religion, especially, has played an important role in this regard, providing forms of consolation that explain or rationalize the depths of human suffering and tragedy. It quickly removes responses of rage or questioning that threaten the foundations of the taken-for-granted world.[45]

Christian hope is not a form of false consolation. It finds its place amid human tragedy and suffering. It takes its bearings from the cross. It acknowledges the tragic depths of John's statement: "He was in the world, and the world came into being through him; yet the world did not know him" (1:10). The cross was no accident, an epiphenomenon on the way to the resurrection. It is the state of God's light in the world. It is light in the midst of darkness. Hope does not see light alone. It sees light in the midst of surrounding gloom. It sees light that often seems little more than a tiny flame enveloped by billowing darkness. But hope also recognizes that the very existence of this light reveals the threats of the darkness as fleeting and unable to withstand the coming of the full light of day. It lives in the light of the breaking dawn. The shadows still linger, but it is clear that they will be banished. So too Christian hope knows that tragedy is not the final word. Indeed, it has no ultimate reality in comparison to the coming redemption of the world. The Holy Spirit's role is to kindle this hope in the minds and hearts of those who believe.

When infants are baptized, they are not capable of understanding any of this intellectually. Experientially, however, all infants know the tragic rupture of symbiosis characterizing birth and the first months of life. They know the "fall" into anxiety and the various threats to the self accompanying its psychological birth.[46] Infants also know the tragic character of life in which growth and loss, self-affirmation and self-negation go hand in hand. They too stand in need of Baptism, even before they can grasp what it means. They need a community of interpretation that can point them again and again to the light that reveals and overcomes the darkness in which they find themselves. They stand in need of Baptism in the name of the Holy Spirit and the future redemption to which this gives witness.

Confirmation represents the moment when this hope is taken up and publicly affirmed in the life of one who has been baptized. This affirmation is *not* primarily the achievement of a psychological state. It is not the adoption of an attitude of positive thinking or an optimistic approach to life. In American society, such stances often are tied in with the attempt to perform well in the face of fierce competition at school or at work. It is especially important for youth and young adults to understand that Christian hope is not this sort of optimism.

Indeed, hope can sometimes be accompanied by the psychological state of depression. If hope finds its true place in the midst of the tragic depths of life, it can be a sobering, even saddening, experience for a youth or young adult to confront tragedy for the first time. Confirmation must not shield persons from these emotions or the realities that engender them. It allows confirmands to confront life in its tragic depths and then points them to the One in whom tragedy has been overcome. Christian hope is light in the midst of darkness, confidence in the face of despair, struggle in the face of oppression, and expectation in the face of impossible odds. It can engender a wide range of psychological states, none of which has anything to do with a shallow optimism.

Accordingly, the profession of hope involved in confirmation must include a strong cognitive component and not merely emotions. It is confidence born of an appropriation of God's covenanting activity, especially as this points to God's future redemption. It is the personal profession by an individual that he or she now understands that this is the true context of life. All of life is lived in the context of God's coming redemption. None of the cycles of death and destruction can remove this reality. Moreover, it is profession of the belief that some small measure of that future redemption can be fashioned within the confines of the present historical moment through the power of the Holy Spirit. This leads to the second baptismal theme that confirmation must take up.

The Spirit's Work in Creating Parables of Redemption

Baptism in the name of the Holy Spirit sets before the one baptized the task of discerning and participating in parables of the coming kingdom. The concept "parable," as used here, does not refer to a literary genre but is used to refer to any enacted sign of God's future redemption. Such signs point beyond themselves, while participating in the reality to which they point. They reflect the character of the Holy Spirit as a down payment of the coming kingdom.

When persons are baptized in the name of the Holy Spirit, they are given the task of aligning themselves with those contemporary movements and struggles in which the Spirit is carrying out its redemptive work already. Although the church is itself called to be a parable of the kingdom, it is not the sole or even primary locus of the Spirit's redemptive activity. As Barth and others have pointed out, the state can be a parable of the kingdom, reflecting in a provisional way the promise of justice and mercy that will come fully when Christ returns. Similarly, political or cultural movements that are struggling against some form of oppression can serve as parables of the kingdom, signs of resistance and hope in the face of cycles of death and destruction. In short, the locus of the Spirit's work is the full range of life, reflecting the cosmic scope of future redemption.

All Christians are given the task of discerning and participating in such parables of the kingdom when they are baptized in the name of the Holy Spirit. This task is self-consciously taken up in confirmation. Confirmation education must help youth acquire or deepen the capacities necessary to read the signs of the times. It must pose the question: Where is the Spirit at work in the world? It must provide confirmands with some sense of how they might go about answering this question.

Confirmation must go beyond this, however. It must encourage confirmands to enter into some concrete activity, movement, or group outside the church that is thought to be parabolic. Out of their participation in such groups or movements, confirmands are to examine the relationship between the church and the world, the Holy Spirit and the human spirit, God's redemption and human transformation. Confirmation thus serves as a point of resistance to modernity's tendency to confine religion to the private sphere. It equips confirmands to grasp the relation of their faith to the public sphere in full recognition that it often is here that the most important and visible parables of the coming kingdom are found.

Confirmation and the Lord's Supper

This section will be much shorter than the previous one because it can assume the theological themes that have been explicated already in relation to Baptism.

Baptism and the Lord's Supper share virtually the same theological content. Both give witness to the saving significance of Jesus' death and the role of the Holy Spirit in creating newness of life that anticipates the coming redemption. Both also presuppose God's election of humanity to covenant fellowship, even if this is not expressed as directly in the scriptural passages in which Baptism and the Lord's Supper are discussed. The larger scriptural framework of the Son's work of reconciliation and the Spirit's work of redemption is one in which God elects to be for humanity in eternity. Reconciliation and redemption are not repair jobs but are consistent with the character of God's inner being.

There is little need then to explicate the theological content of the Lord's Supper. This Sacrament also gives witness to God's electing, reconciling, and redeeming activity. It too is a sign of the covenant of grace. This is not to say, however, that Baptism and the Lord's Supper are identical. As noted earlier, they differ in their temporal character. Baptism is a once-and-for-all event, an unrepeatable sign of initiation into the covenant community. The Lord's Supper is cyclical in nature, a sign of personal and corporate covenant renewal in which persons participate many times over the course of their lives.

In taking up the cyclical nature of the Lord's Supper, confirmation represents one of many moments of covenant renewal on a pilgrimage that will continue as long as a person is alive. Why is this so important to emphasize? Time and time again, scripture points to the tendency of the covenant community to turn the dynamic covenantal relationship between God and God's people into a static institution.[47] Whether this involves an overidentification of the covenant with some form of the law or an ideological use of covenant themes to justify political arrangements (such as the Israelite monarchy), it represents a perversion of the dynamic, eventful character of the covenant relationship.

At their best, the Israelite services of covenant renewal attempted to resist this tendency, doing more than socializing persons into an established institution. Their recollection of the gracious acts by which God established the covenant community were not presented as something that happened in the distant past but as events in which the present generation participates: "Then I sent Moses and Aaron, and I plagued Egypt . . . and afterwards I brought you out" (Josh. 24:5). The rehearsal of this history culminated in a choice confronting the present generation ("choose this day whom you will serve" [v.15]) and placing it under an obligation ("put away the foreign gods that are among you, and incline your hearts to the LORD" [v.23]). Even when the Davidic covenant pattern emerged and came to be closely associated with the cult surrounding the Temple, the dynamic quality of the covenant was not completely lost.[48] This is seen in the Temple entrance liturgy of Psalm 24: "Who shall ascend the hill of the LORD? And who shall stand in his holy place? Those who have clean hands and pure hearts" (vs.3–4a).[49]

Services of covenant renewal took place periodically in order to remind the members of the covenant community that their relationship with God was a dynamic reality, not an established institution. Each generation must stand before God as earlier generations had stood, hearing again the gracious acts by which God established the covenant and accepting its claim upon them. The covenant

relationship cannot be secured simply by membership in a community or participation in its cult, but it is a matter of ongoing trust and obedience.

So too the Lord's Supper functions as a renewal of the covenant of grace in the
Christian community.[50] It involves a recollection of the central events by which
God has established the new covenant. Through this recollection, God addresses
the congregation again and again with the promise, "I will remember your sins no
more," and invites a response of trust and obedience. This turns the community
toward the future and the promise of the messianic banquet, filling it with hope
and strengthening its resolve to participate in those parables of the coming kingdom that the Spirit is creating already within the present historical context.

Viewed along the lines of a service of covenant renewal, the Lord's Supper
graphically sets forth the dynamic nature of God's covenant with the community
of faith. This covenant is a matter of God's ongoing address to the community and
its response in faith and obedience. It is never an accomplished reality, an established relationship based on a once-and-for-all event taking place at some point
in the distant past. It is for this reason that the meaning of the Lord's Supper must
be taken up by confirmation and held in tension with the meaning of Baptism. Initiation into the covenant community involves participation in a community that is
on the way, venturing forth again and again in trust and obedience to the inbreak-
ing Word.

This understanding of the Lord's Supper has important implications for the
way confirmation is defined. First, it provides us with our primary theological reasons for locating the Lord's Supper before confirmation. This Sacrament, like
Baptism, is a means of grace, an instrument used by God to address the present
community of faith. It is not primarily a witness to the participants' understanding or worthiness. For this reason, the classical Reformation pattern that placed
First Communion after catechetical instruction has no more theological justification than the location of Baptism after this instruction. Why is the achievement of
a certain level of knowledge a prerequisite to one but not the other?

In both Sacraments, God is the primary actor, not the human participant. Both
give witness to the prevenience and priority of God in establishing and maintaining the covenant of grace. Both share the same logic, for their theological content
is identical: Become who you are already in Christ for in him you are elected, rec-
onciled, and redeemed! Just as infant Baptism vividly portrays this logic, so too
should the Lord's Supper. Even before children can understand the full meaning
of the body and blood, they already are fed by the tokens of the new covenant in
Christ. Confirmation represents a taking up and grasping of a reality that has already been established in Christ and, following this, in the experience of all the
baptized members of the church, no matter how young they are.

This brings us to our second point. In the proposal being developed in this
chapter, confirmation is described in a way that places the accent on the human
actor. It represents a free, human response to the Word as it is communicated
through Baptism and the Lord's Supper. This emphasis on the human side of confirmation has certain dangers, especially if confirmation is viewed solely in relation to Baptism. It can easily be seen as the all-important profession and pledge

by which a person is saved. At last, the Word declared in Baptism is given an unequivocal yes by the confirmand. This understanding of confirmation could degenerate into something closer to an Anabaptist understanding of decisional regeneration than a Reformed evangelical rite.

Unfolding the meaning of confirmation in relation to the Lord's Supper ameliorates this danger considerably, especially if this Sacrament is viewed along the lines of a covenant renewal. It makes it clear that the confirmand's profession and pledge are human actions that must be undertaken again and again in response to the Word. The covenant relationship with God in which the confirmand is located already is a dynamic relationship. It is not something that can be taken for granted or secured on the basis of a one-time profession. Rather, it is a relationship in which members of the covenant community must trust and obey repeatedly over the course of their lives.

It is on the basis of its relationship to the Lord's Supper that confirmation rightfully is placed amid services that allow the members of the church to reaffirm the covenant over the course of their lives. This is not merely a reaffirmation of the baptismal covenant. Primarily, it is a reaffirmation of the covenant of grace revealed and effected in Jesus Christ. Baptism and the Lord's Supper both are effective witnesses to this covenant. In its orientation to Baptism, confirmation is a singular, unrepeatable event by which the individual ratifies this covenant for the first time. In its orientation to the Lord's Supper, something that the confirmand has repeatedly experienced prior to the confirmation service, confirmation points to the dynamic nature of the covenant relationship. Although confirmation should not lose its distinctive identity as an unrepeatable rite because of its relationship to Baptism, it rightfully is placed among repeatable rites because of its relationship to the Lord's Supper. It too points to the need for future renewals of the covenant and reveals the Christian life as a life of ongoing repentance and conversion.

Confirmation and Catechetical Instruction

One of the hallmarks of the Reformation was its emphasis on catechetical instruction. The Reformers were unequivocally enthusiastic about the importance of establishing catechetical instruction as a vehicle of church reform. As we have seen, when confirmation gradually was accepted in many of the churches coming out of the Reformation, it was located within the pattern that already was established: infant Baptism, catechetical instruction, and admission to the Lord's Supper. Catechetical instruction played a crucial role in this pattern, allowing young Christians to appropriate the faith into which they were baptized as infants and to participate in the Lord's Supper meaningfully.

The breakup of this pattern in many churches over the course of the twentieth century left them ill-prepared to cope with the cultural disestablishment of Protestantism taking place during this same period. Just as Protestantism began to receive less help from the educational institutions of the surrounding culture, it abandoned one of the few educational practices that had proved effective in teaching laypersons the basic doctrinal content of the faith. These churches are now reaping the harvest they have sowed. Biblical and theological illiteracy, a massive decline in denominational loyalty, and a rapid increase in church switching reflect, in part, mainline Protestantism's inability to create new educational patterns by which it can hand on a compelling vision of the Christian life to its children and youth.

In the face of this situation, it is imperative for mainline Protestantism to establish new practices of catechetical instruction that are appropriate to the challenges of the present context. There were two important strengths of the older form of catechetical instruction. First, it provided every member of the church with a basic level of theological literacy. The essential doctrinal tenets of the faith, as articulated in a particular denominational tradition, were handed on to each new generation. At its best, moreover, adults continued to study the catechism, appropriating it at a deeper level as their cognitive capacities matured. Longer, more complex catechisms were written for this purpose. Second, the study of the catechism indirectly reinforced biblical literacy. Many catechisms were accompanied by citations of biblical passages that warranted their material. Study of these passages was encouraged as the catechism was learned.

Two weaknesses of this older approach to catechetical instruction, however, are closely related to these strengths. The first weakness concerns the overemphasis placed on the internalization of the doctrinal teachings allowing confession of the church's faith that insufficient attention was paid to aspects of this material such as personal construction, understanding, and profession. There was a strong tendency to allow mastery of church teaching to overshadow elements of personal appropriation. This weakness was caused by the Reformers' overreliance on the "internalization pedagogies" of renaissance humanism. In order to honor their commitment to the personal and individual aspects of the faith, as well as the corporate aspects, it is important for new forms of catechetical instruction to do two things. First, it should use more interactive pedagogies in its work with children to establish educational practices explicitly designed to help youth and adults critically appropriate the basic tenets of the faith that they received at an earlier age. Second, it should separate catechetical instruction, offered to all children when they reach a certain age, from confirmation, which should be entered only when a person is ready to make a personal profession of faith and pledge of obedience.

The second weakness of the older model of catechetical instruction was its placement of doctrinal material in the foreground and biblical material in the background. Perhaps this is because it could assume a preaching ministry that was solidly focused on the Bible. It is clear that the contemporary church cannot assume a basic knowledge of the Bible among its members. Officers of the church are ignorant of the most simple stories of the Bible. In order to remedy this situation, a new form of catechesis must be developed that focuses primarily on the biblical narrative. This is outlined below in conjunction with a catechetical approach that invites children to learn the basic beliefs of the church in close relation to their understanding of the biblical narrative. The new form of catechetical instruction advocated here would do three basic things.

1. *Confirmation should be separated from catechetical instruction.* In the present proposal, it is the *professional* purpose of confirmation that is primary, with catechumenal and catechetical purposes subordinated to this goal. Concretely, this means that confirmation should *not* represent the culmination of instruction automatically given to youth when they reach a certain age. The close identification of confirmation and catechetical instruction renders confirmation little more than an agency of socialization in the church. It creates a structure of expectation making it highly likely that young people will be confirmed when they have finished their confirmation class. In spite of teachers' attempts to keep this an open process, the overall pattern of this approach is so heavily weighted toward choosing to be confirmed that it is virtually impossible for youth to resist this step. Even the occasional adolescent who refuses to be confirmed often does so because of the current state of his relationship with his parents or his strong identification with a peer group outside the church. For this reason, confirmation should be separated from catechetical instruction, as an age-related educational program.

2. *Establish a new practice of biblical catechesis in conjunction with the teaching of a doctrinal catechism.* During middle childhood, congregations should offer a special series of classes that provide its children with an overview of the narrative structure of scripture. In the educational ministry of the contemporary church, children get scripture in bits and pieces. Church school curriculums treat different parts of the Bible over many years. Sermons focus on isolated texts. Nowhere are children given the opportunity to gain a sense of the overarching unity of the Bible. Consequently, they have little sense of the story of salvation, especially the relationship between the Old and New Testaments. One of the most important purposes of a practice of biblical catechesis would be to help children gain a sense of scripture in its wholeness and integrity.

This new practice of biblical catechesis should be conjoined with the teaching of a new catechism that articulates the basic beliefs of the church. In the way it structures its material, the catechism would follow closely the biblical narrative, helping children begin the task of constructing beliefs that make sense out of the biblical story they have learned already. Beliefs about God's creation of the world and its fall, for example, would be offered before those about Jesus Christ. At their best, the older catechisms did just this, mirroring the biblical narrative in the structure of their material. In a new form of catechetical instruction, this should be done explicitly, with the study of the biblical narrative taking first place.

3. *Offer a more complex form of catechetical instruction to those who have chosen to enroll in confirmation classes.* The present proposal places the accent in confirmation squarely on its *professional* purpose. The brief outline given here will be unpacked more fully in the following chapter. Rather than locating confirmation at the end of an educational process that youth enter when they reach a certain age, individuals will choose to enter confirmation when they are ready to make a public profession of faith. At their own initiative, they will approach the minister or trusted adult and ask to be enrolled in

the confirmation program. They then will appear before the appropriate governing body and state their reasons for seeking to enter confirmation at this time. This will be followed by a brief service of enrollment during Sunday morning worship. Individuals will not be enrolled en masse but as each one expresses the desire to be confirmed. Once enrolled, confirmands will begin a course of individual study, prayer, and reflection under the direction of the minister or an appropriate spiritual mentor.

This will be followed by participation in confirmation classes regularly offered at certain times of the year. The primary purpose of these classes is *professional.* In their content and process, they are designed to help people understand what it means to make a personal profession of faith and pledge of obedience. This means that confirmands must be invited to reflect critically on the biblical and theological material they learned at an earlier age. The purpose of these classes is to create a context in which they can genuinely make the faith their own.

Serious study of theology should be undertaken. It is quite possible that a new catechism, along the lines of the older longer catechisms, would be useful in this regard. It would provide the material for substantive theological reflection. Pedagogically, however, this catechism would not be used as a source of internalization of the church's preestablished beliefs. Rather, it would serve as a springboard for serious reflection, criticism, and dialogue designed to help people construct and articulate their theological understanding of the faith they will confess when they are confirmed. Catechetical instruction thus would be placed in the service of confirmation's central purpose. We turn now to the task of describing in greater detail how this would look as part of a comprehensive practice of confirmation.

8

A Fitting Practice of Confirmation

Is it really possible to reform confirmation in ways indicated in the previous chapter? Are there not great risks involved in the kinds of changes being called for, especially the separation of confirmation from an educational program that youth enter upon reaching a certain age? These questions cannot be avoided. In spite of all the problems with confirmation as it currently exists, it remains an area of church life in which a large percentage of young people continue to participate. Breaking the link between confirmation and a particular age could very well contribute to the well-established trend of declining participation by youth in the church during late adolescence and young adulthood. Why cast out one demon only to have seven take its place? This is a real concern, and it compels us to describe in greater detail how a new practice of confirmation would look and how it might be established. It would be pretentious to believe that all relevant issues can be resolved in this short chapter. Our goal is the more modest one of establishing the plausibility of the proposed reform and opening a dialogue with pastors, Christian educators, laypersons, and other practical theologians. In the end, they will find this proposal needed and compelling or not.

It is important to recall that the early phases of the Reformation were characterized by a great deal of variety and creativity in congregational life. Many catechisms were written; different educational approaches and settings were tried; supplemental resources such as wall placards and children's books were developed; catechetical preaching was integrated into worship in a variety of ways. Only gradually did some approaches to catechetical instruction win widespread assent among congregations of the reform movement. Calvin's Genevan Catechism, for example, never really caught on, whereas the Heidelberg Catechism did.

Congregations today are in a similar situation. They must not think in terms of a "from-the-top-down" approach to church reform. Denominational bureaucracies are ill-equipped to develop innovative programs that will have much influence at the level of the congregation. They are understaffed, underfunded, and subject to widespread distrust. If confirmation is to be reformed, the initiative must come first at the congregational level, and it will include a period of experimentation and creativity. Only gradually, as congregations take the risks involved in reforming the practice of confirmation, will other congregations discern both the need and possibility of change. Accordingly, this chapter represents an invitation to innovation. It will outline the various phases of a new practice of confirmation and attempt to describe how it might be established in church life. It will not solve all problems or answer all questions; it will open a conversation.

The first task is to project the proposed practice of confirmation into a *congregational* context. If people do not automatically enter confirmation when they reach a certain age, what context is needed to invite them to choose to be confirmed? How will they know when they are ready? How can congregational leaders evoke and acknowledge this readiness without lapsing into coerciveness, on the one hand, or fostering individualism, on the other? This section will be followed by a description of each phase of the practice once a person has entered it. During the phase of *enrollment,* persons will choose to enter the confirmation process, begin a dialogue with appropriate church leaders and governing bodies, and participate in a service of enrollment during Sunday morning worship. Once enrolled, they will enter a period of *spiritual mentoring* in which they learn or deepen their use of the spiritual disciplines of personal prayer, Bible study, and vocational discernment. This will take place under the oversight of spiritual guides who are experienced in the use of these disciplines and have proven adept in providing personal direction and guidance to others. During set times of the year, *catechetical instruction* will be offered for those who have been enrolled and have participated in spiritual mentoring for an appropriate period of time. Traditional catechetical material will be used to help confirmands deepen their understanding of what is at stake in taking up the vows of the covenant of grace. Following this instruction, confirmands will enter the final phase, the *confirmation service,* in which they will make a public confession of the church's faith and engage in an act of covenant ratification. The liturgical components of this service are important, for they will give expression to the overriding professional purpose of confirmation.

Confirmation in Congregational Context

Ecclesial practices are interrelated. Reform of confirmation will not be possible without corresponding changes in other areas of church life. As it presently exists, confirmation is entered when young people reach a certain age. They move through a confirmation program and then decide whether or not to be confirmed. One of the major shifts proposed here is to eliminate the quasi-automatic entry into a confirmation program at a certain age and to leave it to the individual to choose to enter confirmation when he or she is ready to make a public profession and pledge. Many will view this as risky, for a high percentage of young people participate in confirmation. Skeptics rightly will ask: Why eliminate one of the few educational programs in the church that seems to be working?

This is a fair question, and it must be taken seriously. But it also is fair to take it one step further and ask: Working to what end? Many young people treat confirmation as a kind of graduation. Upon its completion, they gradually diminish their participation in the church school and youth group and eventually drop out altogether during late adolescence or young adulthood. Confirmation seems to represent the final stage of a childhood faith rather than the first step in a maturer appropriation of the covenant relationship in which they already participate. Nonetheless, the question remains. Is it possible to reform confirmation without inadvertently contributing to the pattern of adolescent departure so widespread in mainline Protestantism today?

There are two important responses to this question. First, if the church is to grant a more important place to the personal appropriation of the faith for theological reasons, then it must be willing to allow the element of personal choice to be real. There can be no pretense when it comes to respecting the freedom and responsibility of others. If parents, for example, really want to teach their children moral responsibility, then they cannot protect them from making real choices and living with the consequences of these choices. So too the church cannot claim to support a genuinely free and personal profession of faith as long as it continues a programmatic approach to confirmation in which young people automatically enter this program when they reach a certain age. Already at the beginning of the process, confirmands are being treated as members of a class. How likely is it that they will feel free to say yes or no when they see their classmates stepping forward to be confirmed, basking in their parents' approval, and enjoying the festivities that accompany this step? The choice must be real or it is not really a choice. The church would do well to become clear about its theological commitments and then shape its practice accordingly.

Second, the change proposed here does not mean that the church must sit by idly waiting for individuals to choose to enter confirmation. Parenting again provides a good analogy. Although parents may respect their child's need to learn responsibility, this does not mean they will abandon their role as teachers and disciplinarians. Even though freedom is real, it is not absolute. Its proper exercise depends on the acquisition of self-discipline and good judgment. The congregation also has a part to play in creating a context in which young people are equipped to make a real decision about the confirmation of their faith. It is at this point that the interrelatedness of the practices of the church becomes apparent. For the proposed reform of confirmation to work, it must be accompanied by other changes in congregational life. Some of the most important of these are the following:

  1. *Baptismal education.* This would involve the institution of a series of classes on Christian parenting offered before and after a couple has its child baptized. The vows made by the parents during the baptismal service are placed within the context of a covenantal interpretation of parenting. Parents promise to raise their offspring as a child of the covenant, providing the appropriate teaching and nurture. Within this framework, confirmation is described as pointing to an important truth: At some point, their child will have to accept the vows of the covenant herself or himself, choosing to continue on the path begun during childhood. Parents can witness to the love God has for their children, but each one must finally decide to go forward on the path initially traveled with the family of origin.

  2. *Education in the Lord's Supper.* Early participation in the Lord's Supper should be followed at some point by a special program that helps children

understand what they have experienced already. A good time to offer this sort of program would be when children are in the six- to eight-year range. Concrete images and simple stories linking this Sacrament with other accounts of covenant-making and renewing in the Bible would allow the Last Supper to be portrayed as pointing to the covenant of grace revealed in Jesus Christ. Children also will have seen confirmation services by the time they have reached this age, and confirmation could be placed in the same covenantal framework. The people standing before the church in confirmation have decided for themselves to accept the covenant in which they have participated since childhood. God has always loved them; at this point they are standing before the whole church and world to say that they accept that love. This could be interpreted to children as part of their education about the meaning of the Lord's Supper.

3. *Biblical catechesis and catechetical instruction.* In the previous chapter, mention was made of a new form of catechetical instruction centered on the Bible, not the confessional doctrines of the church. Offered at some point between the third and fifth grades, this practice would make sure children have mastered the most important stories of the Bible and can weave them together into a larger narrative whole. The church's present life would be described as a continuation of the story the Bible tells. Within this interpretive framework, models of the Christian life would be offered that are linked to current practices of the church, including confirmation. This narrative catechesis would be followed by catechetical instruction that provides doctrinal reflection on the meaning of this story. A more traditional question and answer format would be appropriate only if it were placed in an educational framework that encouraged more than rote memorization and was closely linked to the biblical material already learned.

4. *Youth ministry.* Many churches have developed special programs for youth that center on Sunday evening meetings, periodic retreats, and contact work (the attempt to build personal relationships with youth away from the church). If young people no longer enter confirmation when they reach a certain age, it would be very important that the youth ministry of the church be strong and creative, fully capable of communicating a compelling vision of the Christian life and involving youth in a range of challenging activities. It also would be important that this ministry not fall into the trap of overspecialization. If the church is large enough to have several persons on the staff, all of them should be involved with youth on a regular basis, including the senior minister. Youth should be integrated into the ongoing life of the church, assisting in worship, serving on committees, and taking part in outreach programs. Throughout its ministry to and with youth, the congregation should pose the following questions, both directly and indirectly: Are you ready to take up the vows of the covenant? Is this something you are prepared to do as an individual, not because your parents want you to or your friends have stepped forward to be confirmed? Do you really understand the cost of following Christ? On the basis of your understanding, are you ready to make a profession of faith and pledge of obedience before the church and the world?

5. *College chaplaincies.* If the church truly respects the freedom of young people to make a real choice with regard to confirmation, some will choose not to be confirmed during their high school years. This makes it important that the church develop special ministries with college students that continue the process of inviting them to take up the covenantal realities in which they have long participated. This may prove to be one of the most challenging changes that needs to take place if the reform of confirmation proposed here is to have any real plausibility. As pointed out in Part 1 of this book, research over the past four decades has consistently revealed the secularizing effects of college and university life on its students. College has become a gateway to the religiously unaffiliated sector of the population. During this same period, mainline Protestant churches have cut back their college chaplaincy programs enormously, due to dwindling financial resources. This trend must be reversed. Especially important will be the cultivation of chaplains who have competence in and love for both the academic community and congregational life and are not becoming chaplains because they are alienated from the church. Why is this important? Part of the task of the Christian chaplain in the present university life is to present the claims of the gospel in an increasingly hostile atmosphere. It involves allowing young people to become seekers without abandoning them to the cultural hedonism and careerism so prevalent on college campuses. It involves respecting the life of the mind that the university represents and attempting to pose the question of confirmation in an intellectually defensible manner. It means refusing to concede the most important thing at stake in confirmation: the reality of the covenanting God, whose graciousness precedes all human seeking and undergirds every human response.

6. *Young adult ministries and the affiliation of new members.* Everyone does not attend college, and many of those who do will graduate without being confirmed. Alongside a renewed interest in college chaplaincies, the church also must develop programs in which the question of confirmation is posed for late adolescents and young adults. There are a variety of ministries in which this could take place: singles ministries, premarital counseling, and young couples ministries. A natural place to raise the question of confirmation in each of these areas is in relation to the young person's decision to affiliate with a congregation. The mobile nature of young adults in our society makes it likely that many of the participants in these ministries will be coming from other congregations and will need to transfer their membership. This could serve as a perfect opportunity for the pastor to find out whether they have been confirmed and to explain the confirmation program of the church to them if they have not been.

Undoubtedly, creative pastors and Christian educators can think of other ways in which the question of confirmation could be posed to people throughout their participation in the church. Perhaps the most important of these has only been mentioned briefly: the confirmation service itself. As the unconfirmed people in the congregation see others participate in this service, it will set before them the importance of taking the steps involved in making a personal profession of their faith. This service, along with the changes mentioned above, would work together to create a context in which it would be possible to eliminate the quasi-automatic entry of young people into a confirmation program without abandoning them to the whims of their personal feelings, their peers, or their parents. The church would make it clear that every person baptized as an infant is expected to take up the vows of the covenant in a self-conscious, freely chosen fashion at some point in his or her life.

It is important that this be done in a manner reflecting the church's theological commitments. Confirmation does not represent the moment of personal salvation in the Christian life. It is God who performs the true work of salvation, and this should be the accent from beginning to end. It is God who is the author, executor, and sustainer of the covenant of grace. Nonetheless, this does not rule out a legitimate, secondary place for the human activity of responding to God's prior covenanting activity.

In posing the question of confirmation the church thus must resist all coercion or manipulation. It can approach its baptized children as ones who have been marked with the sign of the covenant and already participate in its benefits. At the same time, however, the church must not fall into indifference or false confidence with regard to its children. Although standing within the circle of the covenant community, the covenant lies before them as something yet to be taken up. The church has the responsibility of continually posing the question of confirmation: Are you personally ready to take up the vows of the covenant, choosing to become who you already are? Are you ready to make a profession of faith and pledge of obedience in response to God's prior covenanting activity on behalf of humanity, the church, and you personally?

Enrollment

What happens when a person steps forward and expresses the desire to be confirmed? The first phase of confirmation is the process of enrollment. It focuses on helping test the person's readiness to take this step. This decision ultimately is left to the individual and the individual alone. The church's role is to raise the important questions that the person should think about. It does not have the right to refuse to admit someone to confirmation who, upon consideration of these questions, feels ready to be enrolled.

There are several steps involved in this process. The first involves *conversation with the pastor*. In many cases, this will be preceded by informal conversations with others: the minister or lay leaders of the youth program, parents, or friends who have already been confirmed. It would be appropriate for one of these persons to accompany the individual seeking enrollment to his or her initial meeting with the pastor. At some point, however, the pastor and potential confirmand should meet by themselves in order to insure privacy and to make sure that the person is really speaking for himself or herself.

The pastor should do everything possible to create a nonthreatening atmosphere, assuring the person that she or he is not being judged and will be free to make the final decision about whether to continue. Something similar to the following should be communicated at the outset: "These are questions the church thinks it is important for us to explore together in order to help you make up your mind." The following then are some of the important questions for the pastor to raise:

1. Why are you seeking confirmation at this time? What prompted you to step forward now?
2. Do you feel under any pressure from others to enter this process?
3. How strong is your Christian education background? Do you think you are well-grounded in the basic beliefs of the church? Are you willing to study in order to strengthen those areas that are weak?
4. Are there aspects of your personal spirituality that you are especially eager to work on right now? How often do you attend public worship? Do you read the Bible and pray regularly? Are you involved in the outreach of the church on a regular basis? Have you ever been given the opportunity to reflect on your financial obligation to the church?

The goal of this pastoral conversation, which may stretch over several sessions, is to help test the person's readiness to move forward. In my view, this decision should not be made at the initial meeting. The person should be asked to continue to think and pray about these questions for several days before giving the pastor a decision about moving to the next step.

The second step in enrollment is *appearing before an appropriate governing body* to state publicly for the first time a desire to be enrolled. This can be an intimidating experience, especially if the group is rather large. For this reason, it is important that a set pattern be followed to let the person know what to expect and to reduce the feeling of an examination. A member of the governing body should meet with this person in advance to find out basic biographical information and to go over the questions that will be asked before the group. This member will introduce the person when the group meets and will ask each of the questions on behalf of the governing body. These should include questions such as the following:

1. Do you understand the meaning of confirmation?
2. Why do you seek confirmation at this time?
3. What excites you most about enrolling in our congregation's confirmation program?
4. What obstacles do you anticipate in participating in this program? How do you plan to overcome them?

It would be appropriate for the respondent to write out answers to the questions and read them to the group, although this is not as desirable as a conversational approach.

If more than one person is appearing before the group, it is important for each one to answer these questions individually. This will signal to candidates from the outset that the process they are entering is a deeply personal one. These questions might be followed by ones asked spontaneously by the group, but only if this can be done with tact and sensitivity. The presider then might ask the governing body the following question:

> **Pastor:** Do you endorse [*name*]'s desire to be enrolled in the confirmation program, and will you do everything in your power to help [*him or her*] accept more fully the covenantal relationship in which [*he or she*] already participates as a baptized member of the church?

Following this meeting with the appropriate governing body, the final step of this initial phase of confirmation is participation in a *service of enrollment* during Sunday morning worship. This is the first opportunity for the individual to stand before the church to declare the desire to be confirmed. It also is the first opportunity for the church as a whole to provide an expression of support for the person.

A word must be said here about the role of the spiritual mentor, because this figure appears in the proposed liturgy that follows. As we have seen, sponsors, exorcists, and godparents have played an important role in confirmation throughout church history. Across the ages, initiation and catechetical instruction have included special figures who have brought a more personal dimension to the process. Such is the case with the spiritual mentor. This role is designed to provide a relationship in which ongoing sharing of some depth can begin to take place during the second phase of confirmation. More will be said of this in the following section.

The service of enrollment might take the following form:

The pastor, confirmands, and spiritual mentors gather at the front of the sanctuary.

> **Pastor:** God chose us in Christ before the foundation of the world to be holy and blameless before him in love. God destined us for adoption as his children through Jesus Christ. Ephesians 1:4–5.
>
> Friends, this day is a special event in the life of the person(s) standing before you. *[Name(s)]* has expressed the desire to enroll in the confirmation program of our church. Having duly considered the seriousness of this step and having appeared before the *[name of governing body]* of our church, *[he or she]* now stands before you to declare *[his or her]* intention.
>
> *[Name]*, is your decision to enroll in the confirmation program of the church made freely through the grace of God?
>
> **Candidate:** It is.
>
> **Pastor:** As a baptized member of the church, you have been marked with the sign of the covenant. Why, then, do you seek confirmation?
>
> **Candidate:** In confirmation, I come before the church and the world to profess my faith in the God of the covenant. I come also to pledge my obedience to this same God and to take up the responsibilities of the covenant relationship by which I am joined to God and neighbor.

Pastor: Confess now the symbol of the church's faith in the triune God.

Candidate: *[The candidate will say the Apostles' Creed, followed by the accompanying phrase.]* This statement of the church's faith I will seek to understand and confess as my own.

Pastor: Pledge now your obedience by stating the laws given by God at Sinai to guide the covenant community.

Candidate: *[The candidate will say the Ten Commandments, followed by this accompanying phrase.]* These commandments I will seek to understand and follow as an expression of my obedience to God.

Pastor: Faith and obedience are part of a relationship with a living God. You must learn to seek God's counsel in all things through prayer. As an expression of your commitment to a deeper understanding of the importance of corporate and personal prayer, say now the prayer the Lord taught his disciples.

Candidate: *[The candidate will say the Lord's Prayer.]*

Pastor: The church stands with you as you enroll in the confirmation program. You will need much support and guidance in the weeks ahead. In order to provide you with this assistance *[Name of spiritual mentor]* has been appointed as your spiritual mentor. May God bless this relationship and bring it to fruition.

Let us pray. Before the foundation of the world, O God, you chose us in love through your Son, Jesus Christ. All of creation is an expression of your covenant love. From age to age, you have entered into special covenants with your people, showing forth your grace and empowering them for your service. We stand before you today as children of the covenant, as did Noah, Abraham and Sarah, Moses and Miriam, Joshua, Deborah, and David. In the fullness of time, you sent your Son Jesus to show us the depths of your love and to serve as the true covenant partner, on our behalf and in our stead.

Congregation: All of us who have been baptized into Christ Jesus were baptized into his death. As he was raised from the dead, so too we are raised to newness of life.

Pastor: Will the candidate(s) please kneel. *[The pastor and spiritual mentor will place their hands on the candidate.]* *[Name]*, you are a child of the covenant, a participant in the death and resurrection of Christ Jesus. May the Holy Spirit, who has long been present in your life, strengthen your resolve in the weeks ahead. May you come to a deeper appreciation of who you already are in Christ and come before this body in the near future to confess your faith and pledge your obedience to the God of the covenant. Amen.

Spiritual Mentoring

Once a person is enrolled, he or she is a confirmand: someone in the process of being confirmed. Because a person does not become a confirmand automatically upon reaching a certain age or grade, enrollment is followed by a second phase, spiritual mentoring. Individuals can enter this phase at any point of the year. It should last from four to twelve months. Anything less than four months is not long enough for the mentoring relationship to develop. It also is not enough time to deal with the weighty intellectual issues that come to the fore during this part of the confirmation program.

Several words of background and explanation are needed to justify this part of the proposed confirmation program, for there is a long-standing suspicion in the Reformed tradition of a preoccupation with personal spirituality. This suspicion stems from the early Reformers' critique of two quite different forms of spiritual expression that confronted them: monastic spirituality and the emergent pietism of the Anabaptists. Monastic spirituality, with its asceticism and otherworldliness, clashed with the Reformers' emphasis on Christian vocation, in which the spiritual life is centered on the service of God in the conduct of one's worldly responsibilities and roles. It also was viewed as encouraging an understanding of the Christian life in which God's favor is earned through an "increase" of an individual's personal spirituality.

The nascent pietism of the Anabaptists also was viewed with suspicion. The Reformers believed there was something inherently wrong with the Anabaptists' preoccupation with personal salvation, an inevitable by-product of their decisional view of regeneration. The true center of the Christian life is the glorification of God and service of God's purposes, not the salvation of one's soul. Likewise, they viewed with suspicion the Anabaptists' efforts to bring about an increase in piety through special meetings and Bible studies. This was seen as fostering spiritual pride and a church within the church.[1]

A suspicion of certain forms of spirituality and pietism thus was present in the reform movement from the beginning. This does not mean, however, that the Reformers rejected altogether the development of personal and corporate practices that could nurture Christian piety. Calvin defined piety as "that reverence joined with love of God which the knowledge of his benefits induces."[2] Lying behind his use of this term was the Latin term *pietas,* which in ancient Roman life implied the honor, respect, and affection children were to hold toward their parents. This was extended by the Romans to the attitudes a citizen was to show toward his country.[3] Calvin retained these connotations in his use of this term, only for him they referred to the honor, respect, and affection Christians were to show toward God.

Piety, in this sense, was a central part of Calvin's understanding of the Christian life, something that is reflected in his theology. When he writes of the knowledge of God in the *Institutes,* for example, he has in mind participatory knowledge, a knowing of God that includes the mind, the affections, and the behavior. True knowledge of God includes an attitude of proper respect, honor, and love growing out of a knowledge of God's benefits. Similarly, his understanding of the third use of the law reflects his appreciation of the positive role it can play as a spur and model for Christian piety. Indeed, he portrays the church as a whole as a context in which the enduring attitudes and behaviors of its members are shaped in a manner appropriate to the purposes of God. Piety was an important part of Calvin's theology. Building on the covenantal framework developed in the previous chapter, I use piety and spirituality interchangeably, defining them as an attitude of awe and gratitude toward the covenanting God disclosed in Jesus Christ. It is the animating force behind a Christian's devotion to the duties and responsibilities of the covenantal life. It is not possible for the church in one brief phase of its confirmation program to compensate for things that are lacking in other parts of its teaching ministry. Ideally, the church shapes the piety of its members through their participation in a wide range of practices. It is appropriate for the church to focus during confirmation on those key practices by which confirmands are given a fuller and more personal sense of their covenant relationship with God. To this end, the second phase of the proposal being developed here focuses on teaching the practices of private prayer, the study of scripture, disciplined sharing with other Christians, and vocational discernment.[4]

How should these practices be taught? The approach recommended here is that of a personal relationship between a spiritual mentor and a confirmand. The term "mentor" is chosen intentionally because it denotes one who can serve as an experienced guide or trusted counselor.[5] It is chosen instead of "spiritual director" because the latter implies a level of competence that is not necessary in the relationship being proposed here. Indeed, it is probably best if spiritual mentors normally are not clergy, for this can make it difficult for some confirmands to enter into the relationship without preconceptions. All that is needed are laypersons who have enough maturity to serve as guides in the practices that are being taught.

Obviously, it is important that mentors regularly participate in these practices themselves and have a sense of what it means to participate in them over a period of time. It also is highly desirable that they have the opportunity to reflect on the history and meaning of these practices in special classes led by the pastor, Christian educator, or some other knowledgeable teacher. Such classes could help mentors reflect on the purpose of these practices theologically and would expose them to the range of approaches that have been used by their participants across the centuries and in different branches of Christianity.

The latter is important because the approach mentors use themselves may or may not prove helpful to the confirmand with whom they are paired. Moreover, it is probably best if a standardized form or method is not taught to each confirmand, as if the only appropriate way to pray or study the Bible were to follow steps one, two, three, and four. The practices being taught have long histories in the Christian tradition and cannot be reduced to simplistic, formulaic patterns. Mentors must walk a fine line between providing concrete guidance about how a practice might be carried out and encouraging experimentation in its use as the confirmand finds a pattern that works for him or her.

The kinds of relationships formed between a mentor and confirmand undoubtedly will take many forms. Ideally, a relationship of trust and respect can develop over time, allowing a mutual sharing of depth. In such relationships, the confirmand can learn at the deepest level, identifying with the mentor and internalizing him or her as a meaningful inner figure.[6] In this kind of relationship, the piety of the mentor is more important than the particular knowledge she or he hands on. The confirmand internalizes the attitudes and visions of the mentor that animate the practices being taught. Not all relationships, of course, will reach this depth. It is enough if mutual respect develops and the mentor comes to serve as a trusted guide and source of accountability.

A few additional comments about the practices that are the focus of this phase of confirmation may be helpful. Two introductory caveats are necessary. First, the establishment of a group of spiritual mentors equipped to provide the kind of guidance described here requires the development of an educational program that is currently not found in many mainline Protestant congregations. The components of this program will become evident as we proceed. Second, it is important to keep in mind the close relationship between the corporate and private forms of the practices described below. As Calvin pointed out many times, those who come to public worship without the benefit of regular private prayer and study of scripture are not ready to hear the Word of God. He also pointed out, however, that the private exercise of these practices was likely to go astray when it was not grounded in correlative practices of the larger church. The "spiritual interpretation" of scripture by the Anabaptists had driven home the point that private study must be disciplined by corporate forms of learning and doctrinal reflection. Likewise, prayer, mutual sharing, and vocational discernment stand within the nurture and discipline of the church. Although our emphasis largely is on the personal form of these practices, it is important to explore how they can remain grounded in congregational life.

Personal Prayer

One of the hardest things for most contemporary people to learn is that prayer is not primarily a matter of asking God for things but is a matter of attuning oneself to God's purposes for the world. The primary purpose of prayer is not utilitarian. God is not to be used to meet the self-centered needs of a person. God is the divine Other, standing over against human sinfulness and finitude. The purpose of prayer is to help us move beyond the circle of our own needs to discern what the sovereign God is asking us to do and be.

At the same time, the practice of private prayer points us in the opposite direction. It not only attunes us to the otherness of God but helps us draw near to God. It is rooted in the sense of intimacy that Jesus brought to the covenant relationship when he taught his disciples to address God as "Abba." This term possesses the connotations of affection and familiarity akin to our term "Daddy."[7] Such intimacy goes far beyond the awe and respect characterizing the piety of ancient Israel. It invites those who enter into a covenant relationship with God through Jesus Christ to view themselves as adopted children who can call on their heavenly Parent to guide them and provide for them as they seek to do God's will.

In short, it is important for confirmands to learn two basic things about the purpose of private prayer: (1) It is not a matter of asking but of listening, of orienting the self to the sovereign God's purposes for the world; and (2) it is grounded in and nurtures the sense of intimacy that Jesus brought to the covenant relationship. One without the other can lead to a distorted view of prayer. Prayer that promotes overfamiliarity with God has lost a sense of God's otherness and the need to bend our wills in prayer to the purposes of God. Much contemporary spirituality in the Anabaptist tradition can be criticized along these lines. Too often, however, contemporary Reformed spirituality falls into the opposite trap, emphasizing the pursuit of moral duties and responsibilities to the exclusion of a sense of intimacy with God. Such piety leads to a dead legalism with little passion and vitality.

It is important for mentors to communicate to confirmands the need to balance both purposes in private prayer. It also is important for them to provide concrete help and guidance in how a regular prayer life might be cultivated. More than is commonly acknowledged, Calvin and other members of the Reformed tradition encouraged the use of set forms and patterns in the practice of private prayer. Calvin appended prayers to his *Genevan Catechism,* for example, that could be used to help persons move through each part of the day with a prayerful attitude.[8] Likewise, he encouraged the revival of singing and praying the psalms in corporate and private worship.[9]

Public and private forms of prayer were brought together in a manner that is important for us to retain today. The larger church provides practical forms that reflect its theological commitments. Using the psalms as a regular part of devotional prayer is a case in point.[10] The psalms teach us how to pray, inviting us to express the full range of emotions in our relationship with God, while placing these emotions in a pattern appropriate to the life of faith. The psalms provide a kind of "grammar of the heart" that is interiorized as the one praying follows their various movements in addressing God.[11] Expressions of anger or despair, for example, typically are followed by an affirmation of confidence in God's providential care.

Advice in how to use the psalms to establish a structure for the practice of private prayer is only one example of the kind of concrete guidance that spiritual mentors should be able to provide their confirmands. Such forms link the individual to the larger repository of patterns the church has developed across the centuries and, even more important, can help establish a practice that is solidly grounded in the central theological commitments of the larger church. Obviously, this requires educational programs for mentors that can equip them with the knowledge and skills necessary to guide confirmands in this way.

Study of Scripture

The study of scripture has long been recognized as one of the hallmarks of Reformed spirituality. If there is one thing that consistently received attention among the early Reformers, it was their emphasis on putting the Bible back into the hands of the people. Their support of general education and catechetical instruction was motivated by their belief that only an educated laity would be able to resist false teachings, participate in the church's ministry, and carry out their vocations in the world. Reformed piety is a scripture-centered piety. This has become deeply problematic, however, over the course of this century, making it important that spiritual mentors have a clear understanding of what is at stake in the study of scripture. Modern biblical scholarship has created a vast chasm between the findings of the academy and the use of the Bible in congregational life.[12] The devotional use of scripture often represents the most extreme example of this chasm, abandoning the contribution of scholarship altogether. One of the most important tasks of this phase of the confirmation program is to help bridge this gap. Here, as elsewhere, confirmation cannot compensate for things left undone in other parts of the teaching ministry. What it can do, however, is make sure that all those participating in the confirmation program are given the opportunity to reclaim the authority of scripture in the Christian life without sacrificing their intellectual integrity. There can hardly be a more important yet more difficult task in the church today.

It is important to remember that the early Reformers were deeply steeped in the scholarship of contemporary humanism and drew on this scholarship to counter scholastic approaches to scripture and theology. They were not compelled to sacrifice the life of the mind to the life of faith. They did, however, subordinate the former to the latter, following Augustine's advice to the preachers of his day. Augustine recommended the use of classical scholarship in the church on an analogy taken from Israel's exodus from Egypt. The Israelites stole from the Egyptians those things needed for the journey but put them to new uses.[13] So too the church should "steal" from classical scholarship those things necessary for its journey toward the city of God but put them to new uses. This is how the Reformers saw themselves as drawing on the findings and tools of humanism. They embraced the cutting edge of contemporary scholarship but put it in the service of their faith. Their piety was an intellectually informed piety. Nowhere is this more evident than in their study and interpretation of scripture. What might this mean today?

First, it means seeing scholarship for what it is. All scholarly research is a fully human, rational enterprise by which arguments are made within a communal context, using established procedures of data collection, rational scrutiny, and falsification. The time is past when scholarship, under the banner of science, can claim for itself an authority as absolute and certain as the religious authority it so often challenges. Scholarship is inherently self-critical, subject to revision on the basis of new findings and new presuppositions. This is as true of biblical scholarship as any other field. One need only take a quick survey of the many paradigms currently operative in this field to recognize the ways its scholarship depends on particular presuppositions. From rhetorical to feminist to historical critical approaches, biblical scholarship is subject to the limitations of any form of scholarship.

Second, such scholarship ultimately is not the basis of faith. Christian faith is derived from God's self-revelation in Jesus Christ, whose power and authority are acknowledged through the inner work of the Holy Spirit. Faith is brought into being through Word and Spirit. It is not subject to the vagaries of human scholarship. This does not mean, however, that scholarship has no role to play. Following Augustine's insight, picked up by the Reformers, its role is the increase of faith's understanding. Faith is impelled from within to understand all things in relation to God. In so doing, it must open itself to the ongoing findings of scholarship, putting those findings to new uses. The coordination of these findings with theology is one of the perennial tasks facing the theologians of the church.

The implications of this discussion for the study of scripture are several. First, no person should complete confirmation without being given the opportunity to understand modern critical perspectives on scripture and to place such perspectives in a broader theological context. If piety is to have intellectual integrity, it must embrace scholarship. If it is to remain faithful, it must put this scholarship in its proper place. Mentors should have at their disposal, books, pamphlets, videos, and other resources that can introduce confirmands to contemporary biblical scholarship or deepen the knowledge they already have. Confirmands should begin to read books appropriate to their level of understanding and should discuss them when meeting with their spiritual mentors. Intellectual discussions should be a regular part of their relationship.

Second, confirmands can best learn the positive contribution of such scholarship by integrating it into the practice of private prayer they are beginning to develop. This involves two distinguishable activities: the study of scripture and the devotional reading of scripture. The former draws on commentaries and other resources to better understand a text from a literary, historical, or some other scholarly perspective. A devotional reading of scripture draws on this scholarship in the attempt to listen for God's Word. Scripture is approached in a prayerful attitude with the expectation that God can and will speak through it. The confirmand should be encouraged by the mentor to establish times of study alongside the devotional reading of scripture that is an important part of prayer. It is quite common for persons to establish a pattern for such times that begins with a brief prayer asking God to ready the heart to hear and receive the Word, moves to the praying of several psalms, shifts to the devotional reading of a passage of scripture, and concludes with a time of spontaneous prayer. The devotional reading of scripture in this context is deeply enriched by times of study at other times. Piety is both intellectually informed and faithful in the attempt to be open to God's Word.

A final word should be offered about the integration of the private reading and study of scripture and its study in corporate worship and teaching. It is a welcome sign that a wide range of Bible study programs have begun to be used in the church in recent years. Such programs could be structured in a way to support both the individual's study and the devotional reading of scripture. It would be quite helpful if spiritual mentors could point to such programs in their conversations with confirmands, encouraging them to join them upon the completion of the confirmation program.

Disciplined Sharing with Other Christians

In large measure, disciplined sharing with other Christians will be the focus of the next phase of the confirmation program, for it is structured around a small group format. A few comments can be offered here, for the mentor-confirmand relationship also is a form of disciplined sharing. The larger issue at stake is the importance of helping confirmands recognize the role that disciplined sharing with other Christians plays in the Christian life. Although respect for individual conscience has always been an important aspect of the Reformed tradition, this has been balanced by an equal regard for the importance of communal checks on the individual. This grows out of the recognition that the capacity for human self-deception is great, making it important for individuals to test their insights by sharing them with others.

During the second phase of confirmation, it is the mentor-confirmand relationship that is the focal point of this sharing. Several guidelines can be offered.

1. *Set meetings should be established at a regular time and place.* No relationship has a chance to grow unless the participants have an opportunity to be together on a regular basis. The mentor-confirmand relationship should be treated with the same seriousness as a therapeutic or spiritual direction relationship. It would be helpful to meet at least every other week for an hour, although longer and more frequent meetings are desirable. It is good to meet on neutral ground, away from either party's home. The meeting place should afford privacy and prevent interruptions.

2. *The meeting should gradually adopt a regular format.* When the mentor and confirmand first begin to meet, it is important that the mentor provide some structure. The confirmand will be looking to the mentor to set the tone for the meeting and to establish the sort of sharing that will take place. At first, these meetings are likely to deal with assigned reading and the practices being taught. The mentor functions as a kind of teacher. It is important that this gradually give way to a meeting pattern that is mutually established and has more balance between guiding and listening, teaching and learning on the part of the mentor.

3. *The meeting should include intellectual discussion and personal sharing.* As the discussion of prayer and the study of scripture has made apparent already, there are important intellectual components to this phase of the confirmation program. All confirmands are to come to terms with modern biblical scholarship, for example, and to place it in a theological framework. This involves serious intellectual work on the part of both mentor and confirmand. At the same time, this relationship is not to focus solely on academic topics. It should include times of personal sharing. As the confirmand begins to establish a regular prayer life, it would be quite natural to make the transition from intellectual discussion to personal sharing by asking questions such as: What sorts of things have been going on in your life this week? Are there particular insights or issues that keep coming up when you pray? What about your relationships? Are there important things going on there? In turning to these areas, the mentor is not becoming a therapist. The goal is to assist confirmands in discerning the Spirit of God in their lives and to better hear the concrete Word that God is speaking to them.

4. *Teach when necessary; guide when suitable; ask when possible.* It is important for the mentor to keep the larger goal of confirmation in mind: allowing the confirmand to take up the vows of the covenant in a qualitatively new way. It is the confirmand's personal understanding and appropriation of the faith that should take center stage, not the mentor's insights or a particular resource. Accordingly, the confirmation program as a whole should use educational approaches that evoke the confirmand's active construction of the topic at hand. This is especially important in the mentor-confirmand

relationship, giving rise to the guideline offered above. Teaching is used here in a rather narrow sense to refer to the handing on of special knowledge and skills.[14]

Obviously, the mentor has been chosen because he or she is experienced in the practices being taught, experience that hopefully has been deepened through participation in special classes for mentors. This knowledge and experience undoubtedly will prove helpful to the confirmand at certain points and should be taught when necessary. Guiding implies a less direct approach on the part of the mentor, showing the way but letting the confirmand travel there himself or herself. Asking implies even less direction on the part of the mentor, raising the right question at the right time but refusing to provide direct guidance about what should be thought or done. In light of the larger goal of confirmation, asking should be an important part of the relationship.

Vocational Discernment

One of the most important theological shifts having a direct impact on the early Reformers' understanding of piety was their reconstruction of the concept of Christian vocation. Luther provided the initial insight, and it soon was picked up by other leaders of the reform movement. Vocation is derived from *vocatio,* meaning calling. Theologically, it describes the Christian calling to serve God in every part of one's life. In the Reformers' minds, this meant there is no special sphere of life that is more sacred than any other. Christians were not to withdraw from the world to serve God but were to serve God in their various worldly responsibilities. They were called as parents, workers, citizens, students, and church members. It was no accident that Reformed theologians later developed the idea of vocation along covenantal lines. All of life was viewed, in the context of the sovereign God's covenanting activity and different life spheres, as placing before the Christian different covenantal responsibilities. Christian vocation involved the proper ordering of one's life in accordance with the roles and responsibilities of the different covenants of which one was a part. It is difficult to retain this understanding of vocation in the contemporary world. As we saw in the first part of this book, modernization has altered markedly the place of religion in society through the processes of institutional differentiation and secularization. In modern life, religion typically is confined to the private sphere, focusing on existential crises and matters of personal morality. It does not offer a comprehensive interpretive framework that is shared by most members of society.

Institutional differentiation and secularization make it difficult for Christians to develop a sense of vocation. Most contemporary Christians have little sense of what it might mean to discern their calling to serve God in the workplace, the political arena, or even the home. As we have pointed out repeatedly, it is not possible for confirmation alone to provide a remedy for a trend this broadly based. This must be done by the church as a whole. Nonetheless, as the beginning of a broader reform of the church, confirmation can point the way. If confirmation is to focus on the individual's self-conscious acceptance of the vows of the covenant, then it must make sure that it does not unwittingly reflect the modern assumption that this covenant only has to do with the private sphere of life. It is more important today than ever that all confirmed members of the church be given the opportunity to understand their calling as embracing the entire range of roles and responsibilities in which they participate.

There undoubtedly are many ways this can be accomplished. The present proposal uses a twofold strategy: exploration of one life sphere in depth and adoption of an action/reflection educational model. The life sphere we have chosen to focus on is the political arena, examining Christians' roles and responsibilities as citizens. By exploring this sphere in some depth from a vocational perspective, it is hoped that confirmands will be able to apply the broadened understanding of calling they gain here to other areas of their life. The use of an action/reflection approach is designed to reinforce the idea that vocation has to do with life outside the church. It also is a particularly powerful way to teach confirmands how to reflect theologically on their experience, a skill that lies at the heart of their ability to carry out their vocation in the world.

The broad contours of this part of the program can be outlined. Under the guidance of the mentor, the confirmand should seek out and become actively involved in a volunteer organization that is attempting to address a pressing social problem like homelessness, hunger, illiteracy, domestic violence, or mental illness. It would be extremely helpful if the organization had a political advocacy dimension to it, because this would bring issues of Christian citizenship to the fore. Ideally, the mentor would work with the confirmand in the program on a regular basis, affording an excellent opportunity to deepen their relationship. If this is not possible, they should work together two or three times at a minimum. This hands-on involvement is to be supported by study and reflection with the mentor that attempts to help the confirmand do two things: (1) reflect theologically on the vocational issues raised by his or her participation in this organization; and (2) explore the systemic dimensions of the particular problem the organization is attempting to address.

This reflection is quite important. It would be easy to lapse into thinking of involvement in organizations of this sort as merely an act of Christian charity. As far as the confirmation program is concerned, however, the Christian's role as a citizen and as a member of a particular state is at stake. What are the appropriate roles and responsibilities of the Christian citizen? What is the role of the state in a theological perspective? How does involvement in volunteer organizations in a democratic society intersect with larger political issues?

Equally important is reflection that helps the confirmand gain a systemic perspective on the problem being addressed. If a confirmand is working with a group that attempts to feed and house homeless people, for example, questions of the following sort would be helpful: What sectors of the population have the highest incidence of homelessness? What is the relationship of homelessness to changes in the economy? What effects do particular public policies (for example, the deinstitutionalization of mental hospitals in the late 1970s) have on homelessness? What is the relationship of homelessness to larger social structures such as racism and sexism?

No doubt this is a tall order. The combination of action and reflection, however, has the potential of making a particularly powerful impact on the confirmand's piety. Just as the confirmand steps forward to accept in a deeper way the vows of the covenant, he or she is given the opportunity to form a much broader and richer understanding of calling to the service of God. Christian vocation includes every area of life. It involves the discernment of the roles and responsibilities entailed by serving a God whose covenanting activity embraces all of creation.

Catechetical Instruction

The third phase of confirmation is catechetical instruction. This phase is designed to build on the patterns established during spiritual mentoring and to deepen the confirmand's intellectual understanding of the profession of faith and pledge of obedience that will be made during the confirmation service.

Depending on the size of the church and the number of people who are likely to participate in the confirmation program in any given year, catechetical instruction should be offered on a yearly basis. If the church regularly has a large number participating in this program, it may want to offer this part of the program during both fall and spring. If taking place in the fall, the confirmation service might occur in conjunction with the new year, an appropriate time for the congregation as a whole to join the confirmands in renewing the covenant vows. If offered in the spring, Pentecost would be an appropriate time for confirmation.

This phase of confirmation maintains continuity with catechetical instruction as it has been carried out across church history. Its subject matter is the traditional catechetical trilogy of the Lord's Prayer, the Apostles' Creed, and the Ten Commandments. This basic material is supplemented with other important teaching (for example, the sacraments and the Sermon on the Mount). The theological contents of the faith are taken seriously, as they traditionally have been in catechetical instruction.

The theological contents, moreover, are located within the context of a broader practice, as in the adult catechumenate. They build on and deepen knowledge and skills acquired through participation in other phases of confirmation: the study of scripture, the discipline of personal prayer, and the discernment of Christian vocation.

In one significant way, however, the present proposal differs markedly from earlier forms of catechetical instruction. Its emphasis on the professional purpose of confirmation leads me to adopt an educational format designed to allow confirmands to grapple with the meaning of the material studied in both a personal and substantive manner. While its goal is to allow confirmands to make an intelligent confession of the church's faith, even more important is the goal of covenant ratification: the individual's personal profession of faith and pledge of obedience. To this end, a small group format is used. Confirmands are placed in groups of eight to ten people meeting on a weekly basis. The use of small groups does two things: (1) provides a context in which the practices of prayer, study, and vocational discernment can be continued and deepened, and (2) affords a setting that is small enough to use a discussion format to study the traditional catechetical pieces. A few words about both dimensions of catechetical instruction are in order.

The spiritual mentoring phase of this program involves disciplined sharing between the mentor and confirmand. If this relationship goes well, there is no reason for it not to continue on a more informal basis during the phase of catechetical instruction. The goal of this phase, however, is helping the confirmand make the transition from a mentoring relationship to one of a peer among peers. It is now time to move from apprenticeship to mature acceptance of the roles and responsibilities of a covenant relationship with God. Participation in a meaningful small group of peers is designed to help this take place.

It also provides support for the disciplines begun during the previous phase. Small group meetings should begin or end with a period of sharing the personal insights and issues that are emerging in their prayer and study. By supporting the practice of these disciplines in a new context, the chances are better that they will be continued beyond the mentor-confirmand relationship and even beyond the confirmation program itself. The insights and systematic analysis associated with vocational discernment also should be integrated into this phase. A weekend retreat would allow each confirmand to teach the group about the project with which he or she worked and what was learned about its systemic dimensions and vocational implications. If a retreat does not seem feasible, each confirmand could be given part of one group meeting to teach others about what has been learned.

The small group format is chosen because it affords a context in which the disciplines of the previous phase can be continued. It also is an excellent setting for the use of a discussion method on a regular basis. In my view, the discussion method should be the predominant one used throughout catechetical instruction, in light of the professional purpose of confirmation. The catechetical pieces are to be studied with one central goal in mind: to help the confirmands understand what is at stake in taking up the vows of the covenant and in making a profession of faith and pledge of obedience. The give and take of a discussion approach is the best way of allowing confirmands to clarify their understanding of the intellectual substance of the catechetical pieces and to explore what it means to be guided by them today.

This task would be greatly facilitated if the group were able to draw on a catechism or catechetical manual that offers a rich and insightful interpretation of the traditional catechetical pieces and raises questions about their contemporary meaning. Ideally, these resources would offer a balance of theological substance, simplicity of expression, and relevance to contemporary life. Various modern theologians have written about one or another of the catechetical pieces, and their writings could be adapted or new ones developed for use in the confirmation program. The best theological minds of the church could be encouraged to write such pieces. While they are actually being used in confirmation programs, those found most compelling and theologically appropriate gradually would come to the fore.

A catechetical manual that draws on the underlying theology of the present proposal might teach the traditional catechetical pieces and supplementary material in the following manner. The Apostles' Creed would be examined in conjunction with the triune faith confessed in Baptism and the Lord's Supper. The confirmands were baptized in the name of the Father, Son, and Holy Spirit and, as such, are children of the covenant. They renew this covenant each time they participate in the Lord's Supper. The Apostles' Creed points to the work of each member of the Trinity and the place of the church within this work. Exploration of each phrase of the creed could take place in conjunction with both traditional and contemporary meanings. Examination of the Father's role as maker of heaven and earth, for example, opens important contemporary questions about the appropriateness of masculine language in describing God and recent developments in cosmology. Similarly, Jesus' suffering under Pilate raises questions about God's relation to suffering in general and the appropriateness of describing any form of suffering as salvific. In short, the Apostles' Creed would be explored in conjunction with the confession of faith in the triune God taking place during Baptism and the Lord's Supper but now explicitly affirmed by the confirmand during the confirmation service. What does it mean to confess faith in the God of the covenant of grace? In conjunction with this examination of the Creed, it also would be highly desirable to examine the prayers of thanksgiving offered in both sacramental services. Here God's covenanting activity is rehearsed in a special way and explicitly related to the sacraments.

The Ten Commandments and material from the New Testament, especially the Sermon on the Mount, would be studied as an expression of the law. What is the role of the law in the Christian's life? Why has it traditionally been viewed in the Reformed tradition as God's gift to the covenant community? Traditional themes such as the relation of the law to the gospel and the three uses of the law could be examined, as well as contemporary questions. Helping confirmands struggle with the place of freedom, conscience, and the guidance of the law in relation to issues such as homosexuality, capital punishment, and medical ethics could also help them construct an interpretive framework by which to respond to ethical concerns. The law is not a dead thing or a legalistic whip, but a living source of guidance in the confirmand's attempt to discern and obey God's will in the present.

The covenantal life is a dynamic, adventurous relationship with God, something that could be explored in relation to the Lord's Prayer. The confirmands have been involved in the discipline of devotional prayer throughout the program. The Lord's Prayer can help them reflect critically on what they have been practicing. What does it mean to ask God for daily bread? Does this authorize asking God for material blessings? Does it teach the one praying to ask God only for the material things necessary for the day at hand, like the gift of manna during Israel's wandering in the wilderness? It is not difficult to see how reflection on questions like these could be developed in a number of directions: the lure of careerism, the fairness of the distribution of contemporary resources in the world economy, or the appropriate level of financial support that a confirmed member ought to make. Virtually any theme having to do with the appropriate use of the material resources provided by God could be explored.

In short, the confirmation program would explore the traditional catechetical pieces in terms of a covenantal framework, with an eye to the profession and pledge the confirmands are about to make. A discussion method would be used much of the time to maximize the confirmands' engagement with the material. In order for this discussion to have depth and to help the confirmands accumulate insight and knowledge over time, it would be important for the small group leader and the catechetical manual to provide appropriate background material at various points. Ideally, a manual offering both substantive commentary and contemporary questions could provide this background in assigned readings. With a minimal amount of new input from the leader, the discussion could begin. If the leader is skillful in guiding the discussion, it will be possible to make sure that the important issues are covered without usurping the group's pursuit of those themes most interesting to it.

The Confirmation Service

The final phase of the confirmation program is the actual service of confirmation. During the final portion of catechetical instruction, the liturgy of the confirmation service should be closely studied This would provide each confirmand with the opportunity to decide whether he or she is ready to make the covenantal vows lying at the heart of the service. Once this is done, a list of those confirmands who have decided to confirm their vows would be announced to the congregation, reminding the whole church of the importance of the occasion and inviting them to use the service as a time to renew their own covenant vows.

In earlier chapters, we have examined certain aspects of the services used by the Episcopal, Lutheran, United Methodist, and Presbyterian denominations. All of these, except the Presbyterian Church, use the rubric "confirmation" to refer to a special service in which individuals are given an opportunity to confess the baptismal covenant. Although the confirmation service is one of several services allowing the reaffirmation of the baptismal covenant, it retains its own identity and special focus. The thrust of this book has been to argue that the Presbyterian Church should join these denominations in using this rubric. Its service for "Reaffirmation of the Baptismal Covenant," in which a profession of faith is made for the first time, is structurally similar to the services used by the other denominations. Elements of profession, renunciation, and pledging are present. The service as it stands in the current *Book of Common Worship* represents an excellent liturgy for confirmation, with several minor alterations. Most important, the service would be identified as a nonrepeatable confirmation service. Confirmation language would be introduced into the service at appropriate points. I would eliminate the use of oil and consignation from the service, for they are descendents of the medieval understanding of confirmation and are closely identified with the bestowal of the Holy Spirit. Anointing has been restored to the baptismal service and has no place here. Laying on of hands was the sign of blessing preferred by Calvin and Bucer, and it is adequate. At first glance, use of the two traditional prayers offered in conjunction with the laying on of hands—the Defend Prayer and the

Prayer for the Sevenfold Gifts of the Spirit—might run into the same problem as the use of oil and consignation: implying bestowal of the Holy Spirit through the service. This is not the case. Both recall Bucer's language as mediated through the early prayer books of the Church of England and place the accent on the "daily increase" of the Spirit. This is appropriate theologically, because it indicates that the confirmand, as a child of the covenant, already participates in the life of the Spirit and that confirmation is in no way either completing Baptism or bestowing something new.

After Confirmation

The period immediately following confirmation is an important one. Confirmands have been participating in an intense practice for many months and have received special support from their mentor and small group. It would be easy for the confirmation service to be followed by a kind of letdown or for the confirmand to lose the sense of involvement and idealism that this practice can foster. How can the church respond to these potential difficulties? Several concrete guidelines can be offered.

1. *Interpret these phenomena to confirmands during the final phase of catechetical instruction.* There are many occasions in pastoral care in which knowing that your experience in the midst of a crisis is normal helps you understand and accept it. Knowing that it is normal for adolescents to question the authority of their parents and to rely on the judgments of their peers can help parents not to overreact when they receive criticism. It may be helpful for confirmands to be apprised of the potential letdown that can accompany the end of confirmation.

2. *Help newly confirmed members get involved in the educational ministry of the church.* If the church has other educational and outreach activities in place, it is important for confirmands to understand what these activities are and how they can get involved. High commitment educational offerings are especially desirable. Many churches have ongoing Bible study programs or well-developed small group ministries that would allow confirmands to build on the disciplines of study, prayer, and sharing established during confirmation. It also would be helpful if the educational ministry of the congregation offered classes giving the opportunity to reflect on different spheres of life from a vocational perspective. One of the key insights the practice of confirmation attempts to evoke is an understanding of every sphere of life as a part of the Christian's calling to serve God. Deepening and concretizing this perspective with ongoing classes in areas such as parenting and work would go a long way toward helping the vocational thrust of confirmation to have more than a short-term effect.

3. *Encourage confirmands to accept a position of leadership and service in the congregation or beyond.* If confirmation has gone well, those who confirm the vows of the covenant will have a new sense of their personal understanding of and commitment to the faith. It is important for the church to pro-

vide newly confirmed members of the church with opportunities to act on this deeper sense of commitment by placing their gifts at God's disposal through service in the congregation or beyond. Confirmands should be expected to assume leadership and are likely to be quite willing to do so. The pastor, Christian educator, and nominations committee should consistently seek to involve newly confirmed members of the church in positions of leadership appropriate to their gifts. The church should be proactive in this regard. The sphere of meaningful service, moreover, should not be viewed as confined to the congregation. Some confirmands may continue to work in the organization with which they were involved during confirmation. Others may have become interested in another organization through the teaching of one of their fellow confirmands. Service and leadership outside the church should be encouraged and viewed as an important expression of the confirmand's sense of vocation.

4. *Develop patterns of follow-up with newly confirmed members.* These new members of the church should not be forgotten as soon as they are confirmed. Congregations should develop appropriate strategies to follow up on a personal level with each participant in the most recent confirmation program. The pastor, spiritual mentor, or small group leader would be the natural ones to carry this out. The purpose of this would be twofold: to show continuing interest in the individual on a personal level and to gain some sense of how well the new member is building on the insights, knowledge, and skills gained during confirmation. A word of encouragement may be all that is needed. Stronger forms of intervention may be warranted, however. During confirmation, the person has taken up the vows of the covenant. If for some reason this has not proven to have a long-lasting effect, it is appropriate for the congregation to gently invite the person to consider the importance of the promises that were made. It also is important that the congregation make sure it has not neglected to provide opportunities for the person to lead and serve in areas in which he or she is interested.

Conclusion

Confirmation should not be viewed as an ending but as a beginning. It is a step forward in a person's appropriation of the covenant of grace in which he or she has long participated. Confirmation does not represent the focal point of salvation. This is properly located in God's decision in eternity to be for humanity in Jesus Christ and the revelation and enactment of this decision in the Son's work of reconciliation. Baptized Christians have been marked with the sign of the covenant and have renewed their allegiance to it each time they participate in the Lord's Supper. Confirmation takes its place within this larger framework. Its emphasis on the individual's confession of faith and pledge of obedience is not the fruit of an individualistic view of salvation or of an occasionalistic view of grace. God's covenant of grace is the larger context in which all of life takes place, and its ongoing discernment and appropriation represents the heart of the Christian life. Confirmation represents a small step forward in this process. The adventure of a life of vocation is just begining. Each time the Lord's Supper is celebrated, the covenant of grace is renewed. On special occasions, reaffirmation of the baptismal covenant also allows this to take place.

Nonetheless, confirmation represents an important moment in the Christian's life. It is the time when the personal and individual dimensions of the faith come to the fore. The church tells those who would enter confirmation: "Now is the time for you to confirm the vows of the covenant, taking them up with understanding and in freedom." Moments of choice and decision are not the heart of salvation, but they do have an appropriate place. One place they find expression is in confirmation.

All this, however, remains prospective. Confirmation presently does not play this role in the life of the church. It wavers uncertainly between theological confusion and practical need. This chapter's proposal represents a call to move beyond the present state of affairs and to begin the pressing business of reform. It is offered in full awareness that such reform ultimately awaits the work of the Holy Spirit and cannot be engendered by human means alone. This affirmation of divine agency is no excuse for refusing to do everything that possibly can be done. To that end, this work is offered. May it be used to God's own ends and in God's own time.

Epilogue

Confirmation in Practical Theological Perspective

Paul Tillich once pointed out that while the section on theological method usually is the first to appear in a book on theology, it often is the last to be written.[1] There is much truth in Tillich's insight, but I have taken the opposite tack in this book. From the very outset of this project, I have been clear that a book on confirmation needed to be written from the perspective of practical theology. Other than a few comments about practical theology at various points in the book, however, relatively little has been said thus far about this form of theological reflection. Why?

Discussions of theological method have been compared to a speaker who rises to give a speech and begins to clear his throat before starting. The audience is willing to indulge a few "Ahems" but if they go on indefinitely, it will begin to think that the speaker does not really want to get on with the presentation. There has been a tendency in modern theology to get stuck in the throat-clearing stage, becoming so preoccupied with theological method that the material and constructive tasks of theology never get performed. I have attempted to avoid this pitfall by plunging into the task of writing a practical theology of confirmation, offering only enough comments on practical theology to provide a general orientation. Here at the end of the book, I hope to provoke "Ahas" and not "Ahems" by articulating briefly the methodological commitments that have informed this work.

Practical theology is not an unproblematic rubric. It often is viewed as that branch of theology with the task of providing "how to" methods for ministers. This is often how it is viewed in seminaries and schools of divinity by those outside this field. An understanding of its history provides insight into the origin of this understanding of practical theology and the reasons it is being rejected by most practical theologians today. Practical theology as a distinct branch of theology first appeared in conjunction with the emergence of the research university of the early modern period.[2] Although its roots are found in the differentiation of moral theology from dogmatics, it emerged as a specialized academic discipline precisely when religion became problematic in the context of modernity and the specialized research orientation of the modern university gave rise to the encyclopedic organization of theology.[3]

Thus there were two catalysts in the emergence of practical theology. On the one hand, the challenges to Christianity posed by modernity forced the church to reflect on its beliefs and practices in the face of an increasingly secular, empirically oriented world. On the other hand, this response took a specific form because of its location in the single most important center of modern intellectual thought: the modern research university.[4] Theology was forced to define itself in relation to the model of rationality beginning to emerge in this setting. Broadly speaking, this model was characterized by three general features: (1) science was viewed as paradigmatic of rationality because of its disinterested, objective stance, its use of mathematical models, and its ability to secure findings that could stand the test of public scrutiny; (2) rationality took the form of increasingly specialized research programs; and (3) practical reason was reduced to the technological task of applying the findings of pure research.[5]

In order to justify its existence in the university, theology began to internalize each of these trends. They are reflected in the thinking of major theologians such as Friedrich Schleiermacher, generally considered the father of modern theology. Theology began by adopting the methods of modern scholarship. It was during this period, for example, that biblical studies began to engage in critical forms of analysis, and church history began to adopt modern forms of historical investigation. With science the paradigm of rationality, theology did not merely engage these scholarly disciplines as dialogue partners but began to view its own "scientific" task exclusively in terms of their methods and procedures. In other words, it had no rationality proper to its own subject matter and practice, at least none that deserves the name science.

Schleiermacher is illustrative of this trend.[6] He described theology as a "positive science," defined as "an assemblage of scientific elements which belong together not because they form a constituent part of the organization of the sciences, as though by some necessity arising out of the notion of science itself, but only insofar as they are requisite for carrying out a practical task."[7] Theology, as such, is not a part of science proper. It is scientific only to the extent that it draws on and coordinates the methods and findings of other scholarly disciplines.

Schleiermacher also is illustrative of theology's response to the second trend characterizing the modern university: the emergence of highly specialized research programs. It was during this period that disciplines in the modern sense first appeared. Scholarship was viewed as carried out in the context of research communities bound together by a defining area of interest, technical language, and specialized procedures of investigation, communication, and proof. As disciplines became more specialized, a specific literary genre emerged to coordinate their findings: the encyclopedia. Two types of encyclopedias were produced: great multi-volume dictionaries, gathering together and organizing the findings of different disciplines, and field-oriented encyclopedias, designed to introduce students to a particular field of study.[8] As theology began to organize itself into specialized disciplines, it too began to produce field-oriented encyclopedias that could introduce students to the theological disciplines and help them understand these disciplines' relation to one another and the theological task as a whole. Schleiermacher's *Brief Outline on the Study of Theology* was one of the most popular of these theological encyclopedias. It identified three branches of theology: philosophical, historical, and practical.

It thus was in the context of this encyclopedic organization of theology that the rubric of practical theology first began to be used on a wide scale. The way practical theology was defined in this context was deeply influenced by the third trend characterizing the modern university: the reduction of practical reason to the technological task of applying the findings of pure research. This understanding of practical reason represented a major departure from the way it had been viewed in the thinking and educational programs of the renaissance humanists immediately preceding the modern period. Harking back to Greek and Roman antiquity, the humanists held in tension both logic-centered and practical notions of reason.[9] The latter was found in areas of study such as medicine, law, rhetoric, the pastoral arts, and moral theology. In these practical fields, reason was viewed as oriented toward the performance of a complex activity within a contingent field of experience. The knowledge it offered was not portrayed as the necessary conclusions of formal arguments but as general guidelines summarizing insights from past practice that could help practitioners discern how to proceed in the face of the particularities of the situation at hand. Reason was seen as moving analogically from paradigmatic to individual cases, providing help in how to perform complex activities such as arguing a legal case, offering moral guidance, making a medical diagnosis, or preaching a sermon.[10]

In contrast, the research university employed an understanding of rationality in which modern science was paradigmatic, leading to the demise of the much richer, classical understanding of practical reason. Practical reason was, now, consigned the much more limited task of formulating methods and techniques that applied the findings of pure research. It was precisely this understanding of practical reason that was used to interpret the role of practical theology in the newly emerging theological encyclopedias. Again Schleiermacher is illustrative of a much broader trend. He describes practical theology as a "technical discipline" charged with the task of formulating the "technology" by which the findings of the other theological disciplines are put to use in the contemporary life of the church.[11] Indeed, he goes so far as to write: "If philosophical and historical theology have been clearly appropriated, and in the right proportion, nothing further remains of a theoretical nature in order to acquire a right conception of these tasks."[12] Practical theology was concerned with mere technique, not with research or theory-construction. It is little wonder that this understanding of practical theology quickly degenerated into a form of craftsmanship by which ministers-to-be were initiated into the conventional lore of congregational life. Retired ministers were brought in to teach courses in this field. A research or theoretical orientation was not expected of its practitioners.

Practical theology has attempted to break out of this limited understanding of its task in a variety of ways. With the rise of the social sciences, it attempted to follow the lead of the other theological disciplines and adopt the methods and findings of fields considered genuinely scholarly. In many cases, it came under domination by these cognate fields. In the United States, for example, the religious education and clinical pastoral education movements focused almost exclusively on education, developmental psychology, psychotherapy, or modern philosophy. While this was an understandable response to the helps-and-hints approach of practical theology, it represented a continuation of the problem, not a real solution. Practical theology as a form of *theology* still had no defining subject matter or modes of rationality of its own. It was left with the false alternative of either accepting a severely reduced understanding of practical reason or adopting the "scientific" (read: truly rational) approaches of other fields.

There is a widespread consensus that we stand at the end of the era in which practical theology initially took shape. The judgment is commonplace that the older understanding of rationality, modeled on an objectivist, hyperspecialized understanding of science and reducing practical reason to matters of application, has collapsed. Whether this is construed as the end of modernity and the movement into postmodernity or as a qualitative shift within modernity itself, the reasons given for this turn are many and complex.[13] The philosophy of science has pointed to science's historical and social grounds, undercutting the possibility of pure objectivity. The role of the imagination, models, and metaphorical knowing in science also has come to the fore. Cultural anthropologists have made us aware of the ethnocentrism inherent in equating human rationality with scientific rationality. Philosophy has moved beyond its "turn toward the subject" in which it was preoccupied with the subject's consciousness and the epistemological focus this entailed. It has turned toward language and communication as the most fundamental mediums of human understanding. This has led to a rebirth of practical philosophy in hermeneuetics, rhetoric, and ethics.

In this new postmodern context, the interested, communally based argumentation of theology no longer is placed in the role of the unwelcome guest in the academic house. The fact that theology has a set of practical precommitments and interpretive frames does not make it different from any other rational enterprise. This is particularly good news to practical theology, which played the poor stepchild of the unwelcome guest in the old academic house. Its position today is virtually reversed, as all forms of theology scramble to indicate the ways that they too are grounded in some form of praxis. Within practical theology itself, a much broader and richer understanding of its nature and purpose has begun to emerge on a truly international scale. Gert Otto, Dietrich Rössler, Johannes van der Ven, Don Browning, Duncan Forrester, Pam Couture, and many others have begun to usher in a new understanding of practical theology.[14] Three characteristics of the emerging paradigm are particularly important.

First, practical theology is no longer confined to the ecclesial-pastoral paradigm in which the ministries of the church and the pastor are its subject matter. It now is seen as examining the church in the context of society as a whole. This entails complex forms of contextual analysis that include the empirical church and its socio-historical context. Second, practical theology is viewed as having its own constructive theoretical task. It examines ends as well as means, generating theoretical models as a regular part of its work. Third, it is concerned more directly with the pragmatics of transformation than is any other form of theology. While all forms of theology may be viewed as practical, practical theology alone is concerned with the construction of knowledge that can guide the members of the church in their attempt to actually perform some aspect of the Christian life. Its theoretical models must issue in concrete guidance at the level of concrete human existence or it has not completed its practical theological task.

The understanding of practical theology informing this book has been deeply influenced by this new paradigm. It begins by situating confirmation practice in the context of modernization and then locates it historically. It offers reflection on the ends governing confirmation and concludes with concrete guidelines for the implementation of the proposed confirmation program. It shares these general characteristics with many other contemporary forms of practical theology. Within the new understanding of practical theology that has begun to emerge, however, this book represents a particular perspective, one that is far more Barthian than most others. The two most influential practical theologians in Germany in recent years, Gert Otto and Dietrich Rössler, stand in the tradition of Friedrich Schleiermacher, even as they transform his understanding of practical theology in significant ways. They place great emphasis on practical theology's examination of the function of religion in shifting socio-historical contexts and the critical assessment of this function. Moreover, Schleiermacher's understanding of theology as a "positive science" also is adopted: the position that theology has no true rationality of its own but adopts the rational methods and findings of the other scholarly disciplines and places them in the service of theological reflection.[15]

In the approach to practical theology informing my work, these Schleiermachian tenets are not accepted as constituitive of practical theology. Although contextual analysis is important, there are grave dangers in reducing the church to the category of *religion,* even for empirical purposes. Theology, moreover, is viewed as a form of rationality that is *sui generis,* its own thing. Theology has its own subject matter and object, which determines its unique methods of investigation, modes of proof, and genres of argumentation. These criticisms are indebted to the insights of Karl Barth.

The legacy of Barthian practical theology is a mixed one. Barth's good friend Eduard Thurneysen may have done him more harm than good in the program of practical theology he projected.[16] With little interdisciplinary sophistication, Thurneysen did not properly acknowledge either the role of contextual analysis or the relative independence of practical theology from dogmatic theology.[17] He too often engaged in a kind of applied theology in which church doctrines formulated at an abstract level were used to determine practice. He was followed in this approach by the Canadian practical theologian, James Smart, the editor of the Presbyterian *Faith and Life* curriculum.[18]

Barth's theology appears to lend itself to a much more dynamic and interdisciplinary understanding of practical theology. Long before the postmodern discussion had arisen, Barth insisted that theology has its own subject matter and object, which give rise to its own unique forms of rationality.[19] His definition of this subject matter was christological, focusing on the one Word of God, Jesus Christ, as the norm of Christian faith and life. This led him to affirm the penultimate authority of scripture as it points to the Word and the living witness of the church. Jesus Christ as the Word of God is viewed both dynamically and paradoxically in all three of these theological sources. The Word is not portrayed as something given straightforwardly in the Incarnation, the words of the Bible, or the witness of the church. God's self-disclosure consists of both a revealing and a concealing.

One of the ways Barth attempted to honor this affirmation was by working in a dialectical fashion in his theology.[20] It was common for him to examine a theme from one perspective and then examine it again from a sharply contrasting perspective, affirming both as necessary and valid. This was his attempt to remain faithful to the multidimensional and incomprehensible nature of theology's subject matter. Theology's task is not to reduce the paradoxical character of God's self-disclosure to a system, organized around an integrated set of ideas or a particular method. Rather, its task is to follow and display the patterns of God's revealing and concealing, holding in tension various elements of thought in order to remain faithful to these patterns.

One of the implications of Barth's dialectical approach to theology was his use of a procedure for ordering its various parts that George Hunsinger calls "dialectical inclusion."[21] Hunsinger describes this as follows:

> Barth's sense of the interrelatedness of all Christian doctrine sometimes leads him to work with patterns of "dialectical inclusion," in which the part is included in the whole, and the whole in the part. Each part is thought to contain, from a certain vantage point, the entire structure. The part includes within itself the entire pattern and way of functioning of the whole. The part is not just a division of the whole but a reiteration of it.[22]

This way of ordering his theology leads to one of the maddening, but important, features of Barth's writing style: his repetition. As he treats each new part of his theology, he repeats the whole. Whether the topic is justification, election, or sanctification, the whole mystery of God's relation to humanity is at stake and must be treated from the perspective of the topic at hand. Each new part of his theology, as such, is not so much a division as a reiteration of the whole that is present in the part. Moreover, Barth's goal is not to achieve a rational synthesis of each part, but to allow each part's perspective on the whole to stand in a tensive, nonreductionistic relation to the other parts of his theology. The part is *only* part, and it finds its proper place only in relation to the whole. The doctrine of sanctification by itself does not represent the full meaning of the Christian life; it is only part of the story. However, its perspective on the whole is not reduceable to some other topic. Indeed, it may even stand in a paradoxical relation to other topics such as justification or election, each of which must be affirmed as equally true.

Although neither Barth nor Hunsinger do so themselves, I believe it is legitimate to extend the idea of dialectical inclusion to the conceptualization of the way different forms of theology carry out their work. Barth accepted, in a qualified way, the need for distinct forms of theological reflection.[23] Less important than the particularities of Barth's way of dividing theology is the help Hunsinger's reading of Barth's work provides in the way we view the task of each of these divisions. Each part of theology should view itself as reiterating the whole from its own perspective. This stands in sharp contrast to encyclopedic approaches to theology organized around the specialized research programs of tightly bounded disciplines. Rather than parceling out the tasks of theology to discrete academic disciplines, each form of theological reflection is viewed as thinking through the whole of the theological task from its own perspective. It represents the whole as it is found in each particular part.

This means that biblical studies cannot avoid asking theological questions, analyzing the social context, or considering the ways its exegesis and interpretation function rhetorically in a particular context. Nor can church history shirk these same type questions. In each case, the whole of the theological task is reiterated from the vantage point of the part and its particular orientation toward the subject matter of theology. Moreover, each form of theology stands in a dialectical, nonreductionist relation to all others. They need one another, not merely to gain specialized knowledge (important as this may be) but as a reminder of the incomprehensibility of the God whom each form of theology attempts to understand. Their perspective on the whole is only partial, and they need others to remind them that no form of theology can capture the mystery of God.

What does this mean for practical theology? It means that practical theology cannot avoid asking the most fundamental questions about God and thus derives its rational orientation accordingly. These are not left to philosophical or dogmatic theology, as in the older encyclopedic approach that consigned practical theology the relatively minor task of forming ministerial methods and techniques. Practical theology must ask questions of the whole theological task from its own perspective. One of the significant differences between the approach advocated here and that offered by Don Browning in *A Fundamental Practical Theology* is that he is attempting to describe the whole of theology. I am attempting to describe the whole from the perspective of practical theology only.

The particular practical theological approach informing this book is based on an understanding of the subject matter of theology as the Word of God. Jesus Christ as the divine self-communication is the paradigm for God's revealing and concealing work in all its forms. This leads me to adopt an approach to practical theology that can be called rhetorical-hermeneutical. By rhetorical, I point to the character of God's Word as a form of address that makes a claim upon its hearers and seeks to transform them through loving persuasion. By hermeneutical, I point to the way this Word accommodates itself to the interpretive situation of its hearers as creatures, bound by finitude, and as sinners, curved in upon themselves. This leads me to define practical theology as that form of theological rationality that examines the church in its present empirical existence, measuring it critically against the norm of its faith and life, Jesus Christ, and providing it with guidance in how it might hear and respond to this Word in its own time and place. The rhetorical-hermeneutical character of practical theology gives rise to several distinct types of knowledge and rational procedures: (1) normative-systematic, (2) contextual-analytic, and (3) preceptive-pragmatic. Each of these is equally important; none either is more fundamental than the others or can be derived directly from them. They coexist and interpenetrate dialectically, provoking and supplementing one another's insights.

The construction of *normative-systematic* knowledge grows out of practical theology's need to determine the nature of the claim God's Word makes upon humanity and the kinds of transformations this implies. It seeks to answer the most fundamental questions of theology: What are God's purposes for the world? What is the nature and role of the church? What is the human vocation? Only as practical theology articulates the ends governing human life can it be clear about the kinds of transformations it seeks to support, enable, and demand. Its articulation of these ends is *systematic* only in the sense of examining these ends in their depth and breadth, not in the sense of logical coherence.

This book offers normative-systematic knowledge in two basic ways. First, it views confirmation in relation to the Sacraments of Baptism and the Lord's Supper and attempts to articulate the larger covenantal framework in which these sacraments have their meaning. Confirmation's meaning is viewed as taking up and reflecting the Trinitarian baptismal formula that was unpacked in terms of God's electing, reconciling, and redeeming activity. In other words, the *end* of confirmation is viewed in relation to other ends that, in turn, point to the larger whole of which they are a part.

A second place this sort of knowledge is offered in this book is in its definition of confirmation as a practice. How is this warranted? It is warranted by an examination of scripture to determine if confirmation had apostolic authority. When this is ruled out, confirmation is viewed as a part of church tradition and thus granted a very different status. The narrative-historical rendering of confirmation's story is not in the service of an idealization of some aspect of the tradition, as frequently is the case in contemporary liturgical theology. Rather, it is used to show that confirmation is a malleable practice communicating different goods over time. It is construed as a part of the *bene esse* of the church, not its *esse*—a practice serving the church's well-being, not a constituitive part of its nature. This grants the church a certain freedom in its appropriation of this practice. Only to the extent that confirmation serves the more fundamental aspects of the church's being does it have a continuing role to play. Confirmation is dispensable, even though the church's witness through worship, nurture, and evangelism are not. Confirmation is seen as serving the more fundamental ends of church life. My attempt to reconstruct this practice is an effort to place it in the service of these ends.

The kinds of ends developed in the normative-systematic dimension of practical theology, however, are not determined in a vacuum. This brings us to the second form of knowledge that practical theology constructs: *contextual-analytic*. This grows out of the recognition that the Word of God is both dynamic and concrete. The witness of scripture and the living proclamation of the church become the Word of God only as God in freedom acts to address persons in a particular time and place. Contextual analysis is an inherent by-product of the freedom of the Word and the recognition that theology must start anew if it is to follow that Word. The rightful place of nontheological resources in the contextual analysis is derivative of this more fundamental theological understanding of contextuality. Accordingly, the contextual-analytic work of practical theology looks in two directions simultaneously. First, it seeks to describe and analyze the contexts that are relevant to the topic it is treating. Second, it seeks to articulate its authorial context and the interests that inform its work.

The first of these is informed by recognizing the importance of time and place. From a theological perspective, temporal contexts include both historical and eschatological elements. Not only are persons, events, and things placed in a historical frame but they also are viewed from the perspective of God's in-breaking future that transforms the present. Contexts of "place" have to do with the various systems in which the subject is "located": systems of gender, class, ethnicity, geography, and so forth. Theology has a stake in these systems, viewing them as expressions or distortions of God's purposes for the world.

In our analysis of confirmation, three contexts figure prominently: the historical development of confirmation as a practice, modernization, and the twentieth-century ecumenical liturgical discussion. Each contributes something significant to the constructive proposal offered in this book. The concept of practice is used to trace the range of goods associated with confirmation over time, enabling us to discern goods still operative, to consider retrieving goods that have been lost, and to project new goods appropriate to the present moment. Recognition of the individualizing and individuating trends of modern life, largely mediated through adolescence, led me to affirm the importance of a professional purpose for confirmation in the present. Liturgical developments in a range of church traditions serve as the context for the discovery of an emerging consensus about a new paradigm that might replace the older pattern of infant Baptism, catechetical instruction, and admission to the Lord's Supper. Such forms of contextual analysis are necessary if practical theology is to assist the church in discerning what it means to serve God in its own time and place. The dynamic, concrete nature of the Word as a form of address inevitably leads theology to take contextuality seriously.

Application of contextual analysis to the authorial situation is a by-product of the insights pointed to above and has been deeply influenced by philosophical hermeneutics and ideology critique in recent years. Practical theologians do their work located in a particular time and place. As white, male, Presbyterian, middle class, and American, I inevitably bring certain biases to my work—biases that contextual analysis can help make evident and perhaps even correct. Here conversation with perspectives other than one's own is essential. Learning from research on women's development and entering into a conversation with persons from other Christian traditions are cases in point.

There is an equally important contextual situation in which the author also is located, one that often is not given much attention when this topic is discussed. This is the hermeneutical situation created by the context of faith. How is it possible for an author to hear the Word and give response to it in theological form? This is not a matter of overcoming a historical, aesthetic, or gender gap, because it involves the gap separating creature from Creator and sinner from sovereign God. There are no hermeneutical moves an author can make to overcome this gap, even if it is the single most important hermeneutical context in which he or she works. The only appropriate response is an attitude of prayer coupled with a healthy dose of epistemological humility.

The final form of knowledge constructed by practical theology is *preceptive-pragmatic*. This has to do with the rules of art that practical theologians offer their readers to guide their judgments in the actual performance of some aspect of the Christian life. Chapter 8 of this book represents preceptive-pragmatic knowledge. It attempts to set forth a program of confirmation in some detail that can guide a minister, Christian educator, or church committee in actually setting up this program. This form of knowledge is inherently open-ended, because it is oriented toward the performance of an activity in its concreteness. All complex activities involve elements of judgment and artistry that cannot be captured in replicable "how to" prescriptions. These kinds of technological models of application have no place in the approach to practical theology advocated here. It is concerned with the formation of judgment, not the communication of a "canned" program.

The orientation of preceptive-pragmatic knowledge toward the formation of judgment is evident in a variety of places in Chapter 8. In the discussion of spiritual mentoring, for example, a general maxim is offered: Teach when necessary; guide when suitable; ask when possible. This was given to help spiritual mentors view their relationship to the confirmands they are guiding as one in which the confirmands are encouraged to claim their own voice and inner authority. How this precept would actually get followed in any concrete relationship cannot be determined in advance. It depends on the judgment and artistry of the mentor. The same is true of the broader elements of the program. There is nothing magical about placing the spiritual mentoring phase before small group catechesis. The program as a whole is inherently open-ended, necessitating judgment, not direct application.

It would be easy to slip into the mistake of viewing *preceptive-pragmatic* knowledge as derived from the first two types of knowledge that have been examined. The larger ends of *normative-systematic* knowledge and the insights of *contextual-analytic* knowledge are seen as yielding a set of practical guidelines deductively. Although all three forms of knowledge are mutually informing, it would be a mistake to view one as derived from the others in this fashion. There is a knowledge-yield that comes from participation in a practice and performance of an action that cannot be gained through the kinds of rational procedures used to project larger ends or analyze contexts.[24] This is knowledge from the inside: a sense of timing and proportion, recognition of relevant elements of contingency, competence in a range of skills, and development of relevant interpretive schemas. This kind of knowledge can only be acquired from the actual doing of a practice. Although it is impossible to capture fully, it can be thematized in the form of precepts as described throughout this section.

Such knowledge, moreover, serves as an independent, critical test of the other forms of knowledge found in practical theology. Only when the confirmation program proposed in this book is actually tested in a number of congregations, and confirmands, parents, mentors, Christian educators, and ministers are given the opportunity to develop informed judgments about its viability will this particular source of knowledge be available. This knowledge has the potential of altering our understanding of the purpose of confirmation and the adequacy of the contextual analysis informing the confirmation program. It becomes clear at this point that practical theology is not the prerogative of academic theologians alone but also depends on the knowledge and insights of those seeking to shape a reflective, faithful response to the address of the Word of God in particular contexts of experience.

Notes

Introduction: Troubling Questions

1. The Anglican study was *Crisis for Confirmation* (London: SCM Press, 1967). The American version, cited below, drew on much of theological material of this book, although it conducted its own research.
2. *Confirmation Crisis* (New York: Seabury Press, 1968).
3. The study uses the term "communicants" to refer to persons who had been confirmed. At that time, the Episcopal Church only admitted persons to communion after confirmation.
4. Dean Hoge, Benton Johnson, and Donald Luidens, *Vanishing Boundaries: The Religion of Mainline Protestant Baby Boomers* (Louisville, Ky.: Westminster/John Knox Press, 1994).
5. Ibid., p. 71.
6. Ibid., p. 67.
7. Ibid., p. 68.
8. Ibid., p. 9.
9. *Effective Christian Education: A National Study of Protestant Congregations—A Report for the Evangelical Lutheran Church in America,* ed. Peter Benson and Caroly Eklin (Minneapolis: Search Institute, 1990), p. 53.
10. Forty people between the ages of forty and fifty-two were interviewed. Twenty were unchurched and twenty were churched, according to the criteria used in *Vanishing Boundaries.* The interviews were designed to allow me to gain a better understanding of the retrospective, subjective meaning of confirmation for those interviewed. They were based on the following questions that were explored in an open-ended manner: How old were you when you were confirmed? How long did the confirmation program last? What stands out about the program? Why did you participate in the program? Why did you choose to be confirmed? In what ways did your choice to be confirmed influence you? As you look back at this program, what kind of long-term impact did it have on your current beliefs and values?

Part 1: Confirmation as a Current Challenge

Notes to Chapter 1

1. Erik Erikson, ed., "Youth: Fidelity and Diversity," *The Challenge of Youth* (Garden City, N.Y.: 1961), p. 13.
2. Those classified as unchurched did not hold official membership in a congregation and did not attend church at least six times a year. Hoge, et al., *Vanishing Boundaries,* p. 67.

3. *The Unchurched American . . . 10 Years Later* (Princeton, N.J.: The Princeton Religion Research Center, 1988), p. 32. This research is a follow-up study based on an earlier volume: *The Unchurched American: A Gallup Study, 1978* (Princeton, N.J.: The Princeton Religion Research Center, 1978).
4. Hoge et al., *Vanishing Boundaries,* p. 147.
5. Ibid., pp. 109–15.
6. *The Unchurched American . . . 10 Years Later,* p. 32.
7. Peter Benson and Caroly Eklin, *Effective Christian Education,* p. 50.
8. R. T. Gribbon, *When People Seek the Church* (Washington, D.C.: Alban Institute, 1982), p. 4. The research reported in *Vanishing Boundaries* (p. 108) confirms this general pattern, reporting that 52 percent of the Presbyterians who are currently active in the church dropped out of the church for a period of time after they were confirmed.
9. This same finding and its relationship to changes taking place during the 1960s is found in Wade Clark Roof and William McKinney, *American Mainline Religion: Its Changing Shape and Future* (New Brunswick, N.J.: Rutgers University Press, 1987), chap. 2. Hoge et al., *Vanishing Boundaries,* p. 8.
10. One of the best treatments of this phenomenon is found in Roof and McKinney, ibid., pp. 162–81.
11. Ibid., p. 170.
12. Hoge et al., *Vanishing Boundaries,* pp. 68–69.
13. In addition to the Roof and McKinney volume cited above, see also Robert Wuthnow, *The Restructuring of American Religion: Society and Faith Since World War II* (Princeton, N.J.: Princeton University Press, 1988), especially chap. 5.
14. Robert Wuthnow has documented the importance of the search for community and a deeper grasp of the sacred in driving the widespread participation of Americans in small groups in *Sharing the Journey: Support Groups and America's New Quest for Community* (New York: Free Press, 1994).
15. Joseph Kett, *Rites of Passage: Adolescence in America 1790 to the Present* (New York: Basic Books, 1977), pp. 29–31.
16. Ibid., p. 146.
17. Ibid.
18. Ibid., p. 245.
19. Ibid., p. 178. The exact figure is 38.4 percent.
20. Ibid., p. 154.
21. Stanley Hall, *Adolescence: Its Psychology and Its Relations to Physiology, Anthropology, Sociology, Sex, Crime, Religion and Education,* 2 vols. (New York: Appleton, 1905).

Notes to Chapter 2

1. Dennis Wrong, "The Oversocialized Conception of Man in Modern Sociology," *American Sociological Review,* 26 (April 1961), pp. 183–93 and *The Problem of Order: What Unites and Divides Society* (New York: Free Press, 1994). See also *Individualism Reconsidered: Readings Bearing on the Endangered Self in Modern Society,* ed. Donald Capps and Richard Fenn (Princeton, N.J.: Center for Religion, Self, and Society, Princeton Theological Seminary, 1992), Monograph Series, No. 1.
2. Peter Berger and Brigitte Berger, *Sociology: A Biographical Approach* (New York: Basic Books, 1975), chaps. 3, 4, 6, 7, 9, 11. J. Clausen, ed., *Socialization and Society* (Boston: Little, Brown, & Co., 1968).
3. Peter Berger and Thomas Luckmann, *The Social Construction of Reality: A Treatise in the Sociology of Knowledge* (Garden City, N.Y.: Doubleday & Co., 1966), p. 76.
4. Victor Turner, *The Ritual Process: Structure and Anti-Structure* (Ithaca, N.Y.: Cornell University Press, 1969), chap. 3.
5. Peter Berger, *The Heretical Imperative: Contemporary Possibilities of Religious Affirmation* (Garden City, N.Y.: Anchor Press, 1979), p. 11.

6. Cornell West, *The American Evasion of Philosophy: A Genealogy of Pragmatism* (Madison, Wis.: University of Wisconsin Press, 1989), p. 79.

7. David Elkind, *The Hurried Child: Growing Up Too Fast Too Soon* (Reading, Mass.: Addison-Wesley Pub. Co., 1981). *All Grown Up and No Place to Go: Teenagers in Crisis* (Reading, Mass.: Addison-Wesley Pub. Co., 1984).

8. Jurgen Habermas, *Legitimation Crisis,* trans. T. McCarthy (Boston: Beacon Press, 1975); Niklas Luhmann, *The Differentiation of Society,* trans. S. Holmes (New York: Columbia University Press, 1982); Peter Berger, Brigitte Berger, and Hansfried Kellner, *The Homeless Mind: Modernization and Consciousness* (New York: Vintage Books, 1973).

9. Luhmann, *Differentiation,* chap. 4.

10. Role distancing is described from the dramatological perspective of Erving Goffman in *The Presentation of Self in Everyday Life* (Garden City, N.Y.: Doubleday & Co., 1959), chaps. 6—7.

11. Emile Durkheim, *The Elementary Forms of the Religious Life,* trans. J. Swain (New York: Free Press, 1915); *Moral Education: A Study in the Theory and Application of the Sociology of Education,* trans. E. Wilson and H. Schnurer (New York: Free Press, 1961); *Emil Durkheim on Morality and Society,* ed. R. Bellah (Chicago: University of Chicago Press, 1973).

12. Robert Selman, *The Growth of Interpersonal Understanding: Developmental and Clinical Analyses* (New York: Academic Press, 1980).

13. Robert Wuthnow, "Religious Loyalty, Defection, and Experimentation: A Longitudinal Analysis of University Men," *Review of Religious Research,* vol. 19, no. 3 (Spring 1978). See also Hoge et al., *Vanishing Boundaries,* which cites unchurched people as pointing to doubts they had prior to entering college as a significant influence on their church participation (p. 157).

14. William Perry, *Forms of Intellectual and Ethical Development in the College Years* (New York: Holt, Rinehart & Winston, 1970).

15. James Davison Hunter, *Evangelicalism: The Coming Generation* (Chicago: The University of Chicago Press, 1987), pp. 165–78; and Wuthnow, *Restructuring,* pp. 168–72.

16. Kenneth Keniston, "Social Change and Youth in America," in *The Challenge of Youth,* ed. E. Erikson (Garden City, N.Y.: Doubleday & Co., 1965), pp. 209–10.

17. For an overview of Weber's understanding of rationalization, see Jurgen Habermas, *The Theory of Communicative Action, Vol. 1, Reason and the Rationalization of Society,* trans. T. McCarthy (Boston: Beacon Press, 1984), chap. 2 and Reinhard Bendix, *Max Weber: An Intellectual Portrait* (Garden City, N.Y.: Doubleday & Co., 1962), chap. 3.

18. Jean Piaget and Barbel Inhelder, *The Growth of Logical Thinking from Childhood to Adolescence: An Essay on the Construction of Formal Operational Structures,* trans. A. Parsons and S. Milgram (New York: Basic Books, 1958).

19. R. Bellah et al., *Habits of the Heart: Individualism and Commitment in American Life* (Berkeley, Calif.: University of California Press, 1985), pp. 32–35, 47, 68–69.

20. Bellah et al., *Habits,* pp. 32–35, 47–50, 142.

21. David Harvey, *The Condition of Postmodernity: An Inquiry into the Origins of Cultural Change* (Cambridge, Mass.: Blackwell, 1989).

22. Erik Erikson, *Childhood and Society* (New York: Norton, 1950); *Identity, Youth and Crisis* (New York: Norton, 1968); and *History and the Historical Moment* (New York: Norton, 1975).

23. Erik Erikson, "Youth: Fidelity and Diversity," in *The Challenge of Youth,* p. 13.

24. Young Pai, *Cultural Foundations of Education* (Columbus, Ohio: Charles E. Merrill Publishing Co., 1990) and William Myers, *Black and White Styles of Youth Ministry: Two Congregations in America* (New York: Pilgrim Press, 1991).

25. Grace Choon Kim, "Critical Issues for Christian Education with the Korean American Second Generation," *Korean-American Educational Ministry: Basic Principles* (Seoul, Korea: Publishing House of the Presbyterian Church of Korea, 1988), pp. 195–209.

26. An overview of some of the recent literature is found in Judith Jordan's "Empathy and the Mother-Daughter Relationship," in Judith Jordan et al., *Women's Growth in Connection: Writings from the Stone Center* (New York: The Guilford Press, 1991), pp. 28–34.

27. Erik Erikson, *Insight and Responsibility: Lectures on the Ethical Implications of Psychoanalytic Insight* (New York: W.W. Norton & Co., 1964), pp. 90–91.

28. Jean Piaget, *The Origins of Intelligence in Children* (New York: International Universities Press, 1952); *Six Psychological Studies,* trans. A. Tenzer (New York: Vintage Books, 1967). Lawrence Kohlberg, *Essays on Moral Development,* vol. 1, *The Philosophy of Moral Development: Moral Stages and the Idea of Justice* (San Francisco: Harper & Row, 1981). James Fowler, *Stages of Faith: The Psychology of Human Development and the Quest for Meaning* (San Francisco: Harper & Row, 1981). Thomas Lickona, *Raising Good Children: Helping Your Child through the Stages of Moral Development* (New York: Bantam Books, 1983). Sharon Parks, *The Critical Years: The Young Adult Search for a Faith to Live By* (San Francisco: Harper & Row, 1986). Robert Kegan, *The Evolving Self: Problem and Process in Human Development* (Cambridge, Mass.: Harvard University Press, 1982); *In Over Our Heads: The Mental Demands of Modern Life* (Cambridge, Mass.: Harvard University Press, 1994).

29. Fowler has found, for example, that a large number of people do not make the transition from Synthetic Conventional Faith to Individuative Reflective Faith. See *Stages,* pp. 164, 172.

30. James Marcia, "Identity in Adolescence," in *Handbook of Adolescent Psychology,* ed. J. Adelson (New York: John Wiley & Sons, 1980); "Development and Validation of Ego-identity Status," *Journal of Personality and Social Psychology,* 35 (1967), pp. 118–33. See my discussion of Marcia's work in "Evangelism and Education: Developmental Perspectives," in *Evangelism in the Reformed Tradition,* ed. Arnold Lovell (Decatur, Ga.: CTS Press, 1990), pp. 104–5. See also Ruthellen Josselson's *Finding Herself: Pathways to Identity Development in Women* (San Francisco: Jossey-Bass, 1989).

31. Both Erikson and Marcia use the concept of diffused identity, close to Robert Jay Lifton's "protean man," a form of modern identity in which persons shift from one set of commitments and relationships to another without forming a clear sense of self. See Robert Lifton, *History and Human Survival: Essays on the Young and Old, Survivors and the Dead, Peace and War, and on Contemporary Psychohistory* (New York: Random House, 1961), chap. 15 and *The Broken Connection* (New York: Simon & Schuster, 1979), pp. 85, 129, 296–97, 393–94.

32. Kegan, *Evolving Self,* p. 100.

33. Lawrence Kohlberg and Carol Gilligan, "The Adolescent as a Philosopher: The Discovery of the Self in a Postconventional World," *Daedalus* 100 (1971), pp. 1051–86.

34. Philip Helfaer, *The Psychology of Religious Doubt* (Boston: Beacon Press, 1972), Part II.

35. Carol Gilligan, *In a Different Voice: Psychological Theory and Women's Development* (Cambridge, Mass.: Harvard University Press, 1982); Carol Gilligan, Kay Johnston, and Barbara Miller, *Moral Voice, Adolescent Development, and Secondary Education: A Study at the Green River School* (Monograph no. 3) (Cambridge, Mass.: Project on the Psychology of Women and the Development of Girls, Harvard Graduate School of Education, 1988); Carol Gilligan and Lyn Mikel Brown, *Meeting at the Crossroads: Women's Psychology and Girls' Development* (Cambridge, Mass.: Harvard University Press, 1992); Carol Gilligan, Nona Nyons, and Trudy Hanmer, eds., *Making Connections: The Relational Worlds of Adolescent Girls at Emma Willard School* (Cambridge, Mass.: Harvard University Press, 1990); Carol Gilligan, Janie Victoria Ward, and Jill McLean Taylor, eds., with Betty Bardige, *Mapping the Moral Domain: A Contribution of Women's Thinking to Psychological Theory and Education* (Cambridge, Mass.: Center for the Study of Gender, Education and Human

Development, 1988). In addition to works cited above, other important research has
been carried out by Mary Belenky, Blythe McVicker Clinchy, Nancy Rule Gold-
berger, and Jill Mattuck Tarule, *Women's Ways of Knowing* (New York: Basic Books,
1986); Jean Baker Miller, *Toward a New Psychology of Women* (Boston: Beacon
Press, 1976).

36. Miller et al., *Women's Growth in Connection,* p. 12. Similar critiques of the prevail-
    ing models of psychology are scattered throughout the book. Compare pp. 36, 53, 60,
    124. Gilligan offers a similar critique of Erikson. See *In a Different Voice,* pp. 11–13.
37. Particularly helpful are three articles in *Women's Growth in Connection,* cited above:
    Jean Baker Miller's "The Development of Women's Sense of Self" and Janet Surrey's
    "The 'Self-in-Relation': A Theory of Women's Development" and "Women's Self
    Development in Late Adolescence."
38. See Jordan, Surrey, and Kaplan, "Women and Empathy: Implications for Psycholog-
    ical Development and Psychotherapy" and Jordan, "Empathy and Self Boundaries."
39. Brown and Gilligan, *Meeting at the Crossroads,* p. 6.
40. Gilligan and Brown describe this as an "inner chasm." Ibid., p. 216.
41. Miller et al., *Women's Growth in Connection,* pp. 60, 127.
42. Margo Culley and Catherine Portuges, eds., *Gendered Subjects: The Dynamics of
    Feminist Teaching* (London: Routledge & Kegan Paul, 1985); especially Frances Ma-
    her, "Classroom Pedagogy and the New Scholarship on Women," pp. 29–48.
43. Miller et al., *Women's Growth in Connection,* pp. 12, 36, 60, 122.
44. Surrey refers to this as relationship-differentiation. Ibid., pp. 59–60.
45. Gilligan, *In a Different Voice,* p. 74.
46. Miller et al., *Women's Growth in Connection,* p. 127.
47. Belenky et al., *Women's Ways of Knowing,* chaps. 5—6. As the authors note, most of the
    women in this position were attending or had recently graduated from college (p. 87).
48. Janet Jacobs, "The Endangered Female Self and the Search for Identity," in *The En-
    dangered Self,* pp. 37–46. Judith Salzman, "Save the World, Save Myself: Responses
    to Problematic Attachment," in *Making Connections,* ed. Gilligan, Lyons, and Ham-
    mer, pp. 110–45.
49. Jacobs, "The Endangered Female," p. 39.
50. This can be seen as part of a larger critique of Gilligan's and Miller's work in which
    the relational self and ethics of care are seen as not articulating sufficiently the socio-
    historical location of the self in relationship. See Ruth Smith, "Moral Transcendence
    and Moral Space in the Historical Experiences of Women," *Journal of Feminist Stud-
    ies in Religion,* 4, (1988), pp. 21–37 and Joan Tronto, "Beyond Gender Difference to
    a Theory of Care," *Signs* 12, (1987), pp. 644–63.

Part 2: Confirmation in Historical Perspective

Notes to Introduction

1. See my discussion of this in "Restructuring Confirmation," *Theology Today* 49, no. 1
   (April 1992), pp. 46–67.
2. Alasdair MacIntrye's examination of the Aristotelian tradition's understanding of
   practice is the "Ur-source" of this discussion. See *After Virtue: A Study in Moral The-
   ory* (Notre Dame, Ind.: University of Notre Dame Press, 1981), especially chap. 14.
   Jeffrey Stout, *Ethics After Babel: The Languages of Morals and Their Discontents*
   (Boston: Beacon Press, 1988). Craig Dykstra, "Reconceiving Practice," in *Shifting
   Boundaries,* ed. E. Farley (Louisville, Ky.: Westminster/John Knox Press, 1991).
   Stanley Hauerwas, *A Community of Character: Toward a Constructive Christian Social Ethic* (Notre Dame, Ind.: University of Notre Dame Press, 1981), chap. 6. Mar-
   garet Miles, *Practicing Christianity: Critical Perspectives for an Embodied Spirituality* (New York: Crossroad Pub. Co., 1990).

3. For further discussion of my understanding of practices, see "Restructuring Confirmation," pp. 49–50.
4. MacIntyre, *After Virtue,* pp. 176–77.
5. The Ur-source of much of this interest is Stephen Crites's "The Narrative Quality of Experience," *Journal of the Academy of Religion* (Cambersburg, Pa.: AAR, 1971), pp. 291–311. See also *Narrative Psychology: The Storied Nature of Human Conduct,* ed. T. Sarin (New York: Praeger, 1986). Charles Gerkin, *The Living Human Document: Re-visioning Pastoral Counseling in a Hermeneutical Mode* (Nashville: Abingdon Press, 1984). Stanley Hauerwas, *A Community of Character: Toward a Constructive Christian Social Ethic* (Notre Dame, Ind.: University of Notre Dame Press, 1981). Stanley Hauerwas and Gregory Jones, *Why Narrative? Readings in Narrative Theology* (Grand Rapids, Mich.: William B. Eerdmans Pub. Co., 1989). Donald Polkinghorne, *Narrative Knowing and the Human Sciences* (Albany, N.Y.: State University of New York Press, 1988).
6. Polkinghorne, *Narrative Knowing,* chaps. 2, 4.
7. The concept "script" comes from recent cognitive psychology. Of special importance in this regard is Jean Mandler's *Stories, Scripts, and Scenes: Aspects of Schema Theory* (Hillsdale, N.J.: Lawrence Erlbaum Associates, 1984).
8. The best discussion of this aspect of practice is found in Dykstra's "Reconceiving Practice."

Notes to Chapter 3

1. Besides Oscar Cullmann and Dom Gregory Dix mentioned below, more recent examples of persons going back to the New Testament for the origins of confirmation are Theodore Jungkuntz, *Confirmation and the Charismata* (New York: University Press of America, 1983) and Paul Turner, *Confirmation: The Baby in Solomon's Court* (Mahwah, N.J.: Paulist Press, 1993).
2. Oscar Cullmann, *Baptism in the New Testament,* trans. J.K.S. Reid (London: SCM Press, 1950), p. 11.
3. Dom Gregory Dix, "Confirmation or the Laying on of Hands?" *Theology, Occasional Papers No. 5,* 1936, p. 1.
4. An excellent overview of the importance of Acts 8 for later interpretation of confirmation is O. C. Edwards, "The Exegesis of Acts 8:4–25 and Its Implications for Confirmation and Glossalalia," *Anglican Theological Review,* Supplementary Series, no. 2, 1973, pp. 100–12.
5. English translations of some material are available in Paul Turner's *Sources of Confirmation: From the Fathers through the Reformers* (Collegeville, Minn.: Liturgical Press, 1993). See G. W. Lampe's comments on this passage in *The Seal of the Spirit: A Study in the Doctrine of Baptism and Confirmation in the New Testament and the Fathers,* (London: Longmans, Green, & Co., 1951), pp. 79–80.
6. The variety of baptismal and Spirit-giving patterns in Acts are described by J.E.L. Outon, "The Holy Spirit, Baptism and Laying on of Hands in Acts," in *The Expository Times,* LXVI (1955), pp. 236–40 and C.S.C. Williams, *The Acts of the Apostles* (London: A. & C. Black, 1957), Appendix 3, "The Giving of the Spirit."
7. C. K. Barrett, *The Holy Spirit in the Gospel Tradition,* (London: SPCK, 1947), pp. 138–39.
8. G. B. Caird, *Saint Luke* (Philadelphia: Westminster Press, 1977), p. 77.
9. I do not subscribe to the tightly organized schema of H. Conzelmann in *The Theology of St. Luke* (New York: Harper & Row, 1961). See Earle Ellis's comments and more satisfactory schema in *Gospel of Luke,* (Grand Rapids, Mich.: William B. Eerdmans Pub. Co., 1981) pp. 15–16.
10. In some places, it is used as a sign of blessing, as in Jesus' blessing of the children (Mark 10:16). In other places, it involves the transfer of power, as in a healing (for example, Mark 6:5; 8:23; 16:18). Closely related are those instances in which it repre-

sents the transfer of power from one Spirit-possessed person to another (for example, Moses' transfer of power to Joshua in Deut. 34:9). It is used in a similar way to authorize individuals to assume certain roles in the life of the community (as in the commissioning of deacons in Acts 6:6 and of Barnabas and Paul in 13:3).

11. Lampe, *Seal,* pp. 69–70. For a similar argument that places the emphasis on Luke's desire to demonstrate the close relationship of each new stage of the church's mission to the Jerusalem church and its apostolate, see Reginald Fuller, "Christian Initiation in the New Testament," in *Made, Not Born* (Notre Dame, Ind.: University of Notre Dame Press, 1976).

12. Lampe, *Seal,* p. 72.

13. Gunter Bornkamm offers an apt comment in this regard: "The admitted uncertainty in the relation between baptism and the reception of the Spirit remains a sign that the Lord of the Church maintains His rule in freedom and that order in the Church must not be perverted to bind Him to itself." Quoted in G. R. Beasley-Murray, *Baptism in the New Testament* (Grand Rapids, Mich.: William B. Eerdmans Pub. Co., 1962), p. 120.

14. Cyril Pocknee, *Water and the Spirit: A Study in the Relation of Baptism and Confirmation* (London: Daron, Longman & Todd, 1967), pp. 24–25.

15. See Jack Kingsbury's discussion of the similarities of John and Jesus in *Matthew as Story,* sec. ed. (Philadelphia: Fortress Press, 1986), p. 49.

16. Joachim Jeremias, *New Testament Theology: The Proclamation of Jesus* (New York: Charles Scribner's Sons, 1971), pp. 80–82.

17. See John Fenton, *Saint Matthew* (Philadelphia: Westminster Press, 1978), p. 60 and Eduard Schweizer, *The Good News According to Matthew,* trans. David Green (Atlanta: John Knox Press, 1975), p. 52.

18. Sigmund Mowinckel, *He That Cometh: The Messiah Concept in the Old Testament and Later Judaism,* trans. G. W. Anderson (Nashville: Abingdon Press, 1954), pp. 37, 67.

19. Ibid., pp. 63–66. Samuel's annointings of Saul and David were paradigmatic in this regard (1 Sam. 10:1; 16:13–14; cf. 1 Kings 1:39 and 2 Kings 11:12).

20. Cullmann, *Baptism in the New Testament,* p. 19.

21. By the time Constantine became Emperor in A.D. 312, it is estimated that at least one-fourth of the population of the Roman Empire was Christian. See Josef Jungmann in *The Early Liturgy: To the Time of Gregory the Great,* trans. F. Brunner (Notre Dame, Ind.: University of Notre Dame Press, 1959), p. 74.

22. See J.D.C. Fisher's discussion of the emergence of the terminology surrounding confirmation in *Christian Initiation: Baptism in the Medieval West—A Study in the Disintegration of the Primitive Rite of Initiation,* Alcuin Club Collections, XLVII (London: SPCK, 1965), Appendix I, pp. 141–48.

23. Joseph Martos provides a nice summary of this variety. See *Doors to the Sacred: A Historical Introduction to Sacraments in the Catholic Church* (Tarrytown, N.Y.: Triumph Books, 1991), p. 183. See also Leonel Mitchell, *Baptism Anointing,* Alcuin Club Collections, XLVIII (London: SPCK, 1966).

24. Thomas Finn, *Early Christian Baptism and the Catechumenate: West and East Syria Message of the Fathers of the Church* 5 (Collegeville, Minn.: The Liturgical Press, 1992), pp. 19–21.

25. Edward Yarnold, *The Awe-Inspiring Rites of Initiation: Baptismal Homilies of the Fourth Century* (Middlegreen, England: St. Paul Publications, 1971), p. 189.

26. Martos, *Doors to the Sacred,* p. 183.

27. I will be using Geoffrey Cuming's text: *Hippolytus: A Text for Students* (Nottingham, England: Grove Books, 1976). For a more complex treatment of the various extant texts, see Dom Gregory Dix's *The Treatise on the Apostolic Tradition of St. Hippolytus of Rome* (London: Macmillan Co., 1937).

28. See Aidan Kavanagh's detailed comparison of *The Apostolic Tradition,* the *Gelasian Sacramentary,* and the *Ordo Romanus XI* of the sixth and eighth centuries. *The Shape*

of Baptism: The Rite of Christian Initiation (New York: Pueblo Publishing Co., 1978), pp. 54–70.

29. Cuming, *Hippolytus,* p. 15.
30. Ibid.
31. Ibid., pp. 16–17, #18.
32. Ibid., p. 17, #20.
33. This instruction seems to be what Hippolytus has in mind when he writes that persons who have been examined and judged fit to proceed toward Baptism should "hear the gospel." Ibid., p. 17, #20. He writes elsewhere that the newly baptized members "have already been instructed about the resurrection of the flesh and the other things as it is written," p. 22, #21.
34. Roger Beraudy, "Scrutines and Exorcisms," *Adult Baptism and the Catechumenate, Concilium,* vol. 22 (New York: Paulist Press, 1967), pp. 57–61.
35. Frederik van der Meer, *Augustine the Bishop: The Life and Work of a Father of the Church* (New York: Sheed and Ward, 1961), pp. 358–59.
36. See Jungmann's discussion of this in *Early Liturgy,* pp. 80–81.
37. Cuming, *Hippolytus,* p. 22, #21.
38. Van der Meer points out that only a few trappings of this period of preparation remained by the year A.D. 400. See *Augustine,* p. 356.
39. F. L. Cross, *St. Cyril of Jerusalem's Lectures on the Christian Sacraments* (Crestwood, N.Y.: St Vladimir's Seminary Press, 1986). William Telfer, *Cyril of Jerusalem and Nemesius of Emesa,* The Library of Christian Classics, vol. IV (London: SCM Press, 1955).
40. *Egeria's Travels,* trans. John Wilkinson (London: SPCK, 1971).
41. As Nathan Mitchell points out: "Throughout this entire period there exists no single western rite of initiation, but rather a collection of local rites similar in structure yet divergent in significant details." See his essay, "Dissolution of the Rite of Christian Initiation," in *Made, Not Born: New Perspectives on Christian Initiation and the Catechumenate* (Notre Dame, Ind.: University of Notre Dame Press, 1976), p. 52.
42. See Leonel Mitchell's comments in "The Development of Catechesis in the Third and Fourth Centuries: From Hippolytus to Augustine," in *A Faithful Church,* p. 56.
43. See Telfer, *Cyril,* p. 33.
44. Wilkinson, *Egeria's Travels,* p. 144.
45. Ibid.
46. See J.N.D. Kelly's excellent account of the emergence of declaratory creed written for this purpose in *Early Christian Creeds,* chap. 2. Yarnold provides a nice summary of the kind of instruction offered in the context of the entire practice of initiation in *Awe-Inspiring Rites,* pp. 11–13.
47. Quoted in Yarold, *Awe-Inspiring Rites,* p. 12.
48. Ibid., p. 145.
49. Augustine, *Confessions,* trans. R. S. Pine-Coffin (London: Penguin Books, 1961), p. 160.
50. Yarnold, *Awe-Inspiring Rites,* pp. 79–80.
51. Ibid., p. 81.
52. Cited in Lampe, *Seal of the Spirit,* p. 224. See his discussion of the way laying on of hands and consignation were fused in the Western church, pp. 219–31.
53. Mitchell in *Made, Not Born,* p. 70.
54. See Lampe's citations, *Seal of the Spirit,* p. 221.
55. As Fisher puts it, there is no "neat chronological table" by which this process can be periodized. *Christian Initiation,* p. xii.
56. Wayne Meeks, *The First Urban Christians: The Social World of the Apostle Paul* (New Haven, Conn.: Yale University Press, 1983). Ramsay MacMullen, *Roman Social Relations* (New Haven, Conn.: Yale University Press, 1974).
57. Fisher, *Christian Initiation,* p. 52. For a discussion of the variety in this practice, see chaps. 2—3.

58. Turner, *Sources of Confirmation,* pp. 53–56.
59. See Pierre Riché's extensive analysis of the decline of classical education in the West and the rise of medieval educational patterns. *Education and Culture in the Barbarian West: From the Sixth through the Eighth Century,* trans. J. Contreni (Columbia, S. C.: University of South Carolina Press, 1976).
60. Fisher, *Christian Initiation,* p. 86.
61. See Rosamond McKitterick, *The Frankish Church and the Carolingian Reforms, 789–895* (London: Royal Historical Society, 1977), chap. 1.
62. Fisher, *Christian Initiation,* p. 52.
63. Ibid., pp. 57, 65–66.
64. Three of the most important contributors to this debate are Joachim Jeremias in *Infant Baptism in the First Four Centuries,* trans. D. Cairns (London: SCM Press, 1960); Kurt Aland in *Did the Early Church Baptize Infants?,* trans. Beasley-Murray (London: SCM Press, 1963); and G. R. Beasley-Murray, *Baptism.*
65. Acts 10:48 and 11:14; 16:15; 16:33; 18:8; 1 Cor. 1:16.
66. Beasley-Murray, *Baptism,* p. 313.
67. One of the best examples of the importance of corporate identity in the New Testament is the sanctity extended from a Christian spouse to a non-Christian spouse and to their children, found in 1 Cor. 7:14. Sometimes Paul simply refers to the head of the household when he has an entire family in mind. For example, in 1 Cor 1:14 he says, "I baptized none of you except Crispus," but in Acts 18:8, we are told that "Crispus . . . became a believer in the Lord, together with all his household."
68. Quoted by Grant in "Development of the Christian Catechumenate" in *Made, Not Born,* p. 35.
69. Fisher, *Christian Initiation,* pp. 86, 109.
70. Ibid., p. 111.
71. Ibid., pp. 112–13.
72. Ibid.
73. Fisher describes these two lines of thinking in *Christian Initiation,* pp. 125–28.
74. Quoted in Fisher, *Christian Initiation,* p. 125.
75. The military analogy was an ancient one. In the early church, Baptism was frequently described as marking Christians with the insignia of Christ, just as soldiers were marked with the insignia of their cohort in the Roman army. Christ's mark allowed him to recognize those who belong to him when he returns in power to execute the final judgment. See Lampe, *Seal of the Spirit,* p. 16.
76. Quoted from Fisher, ibid., p. 126.
77. See Fisher's comments on this. Ibid., p. 128.
78. Turner, *Sources of Confirmation,* p. 36.
79. A collection of the most important theological texts dealing with confirmation in the early and middle phases of scholastic theology is Kilian Lynch, *The Sacrament of Confirmation in the Early–Middle Scholastic Period,* vol. 1: texts ed. E. Buytaert (St. Bonaventure, N.Y.: Franciscan Institute Publications, 1957). This edition only contains the Latin texts.
80. Martos provides a nice summary of these two positions in *Doors to the Sacred,* p. 190.
81. Fisher provides documenting evidence in *Christian Initiation,* p. 126. For an English translation of the pertinent passage in Lombard's *Sentences,* see Turner, *Sources of Confirmation,* p. 40.
82. See Fisher's discussion in *Christian Initiation,* p. 127.
83. Throughout this section I will be drawing on the following edition of the *Summa: The "Summa Theologica" of St. Thomas Aquinas,* vols. 1–3, trans. Fathers of the English Dominican Province (London: Thomas Baker, 1914).
84. Ibid., p. 208.
85. Ibid., p. 231.
86. Ibid., p. 217.

87. Ibid., p. 219.
88. Ibid., p. 211.
89. Ibid., p. 214. See also pp. 217, 225.
90. Ibid., p. 227.
91. Ibid., p. 225.
92. Turner, *Sources of Confirmation,* p. 42.
93. Ibid., p. 66.
94. Ibid., p. 51.
95. Ibid., p. 46.
96. Aquinas, *Summa Theologica,* pp. 226–27.

Notes to Chapter 4

 1. John Calvin, *The Institutes of the Christian Religion,* vol. 2, ed. John McNeill, Library of Christian Classics, 21 (Philadelphia: Westminster Press, 1960), p. 1460.
 2. Luther's comments are quoted by Arthur Repp in *Confirmation in the Lutheran Church* (St. Louis: Concordia Publishing House, 1964), pp. 15–16.
 3. Riché, *Education and Culture in the Barbarian West.*
 4. McKitterick, *The Frankish Church.*
 5. Ibid., p. 192.
 6. J.N.D. Kelly, *The Athanasian Creed: The Paddock Lectures for 1962–3* (London: Adam & Charles Black, 1964), pp. 42–44.
 7. For examples of different episcopal capitularies emphasizing the teaching of foundational material see McKitterick, *The Frankish Church,* pp. 49–75.
 8. Ibid., p. 42.
 9. Ibid., p. 90.
10. Ibid., p. 99.
11. David Knowles, *The Evolution of Medieval Thought* (New York: Vintage Books, 1962). See also Gillian R. Evans, *Old Arts and New Sciences: The Beginnings of Theology as an Academic Discipline* (Oxford: Clarendon Press, 1980).
12. Knowles, *Evolution,* p. 87.
13. Perhaps the single best overview of this is found in Richard McKeon's "Rhetoric in the Middle Ages," in *Speculum: A Journal of Medieval Studies* XVII, Jan. 1942, no. 1. See also C. S. Baldwin, *Medieval Rhetoric and Poetic (to 1400) Interpreted from Representative Works* (New York: Macmillan, 1928); James Murphy, *Rhetoric in the Middle Ages: A History of Rhetorical Theory from St. Augustine to the Renaissance* (Berkeley, Calif.: University of California Press, 1974).
14. *The Lay Folks' Catechism of the English and Latin Versions of Archbishop Thoresby's Instruction for the People,* ed. T. Simmons and H. Nolloth, Early English Text Society (Millwood, N.Y.: Kraus Reprint Co., 1975).
15. In the earliest phase of the reform movement, the Reformers focused primarily on the reform of the Mass. Its portrayal of the sacrifice of Christ was viewed as a major obstacle to the proclamation of the gospel in the church.
16. There is something of a debate over whether the Reformers reacted against or extended the program of the renaissance humanists. My position is that they represented a critical appropriation of renaissance ideas and practices. The humanism of the leading figures of the renaissance could not be taken over by the Reformers uncritically in light of their theology, which accented human sin and the need for God's grace. Several brief but excellent discussions of the influence of the renaissance on the Reformers are Barbara Sher Tinsley, "John Sturm's Method for Humanistic Pedagogy," *Sixteenth Century Journal,* XX, no. 1, 1989, pp. 23–39; Robert Linder, "Pierre Viret's Ideas and Attitudes Concerning Humanism and Education," *Church History* 34, (March 1965), pp. 25–35; and Steven Ozment, "Humanism, Scholasticism, and the Intellectual Ori-

gins of the Reformation," in *Continuity and Discontinuity in Church History: Essays Presented to George Huntson Williams at the Occasion of his 65th Birthday,* ed. Church and George (Leiden, Netherlands: E. J. Brill, 1979). Portrayals of the Reformation as a reaction against humanism are found in Gerald Strauss, *Luther's House of Learning: Indoctrination of the Young in the German Reformation* (Baltimore: Johns Hopkins University Press, 1978) and Benjamin Kohl, "Humanism and Education," *Renaissance Humanism,* ed. Albert Rabil, (Philadelphia: University of Pennsylvania Press, 1988), vol. 3, pp. 5–22.

17. Ozment, "Humanism," pp. 133–34.
18. Sturm's humanistic program at Strassburg is described in Tinsley's, "John Sturm's Method."
19. Henri Marrou, *A History of Education in Antiquity,* trans. G. Lamb (Madison, Wis.: University of Wisconsin Press, 1956).
20. See G. H. Bantock's extremely helpful discussion of this in *Studies in the History of Educational Theory Volume I: Artifice & Nature — 1350–1765* (London: George Allen & Unwin, 1980), chap. 1.
21. Marrou, *Education in Antiquity,* pp. 217–26.
22. The Reformers frequently cited the widespread theory that confirmation began when infant Baptism became normative, and a form of instruction was offered to young people in conjunction with confirmation to help them accept the faith themselves. As our account of the adult catechumenate made clear, this was not accurate. Hughes Old quotes a revealing passage from Zwingli in this regard, see *The Shaping of the Reformed Baptismal Rite in the Sixteenth Century* (Grand Rapids, Mich.: William B. Eerdmans Pub. Co., 1992), p. 183. See also his comments on the origin of this mistaken theory of the origin of confirmation, pp. 213–15.
23. For his influence on Zwingli, see *Ulrich Zwingli (1484–1531): Selected Works,* ed. S. Jackson. (Philadelphia: University of Pennsylvania Press, 1901), pp. xvii–xviii.
24. Peter Kaufman, *Augustinian Piety and Catholic Reform: Augustine, Colet, and Erasmus* (Macon, Ga.: Mercer University Press, 1982).
25. John B. Payne, *Erasmus: His Theology of the Sacraments* (Richmond: John Knox Press, 1970), pp. 178–80. Payne argues that the new rite Erasmus attached to baptismal catechesis during adolescence did not represent a reform of confirmation, as others have argued. See Repp for his influence on the Reformers' understanding, *Confirmation,* p. 20.
26. See Fisher's comments in *Christian Initiation: The Reformation Period,* pp. 169–70.
27. Payne, *Erasmus,* p. 163.
28. Quoted by Payne in ibid.
29. Ibid.
30. See Fisher's translation of a small portion of the *Paraphrase* in *Christian Initiation,* pp. 169–70.
31. Ibid., p. 169.
32. As early as the summer of 1516, for example, Luther began to supply the pulpit of Simon Heinze, where he preached on the Ten Commandments. See Martin Reu, *Catechetics or Theory and Practise of Religious Instruction,* sec. ed. (Chicago: Wartburg Publishing House, 1927), p. 83. My comments on Luther's early work in this area follow Reu's account.
33. *Works of Martin Luther,* vol. 2 (Philadelphia: A. J. Holman Co. and Castle Press, 1932), pp. 354–84.
34. Ibid., p. 351.
35. Ibid., p. 354. See also the section following this passage.
36. That Luther continues to have confession in mind is evident from his reference to this practice at various points throughout the appendix. See his comment on ibid., p. 363.
37. Ibid., p. 368.

38. Martin Luther, *To the Councilmen of all Cities in Germany That They Establish and Maintain Christian Schools*, ibid., vol. 4, pp. 101–130. This was written in 1524. See also his sermon from 1530 "On Keeping Children in School" in which he exhorts Christian parents not to keep their children at home for work but to encourage them to attend the newly formed schools. Ibid., pp. 133–78.

39. Reu, *Catechetics*, p. 87.

40. *Works of Martin Luther*, vol. 6, p. 174.

41. Ibid.

42. *Luther's Small Catechism: A New English Translation Prepared by an Intersyndoical Committee—Jubilee Offering 1529–1929* (Minneapolis: Augsburg Publishing House, 1929), p. 17.

43. Originally, the *Large Catechism* was titled the *German Catechism of Martin Luther*, and it appears to be a companion to the *German Mass*.

44. See Reu's fine exposition of the *Small Catechism* in *Catechetics*, chap. 14.

45. *Small Catechism*, p. 5. *Large Catechism*, p. 40.

46. As he puts it: "Its contents represent the minimum of knowledge for a Christian. Whoever does not possess it can not be reckoned among Christians nor be admitted to a sacrament, just as a mechanic who does not know the rules and customs of his trade is rejected and considered unfit," *Large Catechism*, p. 40. He uses equally strong language in the *Small Catechism*. See p. 5.

47. *Small Catechism*, p. 5; *German Mass*, p. 65.

48. His two prefaces to the *German Catechism*, subsequently called *The Large Catechism*, and his introductory letter to pastors, accompanying *The Small Catechism*, are excellent places to get an overview of his thinking about the role of the catechism in church life.

49. An accessible summary of Luther's comments on confirmation is found in Fisher, *Christian Initiation: The Reformation Period*, pp. 171–73.

50. Quoted in ibid., p. 172.

51. Ibid., p. 172.

52. *Works of Martin Luther*, vol. 2, p. 231.

53. Ibid., p. 173.

54. Fisher, *Christian Initiation*, pp. 182–83.

55. This liturgy was written at a time when Melanchthon was attempting to negotiate a peace between Catholics and Protestants, and his and Luther's willingness to include a service of confirmation can be seen as a concession to political necessity. See Repp's comments on this in *Confirmation*, pp. 17–18. More than political expediency seems to be at stake in this, however. Melanchthon was under the influence of Bucer at this point and takes up Bucer's attempt to formulate a genuinely evangelical order confirmation.

56. Luther had addressed each part of his *Small Catechism* to the "head of the family," and virtually all of the reformers directed some of their catechetical helps to the home context. Hymnals and catechisms designed especially for children also began to appear.

57. Quoted by Haugaard in "The Continental Reformation of the Sixteenth Century,"in *A Faithful Church*, ed. John Westerhoff and O. C. Edwards (Wilton, Conn.: Morehouse-Barlow, Co., 1981), p. 140.

58. The *Nuremberg Sermons* is one of the best examples. See Reu, *Catechetics*, p. 120.

59. Repp describes this as the "catechetical type" of confirmation and, as he points out, it was the normative practice in Scandinavian Lutheran churches for many years. *Confirmation*, pp. 22–28.

60. A translation of the catechetical portion of this service is found in Rodolphe Peter, "The Geneva Primer or Calvin's Elementary Catechism," *Calvin Studies V* (Davidson, N.C.: Davidson College, 1990), pp. 135–61.

61. Fisher, *Christian Initiation: The Reformation Period*, pp. 169–70.

62. See Old's comments on this element of Denk's theology. *Reformed Baptismal Rites,* p. 108.

63. A translation of *Of Baptism* is found in *Zwingli and Bullinger,* trans. G. Bromiley, *The Library of Christian Classics* vol. 24 (Philadelphia: Westminster Press, 1953), pp. 119–75; *Refutation of the Tricks of the Catabaptists* can be found in *Ulrich Zwingli 1484–1531: Selected Works,* ed. S. Jackson (Philadelphia: University of Pennsylvania Press, 1972), pp. 123–258.

64. This is found in vol. 24 of the *Library of Christian Classics,* ed. G. Bromiley (Philadelphia: Westminster Press, 1953), pp. 96–118.

65. Ulrich Zwingli, *Commentary on True and False Religion,* ed. S. M. Jackson and C. Heller (Durham, N.C.: The Labyrinth Press, 1981).

66. Bullinger was in Zurich for each of the disputations of 1525 and, later, spent five months there in 1527.

67. For example, in *Refutation of the Tricks of the Catabaptists,* Zwingli argues that Paul uses a rhetorical device known as synecdoche, in which a part is used to represent the whole, when he writes about justification by faith. Paul's use of justification must be interpreted within the much larger network of themes that describe the totality of God's saving work: election, predestination, and calling. See pp. 237–47.

68. See, for example, his discussion of circumcision and infant Baptism as signs of the covenant in *Of Baptism,* pp. 138–39.

69. Jackson, *Zwingli: Selected Works,* p. 227.

70. Zwingli also treats the covenant in relation to Abraham in *Of Baptism,* pp. 139–40.

71. Ibid., pp. 141ff.

72. I am following Old's translation here. Ibid., p. 148.

73. See Old's discussion in *Reformed Baptismal Rite,* pp. 146–52.

74. Ibid., p. 150.

75. Ibid., p. 205.

76. Ibid., p. 185.

77. By "evangelical" here, I am not drawing on the modern distinction between evangelicals and liberals. Rather, I am using evangelical in the sense used by the early reformers themselves to refer to churches committed to the evangel, to the proclamation of God's gracious forgiveness made known and effective in Jesus Christ and the unmerited acceptance of this grace in faith. Evangelical in this sense often stands in tension with the theology of contemporary forms of American evangelicalism that have an Arminian theological orientation.

78. August Lang, *Der Evangelienkommentar Martin Butzers und die Grundzuge seiner Theologie* (Leipzig, Germany: 1900), pp. 120–24. W. P. Stephens, *The Holy Spirit in the Theology of Martin Bucer* (Cambridge, Mass.: The University Press, 1970).

79. Stephens, *Holy Spirit,* p. 49.

80. Ibid., p. 161.

81. Helpful discussions are Gerrit Jan van der Poll, *Martin Bucer's Liturgical Ideas* (Assen, Netherlands: Van Gorcum, 1954) and Miriam Chrisman, *Strasbourg and the Reform: A Study in the Process of Change* (New Haven, Conn.: Yale University Press, 1967), chap. 14.

82. Ottomar Cypris, *Basic Principles: Translation and Commentary of Martin Bucer's Gund Und Ursach, 1524,* Union Theological Seminary in New York, dissertation for Th.D., 1971, pp. 166–82, 216–66.

83. E. C. Whitaker, *Martin Bucer and the Book of Common Prayer,* Alcuin Club Collections, no. 55 (Great Wakering, England: Mayhew-McCrimmon, 1974), pp. 82–114. The *De Regno Christi* is found in Wilhelm Pauck's *Melanchthon and Bucer* (Philadelphia: Westminster Press, 1969).

84. Ibid., p. 102.

85. Ibid., p. 102.

86. Ibid., p. 104.
87. The appendix of *The Church Order of Cassel* includes an "Order for Confirmation and the Laying On of Hands." This is found in Emil Sehling, *Die evangelischen Kirchenordnungen des XVI Jahrhunderts,* vol. 8 (Tübingen, Germany: J.C.B. Mohr, 1963), pp. 124–26. The confirmation service penned by Bucer and Melanchthon in the *Einfaltigs Bedencken* was translated by John Day in *A Simple and Religious Consultation* in 1547. Both services appear in part in Fisher's *Christian Initiation: The Reformation Period,* pp. 179–81 and 194–203.
88. Ibid., p. 201.
89. Ibid., p. 202.
90. Ibid.
91. Calvin, *Institutes,* p. 9.
92. John Calvin, "Articles Concerning the Organization of the Church and of Worship at Geneva 1537," in *Theological Treatises,* trans. J.K.S. Reid, Library of Christian Classics, vol. 22 (Philadelphia: Westminster Press, 1954), pp. 48–55.
93. Ibid.
94. John Calvin, *Instruction in Faith (1537),* trans. P. Fuhrmann (Richmond: John Knox Press, 1949). Luther's influence is apparent.
95. François Wendel, *Calvin: Origins and Development of His Religious Thought,* trans. P. Mairet (Durham, N.C.: Labyrinth Press, 1950), p. 61.
96. Calvin, *Institutes,* pp. 1281, 1288, 1289, and 1296. The second of these themes frequently is linked by Calvin to the theme of accommodation. The sacraments are agencies established by God to accommodate to our "dull capacity," p. 1281.
97. Luther's view on whether infants have faith was worked out over many years. In the latter part of his life, he came to place more and more emphasis on the power of the Word attached to Baptism to *create* faith in those who are baptized.
98. Wendel, *Calvin,* pp. 324–25.
99. Calvin, *Institutes,* p. 1343.
100. Throughout this final section I am deeply indebted to Hughes Old's argument. See particularly, *Reformed Baptismal Rite,* pp. 140–42, 194–99, and 217–26.
101. Ibid., pp. 202–3.
102. Old's translation, Ibid., p. 202.
103. For English translations of this text other than Old's, see the following: Peter, "The Geneva Primer"; "The Manner to examine Children, before they be admitted to the Supper of the Lord," in *Catechisms of the Scottish Reformation,* ed. Horatius Bonar (London: James Nisbet and Co., 1866), pp. 93–95; *The School of Faith: The Catechisms of the Reformed Church,* trans. Thomas Torrance (London: James Clarke & Co., 1959), pp. 237–42. I am following Old's translation here.
104. Ibid., p. 205.
105. Old has attempted to reconstruct this service and *The Genevan Shorter Catechism of 1553.* Ibid., pp. 207–9, 217–24.
106. Ibid., p. 208.
107. Ibid., p. 218.
108. Calvin, *Institutes,* IV, p. 19.
109. Ibid., pp. 1451–52.
110. Ibid., p. 1452.
111. Ibid., pp. 1460–61.
112. Elsewhere, Calvin reiterates virtually the same argument: "We also should like to see that rite everywhere restored by which the young are presented to God, after giving forth a Confession of their Faith. This would be a not unbecoming approval of their Catechism." *John Calvin's Tracts and Treatises,* vol. III, trans. H. Beveridge (Grand Rapids, Mich.: William B. Eerdmans Pub. Co., 1958), p. 288. He also mentions this practice in *Commentaries on the Epistle to the Hebrews,* trans. J. Owen (Grand Rapids, Mich.: William B. Eerdmans Pub. Co., 1949), pp. 131–34.

113. Fisher, *Christian Initiation: The Reformation Period*, p. 260.
114. Calvin, *Institutes*, p. 1461.
115. Ibid., p. 1452.
116. Ibid., p. 1452.

Notes to Chapter 5

1. See Repp's discussion of this influence in *Confirmation*, pp. 46–47.
2. Frank Klos, *Confirmation and First Communion: A Study Book* (Minneapolis: Augsburg Publishing House, 1968), pp. 64–65.
3. Repp, *Confirmation*, pp. 46–47.
4. This is Repp's nomenclature, and I am following him here, with a few changes. I have changed his "catechetical" to "instructional" in order to make it clear that I am not referring to my use of this term here.
5. See Luther's discussion in *The Babylonian Captivity, Luther's Works*, pp. 36, 91–92.
6. Repp, *Confirmation*, p. 40.
7. Fisher, *Christian Initiation: The Reformation Period*, p. 200.
8. Repp, *Confirmation*, pp. 36–37.
9. For a partial translation, see Fisher, *Christian Initiation: The Reformation Period*, pp. 182–84.
10. Repp, *Confirmation*, pp. 45–46.
11. See Martin Reu's multivolume collection of these in *Quellen zur Geschichte des kirchlichen Unterrichts in der evangelischen Kirche Deutschlands* (Gutersloh, Germany: Druck Verlag von Bertelsmann, 1906) and his excellent overview in *Catechetics or Theory and Practise of Religious Instruction* (Chicago: Wartburg Publishing House, 1921), p. 117.
12. An excellent balanced discussion of Lutheran orthodoxy is Robert Preus's *The Theology of Post-Reformation Lutheranism* (St. Louis: Concordia Publishing House, 1971).
13. See Reu's comments in this regard in *Catechetics*, p. 127.
14. This is Gustaf Wiencke's assessment. See "Confirmation Instruction in Historical Perspective," p. 103.
15. Repp, *Confirmation*, p. 64.
16. See G. H. Bantock's discussion of Comenius in *Studies in the History of Educational Theory*, vol. 1, *Artifice & Nature 1350–1765* (London: George Allen & Unwin, 1980), chap. 9. Daniel Stevick provides a synopsis of Comenius's influence in England in "Christian Initiation: Post-Reformation to the Present Era," in *Made, Not Born: New Perspectives on Christian Initiation and the Catechumenate* (Notre Dame, Ind.: University of Notre Dame Press, 1976), pp. 109–10.
17. Quoted in Repp, *Confirmation*, p. 69. James Stein provides the biographical context of this phrase in *Philipp Jakob Spener: Pietist Patriarch* (Chicago: Covenant Press, 1986), p. 81.
18. This paraphrase of Spener's thought comes from Stein. Ibid., p. 80.
19. Ibid., p. 81.
20. Repp, *Confirmation*, p. 72.
21. Ibid.
22. Stephen Toulmin, *Cosmopolis: The Hidden Agenda of Modernity* (New York: Free Press, 1990), especially chap. 2.
23. Peter Gay, *The Enlightenment: An Interpretation* (New York: W.W. Norton, 1966). Henry May, *The Enlightenment in America* (New York: Oxford University Press, 1976). Douglas Sloan, *The Scottish Enlightenment and the American College Ideal* (New York: Teachers College Press, 1971). Arthur Whitaker, *Latin America and the Enlightenment: Essays* (New York: Appleton-Century, 1942).
24. See Reu's comments and references in *Catechetics*, p. 144.
25. Ibid., p. 141.

26. Repp, *Confirmation,* p. 81.
27. Ibid., p. 82.
28. Ibid., p. 92. In the chapter from which this is taken, Repp describes various attempts at reform.
29. *The Journals of Henry Melchior Muhlenberg,* 3 vols., trans. T. Tappert and J. Doberstein (Philadelphia: Muhlenberg Press, 1942–1958). See Repp, *Confirmation,* p. 97.
30. Repp, ibid., p. 92.
31. Ibid., fn. 4, p. 99.
32. Wiencke, "Confirmation Instruction," p. 105.
33. Quoted in Repp, *Confirmation,* p. 101.
34. Rationalism had a minimal impact on American Lutheranism, although it was reflected in Frederick Henry Quitman's *Evangelical Catechism: or A Short Exposition of the Principal Doctrines of Precepts of the Christian Religion, for the Use of the Churches Belonging to the Evangelical Lutheran Synod of the State of New York,* published in 1814. See Wiencke, "Confirmation Instruction," p. 107.
35. Robert Lynn and Elliott Wright, *The Big Little School: 200 Years of the Sunday School* (Birmingham, Ala.: Religious Education Press, 1971).
36. Jack Seymour, *From Sunday School to Church School: Continuities in Protestant Church Education in the United States 1860–1929* (Washington, D.C.: University Press of America, 1982).
37. See Philip Pfatteicher, *Commentary on the Lutheran Book of Worship: Lutheran Liturgy in Its Ecumenical Context* (Minneapolis: Augsburg Fortress, 1990), chap. 1.
38. The 1970 commission on the theology and practice of confirmation drew on its own survey, *Current Concepts and Practice of Confirmation in Lutheran Churches.* More recently research was undertaken by the Churchwide Confirmation Ministry Study, a study of thirty congregations. See Ken Smith, *Six Models of Confirmation,* The Evangelical Lutheran Church in America, 8765 West Higgins Road, Chicago, Illinois 60631.
39. *The Report of the Joint Commission on the Theology and Practice of Confirmation* (Minneapolis: Augsburg Publishing House, 1970), pp. 11–12.
40. Ibid., p. 2.
41. *Confirmation in the Lutheran Church* was published in 1964.
42. See Frank Senn, "An End for Confirmation?" *Currents in Theology and Mission* 3 (1976), pp. 50–51.
43. *Report,* p. 21.
44. Ibid., pp. 13–20.
45. Ibid., p. 15.
46. Klos, *Confirmation and First Communion.*
47. The Report appears at the end of Klos's book. See p. 207.
48. Ibid.
49. The subcommittee's work first appeared as *Contemporary Worship–8: Affirmation of the Baptismal Covenant.* See Senn's comments about this document in "An End for Confirmation?" p. 45. For an overview of the Inter-Lutheran Commission on Worship, see Pfatteicher, *Commentary,* pp. 4–11.
50. *The Lutheran Book of Worship* (Minneapolis: Augsburg Fortress Press, 1990).
51. *LBW,* p. 198.
52. *The Confirmation Ministry Task Force Report.* ELCA Division for Congregational Ministries, 8765 West Higgins Road, Chicago, Illinois 60631.
53. Ibid., p. 1.
54. The report mentions almost in passing: "Furthermore, a continued emphasis upon learning from the Small Catechism and the Scriptures is an expectation of confirmation." Ibid., p. 7.
55. Ibid.
56. Klos, *Confirmation,* p. 204.

57. *Confirmation Ministry Task Force Report,* p. 7.
58. Ibid., p. 8.
59. This was discussed in the Introduction in relation to the Search Institute report.
60. Brief introductions to Cranmer's life and work are F. E. Hutchinson, *Cranmer and the English Reformation* (New York: Macmillan Company, 1951); David Loades, *Cranmer and the English Reformation* (Bangor, England: Headstart History, 1991); and *Cranmer: A Living Influence for 500 Years,* ed. M. Johnson (Durham, England: Turnstone Ventures, 1990). Much of Cranmer's writing can be found in *The Works of Thomas Cranmer,* ed. J. Cox (Cambridge, England: Cambridge University Press, 1846), vols. 1 and 2.
61. The Sarum rites of Baptism and confirmation can be found in A. J. Collins, *Manuale ad usum percelebris ecclesie Sarisburiensis* (Chester, England: Henry Bradshaw Society, 1958), XCI, pp. 25–43, 166–67. See Marion Hatchett's discussion in "The Rite of 'Confirmation' in the Book of Common Prayer and in *Authorized Services 1973,*" *Anglican Theological Review,* LVI, 1974.
62. The *Censura* was given to Cranmer in 1551, two months before Bucer's death, and privately circulated until 1577. Bucer's role in the formation of the first prayer books was not widely known. See Constantin Hopf, *Martin Bucer and the English Reformation* (Oxford, England: Basil Blackwell, 1954). Allan Gilbert points out Bucer's influence in the field of education, "Martin Bucer on Education," *The Journal of English and German Philology* 18, July, 1919, pp. 1–24.
63. See the introductory chapters by D. G. Selwyn of *A Catechism Set Forth by Thomas Cranmer* (Oxford, England: Sutton Courtenay Press, 1978).
64. Colin Buchanan, *Anglican Confirmation* (Nottingham, England: Grove Books Limited, 1986), p. 21. For Cranmer's thoughts on this matter, see *The Works of Cranmer,* pp. 80 and 115–16.
65. Fisher, *Christian Initiation: The Reformation Period,* p. 95.
66. Ibid., p. 94.
67. The original phrase behind it was *unctio spiritus sancti.* See Marion Hatchett, "The Rite of 'Confirmation',*" p. 300.
68. L. L. Mitchell, *Baptismal Anointing,* p. 179.
69. Fisher, *Christian Initiation: The Reformation Period,* pp. 236–43.
70. Ibid., pp. 236–37.
71. Ibid., p. 241.
72. Ibid., pp. 106–11.
73. Daniel Stevick, *Baptismal Moments; Baptismal Meanings* (New York: The Church Hymnal Corporation, 1987), p. 22.
74. Fisher notes the Lutheran influence in *Christian Initiation: The Reformation Period,* pp. 252–53. Bucer's influence also is clearly present.
75. Stevick, *Baptismal Moments,* p. 23.
76. The language of "daily increase" is found in the Strassburg baptismal service after 1537 and in the confirmation service written by Bucer and Melanchthon for Hermann's Consultation. See Fisher, *Christian Initiation: The Reformation Period,* pp. 39 and 202.
77. Jeremey Taylor, *The Whole Works,* vol. 5, pp. 616–17.
78. Fredrica Thompsett, "Godly Instruction in Reformation England: The Challenge of Religious Education in the Tudor Commonwealth," in *A Faithful Church,* ed. Westerhoff and Edwards, pp. 174–203. David Siegenthaler, "Religious Education for Citizenship: Primer and Catechism," in *The Godly Kingdom of Tudor England: Great Books of the English Reformation,* ed. J. Booty (Wilton, Conn.: Morehouse-Barlow Co., 1981), pp. 219–47.
79. Selwyn, *Catechism by Cranmer,* fn. 9, p. 20.
80. Ibid., pp. 17, 87–88. For the Lutheran origins of this catechism, see chap. 2.

81. Alexander Nowell, *A Catechism,* ed. G. Corrie (Cambridge, England: University of Cambridge Press, 1853). Parker Society.

82. S. L. Ollard, "Confirmation in the Anglican Communion," in *Confirmation: Vol. I— Historical and Doctrinal* (London: SPCK, 1926), pp. 213–20.

83. Peter Jagger, *Clouded Witness: Initiation in the Church of England in the Mid-Victorian Period 1850–1875* (Allison Park, Pa.: Pickwick Publications, 1982).

84. Buchanan, *Anglican Confirmation,* p. 30.

85. Julien Gunn, "Bishop Hobart's Emphasis on Confirmation," *Historical Magazine of the Protestant Episcopal Church* 24 (1955), pp. 293–310.

86. F. W. Puller, *What is the Distinctive Grace of Confirmation?* (London: Rivingtons, 1890). A. J. Mason, *The Theology of Confirmation in Relation to Baptism* (New York: E. P. Dutton, 1891).

87. Gregory Dix, *The Theology of Confirmation in Relation to Baptism* (Westminster, England: Dacre Press, 1946) and J.D.C. Fisher, *Confirmation Then and Now* (London: SPCK, 1978). Interspersing Catholics like Dix in the following discussion is indicative of the way scholarship in the Roman Church was influencing those elements of the Anglican-Episcopal tradition with Anglo-Catholic leanings.

88. L. S. Thorton, *Confirmation: Its Place in the Baptismal Mystery* (London: A. & C. Black, 1954). Cyril E. Pocknee, *Water and Spirit* (London: Darton, Longman and Todd, 1967).

89. See Buchanan, *Anglican Confirmation,* p. 32 and Stevick, *Baptismal Moments,* pp. 68–73, 81–85.

90. G. W. Lampe's *The Seal of the Spirit.* Others following this general line of criticism are: A. T. Wirgman, *The Doctrine of Confirmation* (London: Longman Press, 1887); A.E.J. Rawlinson, *Christian Initiation* (London: SPCK, 1947); and E. C. Whitaker, *Sacramental Initiation Complete in Baptism,* Grove Liturgical Study No. 1 (Nottingham, England: Grove Books, 1975).

91. J.D.G. Dunn's *Baptism in the Holy Spirit* (London: SCM, 1970).

92. Aidan Kavanagh, *The Shape of Baptism: The Rite of Christian Initiation* (New York: Pueblo Publishing Company, 1978).

93. Mitchell, *Baptismal Anointing.* See also Finn's *Early Christian Baptism and the Catechumenate: West and East Syria.*

94. See David Holeton, *Infant Communion—Then and Now,* Grove Liturgical Study no. 27 (Nottingham, England: Grove Books, 1981). Buchanan, *Anglican Confirmation,* pp. 44–46. Stevick, *Baptismal Moments,* chap. 6.

95. Charles Price, *Introducing the Proposed Book of Common Prayer* (New York: Crossroad Books, 1977), pp. 9–10.

96. Ibid., p. 10.

97. Ibid., pp. 10–11.

98. *Baptism, Eucharist, and Ministry,* Faith and Order Paper no. 111 (Geneva: World Council of Churches, 1982). *Churches Respond to BEM: Official Responses to the "Baptism, Eucharist, and Ministry Text",* ed. Max Thurian (Geneva: World Council of Churches), vols. 1–3. *Ecumenical Perspectives on Baptism, Eucharist, and Ministry,* ed. Max Thurian (Geneva: World Council of Churches, 1983). *Baptism, Eucharist, & Ministry 1982–1990: Report on the Process and Responses* (Geneva: WCC Publications, 1990).

99. *The Book of Occasional Services—1991* (New York: The Church Hymnal Corporation, 1991), pp. 112–26.

100. *Holy Baptism with the Laying-on-of-Hands, Prayer Book Studies 18, On Baptism and Confirmation* (Published by The Church Pension Fund, 800 Second Avenue, New York, N.Y., 1970).

101. Ibid., pp. 16–22.

102. Ibid., p. 20.

103. Ibid., p. 18.
104. Daniel Stevick, *Holy Baptism Together with A Form for the Affirmation of Baptismal Vows with the Laying On of Hands by the Bishop, also called Confirmation.* (New York: The Church Hymnal Corporation, 1973).
105. Ibid., fn. 1, p. 100.
106. *The Book of Common Prayer and Administration of the Sacraments and Other Rites and Ceremonies of the Church* (New York: The Church Hymnal Corporation, 1979), p. 298.
107. Stevick, *Baptismal Moments,* p. 138.
108. Ibid., pp. 138–39.
109. *The Book of Common Prayer,* p. 412.
110. This alternate interpretation is described in a variety of places: Stevick, *Baptismal Moments,* pp. 55–56; Charles Price and Louis Weil, *Liturgy for Living* (New York: Seabury Press, 1979), pp. 127–30; Leonel Mitchell, *Praying Shapes Believing: A Theological Commentary on the* Book of Common Prayer (Minneapolis: Winston Press, 1985), pp. 111–12; John Westerhoff, "Confirmation: An Episcopal Church Perspective," *Reformed Liturgy & Music* 24, no. 4 (Fall 1990), p. 199; and Buchanan, *Anglican Confirmation,* p. 42.
111. The language quoted comes from *The Book of Discipline of the United Methodist Church—1992* (Nashville: The United Methodist Publishing House, 1992), p. 126.
112. *The Works of John Wesley,* ed. Thomas Jackson (Grand Rapids, Mich.: Zondervan, 1958–59), pp. 10, 192.
113. *Wesley's Standard Sermons,* ed. E. M. Sugden (London: The Epworth Press, 1961), 1, p. 295.
114. *Works,* 10, p. 151.
115. Gayle Carlton Felton, *The Gift of Water: The Practice and Theology of Baptism Among Methodists in America* (Nashville: Abingdon Press, 1992).
116. Ole Borgen, "Baptism, Confirmation, and Church Membership in the Methodist Church before the Union of 1968: A Historical and Theological Study (Part I)," *Methodist History* 27:2 (January 1989), pp. 107–8.
117. Felton, *Gift of Water,* pp. 142–43.
118. Quoted in Felton, ibid.
119. Ibid., p. 160.
120. Carl Michalson, "Why Methodists Baptize," *New Christian Advocate* 6 (1958).
121. *Proposed Revision of the Book of Worship* (Nashville: The United Methodist Publishing House, 1960).
122. Ibid., pp. 26–27.
123. Ibid., p. 18ff.
124. *Discipline,* 1964, par. 1714.
125. *We Gather Together: Services of Public Worship, Supplemental Worship Resources 10* (Nashville: The United Methodist Publishing House, 1980).
126. Felton, *Gift of Water,* p. 165.
127. *Companion to the Book of Services: Introduction, Commentary, and Instructions for Using the New United Methodist Services, Supplemental Worship Resources 17* (Nashville: Abingdon Press, 1988).
128. Ibid., p. 78.
129. Ibid., pp. 78–79.
130. Ibid., p. 81.
131. *The United Methodist Hymnal: Book of United Methodist Worship* (Nashville: The United Methodist Publishing House, 1989), p. 32.
132. Ibid., p. 37.
133. *Follow Me,* John Gooch, ed. (Nashville: Cokesbury, 1993).
134. *By Water and the Spirit: A Study of the Proposed United Methodist Understanding of Baptism* (Nashville: General Board of Discipleship, n.d.).

135. Ibid., p. 8.
136. Ibid., p. 9.
137. Ibid., p. 13.
138. Ibid.

Notes to Chapter 6

1. *John Calvin's Tracts and Treatises,* vol. 3, trans. H. Beveridge (Grand Rapids, Mich.: William B. Eerdmans Pub. Co., 1958), p. 288. Calvin is operating on the basis of faulty historical information, noted in chapter 4.
2. Julius Melton makes a similar point in *Presbyterian Worship in America: Changing Patterns Since 1787* (Richmond: John Knox Press, 1967), pp. 14–15.
3. As my colleague Elsie McKee has reminded me, liturgy can mean something more inclusive than set forms of worship or prayer: "planned, public, and corporate acts of worship," to borrow her definition (shared in private conversation). By "liturgical worship," I mean something much narrower than this comprehensive definition. I mean a form of worship drawing on a book of common liturgical forms, providing explicit patterns for worship occasions of various sorts, as well as set prayers, calls to worship, responsive readings, and so forth.
4. For use of the concept of paradigm in theology, see T. Howland Sanks, *Authority in the Church: A Study in Changing Paradigms* (American Academy of Religion) Dissertation Series, no. 2 and Hans Küng and David Tracy, *Paradigm Change in Theology,* trans. M. Kohl (New York: Crossroad Pub. Co., 1991).
5. Leonard Trinterud, *The Forming of an American Tradition: A Re-examination of Colonial Presbyterianism* (New York: Arno Press, 1949), p. 15.
6. For a discussion of this point, see the following: Horton Davies, *The Worship of the English Puritans* (Westminster, England: Dacre Press, 1948), p. 21; William Maxwell, *The Liturgical Portions of the Genevan Service Book* (Edinburgh: Oliver and Boyd, 1931), pp. 5–6; and William McMillan, *The Worship of the Scottish Reformed Church, 1550–1638* (London: James Clarke & Company, n.d.), p. 52.
7. McMillan, *Worship of Scottish Reformed Church,* pp. 57–58.
8. Quoted in Charles Baird, *Eutaxia, or the Presbyterian Liturgies: Historical Sketches* (New York: M. W. Dodd, 1855), p. 22.
9. Ibid., p. 32.
10. See Baird's introductory comments to chapters 4, 11, and 12 in ibid.
11. For a discussion of the influence of Knox's service book, see Maxwell, *Liturgical Portions,* and Alexander Mitchell, *The Westminster Assembly: Its History and Standards* (Philadelphia: Presbyterian Board of Publication and Sabbath-School Work, 1897).
12. This was something well advertised in the title of its initial publication: "The form of prayers and ministrations of the Sacraments, etc., used in the English congregation at Geneva, and approved by the famous and godly learned man, John Calvin." McMillan, *Worship of Scottish Reformed Church,* p. 54.
13. Ibid., p. 42.
14. Ibid., p. 60.
15. Ibid., p. 65.
16. John Morgan, *Godly Learning: Puritan Attitudes towards Reason, Learning and Education, 1560–1640* (Cambridge, England: Cambridge University Press, 1986), chap. 1.
17. The Puritans got their name from the ardor with which they pursued the purification of worship. It originally had negative connotations. See Davies, *Worship of the English Puritans,* p. 1.
18. Ibid., chap. 3. Maxwell, *Genevan Service Book,* n. 34, p. 15.
19. Ibid., chap. 7.
20. Mitchell, *Westminster Assembly,* p. 50.
21. Lefferts Loetscher, *A Brief History of the Presbyterians* (Philadelphia: Westminster Press, 1978), 4th ed., p. 38 and Mitchell, *Westminster Assembly,* p. 95.

22. Loetscher, *Brief History,* pp. 96–97.
23. Quoted in Mitchell, *Westminster Assembly,* p. 113.
24. Both can be found in Horatius Bonar, *Catechisms of the Scottish Reformation* (London: James Nisbet, 1866), pp. 177–285.
25. Morgan, *Godly Learning,* pp. 86–87.
26. Leonard Grant, "Puritan Catechizing," *Journal of Presbyterian History* 46 (Philadelphia: Department of History of the United Presbyterian Church in the U.S.A., 1968), pp. 112–13.
27. An example of a Scriptural catechism is Owen Stockton's *A Scriptural Catechism: Useful for all Sorts of Persons, Both such as desire to teach their families and such as desire to learn the principles of the Christian religion out of the Scriptures* (London: H. Brome, 1622).
28. Only 50 percent of the Puritan catechisms included the Apostles' Creed. Grant, "Puritan Catechizing," p. 113. The *Shorter Catechism* includes it only in the Appendix.
29. Samuel Annesley, *A Supplement to the Morning Exercises at Cripplegate* (London: Thomas Cockerill, 1674), p. 173.
30. Baxter, for example, wrote *The Mother's Catechism,* along with a more general help: *The Catechizing of Families; A Teacher of Householders How to Teach their Household; Useful Also to School-Masters and Tutors of Youth* (London: T. Parkhurst, 1683). For the former, see *The Practical Works of Richard Baxter: with a preface giving some account of the author, and of this edition of his practical works: an essay on his genius, works, and times; and a portrait, in four volumes,* vol. 1 (Ligonier, Pa: Soli Deo Gloria Pub., 1990), pp. 1ff. Another example is John Willison's *A Mother's Catechism for the Young Child* (Glasgow: W. Lang, n.d.).
31. The Puritans did not like Nowell's *Catechism* and used their own when they could. See Morgan, *Godly Learning,* pp. 186–87, 210.
32. Richard Baxter, *The Reformed Pastor,* Puritan Paperbacks, (Edinburgh: The Banner of Truth Trust, 1974), pp. 231–56.
33. Quoted in Grant, "Puritan Catechizing," pp. 107–8.
34. Annesley, *Exercises at Cripplegate,* p. 165.
35. Ibid., p. 154.
36. Ibid., p. 156.
37. Mitchell, *Westminster Assembly,* p. 420.
38. Ibid., pp. 346–53. See also John Leith's fine discussion in *Assembly at Westminster* (Richmond: John Knox Press, 1973), p. 65.
39. Mitchell, *Westminster Assembly,* Lectures 10 and 11.
40. Ibid., pp. 432–35. In their reliance on these preexisting catechisms, the Larger and Shorter catechisms differed somewhat. The former more directly depended on the Assembly's confession, while the latter drew many of its questions and answers from preexisting sources. See also Mitchell's *Catechisms of the Second Reformation* (London: James Nisbet & Co., 1886).
41. *The Book of Confessions, Presbyterian Church (USA)* (Philadelphia: Office of the General Assembly, 1983). Shorter Catechism, 7.012–7.021; Larger Catechism, 7.132, 7.140–7.146; Confession, 6.0376–6.042.
42. Shorter Catechism 7.095; Larger Catechism 7.276; Confession 6.141, 6.157.
43. The phrase "are of years and ability to examine themselves" in Larger Catechism 7.287 is indicative of the advent of the reflective capacities associated with the age of discretion.
44. Ibid., 7.283.
45. Ibid., 7.277.
46. John Davidson's *Form of Examination and Catechism,* for example, written in 1599, refers to such a service. See Bonar, *Catechisms of the Scottish Reformation,* pp. 324–56.
47. This can be found in Baird, *Eutaxia,* chap. 9.

48. Richard Baxter, *The Practical Works of the Rev. Richard Baxter* (London: James Duncan, 1830), 15, p. 493.

49. *Confirmation and Restauration, The necessary means of Reformation and Reconciliation; For the Healing of the Corruptions and Divisions of the Churches* (London: Nevil Simmons Bookseller, 1658). The ecumenical intent of the book is expressed in the initial section, "To the Reader." He mentions a similar intent on p. 6.

50. Ibid., propositions 5 and 12.

51. Ibid., proposition 6.

52. *The Westminster Directory being A Directory for the Publique Worship of God in the Three Kingdomes* (Nottingham, England: Grove Books, 1980), p. 20.

53. Ibid., p. 21.

54. Ibid.

55. Trinterud, *American Tradition*, p. 15.

56. Loetscher, *Brief History*, p. 42.

57. Trinterud, *American Tradition*, chap. 2.

58. It is important to point out that the American manifestations of Scotch-Irish and English Puritan impulses do not reflect the full range of their original sources. That is to say, there were elements comparable to Old and New School Presbyterianism in the Church of Scotland, as well as the English Puritans. The American appropriation of each of these streams of the Reformed tradition is only partial.

59. Shelton Smith, Robert Handy, Lefferts Loetscher, *American Christianity: An Historical Interpretation with Representative Documents,* vol. 1, 1607–1820 (New York: Charles Scribner's Sons, 1960), p. 9.

60. Ibid., p. 10.

61. One of the flaws of Elizabeth McCort's fine dissertation, "Changes in Theory and Practice of Confirmation in the (United) Presbyterian Church in the United States of America, 1789–1958" (New York: Union Theological Seminary, 1967), is her characterization of this stream of Presbyterianism as a by-product of the Anabaptist tradition and a form of revivalism. See, for example, p. 20. This ignores the influence of the English Puritans on this wing of early Presbyterianism. The simple conversionism of nineteenth-century revivalism is best viewed as a narrowing and distortion of earlier understandings of piety already present in the Presbyterian tradition.

62. The influence of Theodore Frelinghuysen, a Dutch Reformed pietist, on Gilbert Tennent might seem to contradict this point, but see Trinterud's interpretation, *Shaping of an American Tradition,* pp. 54–59.

63. Trinterud has documented the reliance of the New Light Presbyters on English Puritanism extensively. Ibid., chap. 10.

64. The single best collection and discussion of these accounts is found in Eric Haden's *The History of the Use of the Shorter Catechism in the Presbyterian Church in the United States of America* (Kansas City, Kan.: Central Seminary Press, 1941).

65. Trinterud, *Shaping of an American Tradition*, pp. 304–5. Baird's *Extaxia* contains the proposed draft of the new directory. See pp. 228–44.

66. Horton Davies, *The Worship of the American Puritans, 1629–1730* (New York: Peter Lang, 1990), p. 266.

67. Milton Coalter, *Gilbert Tennent, Son of Thunder: A Case Study of Continental Pietism's Impact on the First Great Awakening in the Middle Colonies* (New York: Greenwood Press, 1986).

68. Gilbert Tennent, *Twenty-three Sermons upon the Chief End of Man* (Philadelphia: W. Bradford, 1744).

69. Ibid., p. 29.

70. Smith, Handy, and Loetscher, *American Christianity,* p. 326.

71. Ibid., p. 519.

72. See McCort's helpful summary of Dwight's attitudes in *Confirmation,* pp. 86–87.

73. Ibid., pp. 68–74.

74. Thomas Haweis, *The Communicant's Spiritual Companion or An Evangelical Preparation for the Lord's Supper* (New Haven, Conn.: Oliver St. & Co., 1810). John Willison, *Young Communicant's Catechism* (Philadelphia: Russell and Martien, 1831). See also Haweis, *A Sacramental Catechism* (Belfast: James Magee, 1753) and *An Example of Plain Catechising, upon the Assembly's Shorter Catechism* (Pittsburgh: Luke Lommis & Co., 1832).

75. Haweis, *Spiritual Companion*, pp. iii–iv. See also "Examination of our Right to the Lord's Table," p. 21. He makes a similar distinction in *Plain Catechizing*, p. 253.

76. The most extensive treatment of sacramental seasons is found in Leigh Eric Schmidt's *Holy Fairs: Scottish Communions and American Revivals in the Early Modern Period* (Princeton, N.J.: Princeton University Press, 1989). I am largely following this account here. E. T. Thompson also provides firsthand accounts of this practice in *Presbyterians in the South, Volume One: 1607–1861* (Richmond: John Knox Press, 1963), pp. 226–34.

77. Thompson, *Presbyterians in the South*, pp. 226–34.

78. Ibid., p. 229.

79. Melton, *Presbyterian Worship*, p. 51.

80. Charles Finney, *Lectures on Revivals of Religion* (New York: Fleming, 1868), chap. 14.

81. Ibid., p. 238.

82. Ibid., p. 322.

83. Lyman Atwater, "The Children of the Church and Sealing Ordinances," *Biblical Repertory and Princeton Review* 29, January 1857, p. 7. Also see "The Children of the Covenant, and their 'Part in the Lord,'" *Biblical Repertory and Princeton Review* 35, October 1863, pp. 622–43.

84. Charles Hodge, "The Neglect of Infant Baptism," *Biblical Repertory and Princeton Review* 29, January 1857, p. 84.

85. Ibid., pp. 89–91.

86. See *Minutes:* 1804, p. 366; 1808, p. 402; 1816, p. 628; 1818, p. 691; and 1835, p. 37.

87. "The Duty of the Church in the Instruction and Discipline of Her Baptized Children," *Report of the Committee of the General Assembly, Appointed to Draught a Plan for Disciplining Baptized Children* (New York: Whiting and Watson, 1812).

88. Ibid., p. 3.

89. Ibid., p. 11.

90. Ibid., p. 23.

91. Ibid., p. 23.

92. Ibid., p. 34.

93. Ibid., pp. 25, 30, 33–34.

94. Ibid., p. 25.

95. Ibid., pp. 49–54.

96. Many of the arguments offered in this report were repeated in a book published in 1835 by one of the report's authors, Samuel Miller, *Presbyterianism: The Truly Primitive and Apostolical Constitution of the Church of Christ* (Philadelphia: Presbyterian Board of Publication, 1835). Whereas the Romeyn Report described an ancient practice of confirmation in positive terms (following Calvin), Miller explicitly rejected confirmation.

97. Haden, *Shorter Catechism*, chap. 3.

98. For example, an attempt to alter chapter 3, section 3 of the Westminster Confession because of its implied "fatalism" was rejected by the presbyteries in 1909 and 1910. See the *Minutes of the General Assembly of the Presbyterian Church in the U.S.* 1909, p. 48, and 1910, p. 67.

99. The General Assembly authorized use of the 1906 *Book of Common Worship* in 1929. It did so again in 1946, allowing churches to use the revised edition of that same year.

100. Albert Barnes, "The Position of the Evangelical Party in the Episcopal Church," *Miscellanies* (1895–97), vol. 1, pp. 195–98.

101. Charles Hodge, "Presbyterian Liturgies," *Biblical Repertory and Princeton Review*, 27 (1855), pp. 445–67.
102. Ibid., p. 446.
103. Ibid., p. 445.
104. Ibid.
105. Baird, *Eutaxia* and *A Book of Public Prayer Compiled from the Authorized Formularies of Worship of the Presbyterian Church as Prepared by the Reformers Calvin, Knox, Bucer, and Others, with Supplementary Forms* (New York: Charles Scribner, 1857). Baird was raised in Europe.
106. Baird, *Public Prayer*, pp. 164–71. See Baird's comments on this liturgy in the "Appendix," p. 353.
107. Ibid., p. 165. The prayer appears on p. 166.
108. Ibid., pp. 167–68.
109. Ibid., pp. 170–71.
110. Archibald Alexander Hodge, *A Manual of Forms for Baptism, Admission to the Communion, Administration of the Lord's Supper, Marriage and Funerals, Ordination of Elders and Deacons, etc. Conformed to the Doctrine and Discipline of the Presbyterian Church* (Philadelphia: Presbyterian Board of Publication, 1882). This manual was published by the Presbyterian Board of Publication and was so popular that a new edition was published five years later, nearly twice as large.
111. Ibid., pp. 16–21.
112. Ibid., p. 17.
113. Ibid., p. 19. In his notes explaining the meaning of this service, Hodge refers to the service several times as "confirmation" and indicates that he is following his father's thinking. See pp. 20–21.
114. See, for example, Herrick Johnson, *Forms for Special Occasions; Marriage, Burial, Baptism, The Lord's Supper, Ordination, Dedication, etc.: with Scripture Selections for The Chamber of Sickness, The House of Mourning, The Service at Funerals* (Philadelphia: Presbyterian Board of Publication, 1900), pp. 78–83.
115. Melton, *Presbyterian Worship*, pp. 131–32.
116. It originally was to be published "by authority of the General Assembly of the Presbyterian Church," but in the end, it was only portrayed as "Prepared by the Committee of the General Assembly."
117. *The Book of Common Worship* (Philadelphia: The Presbyterian Board of Publication and Sabbath-School Work, 1906).
118. Ibid., pp. 40–41.
119. Ibid., p. 47.
120. *The Book of Common Worship (Revised), Approved by the General Assembly of the Presbyterian Church in the United States of America: For Voluntary Use* (Philadelphia: Presbyterian Board of Christian Education, 1932), pp. 72–74.
121. Ibid., p. 59.
122. See Melton, *Presbyterian Worship*, pp. 111–17.
123. *The Constitution of the Presbyterian Church in the United States, Directory for the Worship of God, Including Optional Forms* (Richmond: Presbyterian Committee of Publication, 1894), pp. 113–14.
124. Ibid., p. 115.
125. Ibid., p. 117.
126. Ibid., p. 117.
127. *The Constitution of the Presbyterian Church in the United States.*
128. *The Westminster Question Book: International Series—A Manual for Teachers and Older Scholars* (Philadelphia: Presbyterian Board of Publication, 1875–98).
129. Joseph Engels, *Catechism for Young Children: An Introduction to the Shorter Catechism* (Philadelphia: Great Commission Publications, 1991). Frances Platt, *A Catechism for Little Children* (New York: New York Sunday School Association, 1885).

The Presbyterian Board of Publication reported that over a million copies of Engels's catechism had been sold by 1880. See *Descriptive Catelogue of the Publications of the Presbyterian Board of Publication* (Philadelphia: Presbyterian Board of Publication, 1880), pp. 402–3.

130. Revisions of the Westminster standards were attempted unsuccessfully as early as 1892 and with success in 1903.

131. "Report to the General Assembly of the Committee to Write an Intermediate Catechism," *Minutes of the General Assembly of the Presbyterian Church in the United States of America* (Philadelphia: Office of the General Assembly, 1912), p. 103.

132. Haden, *Shorter Catechism,* pp. 90–93.

133. See the *Minutes* of the southern church for 1884, p. 229; 1885, p. 425; 1892, p. 44; 1894, pp. 224–25; 1926, p. 60; and 1930, p. 55. In 1875, the General Assembly amended the *Directory for Worship* to make it clear that the Sunday school was nothing but "the more formal organization of catechetical classes which have been known to the Church in all ages." *Minutes,* 1875, p. 42. In 1891, it instituted the practice of giving every child who memorized the *Shorter Catechism* a new Bible. *Minutes,* p. 251.

134. For a discussion of Coe and his relationship to Dewey, see my dissertation, "Practical Theology and Contemporary Christian Education: An Historical and Constructive Analysis," Emory University, 1985, chap. 2.

135. George Albert Coe, *A Social Theory of Religious Education,* Arno Reprint Edition, (New York: Arno Press & the *New York Times,* 1969), pp. 320–21.

136. Harrison Elliott, *Can Religious Education Be Christian?* (New York: Macmillan Co., 1940), p. 23.

137. A helpful overview of the emergence of the modern curriculum in the church is found in Craig Dykstra and Bradley Wigger's "A Brief History of a Genre Problem: Presbyterian Educational Resource Materials," in *The Pluralistic Vision: Presbyterians and Mainstream Protestant Education and Leadership,* ed. M. Coalter, J. Mulder, and L. Weeks (Louisville, Ky.: Westminster/John Knox Press, 1992), pp. 180–204.

138. See Shelton Smith's devastating critique in *Faith and Nurture* (New York: Charles Scribner's Sons, 1941).

139. J. R. Miller, *Manual for Communicants' Classes,* prepared at the Direction of the General Assembly (Philadelphia: Presbyterian Board of Christian Education, 1905). The notes are taken from the revised edition, published in 1919.

140. Ibid., p. 5. See also pp. 11, 13, 14, 43, 49. The first paragraph on Baptism in the manual was added by Verkuyl. Prior to Verkuyl's revision, this purpose was not framed in terms of Baptism. See the comments of William Kosanovich, "Confirmation in the Presbyterian Church in the Twentieth Century," Ph.D. dissertation, Princeton Theological Seminary, 1993, pp. 81–82.

141. See, for example, Charles Erdman, *Coming to the Communion: A Manual of Instruction for Preparatory Classes and Private Study* (Philadelphia: Presbyterian Board of Publication and Sabbath-School Work, 1912) and Victor Lukens, *A Pastor's Instruction Class for Children* (Philadelphia: Presbyterian Board of Publication, 1915).

142. Hugh Kerr, *My First Communion* (Philadelphia: Presbyterian Board of Publication and Sabbath-School Work, 1920).

143. Ibid., p. 7.

144. Hugh Kerr, *A Manual of Faith and Life: A Guide for Individual Christians of Communicant Classes* (Philadelphia: Presbyterian Board of Christian Education, 1937).

145. Ibid., p. 93.

146. Ibid., p. ii.

147. Winfred Moody, *A Teacher's Guide for Use with A Manual of Faith and Life* (Philadelphia: Presbyterian Board of Christian Education, 1938).

148. Ibid., p. vii.

149. Ibid., p. viii. It is unclear whether Moody wrote the "Introduction" herself or whether this was written by her editor or a member of the Board of Christian Education. In any case, it reflects the overall perspective of the guide.

150. Ibid., p. ix.

151. Ibid., pp. x–xi.

152. The southern church approved this measure only after much debate. The initial overture came from the Presbytery of Knoxville in 1981 and was approved by Presbyteries the following year.

153. *Minutes of the General Assembly of the United Presbyterian Church in the United States of America,* p. 629.

154. Ibid., p. 630.

155. Ibid., p. 631.

156. Ibid., p. 631.

157. *The Book of Common Worship, 1946, Approved by the General Assembly of the Presbyterian Church in the United States of America* (Philadelphia: Office of the General Assembly, Division of the Board of Christian Education, 1946), p. vi. The confirmation service is on pp. 131–33. For its reliance on the Church of Scotland's confirmation service see Kosanovich, "Presbyterian Confirmation," pp. 109–14.

158. This stands in contrast with the trend toward viewing confirmation in a quasi-sacramental light by notables in the Scottish Church Service Society. See Bruce Nicol's article, "Confirmation," *Church Service Society: The Annual,* May 1929–30 (Edinburgh: William Blackwood & Sons Ltd).

159. *Minutes of the General Assembly of the United Presbyterian Church in the United States of America,* pp. 153–54.

160. *Directory for the Worship and Work of the Church* found in *The Book of Church Order of the Presbyterian Church in the United States* (Atlanta: John Knox Press, 1975).

161. Ibid., #210–1., p. 143. The profession and purpose language is found in #210-4., p. 144. Immediately after the questions, the minister also says: "Inasmuch as you have made profession of your faith and obedience . . ." #210-5., p. 145.

162. *The Worshipbook: Services* (Philadelphia: Westminster Press, 1970).

163. Max Thurian, *Consecration of the Layman,* trans. W. J. Kerrigan (Baltimore: Helicon, 1963).

164. The report on Baptism is found in the 1972 *Minutes* and that on church membership in the 1974 *Minutes.*

165. *Minutes* (1972), p. 330.

166. See, for example, overtures in the *Minutes of the General Assembly of the Presbyterian Church in the United States* for 1955, p. 82 (that sessions remind parents of their catechetical responsibilities), 1956, pp. 30, 64 (that catechisms should be widely studied), and 1958, pp. 34, 72 (that the Board of Christian Education "seek ways and means of more effectively teaching the catechisms").

167. Haden, *Shorter Catechism,* pp. 94–98. Significantly, however, the catechism was presented more as a summary of the church's traditional doctrines than as a living confession of the church's contemporary faith.

168. *An Outline of the Christian Faith in Question and Answer Form for Use in Communicants' Classes, in the Church School, and in the Home, with A Commentary on the Outline* (Philadelphia: Board of Christian Education of the Presbyterian Church in the U.S.A., 1948).

169. Ibid., p. 3.

170. George Kluber, *On Holy Ground* (Hayfield, Minn.: The Hayfield Publishing Co., 1962).

171. Lewis and Helen Sherrill, *Becoming a Christian: A Manual for Communicant Classes* (Atlanta: John Knox Press, 1943).

172. *This Is My Church* (Philadelphia: Board of Christian Education, 1957, 1959). *The Pastor's Guide for the Training of Church Members* (Philadelphia: Board of Christian Education, 1957, 1959).
173. *This Is My Church*, p. 27.
174. Ibid., p. 28.
175. See *Pastor's Guide*, p. 12 for this rationale.
176. Orville Chadsey, "Confirmation-Commissioning," in *Parish Planning for Grades 7–10*, ed. James Simpson (Philadelphia: Board of Christian Education, 1970).
177. Ibid., p. 21.
178. Ibid.
179. *Context for Choice: A Confirmation-Commissioning Manual* (Philadelphia: Geneva Press, 1973), pp. 65–66.
180. See the introductory comments on ibid., p. 5. The various models are discussed in chapter five.
181. Ibid., p. 67. Elsewhere the manual puts it like this: "If a single overarching criticism can be made against the traditional communicant's class, it is that it has emphasized factual data at the expense of experience" (p. 72).
182. Mac and Anne Turnage, *Explorations into Faith: A Course for Youth Preparing to Be Confirmed/Commissioned* (Philadelphia: Geneva Press, 1977).
183. Ibid. It was edited by representatives of both denominations. See "Statement from the Editors" at the beginning of the book.
184. Ibid., p. 10.
185. Ibid., p. 9.
186. Ibid., p. 10.
187. Ibid., p. 102.
188. David Ng, *Journeys of Faith: Confirming and Commissioning Young Members of the Church* (Louisville, Ky.: Presbyterian Publishing House, 1990), p. 14. See also definitions on pp. 16 and 17–18.
189. Ibid., p. 3.
190. *Journeys of Faith: A Guide for Confirmation-Commissioning* (Louisville, Ky.: Presbyterian Publishing House, 1990), p. 1. Henceforth, this document will be referred to as the *Notebook*. Later in this notebook it is the church that is said to confirm: "The congregation . . . must decide whether to confirm Seekers who make professions of faith," p. 225.
191. *Notebook*, p. 1.
192. *Journeys of Faith*, p. 8. This is expanded on the same page.
193. Ibid., pp. 3, 6, 7, 8.
194. Ibid., p. 6. Organic metaphors are used on the same page to describe justification and on the next page, sanctification.
195. Between 1984 and 1992, seven such resources were published under the title "Supplemental Liturgical Resources."
196. *Supplemental Liturgical Resource 2—Holy Baptism and Services for the Renewal of Baptism* (Philadelphia: Westminster Press, 1985).
197. *Book of Common Worship* (Louisville, Ky.: Westminster/John Knox Press, 1993).
198. According to the chair of the committee, Robert Shelton, its members studied the recent baptismal liturgies and supporting scholarship of a wide range of denominations, including the Lutheran, Episcopal, Scottish Reformed, and United Methodist.
199. *Book of Common Worship*, p. 7.
200. *SLR 2*, p. 58. Cf. pp. 17–19.
201. The other occasions are joining a congregation (a shift from the proposal of *SLR 2*), occasions of growth in faith, pastoral counseling situations, and congregational reaffirmation.
202. See *SLR 2*, pp. 22–23.

203. *The Book of Common Worship,* pp. 406–7.
204. *SLR 2,* p. 54.
205. Ibid., p. 55.
206. Ibid., p. 57.

Part 3: A Contemporary Proposal for Confirmation

Notes to Introduction

1. From "The Confessional Nature of the Church," a study document of the Presbyterian Church (USA), 198th General Assembly (1986), reprinted in *Major Themes in the Reformed Tradition,* ed. D. McKim (Grand Rapids, Mich.: William B. Eerdmans Pub. Co., 1992), p. 23.
2. Ibid.
3. See, for example, Leonel Mitchell's comments in *Worship: Initiation and the Churches* (Washington, D.C.: Pastoral Press, 1991), p. 204.
4. Repeatedly, *SLR 2* equates the Blessing portion of the baptismal service with confirmation. *Supplemental Liturgical Resources 2,* pp.17–19, 56–57.

Notes to Chapter 7

1. See, for example, *By Water and Spirit,* pp. 10–11.
2. Two of the most promising signs of a renewed and deeper appreciation of Barth's thought are George Hunsinger's *How to Read Karl Barth: The Shape of His Theology* (New York: Oxford University Press, 1991) and Bruce McCormack's *Karl Barth's Critically Realistic Dialectical Theology: Its Genesis and Development 1909–1936* (Oxford, England: Clarendon Press, 1995).
3. My discussion of Barth's view of the sacraments will focus primarily on the final volume of *Church Dogmatics,* 4, 4. Although Barth wrote about the sacraments over the course of his career, this volume represents his final word on the matter. For a much earlier example of Barth's thinking on the sacraments that remained closer to Reformed teaching, see *The Teaching of the Church Regarding Baptism* (London: SCM Press, 1948), trans. E. Payne.
4. Barth himself refers to his position as close to that of Zwingli. *Church Dogmatics,* 4, 2, p. 128. For excellent overviews of Calvin's position and that of the Reformed Confessions, see Brian Gerrish, *The Old Protestantism and the New: Essays on the Reformation Heritage* (Chicago: University of Chicago Press, 1982), chaps. 7 and 8; and David Willis, "The Development of Baptismal Theology and Practice in the Book of Confessions," in *Guide to the Recommendations on Baptism Made by the 184th General Assembly (1972),* The United Presbyterian Church in the United States of America.
5. Barth, *Church Dogmatics,* 4, 2, pp. 54–55 and 4, 4, p. x. In the latter, Barth acknowledges that he has now abandoned a "sacramental" understanding of Baptism.
6. Ibid., 4, 4, p. 27.
7. Ibid., p. 34.
8. Ibid., p. 43.
9. Ibid., p. 102.
10. Barth discusses the Reformed position throughout this volume. See especially pp. 104–5 and 172–75.
11. Calvin's discussion of the sacraments in the *Institutes* is found in vol. 2, pp. 1277–1448. His treatment of this topic in the *Genevan Catechism* also is important.
12. *Institutes,* pp. 1288–89, 1304.
13. This is Gerrish's helpful formulation on the *Genevan Catechism.*
14. Ibid., 111.
15. Calvin describes the sacraments as means by which we "attest our piety" toward God before humans in several places. *Institutes,* pp. 1277, 1289.

16. Barth, *Church Dogmatics,* 4, 4, pp. 188–89.
17. For a discussion of covenant themes in the New Testament, especially in relation to the sacraments, see Susanne Lehne, "The New Covenant in Hebrews," *Journal for the Study of the New Testament,* Supplement Series 44 (Sheffield, England: JSOT Press, 1990); Alasdair Heron, *Table and Tradition* (Philadelphia: Westminster Press, 1984); Eduard Schweizer, *The Lord's Supper According to the New Testament,* trans. James Davis (Philadelphia: Fortress Press, 1967); Joachim Jeremias, *The Eucharistic Words of Jesus* (London: SCM Press, 1966); and Charles Cousar, *A Theology of the Cross: The Death of Jesus in the Pauline Letters, Overtures to Biblical Theology,* (Minneapolis: Fortress Press, 1990).
18. Jürgen Moltmann, *The Church in the Power of the Spirit: A Contribution to Messianic Ecclesiology* (San Francisco: Harper & Row, 1977), p. 243.
19. See Geoffrey Bromiley's excellent discussion in *Children of Promise: The Case for Baptizing Infants* (Grand Rapids, Mich.: William B. Eerdmans Pub. Co., 1979). See also Joachim Jeremias, *Infant Baptism in the First Four Centuries,* trans. D. Cairns (Philadelphia: Westminster Press, 1960). For opposing positions, see Kurt Aland, *Did the Early Church Baptize Infants?* trans. G. Beasley-Murray (London: SCM Press, 1963) and Paul Jewett, *Infant Baptism and the Covenant of Grace* (Grand Rapids, Mich.: William B. Eerdmans Pub. Co., 1978).
20. Origen (ca. 185–254, provides the earliest direct reference to infant Baptism: "The Church has received a tradition from the Apostles to give baptism even to little children." *Commentary on Romans* in *Patrologia Graeca,* vol. 14 (Migne), p. 1047.
21. Ruth Duck, *Gender and the Name of God: The Trinitarian Baptismal Formula* (New York: The Pilgrim Press, 1991).
22. Cynthia Campbell, "By Any Other Name? The Triune Formula in Baptism," *Reformed Liturgy & Worship,* vol. 29, no. 1, 1995, p. 19.
23. Particularly helpful are the essays collected in Part I of Jürgen Moltmann's *History and the Triune God: Contributions to Trinitarian Theology* (New York: Crossroad, 1992).
24. François Wendel, *Calvin: Origins and Development of His Religious Thought,* trans. P. Mairet (Durham, N.C.: Labyrinth Press, 1950), pp. 263–84.
25. Not only did Barth locate election within his doctrine of God, but he consistently moved from the knowledge given in Christ to his portrait of God *a se.* His understanding of election provides us with a different framework than Calvin's in which to understand the covenant of grace.
26. See his exegetical work in *Church Dogmatics,* 2, 2, pp. 102–3.
27. Ibid., pp. 8–9, 116–17.
28. Barth uses the metaphor of circles in a number of places. See, for example, ibid., 4, 1, p. 26.
29. Ibid., pp. 195–305.
30. Ibid., p. 196.
31. Ibid., p. 321.
32. Barth himself, of course, did not view Baptism in this manner, as I have already indicated. I am adapting the covenantal framework he develops throughout his theology to a classical Reformed understanding of the sacraments. Geoffrey Bromiley, one of Barth's chief translators, has taken some steps in this direction already in *Children of Promise: The Case for Baptizing Infants* (Grand Rapids, Mich.: William B. Eerdmans Pub. Co., 1976).
33. Barth, *Church Dogmatics,* 4, 1, p. 36.
34. Ibid., p. 22.
35. Ibid., pp. 211–83.
36. Philip Reiff, *The Triumph of the Therapeutic* (New York: Harper & Row, 1966); Robert Bellah et al., *Habits of the Heart: Individualism and Commitment in American Life* (Berkeley, Calif.: University of California Press, 1985); and Don Browning, *The Moral Context of Pastoral Care* (Philadephia: Westminster Press, 1976).

37. Barth, of course, follows the progression Christ-church-individual here as in justification. My focus in confirmation is the individual, leading me to deal with this dimension of sanctification.
38. This conflates a royal psalm, 2:7, and Isaiah 42:1, making it clear that the Messiah is
to take the form of a suffering servant.
39. *Church Dogmatics,* 4, 2, pp. 574–77.
40. See Barth's brief distinction between reconciliation and redemption in ibid., 1, 1, pp.
142–43. In each of the moments of God's inner and outer history, the Trinity is fully
involved. Nonetheless, it is important to distinguish the primary roles or work of each
person of the Godhead in order to keep from slipping back into a simple monotheism.
See Jürgen Moltmann's discussion of this in *The Trinity and the Kingdom* (San Francisco: Harper & Row, 1981), Part 5.
41. The New RSV captures each of these aspects in its translation of *arrabon,* using "first
installment" in 2 Cor. 1:22, "guarantee" in 2 Cor. 5:5, and "pledge" in Eph. 1:14).
42. The term "subjective" is Barth's. See *Church Dogmatics,* 1, 1, p. 449.
43. Calvin, *Institutes,* vol. 1, p. 590.
44. For a discussion of the Christian perspective tragedy, see the following: Reinhold
Niebuhr, *Beyond Tragedy: Essays on the Christian Interpretation of History* (New
York: Charles Scribner's Sons, 1937); *The Nature and Destiny of Man* (New York:
Charles Scribner's Sons, 1941), vol. 1; and James Gustafson, *Ethics from a Theocen-
tric Perspective,* (Chicago: University of Chicago Press, 1981).
45. Peter Berger, *The Sacred Canopy: Elements of a Sociological Theory of Religion* (New
York: Doubleday, 1969), Part 1.
46. Paul Tillich, *Systematic Theology* (Chicago: University of Chicago Press, 1957), vol.
2, pp. 3–96; *Theology of Culture* (London: Oxford University Press, 1959), chap. 8.
James Loder, *The Transforming Moment: Understanding Convictional Experience*
(San Francisco: Harper & Row, 1981), chaps. 5–6. Walter Lowe, "Evil and Unconscious: A Freudian Exploration," *Soundings,* Spring 1980; vol. LXIII, no. 1, pp. 7–35.
47. Barth, *Church Dogmatics,* 4, 1, pp. 23ff.
48. For an excellent discussion of the Mosaic and Davidic covenant patterns, see Jon Leven-
son, *Sinai & Zion: An Entry into the Jewish Bible* (San Francisco: Harper & Row, 1985).
49. Similar features are found in Psalm 15:1–3. Ibid., pp. 169–76.
50. See Heron, Jeremias, and Schweizer.

Notes to Chapter 8

1. See Martin Luther's comments in "Concerning Earnest Christians," trans. Charles
White, in *Current Theology of Missiology* (10), pp. 273–82.
2. Calvin, *Institutes,* 1, 2.1.
3. Lewis Ford Battles, "True Piety according to Calvin," *Readings in Calvin's Theology,*
ed. D. McKim (Grand Rapids, Mich.: Baker Book House, 1984), pp. 192–211. See
also John Leith's introduction to John Calvin's *The Christian Life* (San Francisco:
Harper & Row, 1984).
4. This pattern has certain things in common with one suggested by Richard Baxter in
The Reformed Pastor (New York: Robert Cater & Brothers, 1840). Its elements are
found throughout the Christian tradition. Baxter's proposal is creatively appropriated
by Howard Rice in *Reformed Spirituality: An Introduction for Believers* (Louisville,
Ky.: Westminster/John Knox Press, 1991).
5. *The Compact Edition of the Oxford English Dictionary,* s.v. "mentor."
6. The psychological process I have in mind here is analogous to the therapist-client relationship in depth psychology. Particularly helpful in this regard is the conceptualization of how the therapist becomes an "inner object" in the object relations school
of psychoanalysis. See Sheldon Cashdan, *Object Relations Therapy: Using the Relationship* (New York: Norton & Co., 1988) and Otto Kernberg, *Object Relations Theory and Clinical Psychoanalysis* (New York: Jason Aronson, 1976).

7. Joachim Jeremias, *Theology of the New Testament* (New York: Charles Scribner's Sons, 1971).

8. Calvin offered prayers for morning rising, preparation for departure to school, before and after meals, and bedtime. *John Calvin's Tracts and Treatises,* trans. H. Beveridge, vol 2, (Grand Rapids, Mich.: William B. Eerdmans Pub. Co., 1958), pp. 95–99. As Leith notes, the inclusion of these prayers seems to indicate that "Calvin was seeking to establish a pattern for the daily devotions of Christian people." See *Christian Life,* p. xiii.

9. See the introduction to Calvin's *Commentaries: The Book of Psalms,* trans. J. Anderson (Grand Rapids, Mich.: Baker Books, 1984).

10. One of the best examples is Dietrich Bonhoeffer's *Psalms: The Prayer Book of the Bible* (Minneapolis: Augsburg, 1970).

11. Certain contemporary authors refer to this pattern as the "grammar of the heart." See *The Grammar of the Heart: Thinking with Kierkegaard & Wittgenstein,* ed. R. Bell (San Francisco: Harper & Row, 1988). Other helpful books sharing this perspective are Don Saliers's *The Soul in Paraphrase: Prayer and the Religious Affections* (New York: Crossroad Pub. Co., 1980) and Paul Holmer's *The Grammar of Faith* (San Francisco: Harper & Row, 1978).

12. See James Smart, *The Strange Silence of the Bible in the Church* (Philadelphia: Westminster Press, 1970).

13. Augustine, *On Christian Doctrine,* trans. D. W. Robertson, Jr. (Indianapolis: Liberal Arts Press of Bobbs-Merrill Education Publishing, 1958).

14. I realize that teaching is used in a much more inclusive fashion normally, as I do myself in *A Teachable Spirit* and *Teaching for Faith.* Here I am offering a practical maxim, not a full-fledged theory of teaching.

Epilogue: Confirmation in Practical Theological Perspective

1. Paul Tillich, *Systematic Theology: Three Volumes in One* (Chicago: University of Chicago Press, 1951), p. 34.

2. Dietrich Rössler, *Grundriß der Praktischen Theologie,* sec. ed. (Berlin: Walter de Gruyter, 1994), chaps. 1—3.

3. Ibid., pp. 41–60. Richard Osmer, *A Teachable Spirit: Recovering the Teaching Office in the Church* (Louisville, Ky.: Westminster/John Knox Press, 1990), chap. 7. Edward Farley, *Theologia: The Fragmentation and Unity of Theological Education* (Philadelphia: Fortress, 1983), chaps. 3—5.

4. Excellent descriptions of the modern German university, the most influential context in the emergence of practical theology, are found in Friedrich Paulsen's *German Education: Past and Present,* trans. T. Lorenz (New York: Charles Scribner's Sons, 1912) and *The German Universities and University Study,* trans. F. Thilly (New York: Charles Scribner's Sons, 1906).

5. For a discussion of these trends see Stephen Toulmin, "The Recovery of Practical Philosophy," *The American Scholar,* Spring 1988, pp. 337–52 and *Cosmopolis,* cited above.

6. See Walter Wyman's excellent discussion of Schleiermacher's understanding of the organization of science in *The Concept of Glaubenslehre: Ernst Troeltsch and the Theological Heritage of Schleiermacher* (Chico, Calif.: Scholars Press, 1983), American Academy of Religion, 44, pp. 181–84.

7. Friedrich Schleiermacher, *Brief Outline on the Study of Theology,* trans. Terrence Tice (Richmond: John Knox Press, 1966), p. 19.

8. In addition to Farley's *Theologia,* cited above, see Alasdair MacIntyre, *Three Rival Versions of Moral Enquiry: Encyclopaedia, Genealogy, and Tradition* (Notre Dame, Ind.: University of Notre Dame, 1990).

9. Toulmin, *Cosmopolis,* chap. 2.

10. An excellent account of reason working in this fashion is found in Stephen Toulmin and Albert Jonsen, *The Abuse of Casuistry: A History of Moral Reasoning* (Berkeley, Calif.: University of California Press, 1988).

11. In fairness to Schleiermacher, he describes practical theology as constructing "rules of art" that cannot be "applied" in a straightforward manner, but necessitate the "talent" of discerning the fitting thing to do on particular occasions. He discusses these kinds of rules within his aesthetics. His comments about technology and the nontheoretical orientation of practical theology stand, however. Schleiermacher, *Brief Outline*, pp. 93–94.

12. Ibid., p. 92.

13. Richard Bernstein provides two of the best introductions to these trends in *Beyond Objectivism and Relativism: Science, Hermeneutics, and Praxis* (Philadelphia: University of Pennsylvania Press, 1983) and *The New Constellation: The Ethical-Political Horizons of Modernity/Postmodernity* (Cambridge, Mass.: MIT Press, 1991). An excellent introduction to the shifts in science are found in Harold Brown, *Rationality* (London: Routledge, 1988).

14. Rössler is cited above. Gert Otto, *Grundlegung der Praktischen Theologie* (Munich: Kaiser, 1986); Johannes van der Ven, *Entwurf einer empirischen Theologie* (Kampen, The Netherlands: J. H. Kok, 1990). The English translation is *Practical Theology: An Empirical Approach* (Kampen, The Netherlands: J. H. Kok, 1993). Don Browning, *A Fundamental Practical Theology: Descriptive and Strategic Proposals* (Minneapolis: Fortress Press, 1991). Pamela Couture, *Blessed Are the Poor: Women's Poverty, Family Policy, and Practical Theology* (Nashville: Abingdon Press, 1991). Duncan Forrester, "Divinity in Use and Practice," in *Theology & Practice*, ed. D. Forrester (London: Epworth Press, 1990).

15. Schleiermacher, *Brief Outline*, p. 19.

16. Eduard Thurneysen, *A Theology of Pastoral Care*, trans. J. Worthington and T. Wieser (Richmond: John Knox Press, 1962).

17. For a critique of Thurneysen and a far more sophisticated interdisciplinary method based on Barthian convictions, see Deborah van Deusen Hunsinger, "Becoming Bilingual: The Promise of Karl Barth for Pastoral Counseling," doctoral dissertation, Union Theological Seminary, 1993.

18. Two of Smart's writings that describe practical theology are *The Teaching Ministry of the Church: An Examination of the Basic Principles of Christian Education* (Philadelphia: Westminster Press, 1954) and *The Rebirth of Ministry: A Study of the Biblical Character of the Church's Ministry* (Philadelphia: Westminster Press, 1960).

19. Barth, *Church Dogmatics*, 1, 1, p. 5.

20. McCormack's volume on Barth, cited above, provides an overview of the various uses of dialectic in Barth's theology as a whole.

21. George Hunsinger, *How to Read Karl Barth: The Shape of His Theology* (Oxford, England: Oxford University Press, 1991), pp. 58–59, 107–9, 112–14.

22. Ibid., p. 58.

23. Barth described their relation as follows: "Hence theology as biblical theology is the question of the basis, as practical theology the question of the goal and as dogmatic theology the question of the content of the distinctive utterance of the Church." *Church Dogmatics*, 1, 1, p. 5.

24. One of the most helpful discussions of this is found in Rodney Hunter, "The Future of Pastoral Theology," *Pastoral Psychology*, vol. 29, no. 1, Fall 1980. See also Donald Schön, *The Reflective Practitioner: How Professionals Think in Action* (New York: Basic Books, 1983) and *Educating the Reflective Practitioner* (San Francisco: Jossey-Bass, 1987).